DATE DUE

AR 6			
A 4 08			
JE 2 3 08			

DEMCO 38-296

HISTORICAL DICTIONARY
OF THE
SPANISH AMERICAN WAR

HISTORICAL DICTIONARY
OF THE
SPANISH AMERICAN WAR

DONALD H. DYAL

With the editorial assistance of
Brian B. Carpenter *and*
Mark A. Thomas

Advisory Editor
James S. Olson

GREENWOOD PRESS
Westport, Connecticut • London

Library of Congress Cataloging-in-Publication Data

Dyal, Donald H.
    Historical dictionary of the Spanish American War / Donald H.
  Dyal; with the editorial assistance of Brian B. Carpenter and Mark A. Thomas.
        p.   cm.
    Includes bibliographical references (p.   ) and index.
    ISBN 0-313-28852-6 (alk. paper)
    1. Spanish-American War, 1898—Dictionaries.   I. Carpenter, Brian B.
II. Thomas, Mark A.   III. Title.
E715.D93   1996
973.8'9'03—dc20   95-33076

British Library Cataloguing in Publication Data is available.

Library of Congress Catalog Card Number: 95-33076
ISBN: 0-313-28852-6

First published in 1996

Greenwood Press, 88 Post Road West, Westport, CT 06881
An imprint of Greenwood Publishing Group, Inc.

Printed in the United States of America

The paper used in this book complies with the
Permanent Paper Standard issued by the National
Information Standards Organization (Z39.48-1984).

10 9 8 7 6 5 4 3 2 1

Contents

Preface

Among those who know much about the Spanish American War, this episode of American history gets mixed reviews—the arc of historical opinion swings erratically and wide. Commenced in the heat of an idealistic American desire to free Cuba from its oppressive colonial Spanish overlord, the conflict ended with a newly acquired U.S. empire in two hemispheres. In the nineteenth century, empire was not quite the dirty word that it became in the twentieth. Empire had many and influential supporters, but empire was not a monologue. The anti-expansionist movement at *fin de siècle* also had influential supporters. American combatants, flushed with almost universal easy victories, proudly regaled the rest of the population with books and articles about this-or-that heroic action. The press willingly cooperated in this wartime and postwar enthusiasm. Thus, many of the contemporary accounts emphasized the pluck of combatants and perseverance in the face of the adversities of combat. In addition, Theodore Roosevelt, one of the Spanish American War's most ebullient participants, catapulted himself onto the national stage by means of wartime exploit and exploitation. The nation awarded medals, erected monuments, composed songs, wrote stories, paraded its veterans, and in general exuberantly celebrated this brief feat of arms. Veterans' groups sprouted vigorously in this freshly turned soil and retained enough vitality that over four decades later George Dewey's flagship *Olympia* was spared the shipbreaker's torch during the crisis of World War II. Enthusiasm for the war lingered in the 1930s when Richmond P. Hobson received his Medal of Honor and Tom Mix, popular cowboy movie hero, claimed to have ridden with the Rough Riders and to have served in the Philippine Insurrection. Mix did serve in the military during the war, but his unit never left the United States. It is revealing that Mix's publicists of the 1920s and 1930s felt that Spanish American War service was still sufficiently romantic that the manufactured myths surrounding the box office hero included liberal dollops of Spanish American War folklore. There was a warm afterglow from the war in the American memory that lasted several decades.

However, in the late 1920s and early 1930s another and different view of the war emerged. The optimism of the turn of the century and before World War I, first bruised by the realities of worldwide conflict in 1914–1918, was then bludgeoned with economic depression, political strife, hunger, joblessness, and the international failure to halt deteriorating social and economic conditions. A distinct, more cynical view, crept into the collective mind. Exploits once seen as heroic were repainted in cartoonish hue. Snide remarks in the popular press and in films of the period hinted that, somehow, the sacrifices and efforts of Spanish American War veterans were unworthy of the earlier honorifics bestowed upon them. *The Martial Spirit* (1931), Walter Millis's otherwise excellent history, also reads with a subtle condescending tone. The pendulum of popular interpretation now began to swing away from glorification to indifference and even vilification. ''Spanish American War stuff'' described not just the hackneyed, or something from an older or previous generation, but in a pejorative way the phrase also conveyed criticism of unjustified enthusiasm, unwarranted exuberance—even phoniness. The nadir of the social history of the Spanish American War occurred in the years after World War II, culminating, perhaps, in scenes such as that presented in the long-running Broadway and later film hit *Arsenic and Old Lace,* where Mortimer Brewster's lunatic brother Teddy draws his sword and ''charges'' San Juan Hill every time he goes upstairs. Few memories can survive such ridicule, and for several decades after World War II, the Spanish American War almost ceased to exist as a historical phenomenon. History textbooks glossed over the war, and for many it became a historical footnote to the space of time between the Gilded Age and World War I.

Recent scholarship has looked at the Spanish American War, its aftermath, and implications for the new twentieth century in a fresh light. New interpretations contrast startlingly with previous conventional wisdom. President William McKinley, once described as virtually an invertebrate, has of late been described as the first modern president. He not just initiated the political struggle on the national stage but took a newly auditioned balancing act on the world stage. Military reform, significant medical breakthroughs, the healing of the Civil War's scars, modern coordinated logistical systems, and, perhaps most important, the nation's emergence as a global power with global interests have all been attributed to this ''splendid little war.'' Indeed, the U.S. acquisition of Hawaii, the Philippines, Guam, and Wake Island reads like a preview of World War II in the Pacific. It can be stated without exaggeration that the Japanese-American war in the Pacific of 1941–1945 (if there even would have been one) would have been vastly different without the prelude of the Spanish American War. It was the effects of this war that confronted the Japanese with an American intrusion in their own backyard. In consequence, the twentieth-century impact of the American Pacific possessions beggars adequate descriptors. It is possible that the social, economic, and political impact of the Spanish American War upon the United States equals or even exceeds that of World War I.

On Spain's behalf, the war also had profound impact. The year 1898 was one of Spanish despair. Authorities in Spain operated in a state of denial during hostilities, came to the peace negotiations table without arrows in their quiver, and as a result suffered traumatic national humiliation. From the ashes of defeat, Spain reinvented parts of itself. Hispanic consciousness was reinvented. The reverberations of the war affecting Spain, Spain's relationships with former colonies, and Spain's definition of itself continue to find roots in the Spanish American War.

For these reasons and others, the Spanish American War merits more than the one page or less accorded in many history texts. The Spanish American War possesses grit and grist for much further study; it is hoped that the war's centennial will spawn such discussion and that this volume will serve as handy reference for those discussions.

To further such discussion and to facilitate use of this dictionary, asterisks placed within the text of the entries serve as cross-references to related topics. In addition, cross-references guide the user to variant forms of entries. Spanish surnames have been filed by patronymic and are most frequently utilized as patronymics. Maternal surnames are included, however. Since the war was primarily naval in orientation, one can read the naval or ship entries only and get a surprisingly complete overview of the conflict. For that reason, more attention has perhaps been paid to the naval side of the war, including individual ship histories.

Bibliographically, the Spanish American War is a relatively short read. The official reports of the U.S. Army and U.S. Navy published by the Government Printing Office were written in 1898 and the years immediately following. Like almost all such reports, they possess facts but also hint at broader issues. These are the foundational or beginning documents for serious study of military actions during the war. Supplementing these official documents are the numerous firsthand accounts, unit histories, and individual autobiographical accounts of actions. Many of these were written in stirring prose intended for more than mere reportage. Spanish accounts are more fugitive and understandably defensive in tone. Some, such as Admiral Cervera's account, were painfully written as a justification and explanation for defeat. Lastly, a surprising few secondary works, of varying quality, have been published. Foremost among these are David Trask's *The War with Spain in 1898,* G.J.A. O'Toole's anecdotal *The Spanish War,* Graham A. Cosmas's *An Army for Empire,* and several lesser works. These three secondary works should be used as a group, for each supplements the others in critical areas. Cosmas's book is particularly useful for U.S. Army policy and reform issues that develop out of the war. O'Toole emphasizes intelligence operations and brings a useful narrative style to the history of the war. Trask, the best overall summary, binds the whole experience together in a readable and immensely useful text.

I acknowledge the aid and encouragement of many—particularly the staff associated with the military history collections of the Cushing Library at Texas A&M University. In addition, there has been a platoon of dedicated and patient typists—Terry Bridges, Lori Bush, Kim Kizer, Tanya Duggins, Ann Nguyen—who have labored over the manuscript. Special gratitude is due Robin Brandt Huchison. While my debt to these people is great, responsibility for any errors and for interpretation rests solely with the author.

Chronology of the Spanish American War

1892	5 January	José Martí establishes Cuban Revolutionary party
	7 July	Andrés Bonifacio forms Katipunan at Manila, Philippine Islands.
1895	24 February	Grito de Baire, the second Cuban revolution commences
	12 June	President Cleveland issues a proclamation of neutrality in the Cuban Insurrection
1896	16 February	Spain implements reconcentration policy in Cuba
	9 August	Great Britain foils Spain's attempt to form European support of Spanish policies in Cuba
	26 August	Grito de Balintawak, the first cry of the Philippine Revolution
	7 December	President Cleveland declares that the United States may take action in Cuba if Spain fails to resolve the Cuban crisis
1897	4 March	Inauguration of President McKinley
	8 August	Assassination of Spanish prime minister Cánovas forces change in government
	1 November	Emilio Aguinaldo succeeds in creating Philippine revolutionary constitution; Biak-na-Bato Republic formed
1898	1 January	Spain grants limited autonomy to Cuba
	9 February	*New York Journal* publishes Spanish minister Enrique Dupuy de Lôme's letter critical of President McKinley
	15 February	U.S.S. *Maine* explodes in Havana Harbor
	9 March	Fifty Million Bill strengthening the U.S. military passes Congress
	17 March	Redfield Proctor sways Congress and the American business community toward war with Spain

28 March	U.S. Naval Court of Inquiry publishes its findings that U.S.S. *Maine* was destroyed by a mine
21 April	President McKinley orders Cuban blockade; hostilities begin
25 April	United States declares war on Spain
1 May	Commodore Dewey defeats Spanish naval forces at Manila Bay. Andrew Rowan delivers his ''message to [Calixto] García.''
11 May	Charles H. Allen succeeds Theodore Roosevelt as assistant secretary of the navy
10 June	A battalion of U.S. Marines lands at Guantánamo, Cuba
12 June	Philippines declare independence. German squadron under Admiral Diederichs arrives at Manila
15 June	American Anti-Imperialist League organizes. Admiral Cámara's squadron receives orders to relieve the Philippines
20 June	Spanish authorities surrender Guam to Captain Henry Glass
22 June	General Shafter lands troops at Daiquirí, Cuba
1 July	Land battles at San Juan and environs of Santiago commence. Theodore Roosevelt leads charge up Kettle Hill
3 July	Admiral Cervera attempts to break out of Santiago; all his ships are sunk by Admiral Sampson's squadron
7 July	United States annexes Hawaii
17 July	Santiago surrenders to U.S. forces
25 July	U.S. Army lands at Guánica, Puerto Rico
12 August	Spain and the United States sign peace protocol and ceasefire
13 August	Manila surrenders to U.S. forces
26 September	Dodge Commission formed to investigate beef controversy and conduct of War Department
10 December	Treaty of Paris concludes the Spanish American War. Spain cedes Puerto Rico and Guam; sells the Philippines to the United States; Cuba to be independent

1899	17 January	United States claims Wake Island for cable link to the Philippines
	4 February	Philippine Republic declares war on the United States
	2 June	Spanish forces at Baler, Philippine Islands, finally surrender

HISTORICAL DICTIONARY
OF THE
SPANISH AMERICAN WAR

A

ADAMS, BROOKS
(1850–1927)

Son of Charles Francis Adams and Abigail Brown Brooks and grandson of President John Quincy Adams and wealthy Boston merchant Peter Chadron Brooks, Brooks Adams quit the law profession around 1882 to study history. A believer in Social Darwinism, he gave human society a bleak prognosis. His ideas were much influenced by Alfred Thayer Mahan,* author of *The Influence of Sea Power upon History.*

Adams's influential book, *The Law of Civilization and Decay,* was published in 1895. In this work, Adams saw the accumulation and concentration of wealth driving humankind's progress through stages of history; each historical period was distinguished by certain personality types. The "Imaginative Man" marked the early stages—the soldier and artist ruled by the Church, that is, fear of a priesthood. This was supplanted by the "Economic Man," ruled by greed, with two subtypes, the usurer and the peasant. Adams thought the United States and Europe had reached this level and the next stage would be atrophy or disintegration. He did not think any individual or group could affect this destiny. In a review in the January 1896 *Forum,* Theodore Roosevelt* was troubled by this pessimistic thesis and thought Adams to be "a little unhinged."

At the beginning of hostilities with Spain, Adams was skeptical of Roosevelt's gathering together of unrefined cowboys for the fight; after Commodore George Dewey's* victory in Manila,* however, he became jubilant and confident. Adams's Social Darwinist ideas became accepted by the establishment, who no longer considered him "unhinged."

In "The Spanish War and the Equilibrium of the World," published in the August 1898 *Forum,* Adams defends the U.S. role in the Spanish American War. He advocates alliance with England and economic war with the rest of the world. In his view of global politics and economics, the United States and

England (maritime nations) would become allied against France, Germany, and Russia (land-based economies) in competition for trade with the East. To ensure economic efficiency, a strongly centralized state, guided by a well-organized elite, is necessary; war becomes a tool of national policy. Adams's view toward economics has been described as the survival of the cheapest.

Adams's wife, Evelyn (Daisy), was sister to the wife of Senator Henry Cabot Lodge* and daughter of Admiral Charles Davis.*

REFERENCES: Brooks Adams, *The Law of Civilization and Decay: An Essay on History* (New York: Macmillan Publishing Co., 1895); Brooks Adams, ''The Spanish War and the Equilibrium of the Worlds,'' *Forum* 25 (August 1898): 641–651; Arthur F. Beringause, *Brooks Adams: A Biography* (New York: Knopf, 1955).

MARK A. THOMAS

ADAMS, HENRY
(1838–1918)

Brother of historian Brooks Adams,* Henry Adams attended Harvard and studied law in Germany before spending several years in England as secretary to his father, the U.S. ambassador. Returning to the United States in 1868, he became an assistant professor of history at Harvard in 1870, finally settling in Washington, DC, in 1877.

With strong ties to the northeastern establishment, Adams was well established in Washington social circles, part of a group that John Hay* called ''The Pleasant Gang.'' From 1885, shortly after his wife's death, he lived next door to Hay, across from the White House at 1603 H Street; this house became a gathering place for those in Adams's Washington clique.

Adams regarded the Old World as decadent but at the same time saw the nouveau riche of the commercially booming Midwest as greedy and unrefined. His circle was supportive of American expansion and familiar with Frederick Jackson Turner's assertion that American vigor resulted from the existence of a frontier; a new frontier was now needed.

Adams's support of the war with Spain is consistent with his positive view of U.S. imperialism. When forces were massing at Tampa* in spring 1898, Adams, a frequent world traveler, was in Constantinople. In April he analyzed the situation regarding Admiral Pascual Cervera's* squadron sailing from the Cape Verdes,* commenting that the fleet would need to be destroyed entirely or else the U.S. Army campaign might become too drawn out. In letters from Adams to his friend Hay, the usually cynical Adams was atypically jubilant over Commodore George Dewey's* victory in Manila* in May and was eager for the U.S. Navy to take control of the world, thinking it possible. He believed it would be easy to chase Spain out of the Antilles and to acquire Hawaii,* but any more expansion would require careful diplomacy with the major European powers.

In essays after the war, Adams wrote that the rise of Germany as a world power would finally make England embrace the United States, something his family had unsuccessfully tried to do for generations.

REFERENCES: Henry Adams, *The Education of Henry Adams* (Boston: Houghton Mifflin, 1918); Worthington Chauncey Ford, ed., *Letters of Henry Adams* (Boston: Houghton Mifflin, 1938).

MARK A. THOMAS

ADEE, ALVEY AUGUSTUS (1842–1924)

In its 9 February 1898 issue, the newspaper the *New York Journal* published a private letter from the Spanish minister to the United States, Enrique Dupuy de Lôme,* to José Canalejas.* The *Journal* published the letter because it contained Dupuy de Lôme's negative opinions of President William McKinley.* Intended to be confidential and private, the letter created an international scene of some magnitude. Upon seeing the actual letter—which had, of course, been stolen—and realizing its international implications, Secretary of State William R. Day* immediately questioned its authenticity and the motives of the Cuban junta* that had brought it to the attention of William Randolph Hearst's* *Journal* and Joseph Pulitzer's* *New York World.* Day called in the second assistant secretary, Alvey Augustus Adee, to authenticate Dupuy de Lôme's signature. Adee at first believed the signature to be a forgery. However, upon closer examination and comparison with other Dupuy de Lôme signatures in State Department files, he reluctantly concluded that the letter was in fact authentic. Dupuy de Lôme was aware that the publication of the letter made his continued appointment in the United States impossible and had tendered his resignation the previous day, 8 February.

REFERENCE: David F. Trask, *The War with Spain in 1898* (New York: Macmillan Publishing Co., 1981).

ADJUNTAS, PUERTO RICO

Adjuntas is a village about 13 miles north-northwest of Ponce* at about 1,600 feet in elevation. It is a mountainous region with steep ravines and tactically difficult approaches.

Early in the morning of 25 July 1898, General Nelson Miles* came ashore at Guánica,* Puerto Rico,* and took possession of the city and port. Major General James H. Wilson* landed on 27 July with a brigade. On 28 July Miles's and Wilson's forces took Puerto Rico's largest city, Ponce, after only token resistance by Spanish forces. The subsequent landings of Brigadier General Theodore Schwan* on 31 July and Major General John R. Brooke* on 3–5 August completed Miles's preparations. Miles's sophisticated plan to reduce Puerto Rico divided U.S. forces into four separate columns. The second of these columns, led by Brigadier George A. Garretson,* was to proceed north from Ponce on a densely foliated trail unknown to the Spanish but revealed to U.S. forces by collaborating Puerto Ricans. It was to move through Adjuntas to Arecibo* on the north coast. Advance parties of engineers improved this trail, and the second column reached its objective without incident.

REFERENCE: Graham A. Cosmas, *An Army for Empire* (Columbia: University of Missouri Press, 1971).

ADJUTANT GENERAL, U.S. ARMY

It has been said often enough that the Spanish American War was a naval war primarily and that army ineptness on both sides magnified the ad hoc nature of military preparedness, management, and execution. While it is obvious that the military management of some campaigns suffered from mistakes, many of these mistakes require a broader reading than just the incident itself. One such area is that of the Adjutant General's Office.

Within the War Department,* the most important of the three bureaus charged with administering the U.S. Army's affairs was the Adjutant General's Office. This office issued all orders from the secretary of war* and the commanding general, kept the personnel records, supervised the recruiting service, transmitted message traffic or correspondence between all U.S. Army units, supervised National Guard* officers, ran a primitive intelligence service, and during war mobilized all volunteers, militia, and regulars. The adjutant general (Henry Clark Corbin* during the Spanish American War) reported to the commanding general but could take orders only from the secretary of war. The intent of this practice came from federal law that stipulated that the secretary controlled fiscal expenditures—thus the assumed power to control the bureaus. A further complication resulted from the ability of bureau chiefs to issue orders directly to subordinates on detached service. The bureau chief could undermine the generals by issuing conflicting orders to staff. In addition, the secretary of war could give orders to both line and staff officers, thereby creating confusion and even disorder in the prosecution of a campaign. It was possible for the secretary of war to issue commands to units through the adjutant general without the knowledge of the commander. Also, there was no central military staff nor any provision for training one. Such division of authority and absence of a trained military staff strengthened the power of the person responsible for military correspondence, personnel records, recruitment, mobilization, and intelligence, namely, the adjutant general. He could issue orders himself without the knowledge of either the secretary or the commanding general, both of whom were technically his superiors. Such power also invited jurisdictional disputes with other bureaus. These conflicts were both symptom and cause of some command challenges that faced the U.S. Army. Although army reformers such as General John M. Schofield* had done much to dilute the independent tendencies of the bureaus, the reforms stopped short of legislating changes. Nevertheless, the potential existed in early 1898 for a more modern staff organization.

During the war itself the adjutant general helped in war planning and in dealing with recruiting and organizational challenges represented by the politics swirling around the debates over the volunteers,* the National Guard, and the

Hull Bill. The Military Information Division,* subordinate to the adjutant general, played an important supporting role in the war as well.
REFERENCE: Graham A. Cosmas, *An Army for Empire* (Columbia: University of Missouri Press, 1971).

ADULA (ship)

On 23 May 1898 Commodore Winfield S. Schley's* Flying Squadron* lay off Cienfuegos* looking for signs that Admiral Pascual Cervera y Topete* and his ships were in the harbor at Cienfuegos. About noon of the twenty-third, the British steamer *Adula* approached from Jamaica intending to evacuate neutrals from Cienfuegos. *Adula* carried a report that Cervera had gone into Santiago de Cuba* on 19 May (which was correct) and also that he had sailed from Santiago on 20 May (which was not correct). Schley thus erroneously concluded that Cervera was in Cienfuegos Harbor and so delayed his departure awaiting confirmation. Schley's delay caused considerable consternation to Admiral William T. Sampson* and began a rift culminating in the Sampson-Schley Controversy.*

AGONCILLO, FELIPE
(1859–1941)

The hostilities of the Philippine Insurrection* commenced in fall 1896 and paralleled to some degree the Cuban Insurrection.* The Philippine insurgents declared a republic and quickly established an agent or commissioner in neutral Hong Kong.* This agent, Felipe Agoncillo, was a lawyer of notable family from the town of Taal in Batangas, Philippines. In November 1897 Agoncillo called upon the U.S. consul at Hong Kong, Rounsevelle Wildman,* with a proposed alliance between the United States and the insurgent "Republic." The State Department reply was to discourage Agoncillo.

Under instructions from Emilio Aguinaldo,* Agoncillo journeyed to Washington to meet with President William McKinley.* On 1 October 1898, through an interpreter Agoncillo presented his case for Aguinaldo's Philippine independence movement. Agoncillo asked to be represented on the Peace Commission or heard by the commissioners. McKinley negated both requests. Frustrated in Washington, Agoncillo traveled to Paris in an attempt to influence the Peace Commission,* but he failed to receive even a hearing. Agoncillo's failures at every turn to influence others in the cause of Philippine independence underscored the political futility of the enterprise.
REFERENCE: Leon Wolff, *Little Brown Brother* (New York: Kraus Reprint Co., 1970).

AGUACATE, CUBA

Colonel Federico Escario* of the Spanish army led a relief column of 3,752 men from Manzanillo* to Santiago de Cuba*—about 160 miles through torturous terrain. Cuban insurgents* attacked Escario's column repeatedly, with one of the fiercest engagements occurring at Aguacate on 1 July 1898, where Escario's men came under fire from the surrounding hills. Escario formed up his troops "as though on drill," charged the high ground, and took the hills. Spanish casualties included seven dead and forty-three wounded.

Aguacate lies in Havana Province, 36 miles east-southeast of Havana.

REFERENCE: José Müller y Tejeiro, "Battles and Capitulation of Santiago de Cuba," in *Notes on the Spanish American War* (Washington, DC: Government Printing Office, 1900).

AGUINALDO, EMILIO
(Aguinaldo y Farmy, Emilio, 1869–1964)

Emilio Aguinaldo was born on 22 March 1869 at Cavite on Luzon in the Philippine Islands. He was of mixed Tagalog-Chinese ancestry. The Aguinaldo family was part of the local elite, owning substantial property and exercising considerable political power. His father, the mayor of the town of Kawit (Cavite Viejo), died in 1878, and in 1882 the young Aguinaldo quit school for several years, using the free time to travel widely throughout the Philippines. During those journeys Aguinaldo acquired a sense of Filipino identity and a resentment of Spanish imperial authority. Eventually he completed his education at the University of St. Thomas, a college run by Dominican friars in Manila. To avoid required service in the Spanish military, Aguinaldo got a job as a local tax collector, which carried an exemption from the army. In 1895 he became mayor of Kawit, as his father had been before him.

In March 1895 Aguinaldo joined the Katipunan,* a secret, nationalistic fraternal brotherhood founded by Andrés Bonifacio* to bring about Filipino independence. As part of his initiation as a Katipuñero, Aguinaldo took on a pseudonym—Magdalo—after Mary Magdalene. Blessed with a charismatic personality and good tactical skills in guerrilla warfare, Aguinaldo quickly emerged as the Katipuñero leader in Cavite Province. He defeated Spanish forces in a number of engagements that erupted soon after the revolution in 1896. At the same time, Bonifacio encountered a series of military reversals in Manila, which forced him and his followers to flee to the Marakina Mountains. A struggle for control of the Katipunan soon ensued between the two men, but because of his military and political successes, Aguinaldo had the upper hand. In March 1897 Bonifacio came out of his mountain retreat to assert power and regain control of the movement. Aguinaldo would have none of it. In March 1897, in the town of Tejeros in Cavite Province, Aguinaldo had Bonifacio arrested. After six weeks of imprisonment, Bonifacio was tried for treason in a Cavite Katipuñero court. He was found guilty and executed on 10 May 1897. Aguinaldo had become the undisputed leader of the Filipino rebellion.

By the time of Bonifacio's death, the Spanish army had launched an offensive against the Katipunan army. Rebel troops, many of them with their wives and children, retreated to safety in mountain strongholds, but Aguinaldo faced a logistical nightmare there, trying to acquire the food and supplies necessary to support thousands of people. He entered into negotiations with Spanish authorities, which ended in an agreement that Aguinaldo would go into exile in Hong

Kong* in return for 400,000 pesos. He arrived in Hong Kong in January 1898 and almost immediately began negotiating with Chinese and British arms merchants to purchase the weapons his army would need to resume the struggle against Spain. When the United States declared war on Spain on 25 April 1898, Aguinaldo hoped to use the war to achieve Filipino independence. The United States, hoping Aguinaldo would rally Filipinos against Spain and use his troops in the war, invited him back from exile. Aguinaldo arrived in Manila on 19 May 1898.

On 12 June 1898 Aguinaldo declared the independence of the Philippine Islands. On 1 January 1899, after the meetings of a constitutional convention, Emilio Aguinaldo was declared president of the new Philippine Republic. United States authorities refused to recognize the new government, but Aguinaldo was not about to replace Spanish imperial authority with a new American empire. On 4 February 1899 the Philippine Republic declared war on the United States. It was destined to be a bloody conflict. Aguinaldo was captured on 23 March 1901. Under considerable pressure from his family, Aguinaldo agreed to declare allegiance to the United States. Before the war ended in July 1902, more than 4,200 American soldiers were dead, as were 20,000 Filipino soldiers and 200,000 Filipino civilians.

Aguinaldo then retired from public life. However, he wore a black bow in public to symbolize his mourning for the demise of the Philippine Republic. Forty-four years later, when Philippines gained its independence from the United States on 4 July 1946, Aguinaldo removed the tie. His lifelong dream of Filipino independence had been achieved. Emilio Aguinaldo died on 6 February 1964, at the age of ninety-four.

REFERENCES: David Bain, *Sitting in Darkness: America in the Philippines* (Boston: Houghton Mifflin, 1984); Henry Turot, *Emilio Aguinaldo, First Filipino President* (Manila: Foreign Service Institute, 1981).

JAMES S. OLSON

AIBONITO, PUERTO RICO

During the campaign in Puerto Rico* under General Nelson Miles,* U.S. forces were arranged in four different columns to divide the defending Spanish forces. General James H. Wilson* was to lead one of these columns northeast from Ponce* against strong Spanish forces at Aibonito. Intelligence reports on 29 July 1898 informed Miles that the Spanish had reinforced Aibonito, which contained about 4,000 troops, and another 1,000 Spanish troops were in an advance guard at Coamo,* in Wilson's path. One informant, who happened to be the son of the mayor of Aibonito, noted that the Spanish intended to defend Aibonito; cliffs were mined and positions consolidated, he reported. Major General John R. Brooke* advanced his column from Guayama* to Cayey* to threaten Aibonito as well. Brooke received orders to move against Cayey on 8 August in an effort to isolate Aibonito. Meanwhile, on 9 August, Wilson advanced, engaged the Spanish at Coamo, and prepared to assault Aibonito. Miles

encouraged a flanking movement along an old road parallel to the military road. Another flanking footpath was also discovered. On 12 August Wilson sent a force around Aibonito while simultaneously sending a mission to Aibonito to speak with the Spanish commander about possible surrender of the town. A few skirmishes later, Wilson had gathered enough tactical intelligence to plan and prepare for his attack. The struggle for Aibonito promised to be bloody and serious. Wilson planned his attack for early in the morning of 13 August. However, in the afternoon of 12 August, General Miles received a telegram that Spain and the United States had signed a peace agreement and all operators were to cease. Miles informed his subordinates and combat stopped.
REFERENCE: David F. Trask, *The War with Spain in 1898* (New York: Macmillan Publishing Co., 1981).

ALBANY (ship)
(formerly *Almirante Abreu*)
Albany was a 3,437-ton sister-ship to *Amazonas** built in England for the Brazilian navy but purchased 16 March 1898 in a hasty attempt to buttress the American navy on the eve of war. Built as the *Almirante Abreu, Albany* was not completed in time for the opening of the Spanish American War. She therefore remained in England for the duration of hostilities and joined the U.S. Navy only in 1900.
REFERENCE: John E. Alden, *The American Steel Navy* (Annapolis, MD: Naval Institute Press, 1972).

ALEJANDRINO, JOSÉ
(1871–1951)
José Alejandrino served as a general under Emilio Aguinaldo* in the Philippine Revolution that soon became the Philippine Insurrection.* Alejandrino accompanied George Dewey,* commander of the Asiatic Squadron* from Mirs Bay* to Manila* as a representative of the nascent Philippine Republic. Alejandrino was also a participant in an abortive attempt by the Aguinaldo-led revolution to collaborate with the U.S. forces.

During the Philippine Insurrection, General Alejandrino led Philippine forces against the U.S. Army.

ALGER, RUSSELL ALEXANDER
(1836–1907)
Secretary of War (5 March 1897–1 August 1899) Russell Alexander Alger served in a prominent and controversial position throughout the conflict. Reputedly distantly related to Horatio Alger of "risen from the ranks," "slow and sure," and "making his way" rags-to-riches stories, Alger was a success story in his own right. Orphaned at age eleven, he supported himself and two younger siblings by working at a variety of tasks. Eventually he passed the Ohio bar (1857) and two years later moved to Michigan, where he married. Alger fought

gallantly and effectively during the Civil War, receiving promotions to brevet brigadier and then major general. After the war Alger pursued his business interests and became wealthy as well as influential in Michigan social and political circles. National commander of the Grand Army of the Republic, governor of Michigan, and ardent political supporter of rising Republican William McKinley,* Alger coveted the position of secretary of war. McKinley rewarded Alger with that post in 1897.

Alger brought to the appointment excellent political credentials, the respect of veterans, a businesslike common sense, and a concern for his subordinates. Detractors found him emotional, egotistical, and out of touch with the military advances made in the intervening three decades since he last saw action. Alger was also criticized because, despite his war record, he had no real experience in large operations. Alger's forte was with *veterans,* not with contemporary commanders.

Alger also waffled. For example, his interpretation of the Fifty Million Bill* was that only defensive preparations were allowed. John D. Long,* secretary of the navy, had a completely opposite attitude. Nevertheless, Alger ordered equipment and supplies during March and April 1898 that indicated an anticipated large expeditionary force. That Alger thought this force could be rapidly acquired, trained, and dispatched revealed his inexperience with large operations. Alger expected that with a cadre of experienced officers as well as noncommissioned officers, recruits could be made war ready very quickly. Those expectations were not realized, and the War Department received considerable criticism.

Alger also labored to free the bureau chiefs from bureaucratic interference in supply acquisition and distribution. Much of what he did had as its aim efficiency and effectiveness. A developing rift between Alger and General Nelson Miles* erupted into a full-scale feud late in May 1898. Alger, for his part, served honorably, but the details and logistics of the tasks before him severely taxed his abilities. Compounding these trials were a series of press attacks on the War Department alleging incompetence, sloth, and mismanagement. The contrast between the clean, efficient war seemingly waged by the U.S. Navy and the blundering, squalid efforts of the U.S. Army, as reported in the press, cried out for a scapegoat. Alger, as secretary of war, had the dubious distinction of being singled out: ''Algerism'' came to be a synonym for incompetence and venality. The fact that the charges were inflated seemed to have little bearing on the issue, as did Alger's scrupulous but occasionally ineffectual efforts. He relied on his subordinates and made few decisions himself. McKinley obviously distanced himself from his secretary of war, with the result that the president's political maneuvering as well as the Miles feud put fuel onto the growing media fire. Confused and defensive, Alger tried to strike back, but his counterattack sounded strident, occasionally self-righteous, and understandably defensive. Its results were not what Alger hoped. Because of the acrimony of the Alger-Miles feud, McKinley routinely bypassed both men and either made direct decisions himself or allowed Brigadier General Henry Clark Corbin*—commanding general in all but rank and name—to make command decisions. Not unaware of McKinley's maneuvers, Alger resented the president's attempts to make him appear in the wrong and he stubbornly refused to resign. Essentially inactive as secretary, Alger finally left office on 1 August 1899 after his friend, vice-president Garrett Hobart, asked for Alger's resignation on behalf of McKinley.

Despite these bitter feelings or perhaps because of them, Alger produced his own version of the events of the war, *The Spanish American War* (New York: Harper & Brothers, 1901), an interesting volume despite his bias (or because of it) and, among the war's administrators, an almost unique history.

REFERENCE: Graham A. Cosmas, *An Army for Empire* (Columbia: University of Missouri Press, 1971).

ALLEN, CHARLES HERBERT
(1848–1934)

On 11 May 1898 Charles Herbert Allen of Massachusetts succeeded Theodore Roosevelt* as assistant secretary of the navy under John D. Long.* Allen came to the post an experienced administrator and politician, having been a manufacturer, banker, state representative (1881–1882), state senator (1883), U.S. representative (1885–1889), and Massachusetts prison commissioner (1897–1898). Capable, businesslike, systematic, and thorough, Allen served well until 21 April 1900, when he resigned to become the first civil governor of Puerto Rico.* Allen was not just an administrative workhorse; he took an active role in the prosecution of the Spanish American War. Inevitably, however, he was overshadowed as assistant secretary of the navy by his illustrious predecessor, Roosevelt.

ALMIRANTE ABREU (ship).
See ALBANY.

ALMIRANTE OQUENDO (ship)

Almirante Oquendo was an armored cruiser of slightly less than 7,000 tons launched in 1891. Sister-ship to *Vizcaya** and *Infanta María Teresa,** *Almirante Oquendo* mounted two 11-inch guns in lightly armored barbettes and ten 5.5-inch guns without any armor protection except shields. There were many guns of smaller caliber as well. The deck was armored, but without cover or protection for two ammunition hoists leading directly to the 5.5-inch magazines. This last-mentioned design weakness, while not unusual, subsequently proved very damaging.

On 3 July 1898 *Almirante Oquendo* readied for the attempted escape from Santiago de Cuba.* *Oquendo* was short on ammunition and, as American observers had noticed immediately after the destruction of the *Maine,** Spanish captains did not routinely drill their seamen while in port. Thus, *Oquendo*'s readiness for battle may have left something to be desired. The fourth Spanish warship to leave the harbor, *Oquendo* did so after *Infanta María Teresa, Vizcaya,* and *Cristóbal Colón.** The destroyers *Plutón** and *Furor** followed *Oquendo.* All these ships had to pass in line by the U.S.S. *Brooklyn,** *Indiana,** *Texas,** and *Oregon** and the yachts *Gloucester** and *Vixen** waiting at the mouth of the harbor. *Oquendo* received fifty-seven hits and was set ablaze, so that both its magazines exploded. Captain Juan B. Lagaza's ship struggled to reply, but with the crew poorly trained and the ship poorly armed with inoperative guns and inappropriate ammunition, the effort was futile. *Oquendo* turned toward shore at 10:40 A.M., a beached, burned-out hulk.

REFERENCES: Pascual Cervera y Topete, *The Spanish American War* (Washington, DC: Government Printing Office, 1899); José Müller y Tejeiro, ''Battles and Capitulation of Santiago de Cuba,'' in *Notes on the Spanish American War* (Washington, DC: Government Printing Office, 1900); H. W. Wilson, *The Downfall of Spain* (New York: Burt Franklin, 1971).

ALMODÓVAR DEL RÍO, DUQUE DE
(1859–1906)

Juan Manuel Sánchez y Gutiérrez de Castro, the Duque de Almodóvar del Río, was a member of the Spanish Partido Liberal, or Liberal party. The early U.S. military successes of May 1898 caused understandable consternation within the Liberal ministry of Spain. The Liberals supported the decision to fight in part because they believed the Americans to be poor soldiers. The naval successes at Manila* and elsewhere were a crisis-brewing setback, however. Práxides Mateo Sagasta,* head of the Liberal party, took power in Spain late in 1897 after Antonio Cánovas del Castillo* had been assassinated. In May 1898, Sagasta faced the shock of initial Spanish resistance. Part of this effort involved reorganizing the government. The Duke of Almodóvar replaced Pío Gullón as foreign minister. The duke began his work just as Admiral Cervera* arrived at Santiago de Cuba* with his despondent squadron.

Almodóvar's chief role occurred during the peace negotiations,* when he actively involved himself in delaying tactics and proposals in an attempt to strengthen Spain's hand at the table.

REFERENCE: David F. Trask, *The War with Spain in 1898* (New York: Macmillan Publishing Co., 1981).

ALVARADO (ship)

Launched in 1895 and displacing 100 tons, *Alvarado* was a small Spanish gunboat that participated in a number of minor engagements. Its chief significance during the Spanish American War was its capture on 17 July 1898 by American soldiers under General William R. Shafter's* command. When Admiral William T. Sampson* discovered that the U.S. Army had captured a Spanish naval vessel, he sent a hot note to Shafter protesting the army's appropriation of a U.S. Navy objective—thus underlining a persistent conflict between the branches. *Alvarado* was taken into the U.S. Navy as U.S.S. *Alvarado.*

AMAZONAS (ship)
(renamed *New Orleans*)

When it became evident that the United States and Spain would soon be at war, the U.S. Navy Department counted its ships and imagined an inferiority. Hurriedly hunting among foreign builders for possible additions, the navy quickly seized upon two sister-ships being built in Great Britain* for Brazil: *Amazonas,* renamed *New Orleans;** and *Almirante Abreu,* renamed Albany.* On 16 March 1898 the United States purchased both ships. The naval attaché rechristened *Amazonas* the U.S.S. *Amazonas,* quickly reassigned crew from the cruiser *San Francisco* to replace the Brazilian crew, and tried to get steam up for New York. To the surprise of the Americans, all instructions and labeling on the *Amazonas* were in Portuguese; an interesting voyage ensued! Subsequently *Amazonas* served in Cuban waters.

A 3,437-ton protected cruiser originally with six 6-inch and four 4.7-inch rapid-fire guns complemented with three torpedo tubes, *Amazonas* was lightly armored and fast but with limited magazine capacity; it thus received criticism from naval authorities.

REFERENCE: John D. Alden, *The American Steel Navy* (Annapolis, MD: Naval Institute Press, 1972).

AMERICAN FEDERATION OF LABOR

The rising consciousness within the United States of the perceived plight of Cuba and its liberation movement during the 1890s struck responsive chords among a variety of American institutions. Samuel Gompers, as president of the Cigar Makers Union, developed a sympathy for the desires and concerns expressed in the Cuban liberation movement. When Gompers became president of the American Federation of Labor in 1895, these sympathies found voice in a series of three American Federation of Labor resolutions (1895, 1897, 1898) that endorsed the Cuban struggle for freedom and urged the United States to recognize the rights of the belligerent Cubans.

REFERENCE: *American Federation of Labor: History, Encyclopedia Reference Book,* 3 vols. (Westport, CT: Greenwood Press, 1977 [1919].

AMERICAN NATIONAL RED CROSS

While the American National Red Cross had no official standing, the organization was an active participant before, during, and after the Spanish American War. The American National Red Cross first distributed relief supplies to those Cubans suffering under the reconcentration policy.* During the war, the American National Red Cross (better known as the Red Cross) attempted to continue humanitarian aid. The main thrust of aid during the war consisted of strenuous efforts to assist in the camps at Tampa,* Key West,* and other gulf ports and then direct efforts in Cuba and Puerto Rico during the awkward and disorganized time between the surrender and the establishment of military rule. The Red Cross served the military as a nursing and relief auxiliary, helping to provide absent comforts such as mosquito netting, pillows, bedding, food, blankets, and towels. It also began to handle queries from families about sons in the military, ambulance service, and other nonmedical endeavors. Clara Barton* chartered the steamer *State of Texas,* loaded it with supplies, and upon its arrival at Santiago de Cuba* fed approximately 50,000 people in five days from kitchens supplied by the ship. Yellow fever,* rife in Cuba, occupied much of the efforts of medical staffs, nurses, and the Red Cross.

Red Cross female nurses were first used in and around military installations and in Cuba during the war. There had been, however, considerable friction between the Red Cross and the military. Some of it came from ignorance or misunderstanding. It was not until 6 June 1898 that the Red Cross gained acceptance by Surgeon General George Sternberg* and the military.

Compounding these external struggles was a series of crises internal to the organization. Various volunteer organizations, some affiliated with the American National Red Cross and many not so affiliated, appropriated Red Cross insignia and rhetoric. Building on American sympathy for the war and its soldiers, volunteer relief efforts became fragmented and often even competitive. The central administration had little or no control over these agencies.

While in Cuba the Red Cross went into battle with the famed Rough Riders* and, in fact, was better prepared than the army surgeons.

Americans, Cubans, and Spanish were recipients of Red Cross aid after the armistice, but there were also criticisms of its organization and of Barton personally. These criticisms harped on management style, managerial sins of omission and commission, finances, and politics. The American National Red Cross had become powerful and well financed; as such it was the target of criticism as well as praise.

REFERENCES: Clara Barton, *The Red Cross* (Washington, D.C.: American National Red Cross, 1898); Elizabeth Brown Pryor, *Clara Barton, Professional Angel* (Philadelphia: University of Pennsylvania Press, 1987).

AMMUNITION

At the onset of the Spanish American War, the U.S. Army Ordnance Department* struggled to procure enough ammunition to arm its fighting forces. Due to a cutback in congressional funds in previous years, reserve stocks of ammunition in the nation's arsenal were limited. Of great importance were the relatively new smokeless powder cartridges, needed to fire the bolt-action Krag-Jörgensen rifle,* as well as a variety of artillery pieces and navy guns. Black powder,* on the other hand, was in abundant supply and could be relied upon in an emergency. The War Department* frowned upon the black powder because the volume of smoke it produced obscured vision and often betrayed troop positions.

The problem would not be resolved quickly, however, for very few facilities produced the smokeless powder, the manufacture of which was much more complex than that of black powder. Although factories contracted by the government were turning out the ammunition as fast as possible, the commander of the army, General Nelson Miles,* predicted the army would not have nearly enough for the large-scale expeditions planned by the War Department.

Indeed, only three government contractors, two in the East and one on the West Coast, were equipped to produce smokeless powder when mobilization began. A fourth producer's works blew up in March 1898. Other powder manufacturers either constructed new plants or reworked old ones, but they could not meet the immediate demands of the War Department. The army and navy therefore had to work out a priority system for allotting the available smokeless powder. During the first few months of readiness, the smokeless powder was supplied to the U.S. Navy for its battleships' big guns and to the U.S. Army for use in the Krag. The coast defense guns, the field artillery, and the volunteers were given the black powder. Eventually these units received the smokeless powder, but in most cases after most of the fighting had ended. Ironically, the Ordnance Department ended the war with a stockpile of the smokeless powder.

Spanish troops faced a dilemma similar to that of their enemy. Although issued smokeless powder cartridges for their Mauser rifles* and artillery guns, supplies were depleted during the heaviest fighting, forcing a hasty retreat from their entrenched positions.

REFERENCES: Graham A. Cosmas, *An Army for Empire* (Columbia: University of Missouri Press, 1971); William H. Hallahan, *Misfire* (New York: Scribner's, 1994).

                                                                    MITCHELL YOCKELSON

AMPHITRITE (ship)

The *Amphitrite* class of monitors* consisted of the U.S.S. *Miantonomah,* Monadnock,* Terror,* and *Amphitrite. Amphitrite,* for which the class was named, shared the same dimensions with the others in her class: about 250 feet in length on a beam of 55 feet 10 inches. Nine-inch side armor protected its 3,990 tons. Minor differences existed among the ships, but *Amphitrite* had four 10-inch guns and ten guns of lesser caliber. These monitors were old ships, built of iron rather than steel, and their designs dated from the Civil War. Laid down in 1874, *Amphitrite* could make only a little over 10 knots when finally commissioned twenty-one years later on 23 April 1895.

Amphitrite was assigned to Admiral William T. Sampson's* command, but due to the monitor's small fuel capacity and slowness, it was frequently towed by larger ships such as *Iowa.* Amphitrite* participated in the bombardment of San Juan,* Puerto Rico, where she received several hits, losing her after-turret to enemy action.

REFERENCE: John D. Alden, *The American Steel Navy* (Annapolis, MD: Naval Institute Press, 1972).

ANDERSON, THOMAS MCARTHUR
(1836–1917)

Trained as a lawyer, Thomas McArthur Anderson joined the Union forces in 1861 as a private and advanced through time to become a brigadier general.

During the Civil War he fought at Spotsylvania and in the Battle of the Wilderness. Anderson arrived at the Presidio in San Francisco* on 23 May 1898 to be the commander of the vanguard of the Philippine expeditionary force (designated Eighth Army Corps,* or Eighth Corps), some 2,500 men. Since Anderson's troops had to sail on 25 May, he had one day only to inspect his command. Marching from the Presidio to the Pacific Mail dock, Anderson's troops boarded the hastily chartered *City of Peking,* *Australia,* and *City of Sydney* for Manila.* En route, the expedition stopped briefly at Hawaii,* leaving with the cruiser U.S.S. *Charleston* as escort. Captain Henry Glass* of the *Charleston* opened his sealed orders and proceeded to Guam,* where the island was taken without a fight. The expedition finally landed at Cavite,* in the Philippines, on 1 June. The Philippine soldiers coolly received Anderson's command. Emilio Aguinaldo,* president of the nascent Philippine Republic, met only once with Anderson and not at all with General Wesley Merritt,* commander of Eighth Corps, who had arrived by 25 July.

With the arrival of Anderson's troops, the Americans moved to attack Manila. Admiral George Dewey* had controlled Manila Bay* since 1 May. Anderson's troops now moved within proximity of 12,000 Philippine nationalists in what was to become the siege of Manila. By the end of July, troops commanded by General Arthur MacArthur* (father of Douglas MacArthur) had also landed, and the attack on Manila commenced. Merritt organized the whole army into a division of 8,500 troops (with Anderson divisional commander) composed of two brigades commanded by Francis Vinton Greene* and MacArthur. Scrupulously avoiding any contact with Aguinaldo, the commanders moved closer to the Spaniards to engage the fortifications. Unknown to Anderson or his subordinates, the Spanish commander of Manila, Fermín Jáudenes y Álvarez* had negotiated with Merritt and Dewey that after a token struggle, Jáudenes would surrender Manila to the Americans, thus eclipsing Aguinaldo and the Philippine nationalists completely.

Anderson also commanded divisions during the first phases of the Philippine Insurrection*; in 1899 he was replaced by General Henry W. Lawton.*
REFERENCE: Leon Wolff, *Little Brown Brother* (New York: Longmans, 1970).

ANDRÉ, EDOUARD
(1840–1911)

While General Wesley Merritt* continued the planning for the troop assault on the Spanish forces holding Manila,* Commodore George Dewey* attempted to negotiate a surrender of Spanish troops. Unfortunately the night of 31 July 1898 saw a clash between Merritt's forces and the Spanish forces under command of General Fermín Jáudenes y Alvarez.* Jáudenes had replaced General Basilio Augustín Dávila* as commander when Madrid perceived Augustín Dávila's eagerness to surrender, but Jáudenes shared Augustín Dávila's assessment of the hopelessness of the situation as he faced hostile Philippine insurgents and an American army without hope of relief. Yet Spain insisted on resistance in order to save face. Jáudenes's solution to this dilemma was an orchestrated token attack by Merritt's troops with an orchestrated token resistance by Spanish troops and then the surrender of Manila to the Americans. The delicate diplomatic interchanges between Dewey and Jáudenes were carried by the Belgian consul, Edouard André. André would obtain a statement from Jáudenes, write it into a memorandum book, and then go to Dewey and Merritt for response. The Americans' responses would in turn be transcribed and André would make another trip—all this in accordance with customs grown out of communications between opposing commanders. In addition to André's informal dispatch transfers was some formal correspondence between Merritt, Dewey, and Jáudenes.

REFERENCES: Thomas M. Anderson, "Our Rule in the Philippines," *North American Review* 170 (February 1900): 272–283; Ignacio Salinas y Ángulo, *Defensa del General Jáudenes* (Madrid: Impreso y Litografía del Depósito de la Guerra, 1899).

ANGIOLILLO, MIGUEL
(1872–1897)

On Sunday, 8 August 1897, Spanish prime minister Antonio Cánovas del Castillo* was relaxing in the mountains of Basque country in the town of Santa Agueda. While reading his newspaper on the terrace with his wife, he was approached by a young blond man. Without uttering a word, Miguel Angiolillo pulled a pistol and discharged three times into Cánovas. The prime minister was dead within an hour. His successor, Práxides Mateo Sagasta,* inherited the political tightrope of Spanish politics. His solutions (the compromise policy of Cuban and Puerto Rican "autonomy" and the replacement of Cuban governor-general Valeriano Weyler*) attempted to set Spain on a different political path. With Weyler gone from Cuba, the Cuban Insurrection* flamed again, giving Americans who wanted some, fresh excuses to go to war with Spain. Had Cánovas lived, the Spanish American War might never have happened.

Angiolillo sought vengeance for Cánovas's ordering of the execution of numerous comrade anarchists.

REFERENCE: Vincent C. Creux, *Antonio Cánovas del Castillo* (Paris: Love, 1897).

ANNAPOLIS (ship)

The U.S.S. *Annapolis* was the first of her class, commissioned on 20 July 1897. The others were *Vicksburg,** *Newport,** and *Princeton.* Each was a 1,000-ton barkentine rigged single-screw steamer of graceful lines. As gunboats, they were armed with six 4-inch guns and a miscellany of smaller-caliber weapons. The auxiliary barkentine sail rig and clipper bow gave the class a classical or romantic backward glance to the age of sail. For work in the tropics, these gunboats were sheathed and coppered on their hulls.

Annapolis served in the U.S. blockade* of Havana.* On 14 May 1898 *Annapolis, Vicksburg,* and others fired upon the Spanish *Conde de Venadito** and *Nueva España.* On 15 July *Annapolis* engaged the battery at Baracoa, receiving two hits in return. On 21 July *Annapolis,* along with *Topeka,** *Wasp,* and *Ley-*

den, * steamed into Nipe Bay* and exchanged fire with the aging Spanish gun-boat *Jorge Juan,* the latter sinking in the bay.

Annapolis later served in Puerto Rico* in support of General Nelson Miles's* expedition, obtaining the surrender of Ponce.* The ship survived until 1950, when she was scrapped.

REFERENCE: H. W. Wilson, *The Downfall of Spain* (New York: Burt Franklin, 1971).

ANTI-IMPERIALIST LEAGUE

Organized 15 June 1898, the Anti-Imperialist League (later the American Anti-Imperialist League) became the most potent force opposing the annexation of the Philippines. The league opposed annexation on moral, economic, racial, legal, and idealistic grounds and backed its arguments with a publication program of substance. The real power of the Anti-Imperialist League came not from its arguments, (which most Americans disagreed with or ignored), but from the quality of its membership: Andrew Carnegie, Mark Twain, William James, David Starr Jordan, and Samuel Gompers were not individuals who could be dismissed as eccentrics. Edward Atkinson,* the league's honorary director, initiated the huge mailing campaign that promulgated the league's ideas. George S. Boutwell, former secretary of the treasury and Massachusetts senator, served as president. The league flourished from 1898 to 1900, but the Treaty of Paris* effectively snuffed the league's candle.

REFERENCES: Robert L. Beisner, *Twelve against Empire* (New York: McGraw-Hill, 1968); Leon Wolff, *Little Brown Brother* (New York: Kraus Reprint Co., 1970).

ARANGO, CLEMENCIA

In one of the more sensational incidents prior to the Spanish American War—one that inflamed Victorian notions of the sanctity of female modesty—Richard Harding Davis,* a reporter for the *New York Journal,* traveled in Cuba with Frederic Remington,* noted illustrator, seeking interviews with insurgents. As Davis concluded his tour, he booked passage for the States on the steamer *Olivette.* * On the *Olivette,* he met Clemencia Arango, who told him she was being exiled for aiding the insurgent cause. Before their departure Arango and two female companions were searched at their homes by Spanish authorities and then searched again in a customs house. The women were followed aboard the American-owned and -flagged *Olivette* and were undressed and searched again. Davis assumed that male detectives had performed the strip-search on Arango and her companions when in actual fact the search had been performed by women—something of which Davis may have been ignorant. At any rate, the *Journal*'s publisher, William Randolph Hearst,* commissioned Remington to do an illustration for the paper. Remington naturally created a provocative illustration of a naked young woman vainly trying to maintain her modesty while three hirsute Spaniards stood by. The article was front-page news in the 12 February 1897 issue of the *Journal.*

When Arango arrived at Tampa,* she corrected the report—much to her own

embarrassment as well as Hearst's—as Joseph Pulitzer's* *New York World* gloated. The incident seems to have been merely a mistake. Although there had been cases of male Spaniards strip-searching females, this was not one of them.
REFERENCE: Charles H. Brown, *The Correspondents' War* (New York: Scribner's, 1967).

ARECIBO, PUERTO RICO

The Arecibo River flows north from the Cordillera Central or the backbone of mountains that runs through the middle of the island of Puerto Rico.* Arecibo itself is on a small bay at the mouth of the river about 40 miles West of San Juan.* In 1899, Arecibo had a population of around 30,000 inhabitants.

During the war, Arecibo was one of the suspected landing sites of the expeditionary force under General Nelson Miles.* Madrid so informed Governor-General Manuel Macías y Casado.* When the Americans did land at Guánica* on 25 July 1898 and subsequently at Ponce* and Arroyo*, the inhabitants seemed to welcome the Americans. Miles pushed over the mountains after dividing his forces. Brigadier General Theodore Schwan* led one column straight north to Arecibo, taking Lares and Mayagüez* and fighting the Spanish at Hormigueros. The peace protocol signed on 12 August ended hostilities without Schwan's reaching Arecibo.
REFERENCE: Daniel F. Trask, *The War with Spain in 1898* (New York: Macmillan Publishing Co., 1981).

ARELLANO, CAYETANO
(1847–?)

A Philippine jurist, lawyer, and professor of signal prominence, Cayetano Arellano was one of those who attempted to discourage the independence movement led by Emilio Aguinaldo*—and this despite the fact that he was chosen to be secretary of foreign relations in the revolutionary government's cabinet. After the Malolos Constitution of 29 November 1898, he was appointed again to post of secretary of the Department of Foreign Relations, but he was unable to serve.

Arellano was the first supreme court justice of the Philippines under U.S. rule. He also served as a founding member of the Philippine Federal party, a conservative, pro-American organization. Many consider Arellano a practical man who recognized that struggle against the Americans was futile. Others have not been so charitable in their assessment: Teodoro Agoncillo portrays Arellano as one of the betrayers of Philippine independence.
REFERENCE: Teodore M. Kalaw, *The Philippine Revolution* (Kawilihan, P. I.: Jorge B. Vargas Filipiniana Foundation, 1969).

ARMISTICE IN CUBA

One of the more curious diplomatic events in the history of Spain and the United States occurred in the weeks immediately preceding the outbreak of the

Spanish American War on 21 April 1898. Stewart L. Woodford,* U.S. minister to Spain, worked with the new Spanish prime minister, Práxides Mateo Sagasta,* in forming the Liberal party government in Spain. Woodford's as well as President William McKinley's* agenda included an end to the civil war in Cuba. Sagasta and his party walked the politically challenging path of attempting to maintain Spanish honor, satisfy the Spanish who demanded action in Cuba, and pacify an increasingly belligerent United States. Sagasta recalled Governor-General Valeriano Weyler*—called "Butcher"—and announced that all rights and prerogatives of Iberian Spaniards were available to Spanish subjects in the Caribbean. A series of strained diplomatic exchanges expressed Spain's consternation about U.S. filibustering and the continued and augmented violence in Cuba. Meanwhile, the battleship *Maine** journeyed to Havana* and the Spanish minister at Washington, Enrique Dupuy de Lôme* self-destructed when a letter critical of McKinley got into the American press. The destruction of the *Maine* on 15 February 1898 and worsening conditions in Cuba led to a hardening of positions in Washington. In diplomatic dispatches, Washington stipulated an armistice in Cuba between the insurgents and the Spanish forces as an avenue toward peace. On 27 March a communication to Woodford attempted an armistice, a revocation of the *reconcentrado* plan (reconcentration policy*) and a proposal for the U.S. president to serve as arbitrator between Spain and the insurgents. Also, a demand for Cuban independence made the previous day required a Spanish reply by 31 March. Spain acknowledged a willingness to arbitrate the *Maine* sinking, repeal the *reconcentrado* policy in the western provinces of the island, and agree to an armistice should the insurgents ask for it. Woodford reported the reply sadly, expecting the terms to be unacceptable. On 5 April Spain repealed the *reconcentrado* order for the entire island of Cuba, but the armistice was left out of the reply. Papal intervention at this point suggested an armistice, which Spain accepted on 9 April. Thus, by the second week of April 1898, Spain had accepted all the demands Washington had made, a point McKinley noted in his message to Congress on 11 April. The situation in the United States had rapidly deteriorated as war preparations developed. Meanwhile, Congress passed resolutions on 19 April authorizing the president to intervene in Cuba, to recognize the independence of Cuba, and to carry out the resolutions through use of armed force. By 3:00 P.M. on 22 April, Admiral William T. Sampson* had positioned the North Atlantic Squadron* on blockade* off Havana.*

REFERENCES: Alfred L. P. Dennis, *Adventures in American Diplomacy, 1896–1906* (New York: E. P. Dutton & Co., 1928); Walter Millis, *The Martial Spirit* (Boston: Houghton Mifflin, 1931).

ARMY, CUBAN

The Cuban army never numbered more than 30,000 distributed into six army corps opposing the Spanish: Santiago (First and Second Corps),* Camagüey (Third Corps), Havana (Fourth Corps),* Matanzas (Fifth Corps),* and Pinar del

Río (Sixth Corps). The Cuban army lost 10,665 dead, attesting to the ferocity of the conflict between the Spanish and the Cubans. The Cubans served as a roving guerrilla force and, though greatly outnumbered, carried out a hit-and-run strategy that kept Spanish garrisons on the defensive. Armed through captured Spanish weapons or American weapons smuggled into Cuba, these troops operated in small units controlled by regional commanders. General Calixto García* possessed the largest Cuban force in the field and would occasionally engage in pitched battles against Spanish garrisons or towns. The Cuban army also controlled a shadow government of insurrectionists whose civil officials were elected by the army. The Cubans' principal tactic was the raid and ambush, and aided by an excellent intelligence network, they could join or evade the Spanish at will.

Colonel Frederick Funston,* an American, fought with the Cuban army and commanded the artillery in several engagements before the Spanish American War. García's artillery was handled by an American detachment, also.

When the Americans landed, the Cuban army played important tactical roles in numerous actions. Elbert Hubbard's* ''Message to García''* celebrated the working relationship of the Cuban and U.S. armies.

REFERENCES: Graham A. Cosmas, *An Army for Empire* (Columbia: University of Missouri Press, 1971); José Antonio Medel, *The Spanish American War and Its Results* (Havana: P. Fernández & Co., 1931).

ARMY, SPANISH

The Spanish army at the outbreak of hostilities in 1898 had 278,447 officers and men in Cuba. This number includes regulars and volunteers. Puerto Rico* had another 10,005 men. Among regulars and volunteers in the Philippines,* Spain fielded 51,331 men. About 41 percent of the forces in Cuba were volunteer Cubans loyal to Spain and mercenaries. The Spanish army in Cuba was roughly composed of infantry (198,679 men), cavalry (22,548 men), artillery (9,431 men), engineers (6,346 men), and miscellaneous forces of hospital, pack train, marine, mercenary, and police forces (41,453 men). While Spain's armies were numerically impressive, particularly when compared to Cuban and U.S. army forces, Spanish forces received marginal or poor training and suffered from debilitating tropical diseases. Since 1895, some 13,000 Spaniards had died from yellow fever* alone. The ravages of disease meant that only 20–25 percent of the Spanish army was capable of field operations, according to some estimates. The Cuban volunteers (loyalists) were poorly disciplined and by many accounts unreliable.

The effectiveness of the Spanish army was also undermined by an insurmountable strategic weakness and by the naval debacle in the Philippines and in Cuba. The nature of the Cuban Insurrection* gave the revolutionists the countryside while Spain held seaports and large cities. Denied Cuban sources of food and supplies sufficient to maintain their armies in Cuba, the Spanish depended upon a weak navy to ensure a logistical continuity. A similar situation existed in the Philippines. Although sufficient troops were stationed in Cuba to repel any U.S. expeditionary force, they were dispersed in order to deny territory to the insurrection.

Because the Spanish troops were dispersed in several locations throughout the island, they could be harassed separately and attacked piecemeal. When, for example, General José Toral* surrendered the garrison at Santiago,* he also surrendered Guantánamo* and a half-dozen other outlying garrisons that depended on Santiago for supplies and additional troops. Without command of the roads or the seas, Spain could neither reinforce nor resupply its scattered garrisons. Its strategy of dispersing troop assets throughout the regions had been born of the guerrilla warfare characteristic of the Cuban fight for independence. However, the strategy proved ineffectual against the U.S. expeditionary forces in Cuba, Puerto Rico, and the Philippines, where U.S. forces were able to overwhelm small detachments and garrisons almost at will.

Fortifications in Cuba and Manila* were ancient; their lack of modern artillery hampered defensive efforts. With the defeat of the Spanish navy* at Manila on 1 May 1898 and the abortive relief by Admiral Cámara,* the Philippines were lost. The defeat of the squadron of Admiral Cervera* on 3 July meant that Cuba met the same fate. Denied resupply or the hope of rearmament, the Spanish army faced a hopeless situation despite its superior numbers. Spain had resources, great popular enthusiasm at home, and mobilization capability; but without a navy that could defeat its American opponents, none of these resources could be brought to the battlefield.

After the ferocious land battles in and around Santiago,* Spanish resistance wilted in Cuba. In Puerto Rico, Spanish resistance hardly materialized, although General Nelson Miles's* strategy had not run its course before hostilities ceased. In the Philippines, General Fermín Jáudenes* arranged a planned or staged defensive battle to satisfy Spanish honor, and then he surrendered Manila.* This in no way suggests that the Spanish were lacking in bravery; on the contrary, at El Caney* and Santiago the Spanish fought a spirited and determined defense, suffering almost 100 percent casualties at El Caney, either from wounds or disease. Morale was low, however, and after the loss of Cervera's fleet and Commodore George Dewey's* victory at Manila, there seemed little purpose in pursuing the conflict.

REFERENCES: Miguel Alonso Baquer, "The Spanish American War of 1898 and Its Effects on Spanish Military Institutions," in *Proceedings of the 1982 International Military History Symposium* (Washington, DC: U.S. Army Center of Military History, 1984); French Ensor Chadwick, *The Relations of the United States and Spain* (New York: Russell & Russell, 1968); Graham A. Cosmas, *An Army for Empire* (Columbia: University of Missouri Press, 1971).

ARMY, U.S.

The U.S. Army's strength on 1 April 1898 consisted of 2,143 officers and 26,040 men—hardly a formidable force with which to confront the Spanish army* in Cuba or even in the Philippines.* Therefore, on 22 and 26 April, Congress increased the standing army to over 56,000 and authorized 125,000 volunteers (later increased to 200,000 volunteers), including the recruiting of 3,000 men with special qualifications, one regiment of which became the celebrated Rough Riders.* With the 210,000 men called to serve (28,000 regulars, 182,000 volunteers), eight corps were to be established: First Corps was to assemble at Camp Thomas,* Georgia, under Major General John R. Brooke*; Second Corps at Camp Alger,* Virginia, under Major General William R. Graham; Third Corps also at Camp Thomas but under Major General James F. Wade*; Fourth Corps at Mobile, Alabama, under Major General John J. Coppinger; Fifth Corps at Tampa* under Major General William R. Shafter.* Sixth Corps was also to be at Camp Thomas, led by Major General James H. Wilson,* but it never organized; Seventh Corps was to assemble at Tampa under Major General Fitzhugh Lee*; and Eighth Corps at San Francisco* and Manila* under Major General Wesley Merritt.* Under the Fifty Million Bill* of 9 March 1898, much had already been done, such as equipping the regulars with Krag-Jorgensen rifles* and carbines. Volunteers made do with .45-caliber Springfields.*

The speed and energy of the buildup astonished many contemporary observers. By mid-August 1898, the War Department* had outfitted close to 300,000 regular and volunteer troops. This rapid growth of the U.S. Army strained the regular officer corps, the meager supplies available, the supply system itself, and, in consequence, the patience of many soldiers. President William McKinley's* political decisions to accelerate the land war pressured an already-strained system. The result was a series of shortages, equipment boondoggles, transportation tie-ups, sanitation disasters, scandal, and much angry finger pointing. Secretary of War Russell A. Alger* got most of the criticism, including that from the infamous beef controversy.* The army, and the War Department in particular, responded with a trial-and-error approach. Most of the trials derived from the army's unreadiness and the speed of the buildup rather than from ineptitude or negligence. In a few short months, the U.S. Army moved from a small peace-keeping force of 26,000 to more than ten times that number; it also moved from responsibilities only in its own territories to global involvements in unfamiliar climates with unfamiliar peoples. The transitions were breathtaking. And while disease, supply problems, and fluctuating demands on the U.S. Army caused confusion, pressure, and pain, on the whole the organization struggled successfully to accomplish its missions.

REFERENCES: French Ensor Chadwick, *The Relations of the United States and Spain,* 2 vols. (New York: Russell & Russell, 1911); Graham A. Cosmas, *An Army for Empire* (Columbia: University of Missouri Press, 1971).

ARROYO, PUERTO RICO

General Nelson Miles's* plan for capturing San Juan,* Puerto Rico,* called for a four-element advance on San Juan. The most important element was to advance along the road from Ponce,* through Aibonito* to San Juan. Miles expected Spanish troops to dig in or at least contest the American thrust at either Coamo,* the pass at Aibonito, or both. Aibonito lay in the *Cordillera* or mountain ranges that run east to west across the island. Anticipating this defense, Miles planned another advance from Arroyo, a town about 45 miles east of Ponce. Troops would march to Cayey,* on the Ponce–San Juan road north of Aibonito, and thus cut off the expected Spanish retreat from Aibonito.

Accordingly, during 3–5 August 1898, Major General John R. Brooke* landed about 5,000 troops at Arroyo. Brooke was to march through Guayama* to Cayey, link up with Major General James H. Wilson's* column, and then on the outskirts of San Juan join with Brigadier General Theodore Schwan,* who would advance from Ponce to Mayagüez* and Arecibo.*

REFERENCES: Philip S. Foner, *The Spanish-Cuban-American War and the Birth of American War and the Birth of American Imperialism* (New York: Monthly Review Press, 1972); Ángel Rivero Méndez, *Crónica de la Guerra Hispano Americana en Puerto Rico* (New York: Plus Ultra, 1973).

ARTILLERY

At the outbreak of the Spanish American War, the regular army consisted of five regiments of artillery and ten field batteries, which were scattered across the United States. Mobilization for the war increased the regular artillery to seven regiments to be complimented by eight volunteer batteries of heavy artillery and sixteen volunteer batteries of field artillery.

The U.S. Army's Fifth Corps,* under the direction of Major General William R. Shafter,* included a provisional field artillery battalion of four batteries of 3.2-inch field pieces commanded by Major John H. Dillenback, as well as two batteries of siege artillery. In addition, the Ordnance Department* issued to the Fifth Corps twelve Hotchkiss revolving cannons, about sixty Gatling guns*, eight field mortars, an experimental dynamite gun, and assorted other small-caliber rapid-fire weapons.

The guns proved to be of little use because the black powder* used as ammunition produced clouds that revealed their positions to the enemy and slowed down the rate of fire. Another problem surfaced when Dillenback and Shafter failed to take advantage of the centralized command of the field artillery to mass fire upon the enemy positions. Although field artillery tactics stressed mass firing, they used the artillery in a piecemeal fashion that proved less effective. The Spanish, on the other hand, used smokeless ammunition and a rapid-fire technique that proved much more effective than the American technique.

Another concern to the War Department* was manning the coastal fortifications of the United States in event of an attack by Spanish raiders. In many cases, the War Department was forced to improvise due to the lack of modern weapons. The Corps of Engineers* and the Ordnance Department set up temporary batteries by mounting obsolete muzzle-loading rifles, and in the case of Civil War–era forts, they reconditioned the guns and mortars. In addition, twenty-one new 8-inch breech-loading rifles were mounted on the carriages of old 15-inch smoothbores. In April 1898, Secretary Russell A. Alger* sent most of the U.S. Army's big siege guns to the coastal forts, but he removed them in May and June for use in Cuba.

To operate the mounted guns, the War Department received approval in 1898 from Congress for the first increase in the regular army in thirty years. The appropriations boosted the artillery to about 6,000 officers and men. When the war ended, however, none of the coastal artillery had fired a shot. The guns were eventually dismounted and placed in storage for future emergency. Although their efforts were carried out in vain, the coast artillery provided a sound defense on the homefront and provided its citizens with a sense of security.

REFERENCES: Graham A. Cosmas, *An Army for Empire* (Columbia: University of Missouri Press, 1971); Boyd L. Dastrupp, *King of Battle: A Branch of History of the U.S. Army's Field Artillery Program* (Ft. Monroe, VA: U.S. Army Training and Doctrine Command, 1993).

MITCHELL YOCKELSON

ASERRADERO, CUBA

Aserradero lies west of Santiago de Cuba* at 19°59' north 76°11' west. Between 19 June 1898 and 26 June a unique cooperative disembarkment occurred at Aserradero. While cooperation and joint operations between the U.S. Army and the Cuban forces were not unusual, the Aserradero extraction required coordination with the navy and other American units. General Calixto García,* commander of the Santiago Cuban Army Corps, intended a diversion at Cabañas in preparation for the assault on General Arsenio Linares y Pomba* and the Spanish forces in and around Santiago. A detachment of García's forces were to be transferred by sea from Aserradero to Siboney* in secret, so that Linares would not shift his forces. The 3,000 troops with rations and ammunition were transferred completely by Admiral William T. Sampson's* vessels on 26 June.

REFERENCE: David F. Trask, *The War with Spain in 1898* (New York: Macmillan Publishing Co., 1981).

ASIATIC SQUADRON

In 1896 Lieutenant William W. Kimball* completed a study for the Office of Naval Intelligence* that included a plan for the reduction of Spanish forces in the Philippines. Theodore Roosevelt,* assistant secretary of the navy, was an ardent supporter of such a plan. Naturally, Commodore George Dewey* and the Asiatic Squadron were tools to accomplish this mission when war came in 1898. The Asiatic Squadron was based in Hong Kong.* Besides showing the flag, it existed to protect American trade interests in Asia. The squadron possessed no armored ships, but it did count protected cruisers in its complement: *Olympia,* *Baltimore,* *Raleigh,* and *Boston.* The original plan as presented by Kimball had no intention to annex territory; rather, it endeavored to exert pressure on Spain in Asian waters. On 1 May 1898 the U.S. Asiatic Squadron decisively destroyed the Spanish fleet at Manila.* With the subsequent annexation of the Philippines and other islands in the Pacific came an understandable need to strengthen the U.S. military presence in the Pacific. The Boxer Rebellion, the Russo-Japanese War, and the Philippine Insurrection* gave weight to these needs. The Asiatic Squadron soon became the Asiatic Fleet, in 1902, and the Pacific Fleet, in 1907.

REFERENCE: William Reynolds Braisted, *The United States Navy in the Pacific, 1897–1909* (Austin: University of Texas Press, 1958).

ASSOCIATED PRESS

Only the largest U.S. daily newspapers could afford to have their own correspondents in the field. The four largest New York papers—the *World,* the *Journal,* the *Herald,* and the *Sun*—had subscription news services used by many big city papers away from New York, and although a few other independent syndicates existed, most newspapers in the country during the war got stories from the Associated Press telegraphic news service. The Associated Press was at that time the only cooperatively owned, nonprofit press agency in the United States.

Generally, the Associated Press was known for more accurate and less sensational reporting than the big New York papers, certainly than the *World* or *Journal,* although the *World* did have an AP franchise and the *Journal* got one in 1898 upon its purchase of the New York *Advertiser.* The organization was slow in developing coverage in Cuba after the sinking of the *Maine**; its general manager, Melville E. Stone, had pacifist leanings and hesitated stirring up public sentiment for war. He eventually relented somewhat. By the end of April 1898, when Admiral Sampson* began the U.S. naval blockade* of western Cuba, the Associated Press was operating three press boats, the *Wanda,* the *Dauntless,** and the *Dandy,* to bring back news of the hostilities; later, it added the *Cynthia* and the *Kate Spencer.*

REFERENCES: Charles H. Brown, *The Correspondents' War* (New York: Scribner's, 1967); Charles Sanford Diehl, *The Staff Correspondent* (San Antonio, TX: Clegg, 1931).

MARK A. THOMAS

ASTOR, JOHN JACOB
(1864–1912)

The great grandson of the famous fur king, John Jacob Astor graduated from Harvard in 1888 and toured the world for a few years before settling down to business. Said to be worth over $100 million, Astor viewed the outbreak of the Spanish American War in 1898 as a patriotic opportunity. He put *Nourmahal,* his yacht,* at the U.S. Navy's disposal and outfitted an artillery battery for the Philippines at his own expense. He also volunteered and was commissioned a lieutenant-colonel. His first duties were to aid in inspection at Camp Chickamauga under General Joseph C. Breckinridge.* He was later placed of the staff of General William R. Shafter* and saw action in Cuba. At the close of the war, Astor was promoted to colonel.

Capitalist, science-fiction author, and inventor, Astor died courageously in the sinking of the *Titanic* on 15 April 1912.

ATKINS, EDWIN FARNSWORTH
(1850–1926)

Edwin Farnsworth Atkins's father, Elisha Atkins, was a New England sugar merchant, of the firm E. Atkins & Company, and a vice-president of the Union Pacific Railroad during its early years (1860s–1890s). Just after the start of the Ten Years' War* in 1869, as his father became more involved with railroad business, Atkins was sent to Cuba to attend to his father's sugar interests. By 1875, he had complete charge of the company's Cuban operations.

Originally, E. Atkins & Company acted as middlemen, purchasing sugar from refiners and merchants in the vicinity of Cienfuegos,* on the southern shore of the island. By the early 1880s, after a period of hard times in the Cuban sugar industry, the Atkins Company began taking over sugarcane plantations that were unable to pay their debts to the company, acquiring large landholdings in the southern portion of the island.

With such a financial stake in Cuba, Atkins was generally sympathetic to the Spanish government as opposed to the insurgents. A major disruptive tactic of the Cuban insurgents was to burn the sugarcane fields of large landholders. Relying to some extent on large numbers of armed guards to protect his own plantations, when possible Atkins preferred to practice a pragmatic diplomacy, trying to keep peace with both the insurgents who roved the country as well as with the Spanish government. His estates were able to continue production, albeit at lowered levels, at times when most others had to halt operations due to the insurgency.

Atkins opposed U.S. recognition of belligerency status for the Cuban rebels. In 1896, when hearing that delegates of the Cuban junta* would be attempting to persuade Secretary of State Richard Olney* to grant such status to the insurgents in Cuba, he convinced Secretary Olney to reject their request. To fend off congressional pressures for the recognition of belligerency status in the wake of the Morgan-Cameron Resolution, Atkins helped Olney draft a pacification proposal, submitted to Spain on April 7, 1896. Under its terms, Cuba would gain some degree of autonomy,* although Spain would retain sovereignty in Cuba; the United States would mediate the dispute between Spain and the Cuban rebels. Spain rejected this proposal, partly because of political pressures at home, where anti-American sentiments were running high.

After the war Atkins's estates returned to full production. He enjoyed good relations with the Cuban government but favored a strong U.S. presence on the island. Both before and after the war, he devoted much effort to the cause of tariff reductions in the interest of keeping Cuban-grown sugar competitive in the U.S. with domestically grown sugar.

REFERENCE: Edwin Farnsworth Atkins, *Sixty Years in Cuba: Reminiscences of Edwin F. Atkins* (Cambridge, MA: Riverside, 1926).

MARK A. THOMAS

ATKINSON, EDWARD
(1827–1905)

Edward Atkinson of Boston, Massachusetts, was already a well-known speaker for a variety of political causes by the time the events of the Spanish American War cast shadows on his path. He was an agitator for sound money, a cotton manufacturer, fire insurance executive, statistician, economist, and inventor, among other things.

Atkinson applauded the efforts of President William McKinley* to keep the country out of war. Although he sympathized with the plight of the Cubans, he felt that war with Spain would be devastating to the economy. Once war was declared, Atkinson, surprisingly, took the stand that such a war was inevitable. He apparently took little interest in the prosecution of the war until he was convinced of the War Department's* mismanagement of the affair and the ineptitude of some of the U.S. commanders. He became particularly alarmed by the reports of malarial victims and by the ravages of venereal diseases. Meanwhile, the issues surrounding what to do with the Philippines* began to occupy his attentions. To Atkinson, the Spanish American War was a contract not to seize Cuba but to free it from Spanish domination. The growing desire to obtain the Philippines was unacceptable to Atkinson. He viewed the question of imperialism as a sullying of American principles. He favored establishing a joint protectorate of the Philippines by treaty with the other naval powers of the region. He also worried that a large U.S. force in the Philippines would be subject to tropical diseases and other ravages.

A founding member of the Anti-Imperialist League,* Atkinson served as vice-president of that organization and organized an ambitious pamphlet distribution system that achieved considerable controversy. He attempted to address the troops at Manila* with direct mailings, but the postmaster at San Francisco* interdicted the mailings. The Treaty of Paris* stole much of Atkinson's steam, but he continued to work with Senator George Hoar* and Senator Donelson Caffery to attempt a withdrawal from the Philippines.

Atkinson was also a critic of the manner of the investigation into the sinking of the *Maine,* * but the McKinley administration refused to reopen the inquiry. As an antiwar agitator, he also attacked the navy's battleship-building program, dubbing these ships "commerce destroyers," not battleships. Atkinson's capitalist-centered antiwar rhetoric won him many adherents among Democrats and Republicans alike.

REFERENCE: Harold Francis Williamson, *Edward Atkinson* (New York: Arno Press, 1972).

ATROCITIES AND BRUTALITIES

The twin specters of atrocity and brutality seem to be omnipresent in the history of human conflict. A large amount of contemporary writing chronicled or alleged atrocities by Spaniards, Cubans, and insurrectionists alike. Worse was a longstanding practice of emphasizing such brutality for political purposes that dated at least from the Cuban War of 1868. The *reconcentrado** problem exacerbated the debate and inflamed emotions. Clearly, both Spaniards and Cubans behaved, on occasion, in a brutal fashion. However, it is exceedingly difficult to distinguish stories based upon fact and stories marshalled to support a particular viewpoint. The yellow press (*see* The Press and The War*) indicted the Spanish and dismissed rebuttals as propagandist defensiveness. A turning point occurred on 17 March 1898 when Senator Redfield Proctor* addressed the Senate after a fact-finding mission to Cuba. Proctor was known not as a jingoist but as a skeptic of the alarms trumpeted by the press. His address and report were temperate and unemotional and as such had greater effect, say some authors, than all the efforts of the press* combined. Wall Street became convinced, along with other skeptics, that Cuba had to be saved from Spanish misrule.

REFERENCES: Walter Millis, *The Martial Spirit* (Boston: Houghton Mifflin, 1931); George Bronson Rea, *Facts and Fakes about Cuba* (New York: George Munro's Sons, 1987).

AUGUSTÍN DÁVILA, BASILIO
(1840–1910)

The Spanish governor-general of the Philippines,* Basilio Augustín Dávila, was chosen to replace General Fernando Primo de Rivera*—a decision that some felt was a mistake. In any event, Augustín Dávila was installed a few days before war was declared and so had little time to effect a defense. Although Augustín was willing, the resources to defend the Philippines against the expected American naval attack were not forthcoming. Augustín Dávila attempted to establish a military government and to enlist in Manila's* defense civilians and others partial to Spain, but it was a matter of too little, too late. Augustín Dávila vigorously opposed any plan by Admiral Patricio Montojo y Pasarón* that did not include the defense of Manila. So in effect, Augustín dictated the naval defense as well. Augustín attempted by compromise to maintain the loyalty of the Filipinos. He set up an advisory assembly with Pedro A. Paterno* at its head. This assembly called upon all Filipinos to support Spain. Augustín also organized a militia; but as with the assembly, Philippine insurgents infiltrated the group. The assembly lasted only about three weeks before disbanding; and under the pressure of an uprising, the militia melted away.

Augustín failed to utilize the Spanish troops effectively, leaving them in their several locations because of past insurgent activity. Thus insurgents could move freely and overcome garrisons piecemeal. In addition, Filipino troops went over to Emilio Aguinaldo's* forces wholesale. Discouraged by the lack of relief from Spain and the futility of his position, Augustín attempted to surrender to Commodore George Dewey.* Sensing defeatism from Augustín's dispatches, Spain replaced him with Fermín Jáudenes* who Madrid hoped would act with greater resolution.

REFERENCE: David F. Trask, *The War with Spain in 1898* (New York: Macmillan Publishing Co., 1981).

AUÑÓN Y VILLALÓN, RAMÓN
(1844–1925)

After George Dewey's* May day victory at Manila,* the government of Spain decided that some changes needed to be made. Segismundo Bermejo y Merelo* was replaced as minister of marine on 18 May 1898 with Captain Ramón Auñón y Villalón. Auñón's first challenge was to mediate a dispute between Captain General Ramón Blanco y Erenas* who had replaced General Valeriano Weyler* as governor-general on 31 October 1897, and Admiral Pascual Cervera y Topete,* commander of the Spanish squadron in Cuba. Desiring Cervera to sail out of Santiago,* if for no other reason than to maintain Spanish honor, Blanco felt that to go down fighting was preferable to scuttling the squadron in Santiago Harbor. Cervera's assessment was even more pessimistic. Given the deficiencies of his ships, he saw a sortie out of Santiago as a voyage to destruction, a useless sacrifice of 2,000 lives. Auñón agreed with Blanco and made the debate academic when on 23 June he ordered Cervera to sortie from the bay at Santiago de Cuba. Cervera was also placed under Blanco's command.

Auñón also ordered Manuel de la Cámara y Libermoore* on 15 June to sail to Manila for the relief of the Philippines.* Cámara sailed the next day. It was also Auñón who ordered Cámara's return to Spain on 7 July 1898.

REFERENCE: G.J.A. O'Toole, *The Spanish War* (New York: W. W. Norton & Co., 1984).

AUSTRIA

The imminent war between Spain and the United States spawned a variety of diplomatic initiatives and attempts at diplomatic intervention—some with noble intentions, but most from self-interest. Many European powers viewed U.S. pressure on Spain to resolve the Cuban situation as a threat to the principle of monarchy. For a variety of reasons, Germany* endeavored to enlist Great Britain,* Russia, France,* Italy,* and Austria into making a diplomatic intervention into the developing friction between Spain and the United States. Because these European powers distrusted each other's motives considerable jockeying ensued to determine which should be involved and, more importantly, which should lead. Leadership perceived as unfriendly to the United States might provide advantage to one of the other contenders for diplomatic precedence. Germany's solution was to have Austria take the lead, since the queen regent of Spain was

Austrian. Thus the German *chargé* in Vienna duly approached Austria. However, wrangling between France, England, and Germany—and the reluctance of Austria to play the part—doomed the initiative.

REFERENCE: J. Fred Rippy, ''The European Powers and the Spanish American War,'' *James Sprunt Historical Studies* 19, no. 2 (1927): 22–52.

AUTONOMY, IN CUBA AND PUERTO RICO

The strife between Spain and the United States and Cuba that resulted in the Spanish American War had political manifestations before the outbreak of hostilities between Spain and the United States. One of these revealed itself in the development of an autonomy movement. The Spanish government under the leadership of Práxides Sagasta* proposed a compromise between the Cuban insurrectionists' demand for independence and the Carlists' demand to maintain the status quo. The intent of the proposal was to enable Cuba to enjoy self-government while remaining part of Spain. Under its terms, Spain would continue to provide for defense, judicial needs, and foreign affairs, for example. Although the insurgents in Cuba viewed autonomy as a half-loaf proposition and resisted the idea violently, autonomy achieved a measure of support in the United States. In January 1898, autonomist governments were in place in Cuba and Puerto Rico. However, reform had come too late. The next month saw the publication of a letter critical of President William McKinley* by Enrique Dupuy de Lôme,* and within a week of that embarrassment the U.S.S. *Maine* * exploded in Havana* harbor, precipitating a crisis in U.S.-Spanish relations.

REFERENCE: Louis A Pérez, Jr., *Cuba between Empires, 1878–1902* (Pittsburgh: University of Pittsburgh Press, 1983).

AUXILIARY NAVAL FORCE.
See MERCHANT AND NAVAL AUXILIARIES.

B

BACOOR BAY, PHILIPPINES

Bacoor Bay is an inlet or indentation on Manila Bay about 10 miles south of Manila.* Bacoor Bay and the small town of Bacoor played minor roles in the battles in and around Manila. Admiral Patricio Montojo y Pasarón* had placed two Spanish gunboats, *General Lezo* and *Velasco,** in Bacoor Bay before the approach of Commodore George Dewey* and his squadron. The Spanish boats were not in good repair and were moored with the transport *Manila.** The U.S. Asiatic Squadron* attacked Montojo's ships on 1 May 1898 in the Battle of Manila Bay. At 8:00 A.M., Montojo ordered all ships that could get under steam to move to Bacoor and make a last stand. The ships at Bacoor were burned, except *Manila,* which was captured.

The town of Bacoor also served as a retreat for Emilio Aguinaldo* and his troop when evacuating Cavite.* Distrustful of American intentions, Aguinaldo remained at Bacoor during the early phases of the land battle at Manila in early August.

REFERENCE: David F. Trask, *The War with Spain in 1898* (New York: Macmillan Publishing Co., 1981).

BADGER (ship)

The U.S. Navy possessed a long tradition of converting merchant vessels to warships on short notice in wartime. Privateers and other commerce raiders have had a lengthy and illustrious history. *Badger,* a 4,800-ton passenger steamer originally named *Yumuri* was quickly purchased by the navy in 1898 for use as an armed auxiliary cruiser for convoy duty in the Caribbean. *Badger* was also to be part of the Eastern Squadron* to counter Admiral Cámara's* sailing for the Philippines.*

REFERENCE: John D. Alden, *The American Steel Navy* (Annapolis, MD: Naval Institute Press, 1972).

BAGLEY, WORTH
(1874–1898)

On 11 May 1898, the torpedo boat *Winslow** steamed a second time into Cárdenas Bay* accompanied by *Hudson,** *Wilmington,** and *Machias.* J. B. Bernadou,* the *Winslow*'s commander, reported that he was ordered to investigate a gunboat moored near the town. The gunboat commenced firing in conjunction with a battery on shore, and the *Winslow* took several hits disabling steering gear and felling officers and men. Ensign Worth Bagley died along with seamen John Varveres, J. Deneefe, J. V. Meek, and Josiah Tunell. Bagley was the first officer killed by the Spanish in the war.

REFERENCE: *Appendix to the Report of the Chief of the Bureau of Navigation, 1898* (Washington, DC: Government Printing Office, 1898).

BALER, PHILIPPINES, SIEGE OF

The Spanish American War saw numerous incidents of individual gallantry and bravery, but few could match the tenacity of the Spanish garrison at Baler in the Philippines.* Baler is a somewhat remote coastal town on Luzon.* Philippine troops, revolutionists, began a siege of Baler and its Spanish garrison on 1 July 1898. Spanish captain Enrique de las Morenas commanded forty-seven men, who at the commencement of the assault retired to a stone church, which they used as a fortress. Morenas died early in the siege, and Lieutenant Saturnino Martín Cerezo* carried on the defense. Through assaults, privations, sickness, and death, Martín Cerezo held for 337 days. On 12 April 1899—long after cessation of hostilities—a U.S. rescue force was sent under Marine Lieutenant J. C. Gillmore. Unfortunately, Gillmore and his force were ambushed and captured. Finally, on 2 June 1899, Martín Cerezo surrendered, only recently having received news of Spain's defeat and the loss of her colonies. Because of their evident heroism, the thirty remaining Spanish troops were marched with military honors and feted when they returned to Spain.

REFERENCE: Saturnino Martín Cerezo, *Under the Red and Gold: Being Notes and Recollections of the Siege of Baler,* 2nd ed. (Kansas City, MO: Franklin Hudson Publishing Co., 1909).

BALFOUR, ARTHUR
(1848–1930)

British politician and statesman, and author of the Balfour Declaration, Arthur Balfour had a distinguished career as a member of Parliament for twenty-five years before becoming prime minister in July 1902. He was secretary of Scotland (1886), Irish chief secretary (1887), first lord of the treasury (1891), and leader in the House of Commons. In 1895, Balfour was again first lord of the treasury after regaining his position when the Unionist party returned to the majority in 1895.

During the Spanish American War, Balfour was acting head of the Foreign Office for the prime minister, Lord Salisbury, who had adopted a neutral stance when the Cuban crisis erupted between the United States and Spain. Balfour was more inclined to favor the United States. This was evident when Spanish requests for diplomatic assistance were met with caution by Balfour. At the same time, he assured the U.S. ambassador in England, John Hay,* that all measures taken by Britain relating to the Cuban situation would first have to be acceptable to the United States. Balfour also refused the request of the British ambassador to the United States, Sir Julian Pauncefote, to lodge a protest against the possible declaration of war by President McKinley.* Accordingly, the relationship between the United States and Britain was stable throughout the conflict.

REFERENCE: Sydney H. Zebel, *Balfour: A Political Biography* (Cambridge: Cambridge University Press, 1973).

RICHARD W. PEUSER

BALINTAWAK, GRITO DE

The Grito de Balintawak was the first cry of the Philippine Insurrection* made by Andrés Bonifacio* at Balintawak on 26 August 1896. Bonifacio called the Philippine populace to revolt and to begin military initiatives against the Spanish. Bonifacio's early military endeavors met with failure, however. Bonifacio had become president of the Katipunan* on New Year's Day of 1896, and with the increased revolutionary activities he became a threat to Spanish authority. A revolutionary organization that plotted to overthrow Spain, the Katipunan was betrayed to an Augustinian priest, Mariano Gil, and by a Katipuñero, Teodoro Patiño. A search by Spanish authorities revealed incriminating documents and caches of arms. Apprised of the arrest of Katipuñeros and seizure of arms, Bonifacio fled to the hills and proclaimed his famous "Grito de Balintawak."

REFERENCE: Gregorio F. Zaide, *The Philippine Revolution* (Manila: Modern Book Company, 1968).

BALLOON

At the commencement of the Spanish American War, the U.S. Army knew little of Cuba and its terrain. Maps were old, incomplete, or missing entirely. In an effort to amend these deficiencies, Major (later Lieutenant Colonel) Joseph E. Maxfield* brought his Balloon Corps to the attention of Signal Corps* senior officers, and Maxfield and his men were rushed to Cuba with their Civil War–era balloon to make aerial observations of the ensuing battles at San Juan Hill* and its blockhouse. The results of Maxfield's and Lieutenant Colonel George Derby's* ascents brought mixed reviews. On the one hand, the balloon offered a clear view of the Spanish lines and forces and revealed that they were stronger than U.S. intelligence had known. Because of this knowledge, the attacking force was doubled and may have saved the day.

On the other hand, the balloon acted as a magnet for Spanish fire and gave away U.S. positions. Indeed, the Spanish artillery used the balloon as a range marker. The balloon pointed to the location of U.S. troops, so doubtless there

were casualties because of the balloon. Nevertheless, Maxfield and Derby's movement with the advance on San Juan Hill represented the first and the last time a balloon ascent was made coincident with the front lines of battle.
REFERENCE: *A History of the U.S. Signal Corps* (New York: G. P. Putnam's Sons, 1961).

BALTIMORE (ship)

Commissioned in 1890, the 4,600-ton steel-protected cruiser U.S.S. *Baltimore* boasted four 8-inch guns, six 6-inch, and twelve smaller calibers; she also featured torpedo tubes. The cruiser could make 20 knots and in fact earned a bonus for her builders by exceeding her contract speed. This *Baltimore* was the ship of the much-publicized ''*Baltimore* Incident'' of August 1891 when later-Captain Winfield S. Schley* allowed a large liberty party ashore during a civil war in Chile. The sailors got into a fight and two were killed, precipitating an international incident. During the Spanish American War, *Baltimore* first became part of George Dewey's* squadron arriving at Hong Kong* on 22 April 1898. *Baltimore* then formed an integral part of Dewey's squadron engaged in the reconnoiter and destruction of the Spanish naval forces in and around Manila Bay.* *Baltimore* suffered eight wounded in the main engagement—more than any other U.S. warship.

Baltimore along with *Raleigh** caused the batteries at Corregidor* to surrender on 2 May 1898 and supported troop movements by suppressing Spanish artillery fires during the investment of Manila and Fort San Antonio* on 13 August.

The cruiser helped lay the North Sea mine barrage in World War I but lay inactive at Pearl Harbor* from 1922 until 1942, when she was sold. *Baltimore* was the first U.S. warship with telephone, and one of the first with wireless.
REFERENCE: John D. Alden, *The American Steel Navy* (Annapolis, MD: Naval Institute Press, 1972).

BANCROFT (ship)

The U.S.S. *Bancroft* was originally laid down as a U.S. Navy training ship. Commissioned in 1893 at 839 tons, *Bancroft* carried two torpedo tubes and four 4-inch guns (plus smaller calibers) for training purposes. She also carried an auxiliary barkentine rig. Lamentably, she proved too small for the Naval Academy and was employed as a gunboat after 1896. *Bancroft* was part of the naval escort that sailed from Tampa* on 14 June 1898 accompanying army troop ships for Cuba.

Bancroft also engaged the Spanish on 2 August 1898 while trying to free a grounded Spanish schooner near Cortes Bay on the south coast of Cuba. One U.S. seaman was killed in the encounter.

After the war, *Bancroft* served as a survey vessel in the Caribbean and in 1906 was transferred to the Revenue Cutter Service* and renamed *Itasca*. *Itasca* was scrapped in 1922.

REFERENCE: John D. Alden, *The American Steel Navy* (Annapolis, MD: Naval Institute Press, 1972).

BANES, CUBA, PUERTO DE

The Port of Banes, on which lay the Embarcadero de Banes, is located on a narrow, almost landlocked bay that is about thirty-five miles east of Holguín and almost due north of Santiago de Cuba.* The bay is small with a very narrow channel in the eastern part of Cuba in Oriente Province, which in 1898 was named Santiago.

Puerto de Banes played a minor role as the planned destination of General William R. Shafter* after the land battle of Santiago. More importantly, the port served as the first land operation in Cuba when Captain Joseph H. Dorst* landed with troops on 26 May 1898 to deliver supplies to Cuban insurgents.

BARBOSA, JOSÉ CELSO
(1857–1921)

A descendant of African slaves, José Celso Barbosa studied medicine at the University of Michigan and then returned to his native Puerto Rico,* where he became a member of the Liberal Reform party and a staunch and vocal advocate of Puerto Rican autonomy. In temperament and in allegiance to Spain he differed from Luis Múñoz Rivera, who in the years just before 1898 also favored autonomy.* Barbosa, who led the Republican party in Puerto Rico, wanted close ties with the United States. He accepted the role of U.S. sovereignty in 1899, after the Foraker Act, and until his death in 1921 worked for statehood for Puerto Rico. He also served as a member of the Executive Council, the governing body of Puerto Rico, and later the Puerto Rican Senate.

REFERENCE: Antonio Salvador Pedreíra, *Un hombre del pueblo: José Celso Barbosa* (San Juan: NP, 1937).

BARCELONA, SPAIN

Barcelona, the large port on the Mediterranean or northeast side of Spain, figured in both U.S. and Spanish strategy during the Spanish American War. Even before the war, the irrepressible Theodore Roosevelt* urged that a Flying Squadron* of ships could wreak havoc in Spain through raids on Barcelona, Cádiz, and Málaga. In fact, such plans were in place. Spain, for its part, felt keenly the need to protect Barcelona. When Admiral Manuel de la Cámara's* Eastern Squadron* sailed for the Philippines to relieve Manila,* the implied threat of a possible U.S. bombardment of Spain, planted in European capitals by intelligence operations,* initiated a return to the mother country. Indeed, A. T. Mahan* argued that Cámara's squadron was an elaborate bluff, that Spain would never leave its coasts unprotected.

REFERENCE: David F. Trask, *The War with Spain in 1898* (New York: Macmillan Publishing Co., 1981).

BARTON, CLARA (CLARISSA) HARLOWE
(1821–1912)

Almost legendary by the time the Spanish American War began, Clara Harlowe Barton plunged into relief work in Cuba* even before hostilities commenced. However determined and energetic the renowned nurse might be, her efforts in the Spanish American War were marred by internal political squabbling within the American National Red Cross* and the inevitable trials associated with a foreign war. Barton had lost political control of the Red Cross within the United States, and although she exhibited her characteristic ingenuity, organizational skills, and innovativeness, she was, after all, in her late seventies and the years had made her more autocratic, demanding, and independent. She succored *reconcentrados,** Spaniards, Americans, and civilians, yet she came into controversy and criticism because of military concerns, reports from the press, and rivals within the Red Cross organization. She was also frustrated by the military, which did not give the Red Cross access to the wounded upon request. The working relationship of the Red Cross, Barton, and military elements was frequently rocky, at best. Although the Red Cross and Barton herself did much good and received much praise, the insinuations about Barton's age, competence, and financial affairs stung her, and she retreated into a wounded anguish to sort out her trials. William McKinley,* then president, remained a staunch admirer and signed a bill on 6 June 1900 incorporating the American National Red Cross as a partial recognition to Barton's efforts during the war.
REFERENCE: Elizabeth Brown Pryor, *Clara Barton, Professional Angel* (Philadelphia: University of Pennsylvania Press, 1987).

BASES

The need of nineteenth-century steamships for frequent refueling and repair led to several strategic plans for the acquisition of naval bases in a variety of global locations. From an American point of view, the lack of bases was an important early strategic concern. One of the first plans entertained by U.S. forces was to seize Matanzas,* on the Cuban coast, for use specifically as a naval and resupply base. Although this plan was not implemented, its existence highlights the problem. Britain's invitation to U.S. forces to help stave off German ambition in the Far East also necessitated U.S. naval bases. The German need, like the American, was for overseas coaling* stations that would enable naval units to operate far from their native land. The seizure of Guam,* for example, sprang from this need. A. T. Mahan* had predicted the need for coaling bases in 1890, and, to a large extent, the war effort in the Pacific and subsequent peace negotiations endeavored to provide these bases.
REFERENCES: William Reynolds Braisted, *The United States Navy in the Pacific, 1897–1909* (Austin: University of Texas Press, 1958); H. W. Wilson, *The Downfall of Spain* (New York: Burt Franklin, 1971).

BATES, JOHN COALTER
(1842–1919)

John Coalter Bates was born in Missouri and served with the Army of the Potomac during the Civil War. He was promoted several times and became General George G. Meade's aide-de-camp. Bates remained with the army after the Civil War and served in the American West for thirty years, being promoted to colonel in 1892. At the outbreak of the Spanish American War Bates was again promoted to brigadier general of volunteers and given a brigade of the Third Division of General William R. Shafter's* Fifth Corps. It was called Bates's Independent Brigade, or the Independent Brigade. He also commanded at Siboney* briefly before joining General Henry W. Lawton's* command (Second Division) on 1 July 1898 for the attack on El Caney.* Bates's brigade formed the reserve to the Second Division, Fifth Corps; but upon Bates's arrival, General Joseph Wheeler* placed Bates to the left of the line. Bates's brigade engaged the Spanish all day on 2 July.

During the last days of the war in Cuba, Bates (now a major general) commanded the Third Division.

After the war he served in the Philippines* and again in Cuba. He was named chief of staff in 1906.

REFERENCE: Joseph Wheeler, *The Santiago Campaign* (New York: Drexel Biddle, 1899).

BAYAMO, CUBA

Bayamo (originally San Salvador de Bayamo) was the site of the first conflict of the Ten Years' war* (1868–1878) and the 1895 Cuban Insurrection.* By 1898, Bayamo was in the hands of insurgents, and it was here that Andrew Rowan* delivered his famous "message to [Calixto] García"* on 1 May 1898. Bayamo is about 60 miles west-northwest of Santiago.*

BEEF CONTROVERSY

The Spanish American War became associated in the minds of many with valorous deeds, empire building, and scandal. In the latter category stands the beef controversy. William H. Daly,* a surgeon on General Nelson Miles's* staff, investigated complaints by troops of tainted canned roast beef. Daly thought he found traces of acid in tinned beef he tested chemically, and he reported his findings to Miles.

For his own political motives, General Miles kept the information to himself until late fall 1898, when he unleashed a barrage of charges against General William R. Shafter,* Secretary of War Russell A. Alger,* and General Charles P. Eagan,* among others. The scandal was front-page news for weeks. An investigative commission headed by General Grenville M. Dodge* looked into complaints by soldiers and heard testimony about beef rations. The testimony, sometimes lurid, charged that while the beef appeared wholesome it had been injected with something to give it a nauseous odor described as similar to that of a dead human body injected with preservatives. In testimony to the comission, the beef was labeled ''embalmed beef,'' and members of the press naturally got their teeth into it. The Dodge Commission* found no corruption or intentional wrongdoing but claimed there had been mismanagement.

The beef scandal flared openly for some six months and offended overseas importers as well as domestic consumers. It also created a heightened awareness in the army of the need for food inspection. Consequently, in 1901 Congress authorized the secretary of war to contract veterinarians to inspect foodstuffs. The following day, 8 July 1901, the army hired the first graduate veterinarian and began a process that eventually led to the finest and most effective food inspection service in the world. Another unlooked-for result of the beef controversy was that it sensitized the American public to food-processing abuses, thus paving the way for the success of Upton Sinclair's best-selling exposé *The Jungle* (1906) and the Meat Inspection Act passed by Congress in 1906 and the Pure Food and Drug Act of the same year.

REFERENCES: Graham A. Cosmas, *An Army for Empire* (Columbia: University of Missouri Press, 1971); Henry C. Dethloff and Donald H. Dyal, *A Special Kind of Doctor* (College Station: Texas A&M University Press, 1991); *Food Furnished by Subsistence Department to Troops during Spanish American War: Record of a Court of Inquiry,* 3 vols., Senate Doc. 270 (Washington, DC: Government Printing Office, 1900).

BELLIGERENCY

The people of the United States, and its representatives, the Congress, argued the issue of whether to recognize Cuban belligerency for some time before the war began in 1898. Among the reasons for not recognizing belligerency was concern for the significant American investment in Cuban plantations, mines, and commerce. A recognition of belligerency would deny American investments the protection of the Spanish authorities. There was also the debatable issue of whether the insurgents* represented a government, under any definition. On the other hand, Congress was deluged with petitions from citizens' groups requesting that Congress grant belligerent rights to the Cuban Republic. During 1895 alone, congressmen sent eighteen resolutions to committees calling for a recognition of Cuban revolutionaries as an independent government. The Senate Committee on Foreign Relations presented a resolution on 28 January 1896, the Morgan-Cameron Resolution,* that argued the case from several legal and political perspectives but in sum called for the recognition of Cuban belligerency. The Senate voted overwhelmingly—and in a bipartisan manner—for the resolution on 28 February. By 2 March, the House had its own versions of the Morgan-Cameron Resolution and they were also passed decisively. Thus by 1896, after a few months of debate, Congress recognized the Cuban belligerency and also offered Spain the services of the executive branch of the U.S. government to work toward a peace that would grant Cuban independence.

REFERENCE: Philip S. Foner, *The Spanish-Cuban-American War and the Birth of American Imperialism* (New York: Monthly Review Press, 1972).

BENNINGTON (ship)

The U.S.S. *Bennington* was a *Yorktown*-class gunboat of 1,710 tons. The ship was commissioned in 1891 and suffered a tragic boiler explosion at San Diego that scalded to death sixty of her crew.

Although *Bennington* played no direct role in the Spanish American War, Commander Edward Taussig did sail *Bennington* to Wake Island,* which he claimed on 17 January 1899—this, despite the protests of Germany,* which claimed Wake as part of the Marshall Islands. Wake provided the United States with a useful location for a Honolulu-to-Wake-to-Guam*-to-Manila* trans-Pacific cable. Such a cable was possible only because of the acquisition of the Philippines.

REFERENCE: William Reynolds Braisted, *The United States Navy in the Pacific, 1897–1909* (Austin: University of Texas Press, 1958).

BERÁNGER Y RUIZ DE APODACA, JOSÉ MARÍA (1824–1907)

José María Beránger y Ruiz de Apodaca was a Spanish naval officer who also possessed political credentials. Having participated in the September Revolution (1868), he became minister of the marine during several administrations well into the 1890s. He was not elevated to admiral until 1903, however.

Beránger's role in the Spanish American War was minor: He served on a war council under Segismundo Bermejo,* minister of the marine, who ordered Admiral Cervera* to Cuba. Cervera demurred knowing that his ships were in but fair condition. Beránger made Cervera's position difficult with a lengthy rodomontade about the superiority of Spanish sailors, the result of their being of one nationality in contrast to the inferiority Americans, a consequence of their multinational makeup. Beranger was a staunch supporter of Bermejo's plan to send Cervera to the Caribbean.

REFERENCE: French Ensor Chadwick, *The Relations of the United States and Spain* (New York: Russell & Russell, 1911).

BERMEJO Y MERELO, SEGISMUNDO (1832–1899)

An unusual man, Admiral Segismundo Bermejo y Merelo was fluent in many languages and adept at writing, authoring science-fiction novels *(El Doctor Juan Pérez)* while pursuing his naval career. He had the misfortune to be Spain's minister of the marine in 1898. Bermejo, a friend of Pascual Cervera y Topete,* was also the latter's commander. When Cervera attempted to assess the Spanish naval forces and the U.S. naval forces using information provided in part by Bermejo, he quite accurately realized the difficulty facing Spain. Calling a naval council that included José María Beránger,* Bermejo was inclined to be optimistic. As such, he ordered Cervera to Cape Verde* and to his doom. In addition, Bermejo mistakenly believed that the Spanish Asiatic Squadron in the Philippines posed a sufficient threat to American West Coast ports as to neutralize activity there. Bermejo was also chary of what he shared with the cabinet and so lost the benefits of its counsel. Cervera's warnings, for example, never got past his desk. Admiral Patricio Montojo y Pasarón,* Spanish naval commander in the Philippines,* had the same difficulties with Bermejo as did Cervera. In the face of material shortages for waging war, Bermejo encouraged Montojo to be enthusiastic and full of activity. Without time, arms, and supplies, Montojo had difficulty being enthusiastic.

On 12 May 1898 Bermejo had second thoughts about Cervera's squadron and cabled him to return to Cádiz. The cable never reached Cervera, but it caused widespread panic among Spanish officials in Havana* and San Juan.* The source of these second thoughts came from Commodore George Dewey's* stunning defeat of Montojo's forces on 1 May at Manila.* Práxides Sagasta's* government was rocking precariously, and much of the Spanish populace pointed accusatory fingers at the minister of the marine. Shortly thereafter, on 16 May 1898, Sagasta removed Bermejo from office after a series of riots in Madrid brought the issue to crisis proportions.

REFERENCES: Pascual Cervera y Topete, *The Spanish American War* (Washington, DC: Government Printing Office, 1899), G.J.A. O'Toole, *The Spanish War* (New York: W. W. Norton & Co., 1984).

BERNADOU, JOHN BAPTISTE
(1858–1903)

John Baptiste Bernadou was born in Philadelphia and graduated from the Naval Academy in 1882. He was promoted to lieutenant in 1896. Bernadou commanded the U.S.S. *Winslow** in a harrowing engagement in the bay of Cárdenas.*

Bernadou was told that the channel was mined, and so *Winslow* was ordered to sweep for mines. A small Spanish gunboat was sighted, and Bernadou advanced to engage her. The gunboat opened fire first, as did a hitherto unobserved shore battery. *Winslow* received numerous hits and Bernadou was wounded. His ship could maintain neither direction nor speed and had to be towed out of action. Although Bernadou suffered five killed, he was enthusiastically commended for this action; in hindsight, however, the results seem out of proportion to the deed.

After the war, Bernadou was again promoted and worked on ordnance studies—particularly evaluating smokeless powder—and authored several treatises.

REFERENCE: H. W. Wilson, *The Downfall of Spain* (New York: Burt Franklin, 1971).

BERRY, GEORGE
(?–1906)

Sergeant George Berry of the Tenth Cavalry* saw the color bearer of the Third Cavalry falter when shot in the charge up San Juan Hill.* Berry, about halfway up the slope, rushed over to the fallen Third's colors and raised them along with the Tenth's. Shouting to both units, Berry and the colors advanced together to the crest of the hill. Unique at that time, Berry's exploit earned high commendation.

REFERENCE: E.L.N. Glass, *The History of the Tenth Cavalry, 1866–1921* (Tucson, AZ: NP, 1921).

BIAK-NA-BATO, PHILIPPINES

Biak-na-Bato is rocky and difficult terrain near Bulacan in the Philippines.* Emilio Aguinaldo* removed his revolutionary movement to Biak-na-Bato after the fall of organized Filipino resistance to Spain in summer 1897. While in Biak-na-Bato, Aguinaldo reinstituted guerrilla war against Spain. He also convened a constituent assembly and on 1 November 1897 approved a revolutionary constitution modeled after the Cuban constitution of 1895. On the same day, the so-called Biak-na-Bato Republic was formed under its constitution as an effort at independence while the revolution gathered momentum.

Spain reacted quickly to the news of the new republic and sent representatives to negotiate with the revolutionaries. The Pact of Biak-na-Bato, signed on 14–15 December 1897, paid indemnities to the revolutionaries, provided amnesty, and allowed for Aguinaldo's exile to Hong Kong.* This pact, however, addressed none of the issues driving the revolutionary fervor.

REFERENCE: Gregorio F. Zaide, *The Philippine Revolution* (Manila: Modern Book Company, 1968).

BIGELOW, POULTNEY
(1855–1954)

Born in New York City, Poultney Bigelow inherited his journalistic talents from his father, John, who was managing editor of the New York *Evening Post.* Bigelow studied at Yale and Columbia, receiving degrees in 1879 and 1882 respectively; but rather than settle down, he began a traveling education that served him well throughout his long life. In 1885, he founded and edited *Outing,* the first American magazine treating outdoor sports. Because of his travels he wrote several books on Germany,* Japan,* and South Africa. During the Spanish American War, he was employed as a correspondent for *Harper's Weekly* and other magazines and also for the London *Times.* He worked as a reporter with Frederic Remington,* Rufus F. Zogbaum,* Richard Harding Davis,* and others and caused something of a sensation when on 28 May 1898 he reported on the laxity of command at Tampa* and later when he reported the first uncensored impressions of Americans in battle at Cabañas.* He was a critic of Theodore Roosevelt* and of the volunteer armed forces but a supporter of the regular army. Later writers such as Walter Millis used Bigelow's reports to depreciate the entire military experience of the Spanish American War, although Bigelow himself never went that far.

REFERENCE: Poultney Bigelow, *Seventy Summers,* 2 vols. (New York: Longmans, Green & Co., 1925).

BLACK, WILSONE
(1837–1909)

Sir Wilsone Black, K.C.B., had a distinguished army career in the Crimea, the Kaffir War, the Zulu War, and Jamaica; he also commanded troops in China and Hong Kong.* At the outbreak of the Spanish American War, Black was acting governor of Hong Kong. On 23 April 1898 Black notified Commodore George Dewey* of the U.S. Asiatic Squadron* that a state of war existed between the United States and Spain. Great Britain,* sympathetic to the United States in its conflict with Spain in part because, of an attempt to foster an alliance among powers in China,* nevertheless strictly adhered to the laws of war and neutrality. Beneath his official notification, however, the acting governor wrote: "God knows, my dear Commodore, that it breaks my heart to send you this notification."

REFERENCE: Laurin Hall Healy and Luis Kutner, *The Admiral* (New York: Ziff-Davis, 1944).

BLACK POWDER

A shortage of modern weapons and ammunition at the onset of the war forced the United States to use black powder for its large naval guns, artillery,* and infantry rifles. As a holdover from the Civil War era, black powder was considered by many as archaic because of its corrosive nature and the clouds of smoke it emitted after igniting.

Much preferred to black powder was the smokeless powder perfected by the Ordnance Department.* However, it was also in short supply because limited appropriations in previous years had prevented stockpiling by the War Department. Unlike black powder, smokeless powder could not be produced in vast quantities in a short amount of time because its chemistry and manufacture were complex. Government supplies of the modern explosive were sufficient only for the regular infantry. The artillery, all the National Guard* weaponry, and the small-caliber navy guns used nothing but black powder for most of the war.

The ground troops complained that the clouds from the powder revealed their positions to the Spanish army. For this reason, two volunteer units attached to the Fifth Army Corps* were forced to withdraw from action in the Santiago* campaign. The Spanish American War was the last sizable conflict to use black powder. Further technological advances in ammunition would make this form of ammunition obsolete.

REFERENCES: Graham A. Cosmas, *An Army for Empire* (Columbia: University of Missouri Press, 1971); Norman B. Wilkinson, *Explosives in History: The Story of Black Powder* (Chicago: Rand McNally, 1966).

MITCHELL YOCKELSON

BLACK UNITS

Before the outbreak of the Spanish American War, the U.S. Army* included four black units among its ranks. Often called "Buffalo Soldiers" by the Indians they contested on the Plains, the regular units consisted of the Ninth and Tenth Cavalry Regiments and the Twenty-fourth and Twenty-fifth Infantry Regiments. The first call for volunteers to fight the Spanish brought an additional 8,000 to 10,000 more African Americans. Many of them joined the Seventh, Eighth, Ninth, and Tenth U.S. Volunteer Infantry Regiments. These units were known as immunes* because the principal criteria for enlisting in these units, other than race, was residence in an area where tropical disease prevailed. Volunteers from these areas were thought to be immune to the tropical diseases* of Cuba.

In addition to regular and volunteer units, from individual states came a number of fighting men of color: They were the Third Alabama Infantry, the Eighth Illinois Infantry, Companies A and B of the Indiana Colored Infantry, the Twenty-third Kansas Infantry, Company L of the Sixth Massachusetts Infantry, the Third North Carolina Infantry, Ninth Battalion, Ohio Infantry, and the Sixth Virginia Infantry.

Only three of the state volunteer units permitted black officers: the Eighth Illinois, the Twenty-third Kansas, and the Third North Carolina. The regular army did not commission any black officers. After assembling at Tampa,* the regular black units participated with the Fifth Army Corps* during the Santiago* campaign. Of the volunteer units, only Company L of the Sixth Massachusetts experienced combat during the war. At the end of the conflict, black soldiers received considerable praise from the white officers as well as from Spanish soldiers, who nicknamed them the "smoked Yankees." Black regulars were generally better trained and more experienced on the battlefield than white regulars because of their veteran status from the Indian wars of the West. Five black regulars received the Medal of Honor for service in Cuba.

REFERENCES: Herschel V. Cashin, *Under Fire with the Tenth U.S. Cavalry* (New York: F. T. Neely, 1899); Bernard C. Nalty, *Strength for the Fight: A History of Black Americans in the Military* (New York: Free Press, 1986).

MITCHELL YOCKELSON

BLANCO Y ERENAS, RAMÓN
(1833–1906)

Captain General Ramón Blanco y Erenas had distinguished himself in the Carlist struggles and had also served in the Philippines before being appointed captain general in Cuba as a replacement for Valeriano Weyler.* Where Weyler had been focused and decisive, Blanco was something of an appeaser. Just before the intervention of the United States, he proposed that Spanish forces and Máximo Gómez's* insurgent forces ally themselves to repel the U.S. invader. Gómez refused. Blanco had been unable to secure peace in Cuba.

When hostilities commenced, the Spanish minister of the marine placed Admiral Pascual Cervera* and his squadron directly under the command of Blanco, who felt that it would be better to lose the Spanish fleet entirely in battle rather than to lose it by scuttling at Santiago.* Cervera remonstrated against the inevitable loss of life, as well as the loss of ships, but Blanco ordered the sortie from Santiago. With Blanco the issue was one of honor, not tactics nor even strategy. Blanco attempted to enlist the Spanish army commander at Santiago, General Arsenio Linares,* to his own point of view, but Linares remained aloof. Nevertheless, determined to have his martyrs, Blanco persevered and Cervera did indeed try to break out on 3 July 1898.

REFERENCES: Pascual Cervera y Topete, *The Spanish American War* (Washington, DC: Government Printing Office, 1899); Hugh Thomas, *Cuba: The Pursuit of Freedom* (New York: Harper & Row, 1971).

BLISS, TASKER HOWARD
(1853–1930)

Tasker Howard Bliss gained renown as the founding president of the U.S. Army War College and as a commissioner at the Paris Peace Conference of 1919. Before all that, Bliss worked his way up the ranks.

Born into a large family with a modest income, Bliss nevertheless had some powerful advantages. Son of a Baptist preacher and professor of some distinction, Bliss benefited from an extensive education. His knowledge of history, the classics, Latin, Greek, and French aided him throughout his career. Noting the slender economic opportunities afforded him, Bliss sought appointment to the service academies. His first choice was Annapolis, but no appointments being available, he cheerfully accepted one to West Point. A scholar by character as well as training, Bliss excelled in his coursework and graduated in 1875. His early career was somewhat unusual because of his scholarly bent. As a junior officer, he taught at the Naval War College for two years and seized the attention of General John M. Schofield,* commander of the army. He worked at a miscellany of staff jobs in Washington, becoming well known among the small officer corps of the army.

With the election of President William McKinley* came a change in personnel in foreign offices. The tensions developing with Spain demanded cool and knowledgeable heads. That Bliss, a junior officer, was chosen to accompany Stewart L. Woodford,* the new minster to Spain, argued for Bliss's accomplishments. Bliss plunged into the task of making himself proficient in the Spanish language, which he would need as military attaché. Bliss was active in compiling data about the Spanish buildup in Cuba, which he forwarded to the Military Information Division,* where it in turn became the foundation of further intelligence operations.*

During the war itself, Bliss (now a colonel) served as chief of staff for the First Division under Major General James H. Wilson.* He participated with Wilson in the campaign in Puerto Rico* and was about to engage in a serious struggle at Aibonito* when Wilson received word on 12 August 1898 that a peace protocol had been signed. No more combat occurred in Puerto Rico.

Because of Bliss's fluency in Spanish, he was chosen collector of customs for the occupying U.S. forces.

REFERENCE: Frederick Palmer, *Bliss, Peacemaker* (Freeport, NY: Books for Libraries Press, 1970).

BLOCKADE

Early in the prewar planning scenarios, a naval blockade of Cuba and Puerto Rico figured prominently. A blockade, of course, closes enemy ports or coasts to trade, traffic, and communication with the intent to deny essential material and reinforcements and weaken the opposing force. To command the blockading force, the North Atlantic Squadron,* the U.S. Navy passed over more senior officers to select Captain (later Rear Admiral) William T. Sampson.* President William McKinley* issued the blockade order early in the conflict (21 April 1898) to blockade Cuba from Cárdenas* to Bahía Honda. Sampson had already issued a memorandum to his fleet on 18 April with detailed instructions on the Cuban blockade, so the first elements of the fleet were able to steam for Cuba in the early morning darkness of 22 April.

Initially, *New York,* *Iowa,* *Wilmington,* *Helena, Dolphin,* *Mayflower,* *Vesuvius,* *Ericsson,* and *Porter** were ordered to Havana.* *Nashville** and *Castine** were to cruise off Mariel.* *Amphitrite,* *Cincinnati,* *Du Pont,* and *Winslow** were dispatched to Matanzas,* and Cárdenas* would be besieged by *Newport,* *Machias, Foote,* and *Cushing.** Naturally, the composition of these elements changed in the course of the blockade and especially when the navy's first offensive priority, Admiral Pascual Cervera's* Spanish fleet, was finally located at Santiago.* No blockade of Santiago (or Manila, either) was ever announced. A blockade of the southern coast was proclaimed on 28 June, but the scarcity of ships meant it was poorly enforced. Cienfuegos* was also blockaded, but intermittently.

Work in the blockading force was arduous for a variety of reasons, not the least of which was tedium. The occasional blockade runner and miscellaneous cutting-out efforts, particularly in the smaller ports, were the only relief from the monotony of coaling, vigilance, and more coaling.

The effectiveness of the blockade was compromised by the scarcity of ships and multiple missions assigned to the units on blockade. Such was but to be expected, since the blockade was Sampson's secondary mission. The blockade did, however, draw Cervera's fleet to Cuba and destruction, thus fulfilling one of its strategic aims.

REFERENCES: French Ensor Chadwick, *The Relations of the United States and Spain* (New York: Russell & Russell, 1911); Joseph G. Dawson III, ''William T. Sampson and Santiago: Blockade, Victory and Controversy,'' in James C. Bradford, ed., *Crucible of Empire: The Spanish American War and Its Aftermath* (Annapolis, MD: Naval Institute Press, 1993).

BLUE, VICTOR
(1865–1928)

The U.S. Navy inserted Lieutenant Victor Blue into Cuba to travel with the Cuban revolutionary army and report on Spanish ship movements. He went ashore from the *Suwanee** on 11 June 1898 at Aserraderos and obtained the services of Major Francisco H. Masaba y Reges to guide him through Spanish lines in order to observe the harbor of Santiago.* On 12 June, Blue was able to identify Admiral Pascual Cervera's* fleet in the harbor. Blue's report removed all doubt as to the location of Cervera's ships and paved the way for the Battle of Santiago Bay.*

REFERENCE: French Ensor Chadwick, *The Relations of the United States and Spain* (New York: Russell & Russell, 1911).

BOCA GRANDE, PHILIPPINES

There are two channels leading into Manila Bay.* The bay entrance is about 10 miles in width interrupted by three islands. The largest of these is Corregidor,* about 2 miles from the northern coast; this passage is called Boca Chica. The remaining channel, Boca Grande, is about 7 miles across, interrupted by two very small islands, El Fraile and Caballo. Boca Grande was the channel through which Commodore George Dewey* led the Asiatic Squadron.* Supposedly, the Spanish had attempted to mine both Boca Chica and Boca Grande. There were also batteries on Corregidor and El Fraile. Dewey sailed through the 3-mile-wide deep-water channel, electing to ignore any possible mines. Dewey's instincts served him well, as danger from the mines proved illusory.

REFERENCE: H. W. Wilson, *The Downfall of Spain* (New York: Burt Franklin, 1971).

BONIFACIO, ANDRÉS
(1863–1897)

Andrés Bonifacio was born in the Tondo section of Manila,* the Philippines, in 1863. His mother was of mixed Spanish-Filipino ancestry, and his father was city official—a *teniente mayor*—for the Tondo district. The family enjoyed middle-class prosperity until the 1870s, when both of Bonifacio's parents died. Bonifacio had to quit school to provide financial support for his five brothers and sisters. However, he did not let the lack of formal schooling put an end to his education. A native speaker of Tagalog, Bonifacio became fluent in Spanish as well, also becoming an avid student of politics and history. From his teens, Bonifacio nurtured an intense resentment of Spanish imperial power. By the mid-1880s, he was closely associated with José Rizal* and the budding Filipino nationalist movement. He was a charter member of the Liga Filipina* when Rizal established the organization in 1892.

In July 1892, when Spanish authorities arrested Rizal and charged him with sedition, Bonifacio concluded that only revolution, violent if necessary, would break the chains of Spanish imperialism. On 7 July 1892, at a secret meeting on Azcarrage Street in Manila, Bonifacio founded the Katipunan,* a revolutionary nationalist organization dedicated to Filipino liberation. Influenced by the Masonic Order, Bonifacio established the Katipunan as a secret, fraternal society, complete with Masonic rituals, blood oaths, coded passwords, and an aura of religious mystery. He opened the organization to Filipino peasants as well as to the middle class, and in doing so he tapped into a powerful stream in Filipino popular culture. Throughout the nineteenth century, a variety of millenarian religious cults appeared in the Philippines, promising a variety of redemptive salvations, temporal and spiritual. Andrés Bonifacio's Katipunan made Filipino nationalism and anti-Spanish nationalism the redemptive goals, creating in the process a powerful, almost messianic nationalistic movement. The Katipunan also established mutual aid societies and schools for the poor. By 1896, more than 30,000 Filipinos had joined the Katipunan, and Bonifacio had established a highly effective organization at the national, provincial, and municipal levels.

When Spain executed José Rizal in 1896, the movement toward revolution accelerated. Andrés Bonifacio and the Katipunan declared Filipino independence from Spain on 23 August 1896. The revolution was underway. Spanish authorities closed in on Bonifacio, forcing him to flee Manila for the Marikina Mountains. At the same time, however, another group of Katipuñeros in Cavite Province, who were led by Emilio Aguinaldo,* defeated Spanish forces on the battlefield and seized control of several towns. Leadership of the revolution began to shift to Aguinaldo, and the factionalism within the Katipunan turned violent. When Bonifacio tried to assert his authority over Emilio Aguinaldo and the Cavite Katipuñeros, they arrested him. Charged with treason and sedition, Bonifacio was tried and convicted in a Cavite Katipuñero court. He was executed on 10 May 1897. Today, Filipinos celebrate Andrés Bonifacio as a national hero.

REFERENCES: John Foreman, *The Philippine Islands* (Manila: Cacho Hermanos, 1985); César Majul, *The Political and Constitutional Ideas of the Philippine Revolution* (Quezon City: University of the Philippines Press, 1967); Robert Reed, *Colonial Manila* (Berkeley: University of California Press, 1978); Alejo L. Villanueva, *Bonifacio's Unfinished Revolution* (Quezon City: New Day Publishers, 1989).

JAMES S. OLSON

BOSTON (ship)

The U.S.S. *Boston* was an *Atlanta*-class protected cruiser of 3,189 tons commissioned 2 May 1887. *Boston* had an auxiliary brig sailing rig, two 8-inch, six 6-inch, and 10 smaller-caliber guns. She had a 1.5-inch protected deck and a double bottom.

Boston served in the Asiatic Squadron* and deployed to Mirs Bay* on 24 April 1898. *Boston, Baltimore,* and *Concord* were then sent ahead of the squadron to reconnoiter Subic Bay,* where commodore George Dewey* believed the Spanish fleet to be anchored. The Spanish admiral Montojo* had, in fact, originally planned to defend at Subic, but he withdrew to Manila,* and *Boston* and other observers so reported the change.

Boston fought in the battle of Manila Bay,* receiving four hits, one of which exploded in a cabin at water line and started a fire. The cruiser also supported troop landings during May and served as convoy escort. During the siege of Manila, *Boston* provided supporting fires.

Boston was the "B" of the "ABCD ships" of the new steel navy, *Atlanta, Chicago,* and *Dolphin** being the others. Having served as a receiving ship at Mare Island in San Francisco Bay from 1918 until 1946, *Boston* was scuttled at sea on 8 April 1946.

REFERENCE: H. W. Wilson, *The Downfall of Spain* (New York: Burt Franklin, 1971).

BRADFORD, ROYAL BIRD
(1844–1914)

Commander Royal Bird Bradford was chief of the Bureau of Equipment, knowledgeable about coaling stations, about the Philippines,* and about naval needs and strategic concerns. In short, he knew coal*—the U.S. Navy lived on coal—the Philippines, and the system. He was also an ardent expansionist. As naval attaché to the U.S. Peace Commission* in Paris in 1898, he had an important impact in the thinking of President William McKinley.* Bradford argued that the economic and strategic interdependence of the Philippine Islands required that they be administered by one power. Japan,* Russia, Germany,* and Great Britain* wanted to partition the Philippines, something that would have grave repercussions in the international community as nations flocked to the carcass of Spain's colonies. Only American possession would stave off these powers. Great Britain, in particular, was a fervent supporter of U.S. possession of the Philippines. The other powers would accept American annexation, but no one else's. Thus, all avenues seemed to lead to annexation. It was Bradford who coalesced these ideas into one argument and presented it in its strategic theater.

REFERENCES: William Reynolds Braisted, *The United States Navy in the Pacific, 1897–1909* (Austin: University of Texas Press, 1958); Margaret Leech, *In the Days of McKinley* (New York: Harper & Row, 1959).

BRECKINRIDGE, JOSEPH CABELL
(1842–1920)

Joseph Cabell Breckinridge was born in Baltimore, and like so many U.S. Army officers in the Spanish American War, he obtained his commission while serving with volunteers in the Civil War. Breckinridge was the inspector general of the army (1889–1904) and left administrative duties in 1898 to go to Cuba. He was brevetted major general of volunteers in 1898 and fought at Santiago,* having a horse shot out from under him on 2 July. Breckinridge was a friend of General Nelson Miles* and, as inspector general, became involved in the scandals at the close of the war. Breckinridge was ordered by Secretary Russell A. Alger* to command Camp Thomas,* Georgia, and restore order. Also a supporter of Miles in the beef controversy,* with the latter's fall from influence, Breckinridge's career was in some jeopardy. He retired in 1904.

Breckinridge's son, Joseph C. Breckinridge, Jr., fell overboard and drowned from the *Cushing** on 11 February 1898.

REFERENCES: Graham A. Cosmas, *An Army for Empire* (Columbia: University of Missouri Press, 1971); Ethelbert Dudley Warfield, *Joseph Cabell Breckinridge, Junior: A Brief History of a Short Life* (New York: Knickerbocker Press, 1898).

BROOKE, JOHN RUTTER
(1838–1926)

As with many of his contemporaries, Major General John Rutter Brooke was commissioned during the Civil War while serving in a volunteer infantry unit. After the Civil War, Brooke resigned from volunteer service, a brigadier by 1865, and was commissioned lieutenant colonel in the regular army on 28 July 1866. He was promoted to brigadier in 1888 and to major general on 22 May 1897. Brooke commanded at Camp Thomas,* also known as Chickamauga, a training command. He was also commander of the Department of the Gulf and First Corps. Later Brooke commanded 5,000 men under General Nelson Miles* in the Puerto Rico* campaign. Brooke advanced from Arroyo* north in an attempt to cut off the Spanish behind Aibonito.* He also served as the first U.S. military governor of Puerto Rico, retiring in 1902.

REFERENCES: Edward J. Berbusse, *The United States in Puerto Rico, 1898–1900* (Chapel Hill: University of North Carolina Press, 1966); Graham A. Cosmas, *An Army for Empire* (Columbia: University of Missouri Press, 1971).

BROOKLYN (ship)

The U.S. Congress authorized the armored cruiser *Brooklyn* in 1892 as part of the new U.S. Navy. *Brooklyn* was an improved design over *New York,** incorporating hull and armament refinements that made *Brooklyn* a sought-after command. *Brooklyn* featured an extreme tumble home derived from French warship theory. At 9,125 tons and over 402 feet in length with three tall and thin funnels, the *Brooklyn* was able to mount eight 8-inch and twelve 5-inch guns, thus commanding greater offensive power than any other armored cruiser at the time of her commissioning. At that time, the then-chief of the Bureau of Ordnance, William T. Sampson,* investigated the use of electrically operated turrets. After Lieutenant Bradley Fiske, who did the actual testing, wrote the report, *Brooklyn* incorporated the new technology and entered service on 1 December 1896, with Captain Francis Cook* commanding.

During the Spanish American War, *Brooklyn* served as the flagship of the Flying Squadron.* In that capacity she steamed to Cienfuegos* to blockade the Spanish fleet. This effort was wasted inasmuch as the Spanish fleet entered Santiago de Cuba* on 19 May 1898, the same day Commodore Winfield Scott Schley,* commander of the Flying Squadron, left Key West* for Cienfuegos. Receiving orders to steam for Santiago on the twenty-fifth, Schley did not arrive at Santiago for three more days. Schley's perceived dawdling aroused Admiral William T. Sampson* and became an instigant in the Sampson-Schley Controversy.* *Brooklyn* steamed in the blockade* until the sea battle off Santiago on 3 July.

With the North Atlantic Squadron* at the Battle of Santiago Bay, *Brooklyn* lay fortuitously directly in the path of the sallying Spanish. The fastest ship of the fleet, *Brooklyn* was in the van and able to engage the lead ship as she emerged from the bay. At this point, *Brooklyn* made a 360-degree turn, narrowly missing the *Texas.** The purpose of the turn was to avoid being rammed by the Spanish flagship *Infanta María Teresa** and to pursue the Spanish westward on a parallel course. This successful maneuver enabled close engagement of the Spanish fleet, with telling results: shattered and burning, the *Infanta María Teresa, Almirante Oquendo,** and *Vizcaya* beached themselves. *Brooklyn* and *Oregon** also worried *Cristóbal Colón** with continuous fire until she also ran ashore and surrendered.

Brooklyn received about twenty-five hits, mostly in the upper works. The U.S. fleet suffered two casualties, both in *Brooklyn.* A shot decapitated Chief Yeoman George Ellis, and a fireman was wounded.

Brooklyn continued with the North Atlantic Squadron through 16 October 1899, when she left for service in the Far East as flagship of the Asiatic Squadron.* In that capacity, until 1902 the cruiser supported American efforts in the Philippines during the Philippine Insurrection.* *Brooklyn* was decommissioned at Mare Island* on 9 March 1921.

REFERENCE: Ivan Musicant, *U.S. Armored Cruisers: A Design and Operational History* (Annapolis, MD: Naval Institute Press, 1985).

BRYAN, WILLIAM JENNINGS
(1860–1925)

Bible-quoting orator and presidential hopeful, William Jennings Bryan needs little introduction. Bryan was a supporter of the Fifty Million Bill,* and although he ran against William McKinley* in 1896, the Democratic platform was almost identical to the Republican in support of Cuban rights against Spain. The major issue in the election was, of course, the silver issue, and the Cuban revolution was almost completely eclipsed.

Bryan supported McKinley in the Spanish American War and volunteered for service. Joining the Third Nebraska Volunteers and commissioned a colonel, Bryan hoped to get into the fray. McKinley, however, ensured that his political opponent did not have an opportunity for heroics, and the Third languished in Florida.

Bryan was a practical anti-imperialist. He favored the war to break the yoke of the Spanish, but he opposed annexation. Oddly, he favored the Treaty of Paris,* believing that the complexities of multinational intrigue in the Philippines,* for example, would find solution easier if the United States annexed the islands and then liberated its population. Nevertheless, he felt that coaling stations were necessary, that commerce must expand. Inexplicably, he felt that annexing Puerto Rico* would be acceptable. Other anti-imperialists found this mixed message confusing, and it hurt him in the election of 1900. However, Bryan seemed to operate on the principle that the U.S. government should be free of foreign influence, free of alien races (thus Puerto Rico was acceptable but the Philippines were not). These seemingly contradictory messages were not easily understood by colleagues in the Anti-Imperialist League,* and they baffled others who then suspected him of unworthy motives. Complicating the issue further, his friends in the Anti-Imperialist League did not share his views on the silver issue. Thus he became the grudging candidate of many and the whole-hearted candidate of very few.

REFERENCES: David D. Anderson, *William Jennings Bryan* (Boston: Twayne Publishers, 1981); A. Clements, *William Jennings Bryan, Missionary Isolationist* (Knoxville: University of Tennessee Press, 1982); Louis W. Koenig, *Bryan: A Political Biography of William Jennings Bryan* (New York: G. P. Putnam's Sons, 1971).

BUCK, WILLIAM H.
(1868–1924)

A graduate of Annapolis in 1890, Ensign William H. Buck participated in covert intelligence operations* to gather information on Admiral Manuel de la Cámara's* squadron. Buck posed as a wealthy civilian meandering from port to port on holiday aboard the yacht *Juno*. In reality sniffing for intelligence on Cámara's movements, Buck followed the Spanish squadron through the Mediterranean and reported on its progress, thus enabling the Office of Naval Intelligence* to assess the developing situation.

REFERENCE: Jeffery M. Dowart, *The Office of Naval Intelligence* (Annapolis, MD: Naval Institute Press, 1979).

BUENAVENTURA (ship)

When war broke out between the United States and Spain, the United States instituted a naval blockade* of Cuba as part of its strategy. The blockade was covered journalistically by many, including Stephen Crane.* The blockade originally stretched from Bahía Honda to Cárdenas* on Cuba's northern coast and the port of Cienfuegos* on the south coast. On 22 April 1898 a line of U.S. warships sighted the Spanish merchant ship *Buenaventura* voyaging from the gulf port of Pascagoula, Mississippi, to Holland. Blissfully unaware that war had been declared, the captain of the *Buenaventura* hoisted his flag to salute the warships. A shot across *Buenaventura*'s bow by the U.S.S. *Nashville*—the first shot of the war—quickly rearranged reality for *Buenaventura:* She became the first prize of the war.

REFERENCE: G.J.A. O'Toole, *The Spanish War* (New York: W. W. Norton & Co., 1984).

BÜLOW, BERNHARD HEINRICH VON
(1849–1929)

Prince Bernhard Heinrich von Bülow, German statesman, served as foreign secretary for Germany* during the Spanish American War. Appointed in 1897,

Bülow took a leading role in the attempts to mediate between the United States and Spain. He opposed German intervention in the dispute over Cuba. He also proposed sending a German admiral to Manila* to gather information. The result of this proposal was Vice Admiral Otto von Diederichs's* mission to Manila.

Bülow's motives during the Spanish American War came from Germany's desire to preserve the principle of monarchy, expand German presence, particularly in the Far East, and to avoid realigning the European powers. Although he succeeded in the main, the success was not without cost. The German Asiatic Squadron* commanded by Diederichs created considerable friction with the Americans, but Germany did acquire additional islands in the Pacific (subsequently lost in World War I).

REFERENCE: Alfred L. P. Dennis, *Adventures in American Diplomacy, 1896–1906* (New York: E. P. Dutton, 1928).

C

CABAÑAS, CUBA

The town of Cabañas lies on Cabañas Bay about 38 miles west of Havana.* Cabañas had a Spanish fortress with approximately 2,000 troops. Early in the planning, Cabañas was considered a possible landing point for U.S. forces to link with Cuban insurgents* for an assault on Havana. This plan, however, was never implemented. When Admiral William Sampson* left Key West* to commence the blockade,* Cabañas Bay was one of the first ports placed under blockade. On 22 June 1898, General William R. Shafter* landed 16,000 U.S. troops at Daiquirí* to invest Santiago.* A force of 500 Cubans launched a demonstration attack at Cabañas supported by naval shelling; these efforts at Cabañas would be led by Cuban general Calixto García* as a diversion.

A naval action occurred at Cabañas on 17 June when two steam cutters from the *New York** and *Massachusetts** attempted to reconnoitre Cabañas Bay. Steaming slowly past the old fort, both cutters received such heavy fire they had to retreat. Although the two cutters received seventeen hits, no one was injured. *Texas** and *Vixen** steamed forward and with rapid fire suppressed the Spanish fires.

REFERENCES: French Ensor Chadwick, *The Relations of the United States and Spain* (New York: Russell & Russell, 1911); David F. Trask, *The War with Spain in 1898* (New York: Macmillan Publishing, Co., 1981).

CADARSO, LUIS
(1844–1898)

There was no lack of courageous and gallant Spanish warriors during the Spanish American War. Frequently outgunned and often fighting with severe technological disadvantages, the Spanish navy in particular produced a crop of heroes that would fill a lengthy list. Luis Cadarso, captain of the *Reina Cristina,** was one of these. Besides having the responsibility of conning his ship, Cadarso had to deal with the presence of Admiral Patricio Montojo* on the *Cristina*. *Cristina* was not a new ship, having been launched a dozen years previously, but during the naval battle of Manila,* Cadarso maneuvered his ship to fire on George Dewey's* Asiatic Squadron.* *Cristina* was met with such a hail of fire from *Olympia** and others that she had to retire. With his ship aflame and sinking, the intrepid Cadarso died while exposed in the attempt to rescue what remained of his crew. The *Cristina*, so battered that almost all superstructure was gone, sank. Dewey's men later counted over seventy hits in the hull and found eighty skeletons in the sunken ward room.

REFERENCES: *Notes on the Spanish American War* (Washington, DC: Government Printing Office, 1900); *Appendix to the Report of the Chief of the Bureau of Navigation, 1989* (Washington, DC: Government Printing Office, 1898).

CAIMANERA, CUBA

Caimanera is a port on Guantánamo* Bay on the western shore. As such, Caimanera figured in actions near and around Guantánamo, of which two actions stand out. On 7 June 1898, *St. Louis,* Yankee,** and *Marblehead** shelled Caimanera and cut the cable from Caimanera to Haiti.* Some 500 Spanish troops were seen in the vicinity, and on 10 June, a battalion of U.S. Marines landed near Caimanera and dug in. The Spanish attacked, but with supporting fire from U.S. Navy ships the attack was repulsed. On 14 June the marines attacked and captured a blockhouse with the aid of fire from *Dolphin.**

REFERENCE: H. W. Wilson, *The Downfall of Spain* (New York: Burt Franklin, 1971).

CALLAO (ship)

Callao was a small Spanish gunboat of about 200 tons that on 12 May 1898 returned to Manila* from an extended cruise among the Philippine Islands. Unaware that war had been declared, *Callao* blithely steamed into Manila Bay.* When one of the U.S. ships fired a shot, *Callao* instantly surrendered.

The U.S. Navy commander, George Dewey,* added *Callao* to the U.S. squadron. On 13 May, the newly acquired *Callao* supported U.S. troops ashore by rapid fire against Fort San Antonio.*

REFERENCE: H. W. Wilson, *The Downfall of Spain* (New York: Burt Franklin, 1971).

CÁMARA Y LIBERMOORE, MANUEL DE LA (1836–1920)

Commodore George Dewey's* defeat of the Spanish fleet at Manila Bay* on 1 May 1898 ignited impassioned nationalistic feelings in Spain.* Admiral Manuel de la Cámara y Libermoore (sometimes spelled "Livermoore") was placed in command of a Spanish fleet to relieve the Spanish garrison in the Philippines. His fleet consisted of the battleship *Pelayo,** the armored cruiser *Carlos V,** the auxiliary cruisers *Rápido* and *Patriota,* and the torpedo boats (sometimes classed as destroyers) *Audaz, Osado,* and *Proserpina,* along with the transports *Isla de Panay, San Francisco, Cristóbal Colón,* Covadonga,* and *Buenos Aires.* Some of the transports, however, were to return to Spain after escorting the fleet to Suez.

Cámara's orders left him considerable leeway. Cámara's superiors and the new minister of marine Ramón Auñón y Villalón* knew that Cámara could not cope with Dewey's squadron; instead, Cámara was to try to retain the Philippines by a show of force. Auñón also knew that by dispatching Cámara, Spain proper was essentially defenseless against naval attacks.

On 16 June Cámara began his voyage. When the U.S. Navy Department realized Cámara's squadron had sailed and ascertained its destination, it put into action a plan of its own. On 18 June Secretary of the Navy John D. Long* ordered Commodore (later Admiral) William T. Sampson* to create a new squadron, which became known as the Eastern Squadron,* for possible raiding and bombardment missions along the coasts of Spain.* Lieutenant William S. Sims,* U.S. naval attaché in Paris, was ordered to "leak" news of the formation of the Eastern Squadron and its probable mission to agents who would inform Spanish authorities. The obvious intent was to force the return of Cámara's ships—the threat being the unopposed shelling of Barcelona or other Spanish port cities. The State Department on 20 June also attempted to impede Cámara's progress by protesting the coaling of the Spanish ships in neutral ports. Collusion by the U.S. consul prevented coaling by Cámara at Port Said. Unknown to the U.S. consul, the British proconsul in Egypt received instructions from the Foreign Office to disallow the coaling of Cámara's ships.

Sampson's defeat of Pascual Cervera's* squadron in Cuba on 3 July ended speculation on Cámara's real mission. On 7 July Auñón ordered Cámara back to Spain.

The effect of Cámara's squadron on the Americans was considerable. Beleaguered with what he perceived as German pressure in Manila, Dewey was not in a position to repulse Cámara's fleet with certainty. For that reason, as well as others, the monitors *Monterey** and *Monadnock** were dispatched to Dewey's aid. Blockading Cuba, Sampson could not dispatch vessels from his fleet without deleteriously affecting his squadron's many missions. Cámara's squadron presented a dilemma.

For the Spanish, some like A. T. Mahan,* for example, have suggested that Cámara's eastward voyage was an elaborate bluff—the intended result of the bluff was, however, somewhat uncertain. The departure of the fleet did leave the Spanish coasts unprotected. The creation of the Eastern Squadron called the bluff, and the defeat of Cervera again put Spain into a defensive posture.

REFERENCE: David F. Trask, *The War with Spain in 1898* (New York: Macmillan Publishing Co., 1981).

CAMBON, JULES MARTIN
(1845–1935)

Jules Martin Cambon, French ambassador to the United States, had a varied career as an officer in the Franco-Prussian War and with various diplomatic posts and government appointments. He served in Constantinople and Algiers, and on 14 October 1897, he was appointed ambassador to the United States. He presented his credentials on 15 January 1898, just before the outbreak of war between Spain and the United States.

Práxides Mateo Sagasta* decided on 18 July 1898, the day after the fall of Santiago,* to sue for peace. Jules Cambon was asked to serve as intermediary between Madrid and Washington in hammering out a peace protocol. He served well and faithfully represented the Spanish interests. Realistically, however, President McKinley's* strategy to assault outlying Spanish areas (the Philippines and the impending campaign in Puerto Rico, for example) left Spain in a precarious position. As delays mounted, U.S. forces seized greater territory and made inevitable McKinley's stronger bargaining position. Cambon's role was to strive to speed the process as much as possible to preserve Spanish options.
REFERENCES: Margaret Leech, *In the Days of McKinley* (New York: Harper & Row, 1959); Whitelow Reid, *Making Peace with Spain: The Diary of Whitelow Reid* (Austin: University of Texas Press, 1965).

CAMP ALGER, VIRGINIA

Across the Potomac River and south of Washington, Camp Alger was one of the larger training camps for volunteers. From Camp Alger, trained troops were to be dispatched to the Caribbean for duty. Named after Russell A. Alger,* secretary of war, the camp unfortunately became linked with the scandals surrounding the secretary. Early in May 1898 Alger, General Nelson Miles,* and Adjutant General Henry Corbin* abandoned earlier plans to keep volunteers in their respective states. Instead, on 14 and 15 May 1898 the War Department began concentrating troops in camps according to future destination: San Francisco for the Philippines, and Camps Alger,* Thomas,* and Tampa* for the Caribbean. Camp Alger rapidly filled with thousands of volunteers who were ill equipped, poorly trained, and often poorly led. Disease ravaged the camp, and Alger became a synonym for scandal.

By August Camp Alger swelled to 23,500 troops of the Second Corps. Only two brigades from the camp were sent to the Caribbean, so most of the troops stayed in camp. At Alger, camp life became an existence unto itself, and a peripheral "business district" of saloons, prostitutes, restaurants, and the like soon surrounded the camp. Poor drainage and poor conditions soon spawned disease, which was the unfortunate legacy of Camp Alger.
REFERENCE: Graham A. Cosmas, *An Army for Empire* (Columbia: University of Missouri Press, 1971).

CAMP CUBA LIBRE, FLORIDA

Camp Cuba Libre was one of the expansion camps for volunteers and regulars made necessary by the tremendous growth of the military in the first phases of the war. Originally, the Fifth Corps* and Seventh Corps* were to be the first to fight in Cuba, and they were ordered to assemble at Tampa.* However,

Tampa quickly became overcrowded. General William Shafter* felt that Seventh Corps needed another location, and so Camp Cuba Libre, under the command of Major General Fitzhugh Lee,* was created near Jacksonville,* Florida, to alleviate the overcrowding at Tampa. Like other army camps,* Jacksonville suffered from shortages due to the rapid buildup. Eating off shingles with fingers was common at Cuba Libre: There was plenty of food but a scarcity of utensils and implements for food preparation. Nevertheless, Jacksonville was better than most, primarily because of General Lee's efforts. He selected the ground for the camp himself and oversaw the installation of plumbing, tents, lumber purchases, and so on. These efforts helped Jacksonville to escape the worst of the typhoid epidemics that so devastated the rest of the large camps. General Lee's efforts resulted in one of the better-run and better-equipped camps of the period.
REFERENCE: Graham A. Cosmas, *An Army for Empire* (Columbia: University of Missouri Press, 1971).

CAMP DEWEY, PHILIPPINES

As Brigadier General Thomas M. Anderson* led some 2,500 troops from Cavite* (the first contingent of Eighth Army Corps*) to position his men for an assault on Manila,* he realized that Cavite was too far away—27 miles—and he needed a base closer to the area of operations. Anticipating a better position from which to attack, on 15 July 1898 Anderson transferred a portion of his force by water to a point 3 miles from Manila named Camp Dewey, after the victorious George Dewey.* Camp Dewey became the base from which the assault of Manila would originate. It also became the disembarkation point for the rest of Eighth Corps as it arrived at the end of July under Generals Wesley Merritt* and Arthur MacArthur.*

From Camp Dewey, Brigadier Francis V. Greene* was able to negotiate the removal of insurgent forces to his front on 28 July. So by the end of the month Camp Dewey stretched an additional 1,300 yards toward the Spanish lines. From Camp Dewey, Merritt was able to complete his preparations for the assault on Manila.
REFERENCES: R. A. Alger, *The Spanish American War* (New York: Harper & Brothers, 1901); Graham A. Cosmas, *An Army for Empire* (Columbia: University of Missouri Press, 1971); William Thaddeus Sexton, *Soldiers in the Sun* (Harrisburg, PA: Military Service Publishing Co., 1939).

CAMP THOMAS, CHICKAMAUGA, GEORGIA

Camp Thomas possessed the dubious distinction of having the largest concentration of troops among the various camps*; by June 1898, it contained over 60,000 troops of First and Third Corps. Major General J. R. Brooke* commanded at Thomas, and he was woefully understaffed with officers to handle the massive influx of men and the tons of supplies arriving by trainloads daily. Evidence suggests that Brooke's span of control was exceeded: He commanded not only Thomas but also the First Corps and the Department of the Gulf. As a consequence of these burdens, Camp Thomas suffered from poor sanitation and poor organization. An Illinois regiment mutinied and discipline became difficult. Disorganization, poor discipline, and poor sanitation contributed equally to one of the largest scandals of the war: Typhoid cases doubled in the three weeks after 25 July 1898 to 4,400. Overcrowded hospitals, plagued with shortages of everything from linens to staff, were unable to deal with the crisis. Secretary of War Russell A. Alger* and Surgeon General George M. Sternberg* attempted remedial creation of hospitals in August and the dispersal of troops from Camp Thomas to Kentucky in a much-needed effort to stem the advance of disease, but by August when these measures were implemented, much of the damage had already been done.

Not all blame for the disaster can be placed at General Brooke's feet; he was replaced as Camp Thomas's commander on 23 July, when General James F. Wade* took over. On 2 August Wade was replaced by Inspector General Joseph C. Breckenridge,* who commanded until the camp was abandoned at the end of the month. Because of the enormity of the health crisis at Camp Thomas, it became a centerpiece of war investigation and subsequent defense by Alger and others.

REFERENCES: R. A. Alger, *The Spanish American War* (New York: Harper & Brothers, 1901); Graham A. Cosmas, *An Army for Empire* (Columbia: University of Missouri Press, 1971).

CAMP WIKOFF, NEW YORK

Camp Wikoff, named for Colonel Charles Wikoff, who died while leading a brigade at San Juan,* lay about 125 miles from New York City at Montauk Point on eastern Long Island. Camp Wikoff was a response to fears about disease,* yellow fever* in particular. Ignorance about the transmission of yellow fever and a fear of epidemic from returning soldiers caused Secretary of War Russell A. Alger to formulate a plan to quarantine the infected troops in Cuba. In fact, malaria, not yellow fever, began to sweep through the troops in Cuba. Nevertheless, as late as the end of July 1898, there was no intimation of incipient disease, and Theodore Roosevelt,* for example, reported that his troops were fit and ready to fight in General Nelson Miles's* campaign in Puerto Rico.*

On 2 August General William R. Shafter* cabled the War Department that a yellow fever epidemic was likely and that the Fifth Corps* should go back to the States as soon as possible. A long telegram the following day detailed that 75 percent of Shafter's command had been sick and that it was, in consequence, an ineffective fighting force. Yellow fever had not yet struck, Shafter wrote, but when it did the death rate would be excessively high. He urged immediate evacuation of convalescents to the States. Shafter's missives effectively changed the War Department policy, and Alger authorized the immediate transfer of troops to Montauk Point on 3 August 1898. Alger placed General S.B.M. Young* in command of Montauk, and he arrived on 5 August. On 6 August building supplies arrived, and in less than a week wells had been bored, water piped to the sites, and 10,000 tents erected.

Meanwhile back in Cuba, at his request Shafter's subordinates wrote a letter supporting Shafter's claims, and the general forwarded the letter to Washington. This letter, the infamous "Round Robin,"* somehow got into the hands of an Associated Press* correspondent who cabled it to the news bureau. The "Round Robin" and its associated commentary left in the public's mind the image of the heroes of San Juan heartlessly left to die of pestilence on foreign soil. The veterans' arrival at Camp Wikoff confirmed the worst suspicions. Alger's zeal exceeded his resources, and the camp was not ready for the massive influx of troops. No amount of damage control could remedy the confusion and lack of facilities at Camp Wikoff. The troops arrived, often without their baggage, to a beehive of activity, carpenters hammering, and general disorder. The congestion and inevitable supply and construction delays left a poor impression. Scandal and misunderstandings plagued the War Department from the beginning. General Joseph Wheeler* assumed command on 15 August and remained until Shafter's arrival in early September. The War Department earnestly tried to ameliorate conditions, but the combination of misunderstandings, confusion, and congestion left a bad odor hanging over the department. President William McKinley* visited the camp, as did Alger and Surgeon General Sternberg.* Much was done to alleviate the situation, and, indeed, the conditions slowly improved. Nevertheless, it was equally clear that the army had bungled the return of the troops, and Alger, in particular, caught the blame.

REFERENCES: R. A. Alger, *The Spanish American War* (New York: Harper & Brothers, 1901); Graham A. Cosmas, *An Army for Empire* (Columbia: University of Missouri Press, 1971).

CAMPS, U.S. ARMY

The exceedingly rapid buildup of troop strength after the commencement of hostilities created stresses to the military training system that reached gigantic proportions. These strains came not only from the rapid increase of the number of men under arms but also from intense political pressure, a result of the political and idealistic fervor manifested by many, to include volunteer units from the states. On 26 April 1898 Major General Nelson Miles* proposed that volunteer units assemble in their respective states, where they would be outfitted, trained, and after 30 days transported to Chickamauga Park (later Camp Thomas* in Georgia) and to an area in Virginia south of Washington, DC (later named Camp Alger*), to be deployed to Cuba. However, in early May, President William McKinley* so expanded the war aims as to dramatically increase the perceived demand for troops and training facilities. Other orders were issued at the end of May to concentrate these new troops into a series of camps that also served as military administrative headquarters for the various corps. Thus the First, Third, and Sixth Corps marshalled at Camp Thomas at Chickamauga. The Second Corps assembled at Camp Alger. Fourth Corps headquarters were at

Mobile,* Alabama, and other locations on the gulf. Tampa* was headquarters of those going to Cuba first: Fifth and Seventh Corps. Later, on 21 June, the War Department* organized an Eighth Corps for service in the Philippines; it was headquartered at San Francisco.* Only the Fifth Corps* was largely composed of regulars; the others were a mixture of regular and volunteer units. By the end of July 1898, approximately 270,000 officers and men were in service in the U.S. Army. Because of the rapid growth of this mass of soldiery, the camp system expanded. Seventh Corps was supposed to go to Cuba, but Tampa could not handle both its corps, so the Seventh was sent to Camp Cuba Libre* near Jacksonville.* Besides these national camps, each state also maintained state camps. Units mustered late in the war never left their state camps or were diverted to maintenance duties and perform other services after the hostilities.

The camps were uniformly dirty, crowded, and disorganized. Supply and transport bottlenecks contributed to the chaos already in place and logistical delays. The volunteer units in particular suffered because the Fifth and Eighth Corps, which were to be first in combat, got the first supplies. In addition, they had the most experienced officers. Most of the volunteer units had neither adequate supplies nor experienced officers. William Jennings Bryan,* for example, was commissioned a colonel in a Nebraska regiment, inevitably named the "Silver Regiment," but he had no military experience whatever.

One of the bright spots in the camps was the responsiveness of the railroads.* Traffic managers, engineers, and directors worked in concert, often at added expense to the railroad, to cope with increased traffic and increased depot unloading. Unfortunately, this bright spot was offset by myriads of charges of malfeasance, poor sanitation, poor training, poor food, and poor health. Camp Wikoff* at Montauk Point, New York, was intended as a quarantine camp after the conflict but gained greater notoriety as a place of unnecessary suffering.

REFERENCE: Graham A. Cosmas, *An Army for Empire* (Columbia: University of Missouri Press, 1971).

CANALEJAS MÉNDEZ, JOSÉ
(1854–1912)

A distinguished Spanish lawyer, politician, and Liberal party advocate, José Canalejas Méndez was a critic of the government led by Práxides Sagasta.* He particularly criticized the Spanish military's unpreparedness, which became increasingly evident. Canalejas was also the intended recipient of Enrique Dupuy de Lôme's* infamous letter criticizing President William McKinley.*

Despite Canalejas's involvement in the Spanish American War, he survived politically and became prime minister of Spain. An assassin, Manuel Pardiñas, murdered him on 12 November 1912 in front of a bookstore.

REFERENCE: *Diccionario de historia de España,* 2 vols. (Madrid: Revista de Occidente, 1952).

CANARY ISLANDS

Containing a group of seven major islands, the Canaries lie about 70 miles west of Morocco in the North Atlantic. Whereas the Canaries played no direct role in the Spanish American War, they did have an indirect role that preoccupied Admiral Pascual Cervera,* Segismundo Bermejo,* Spain's minister of the marine, and various American naval planners. In at least one of the prewar plans that came out of the Naval War College,* the Canaries were to be used as a base for harassment raids against Spain. Spain also realized this possibility, and part of the dickering over whether to send Cervera's squadron to Cuba centered on the advisability of protecting the Canaries—and ultimately Spain. In fact, in July 1898, Práxides Mateo Sagasta,* Spain's prime minister, explained Spain's need to capitulate in part because the Balearic Islands, the Canaries, and Spain were all in danger. This threat hung over Spain even during peace negotiations,* and the United States did indeed contemplate action in this third theater.

REFERENCE: David F. Trask, *The War with Spain in 1898* (New York: Macmillan Publishing Co., 1981).

EL CANEY

The small village of El Caney was, in 1898, about 6 miles northeast of Santiago de Cuba.* The battles of San Juan Hill* and El Caney were the two principal land battles in Cuba.

By the end of June 1898, the Spanish General Arsenio Linares y Pomba* had at his command at Santiago less than 10,000 troops. He was unable to reinforce them because Cuban insurgents dominated land routes and the naval blockade* sealed off access to Santiago by sea. Life in the besieged city had as a result become hard; the last food landed in April 1898, and access to food from the countryside had been halted by insurgent activity. Linares completed his defensive preparations of Santiago with a three-tiered defense: an outer skirmish line that was not expected to hold against a determined U.S. assault; an inner line of fortifications that included over 520 men at El Caney, in addition to San Juan Hill, Kettle Hill,* and eight other fortified areas; and as a last line of defense, the city itself. Some have criticized Linares for his dispersal of troops, leaving only a small number of troops available to defend against the probable avenues of American approach.

General William R. Shafter* also made mistakes in communication and planning, and he suffered from the mistakes of others. He behaved as if the U.S. naval force did not exist, when, in fact, naval bombardment could have halted the Spanish buildup at El Caney and San Juan. Unable to unload transports and move equipment, Shafter had to leave heavy guns and camping equipment behind.

On 28 June Shafter became aware of the relief force led by Colonel Federico

Escario* marching toward Santiago. Determined to take Santiago before this relief arrived, Shafter initiated hurried plans for an assault.

Reconnaissance on 28, 29, and 30 June was spotty. Shafter believed that El Caney, on the road to Guantánamo,* was of tactical significance. He also intended to reduce El Caney in two hours or less, take San Juan Hill, and seize Santiago in one sweeping attack. The plan and reality never met. Brigadier General Henry W. Lawton* and his division were not completely bivouacked until midnight. The planned assault commenced at 7 A.M. on 1 July, but the lack of effective artillery support and the tenacious defense by General Joaquín Vara del Rey's troops developed into a battle of over eight hours. Vara del Rey had no artillery, and his troops were armed only with Mausers.* Lawton's division, all regulars with Krag-Jörgensen rifles*—except for the Second Massachusetts Volunteers, who were armed with Springfields and black powder*—took a great many casualties while inflicting a great many. Not until the artillery moved to concentrate fire on the stone fort of El Viso did the U.S. attack make headway.

The delay in taking El Caney understandably halted the planned momentum for the successive attacks. At one point Shafter ordered Lawton to withdraw, but Lawton argued that he was too closely engaged. General Adna R. Chaffee's* Twelfth Infantry Brigade took El Viso in the afternoon as Spanish resistance crumbled. Less than 100 Spanish troops were able to effect a retreat; 120 were made prisoners, and about 235 were killed or wounded. Among the Spanish dead were General Vara del Rey and two of his sons. The U.S. attacking force of about 5,400 men suffered 44 killed and wounded.

Although the U.S. troops took El Caney, it was a costly victory. The encounter not only took its toll in human casualties but also unraveled Shafter's plan for sweeping through Santiago. The Americans at El Caney fought not as a cohesive Fifth Corps but as separate units. Command and control, already debilitated, weakened further. The already desperate plight of the Spanish in Santiago and the destruction of Admiral Pascual Cervera's* squadron on 3 July did as much or more as the land battle at El Caney to bring an American victory.

Over 521 Spaniards held against ten times their number at El Caney, which passed into military history as an example of manly courage. So vigorous had been the defense of El Caney and San Juan Heights, that Shafter chose to dig in and lay siege to Santiago rather than to risk excessive casualties.

REFERENCES: John Bigelow, *Reminiscences of the Santiago Campaign* (New York: Harper & Brothers, 1899); French Ensor Chadwick, *The Relations of the United States and Spain* (New York: Russell & Russell, 1911); Graham A. Cosmas, *An Army for Empire* (Columbia: University of Missouri, 1971); David F. Trask, *The War with Spain in 1898* (New York: Macmillan Publishing Co., 1981); Joseph Wheeler, *The Santiago Campaign, 1898* (New York: Drexel Biddle, 1899).

CANNON, JOSEPH GURNEY
(1836–1926)

Joseph Gurney Cannon's career in the U.S. Congress spanned forty years, with eight years as speaker of the House. At the commencement of 1898, Joe Cannon was chairman of the House Appropriations Committee. President William McKinley* was walking a cautious line trying to avoid war with Spain; then on 9 February a letter critical of McKinley by Enrique Dupuy de Lôme,* Spanish ambassador, was published. On 15 February the *Maine** exploded in Havana* harbor, creating a massive international incident with serious implications for domestic and foreign politics. American feeling ran high in many circles, but McKinley wanted to preserve some political distance from this political rockslide to work with foreign powers. Reluctant to broach the issue with Congress directly, on 6 March he summoned Cannon, who agreed to sponsor a bill to arm the army and navy at $50 million. Cannon championed the Fifty Million Bill,* which passed overwhelmingly 313 to 0, with 44 abstentions. McKinley now had funding to build and operate the armed forces, and agents were sent to purchase warships in Great Britain.

REFERENCES: L. White Busbey, *Uncle Joe Cannon* (New York: Henry Holt & Co., 1927); William Rea Gwinn, *Uncle Joe Cannon, Archfoe of Insurgency* (NP: Bookman Associates, 1957).

CÁNOVAS DEL CASTILLO, ANTONIO
(1828–1897)

Antonio Cánovas del Castillo came to head the Spanish government when monarchy was restored in 1874. He did so until 1881, and again from 1883 until 1885. A conservative politician and monarchist, Cánovas was the power behind the Spanish throne. He suppressed the Cuban Insurrection* in 1878 and thereafter attempted to treat the troubles in Cuba. He became a proponent of Cuban autonomy,* a solution similar to that proposed by Grover Cleveland.* Cánovas was assassinated by Miguel Angiolillo,* thereby allowing Práxides Mateo Sagasta* to reoccupy the prime ministership.

REFERENCE: José Luis Comellas García-Llera, *Cánovas* (Madrid: Ediciones Cid, 1965).

CAPE TUNAS, CUBA

Planning is difficult under any circumstances; in war, it can be a nightmare. Intelligence operations* gather data, and given new data, commanders change their minds. Originally, General William R. Shafter* was going to initiate hostilities in Cuba with a force of 6,000 men who would land at or near Cape Tunas, Cuba, and march inland to connect with the insurgents* under General Máximo Gómez.* Linking up with blockade* forces, Shafter would then move to the north to support and supply insurgents there. These orders were issued 29 April 1898 but were cancelled the next day when news of the sailing of

Admiral Pascual Cervera y Topete's* squadron became known. As a result, the planned expedition to Cape Tunas never occurred.

The cape lies about 70 miles east of Cienfuegos,* on the southern coast of Cuba.

REFERENCE: David F. Trask, *The War with Spain* (New York: Macmillan Publishing Co., 1981).

CAPE VERDE ISLANDS

The Cape Verde Islands lie in the Atlantic Ocean off the western bulge of Africa, commencing about 300 miles from the African coast. During the Spanish American War, this archipelago—principally St. Vincent—served as a staging area for Admiral Pascual Cervera's* ill-fated Spanish squadron.

The Cape Verdes belong to Portugal, and that country declared neutrality on 29 April 1898, forcing Cervera and his ships to depart the same day.

In the postwar discussions about strategy, the decision to sail to the Caribbean from the Cape Verdes is pivotal. Some have argued that once Cervera sailed, his squadron was doomed. Caution counseled for strengthening the Spanish squadron with ships not ready for sea in April. Regardless, he sailed, the squadron battled at Santiago,* and the squadron was destroyed.

REFERENCE: French Ensor Chadwick, *The Relations of the United States and Spain* (New York: Russell & Russell, 1911); Víctor M. Concas y Palau, *The Squadron of Admiral Cervera* (Washington, DC: Government Printing Office, 1900).

CÁRDENAS, CUBA

Cárdenas lies east of Havana* and south of Key West,* Florida. The bay and city of Cárdenas were hubs of fishing activity but only for shallow vessels; in 1898, the bay had not been dredged. Admiral William T. Sampson* included Cárdenas in the U.S. blockade* for several reasons: Many of the smaller vessels of Sampson's fleet had small fuel capacities; the proximity of Florida to Cuba's north coast enabled frequent refueling and re-provisioning. In addition, the Navy Department's early orders emphasized the blockade of northern Cuba with areas around Matanzas* and Cárdenas specifically mentioned. Without access to colliers, the blockade of southern ports like Santiago de Cuba,* Manzanillo,* and Cienfuegos* would be impractical.

The first encounter at Cárdenas occurred on 25 April 1898, when the 142-ton American torpedo boat *Foote** had a brief running battle with the 43-ton Spanish gunboat *Ligera*. Little damage occurred to either side.

On 8 May *Winslow,** the 142-ton sister-ship to *Foote,* steamed into Cárdenas Bay. Apparently with the intent of luring *Ligera* and a few smaller armed vessels out of the shallows where the gunboats *Wilmington** (1,397 tons) and *Machias* (1,177 tons) were lurking, it attacked the Spanish vessels. The Spaniards did not cooperate in this plan, however, and *Winslow* was damaged.

On the eleventh the Americans returned; their squadron consisted of *Winslow,* a revenue cutter, *Hudson,** and *Wilmington* and *Machias. Winslow* advanced to investigate the small armed tug *Antonio López,* moored at the mole. A Spanish concealed battery pummeled *Winslow,* completely incapacitating her. *Wilmington* and *Machias* returned fire, but somewhat inaccurately. *Hudson* steamed into the fray and got a towline aboard *Winslow* to drag her from danger. *Winslow* suffered heavy casualties (ten of her crew of twenty-five, including five mortalities), whereas the Spanish lost seven among militia and civilians of the town during the shelling. Two more were wounded aboard the *Antonio López,* which was severely damaged. The Americans never returned to attack Cárdenas.

REFERENCES: Augustín Rodríguez González, ''Operaciones menores en Cuba, 1898,'' *Revista de Historia Naval* 3, no. 9 (1985): 125–146; H. W. Wilson, *The Downfall of Spain* (New York: Burt Franklin, 1971).

CARLOS V (ship)

An armored cruiser that displaced 9,235 tons, *Emperador Carlos V* was almost never called anything but *Carlos V.* The ship played two subordinate roles in the conflict called the Spanish American War. At the commencement of activities, *Carlos V* was in the yard being overhauled. She was thus unable to sail to the Antilles with Admiral Cervera's* squadron. Nevertheless, Admiral William Sampson* knew of her existence and monitored her whereabouts because he was worried she might join Cervera's squadron. Planning for the blockade* included the possibility of the arrival of additional Spanish warships such as *Carlos V.*

The Spanish cruiser also participated in Admiral Manuel de la Cámara's* abortive attempt to relieve the Philippines with the Eastern Squadron.* The possibility that *Carlos V* or *Pelayo** or both might go to the Philippines worried Commodore George Dewey* because together, *Carlos V* and *Pelayo* represented a potent threat to Dewey's meager squadron. In response, the U.S. Navy sent the monitors *Monterey** and *Monadnock** to strengthen Dewey's force at Manila.* Neither *Pelayo* nor *Carlos V* ever arrived.

Launched in 1895 and hurriedly completed during the war, *Emperador Carlos V* carried six torpedo tubes, two 11-inch and eight 5.5-inch guns, plus miscellaneous smaller calibers. She had a speed of 19 knots.

REFERENCE: Alfredo Aguilera, *Buques de guerra españoles, 1885–1971* (Madrid: Librería Editorial San Martín, 1972).

CARRANZA, RAMÓN

Lieutenant Ramón Carranza had served as Spanish military attaché in Washington, DC. With the commencement of hostilities, he was sent to Canada to create and operate a Spanish intelligence operation* using Canadians and disaffected Americans. These would join U.S. military units and serve as Spanish agents. Carranza went to a private detective agency to recruit these agents. One of the recruits, an Englishman, informed the British consul, who informed the U.S. State Department. However, the U.S. Secret Service head, John E. Wilkie,* already knew of Carranza's activities.

Carranza was able to provide the Spanish governor general of Cuba, Ramón Blanco, with valuable information on U.S. naval movements. Through a ruse, U.S. agents obtained evidence that Carranza had violated British neutrality. About the same time, he was also sued by one of his hired detectives, thus ending this career as an espionage agent.

REFERENCE: Donald Weare Wilkie, *American Secret Service Agent* (New York: Frederick A. Stokes, 1934).

CASTILLA (ship)

The *Castilla* was a Spanish wooden cruiser of 3,300 tons built in 1881. She was steam powered with auxiliary sailing bark rig. Mounting eight guns, of which only three were 5–6-inch Krupp and the remainder very small caliber, she was followed by two sister-ships, *Aragón* and *Navarra*. *Castilla* was the eighth Spanish ship to bear the name. In 1898, she was stationed at Cavite,* in Manila Bay.*

A leaking hull rendered *Castilla*'s machinery inoperable, but Captain Alonso Morgado Pita da Viega prepared to defend regardless of her condition. When the semaphore on Corregidor* signaled on 30 April 1898 that George Dewey's* Asiatic Squadron* had been sighted, *Castilla* was as prepared as possible for the coming battle. Such preparations were valiant but useless. At 5 A.M. on 1 May, the Spanish opened fire amid exclamations of "Viva España" and "Viva el Rey." However, as the U.S. forces returned fire, the *Castilla* was shot to pieces and sunk, burning. After receiving permission to abandon the hulk, *Castilla*'s captain transferred the crew to shore, destroyed his signal books, and departed. It was a heroic but hopeless effort. *Castilla* suffered twenty-five dead and over thirty wounded.

REFERENCE: Jesús Salgado Alba, "El crucero *Castilla:* héroe y holocausto en Cavite," *Revista General de Marina* 191 (December 1976): 637–645.

CASTINE (ship)

The U.S.S. *Castine* was a *Machias*-class gunboat authorized on 2 March 1889 and commissioned on 22 October 1894. Part of the reason for the lengthy duration of construction resulted from the discovery that, as designed, these gunboats evidenced some instability. As a cure for this problem, the ships were lengthened from 190 feet to 204 feet; the extra 14 feet, used primarily for bunkers, not only increased stability but lengthened range and cruising ability. *Castine* received as armament eight 4-inch guns, four 6-pounders, two 1-pounders, two Gatling guns, and one torpedo tube. A twin-screw design, she could steam at over 15 knots. *Castine* displaced 1,177 tons.

In Cuban waters, by orders from Admiral William T. Sampson* *Castine* joined Commodore Winfield S. Schley* and his command on 19 May 1898 to cruise near Cienfuegos* in pursuit of intelligence about Admiral Pascual Cervera y Topete's* Spanish fleet. The intent of Sampson's order was that Schley locate the Spanish fleet and contain it. Schley misunderstood his orders, believing he was to blockade* Cienfuegos; this was one of the misunderstandings that eventually led to the Sampson-Schley Controversy.* *Castine* joined Schley's squadron at Cienfuegos on 23 May 1898 and coaled from the collier *Merrimac.** At noon of the same day, the British steamer *Adula** entered the port. Meanwhile, *Castine* developed trouble with her machinery, and in light of further directives from Sampson, Schley directed *Castine* to stay to watch Cienfuegos while *Iowa,** *Texas,** *Massachusetts,** *Brooklyn,** *Marblehead,** *Vixen,** *Hawk,** *Eagle,** and *Merrimac* withdrew from Cienfuegos and steamed east.

Then *Castine* steamed to Tampa,* Florida, where she formed part of the naval force providing escort for General Shafter's* army from Tampa to Santiago de Cuba.* She next participated in naval bombardments, specifically at Daiquirí* in conjunction with the *Detroit** on the western flank and *Wasp* and *New Orleans** on the eastern flank.

After the war *Castine* was posted to the Asiatic Station. During 1908 to 1913, Lieutenant Chester W. Nimitz commanded *Castine* while she served as a submarine tender. She was sold in 1921.

REFERENCES: John D. Alden, *The American Steel Navy* (Annapolis, MD: Naval Institute Press, 1972); H. W. Wilson, *The Downfall of Spain* (New York: Burt Franklin, 1971).

CASUALTIES

One of the great tragedies of the Spanish American War, and one that spawned much ugly press as well as U.S. government investigation, was that for every combat casualty there were almost ten casualties caused by disease.* From combat, 345 American officers and men died; from disease, 2,565. The U.S. Army suffered the majority of these: 280 killed; 1,577 wounded. The greatest loss of life occurred in Cuba among Fifth Corps.* However, almost as many men died at Chickamauga (Camp Thomas*) as died with the expeditionary forces. The U.S. Navy suffered only sixteen killed and sixty-eight wounded; a total of eighty-four.

The Spanish forces fared much worse, but their losses are much more difficult to identify accurately. Officers and men who died in the Spanish navy numbered about 560, with an additional 300–400 wounded. Numbers reported after the action by the Spanish were considerably higher and have been revised downward.

Spanish losses in the land battles remain difficult to assess. In the battles of El Caney* and San Juan Heights,* the Spanish suffered 215 killed and 376 wounded—far fewer than the losses of the attacking Americans. In addition, the Spanish suffered a constant drain from insurgent activity both in Cuba and in the Philippines, although no accurate count has been made of these.

REFERENCE: French Ensor Chadwick, *The Relations of the United States and Spain* (New York: Russell & Russell, 1911); Jack Cameron Dierks, *A Leap to Arms: The Cuban Campaign of 1898* (Philadelphia: J. B. Lippincott Co., 1970); José Müller y Tejeiro, *Battles and Capitulation of Santiago de Cuba* (Washington, DC: Government Printing Office, 1899).

CAVITE, PHILIPPINES

Located 10 miles southwest of Manila,* Cavite is a small inlet and old walled town. The Spanish fortified Cavite, and these fortifications figured in Admiral Patricio Montojo's* plans for the defense of the Philippines in case of war, for Cavite was also the Spanish naval arsenal. Like Admiral Pascual Cervera,* Montojo lacked the mines and guns to make a really effective defense. He fought Commodore George Dewey* in sight of Cavite in the Battle of Manila Bay* on 1 May 1898. Cavite struck its flag shortly after noon.

After the war Montojo was criticized for giving battle at Cavite; but given the fortifications there and the absence of effective fortifications elsewhere, effective options were lacking.

On 30 June the first group of U.S. troops arrived at Cavite under the command of Brigadier General Thomas M. Anderson.* Cavite had also been an insurrection stronghold when Emilio Aguinaldo* returned from Hong Kong in May 1898.

REFERENCE: William Reynolds Braisted, *The United States Navy in the Pacific, 1897–1909* (Austin: University of Texas Press, 1958).

CAYEY, PUERTO RICO

Cayey lies 25 miles south of San Juan in east-central Puerto Rico. Major General John R. Brooke* commanded the right flank of General Nelson Miles's* offensive in Puerto Rico.* On 8 August 1898, Brooke received his orders to take Cayey. The purpose of the assault was to flank Aibonito.* On the afternoon of 12 August, Brooke made preparations to attack Cayey in consort with General James Wilson's* attack. The next day, Brooke's attack commenced with the maneuvering of artillery batteries but was stopped by the arrival of a telegram indicating a suspension of hostilities. Brooke then retired to Guayama.*

REFERENCE: Ángel Rivero Méndez, *Crónica de la Guerra Hispano Americana en Puerto Rico* (New York: Plus Ultra, 1973).

CERVERA Y TOPETE, PASCUAL
(1839–1909)

Among the tragic figures of the Spanish American War, Pascual Cervera y Topete was perhaps the most notable. An experienced Spanish naval commander, he had participated in operations in Africa, the Philippines, and Cuba and engaged in the Carlist fracas. He commanded the *Pelayo** in 1885, and when Práxides Mateo Sagasta's* government came to power, Cervera was made minister of the marine in 1892. On 30 October 1897, Cervera, now a rear admiral, succeeded Segismundo Bermejo* as commander of the Spanish squadron at Cádiz. Cervera saw on the horizon the impending conflict with the United States, and it filled him with misgivings. The Spanish navy was not in a state of repair, nor was it trained to acquit itself well against the U.S. navy. Cervera requested instructions from Bermejo, then minister of the marine, in January and February 1898 in the case of war. Cervera pointed out that the U.S. forces were significantly stronger than the Spanish naval forces. Nevertheless, Bermejo's plan incredibly expected Cervera to destroy Key West* and to blockade* the U.S. Atlantic coast. The voice of patience and reason throughout, Cervera reiterated that with the forces available to them, a defensive posture was the most anyone could expect. Cervera surveyed his squadron to find two of the ships, *Pelayo** and *Carlos V,** unavailable. The vessels at Havana* that Bermejo felt would augment the Cádiz squadron in the Caribbean were assessed by Cervera as of negligible war value, being old, underpowered, and unarmored. He communicated all this before the *Maine** explosion. Nevertheless, Bermejo responded with enthusiasm and encouragement, for he expected other European powers to support Spain. Cervera, the realist, pointed out that even if the weight of arms did not favor the U.S. Navy, the strategic situation remained an overwhelming obstacle. Spain had no effective ship-repair facilities in the New World, and damage to the Spanish ships would force them out of the theater of conflict. The U.S. Navy, on the other hand, possessed repair facilities in numerous ports, and even if the Americans lost the first engagement, Cervera saw that Spain could not win ultimately. He saw plainly that the Spanish navy could neither blockade U.S. forces nor defeat them in open conflict. He further saw that the persistence with which Spain clung to its colonial territories stemmed from a self-defeating romanticism. He worked for peace from a rational assessment of Spain's weakness—not from defeatism. Thus Cervera, having assessed the tactical and strategic powers of the Spanish navy and found them wanting, had been called upon to wring victory from his own certainty of defeat. On 7 April 1898 Bermejo issued orders for Cervera's squadron to sail from Cádiz to the Portuguese Cape Verde Islands.* Cervera obeyed. When Spain declared war on 23 April, Cervera was supposed to sail from that neutral port within twenty-four hours; however, he did not head for the Caribbean until 29 April.

Peace had been a forlorn hope for some time, and Cervera had concentrated his arguments on preserving the Canaries* and the Spanish mainland from harassing raids by a U.S. Flying Squadron.* He regarded Cuba as already lost and fretted about the vulnerability of the Philippines, as well as about the absolute absence of any threat to the Pacific coast of the United States. Cervera was not alone in his assessments, but his was the loudest voice.

Bermejo ordered Cervera to Puerto Rico* because of the expectation that San Juan* would be the first objective of the Americans. Cervera's base of operations became the Canaries, which were too far away to be of practical use. The Spanish fleet was now divided: Cervera cruised toward the Caribbean with a squadron too weak to challenge effectively the U.S. squadron, and the force left in Spain was also too weak for offensive action. Faced with the inevitability of the loss of Cuba, Spain also decided to lose its ships. Cervera plainly foresaw all this and became one of the major players in the fiasco.

When the U.S. Navy became aware of Cervera's sailing, there began a great sea chase. *Harvard,** *St. Louis,** and *Yale,** fast auxiliary cruisers, steamed to sniff out prey for Admiral William Sampson's*s* warships. On 12 May, Captain

Fernando Villaamil* with the torpedo boats *Terror*‌ and *Furor*‌ reported to Cervera that the Americans were at San Juan, there was no coal for Cervera's depleted ships at Martinique, and Havana was under blockade.* Cervera steamed to Curaçao, a neutral Dutch port where he could obtain only 600 tons of coal. In the absence of any other alternatives, Cervera then sailed for Santiago de Cuba,* which was not under blockade. He arrived on 19 May. Coincidentally, a message from Bermejo arrived the same day that allowed Cervera to return to Spain. Apparently, the loss of the Spanish at Manila* on 1 May and Sampson's aggressive pursuit convinced Bermejo that Cervera had been right all along. However, it was too late. Without colliers, and there were none, there was no coal to make the voyage. Meanwhile, a new minister of the marine had been installed: Ramón Auñón y Villalón.* Faced with pressure from the governors-general of Puerto Rico and Cuba, who felt that if Cervera's squadron sailed, the fighting will of the Spanish troops would go with it, the new minister sent word on 19 May to rescind the option to return to Spain.

It took the Americans ten days to discover that Cervera was in Santiago harbor. Postwar recriminations, such as the Sampson-Schley Controversy,* centered around some of the blunders committed while trying to locate the Spanish squadron and the failures of initiative once it was located at Santiago.

Once apprised of the dozen vessels off Cienfuegos,* Cervera discussed with his captains the possibilities of sailing to San Juan. The discussions surfaced over several days, but always the consensus was to stay at Santiago. Cervera had options, but with his viewing his predicament as hopeless, these options never gained momentum. At any event, when Schley arrived off Santiago on 29 May, the options mostly disappeared. On 8 June Cervera discussed with his captains a night breakout led by destroyers, but again his captains opposed the plan. Events had overtaken Cervera and his squadron.

On 22 June the U.S. expeditionary force landed at Daiquirí.* Auñón ordered Cervera under Governor-General Ramón Blanco y Erenas's* command on 25 June. Cervera lost no time in reiterating to Blanco the list of the fleet's deficiencies: He possessed only one-third of the ammunition he needed; the *Vizcaya*‌ was so foul she could not make any speed; there was insufficient coal for virtually any conceivable operation; there were no mines to sow in the channel; the blockading fleet was ''four times superior'' to his own, thus inviting certain destruction if Cervera sortied. After the land battles of 1 July at El Caney* and San Juan Hill,* matters became even worse. The capture of Cuabitas meant the loss of Santiago's water supply. Cuban insurgents* and U.S. troops so controlled the countryside that there were no provisions. Fewer than 200 rounds per Spanish soldier were available. If large-caliber guns were brought forward, they could shell Cervera's ships in the harbor with impunity. Although many if not most of Cervera's officers felt the squadron's sortie against Sampson would end in disaster, options such as surrender or scuttling would deface national honor. One of Cervera's concerns, which he expressed forcibly to Blanco, was that national honor, which Cervera characterized as vanity, seemed more important than national defense or the lives of his men. Regardless of Cervera's arguments, Blanco ordered the sortie with the idea of escaping to either Cienfuegos or Havana. This direct order was given on 28 June; Blanco received support for his order from Auñón, who cabled that he wanted the squadron to sortie. Both recommended that the sortie take place at night during inclement weather. Since the narrow channel permitted only one vessel to exit at a time, and also since the Americans kept the channel brilliantly lit at night with searchlights, Cervera instead chose to sortie at 9 A.M. on 3 July. He gave orders to that effect on the previous evening with instructions to steam for either Havana or Cienfuegos.

In the action, all ships chose to run for Cienfuegos; none succeeded. Cervera's entire squadron was sunk or run ashore.

From Playa del Este, Cervera cabled Blanco on 4 July with the sad news that the entire squadron was destroyed and commented on the recognition by the Americans of the gallantry of his crews. As a captive aboard the U.S.S. *St. Louis,* Cervera sent a longer report to Blanco. Cervera lived comfortably at Annapolis until he was repatriated in September 1898.

Cervera was brought before a military tribunal and was absolved of any culpability. Regardless of his absolution, Cervera became bitter and retired from public life.

REFERENCES: Pascual Cervera y Topete, *The Spanish American War* (Washington, DC: Government Printing Office, 1899); Víctor M. Concas y Palau, *The Squadron of Admiral Cervera* (Washington, DC: Government Printing Office, 1900).

CHADWICK, FRENCH ENSOR
(1844–1919)

French Ensor Chadwick, noted American naval officer and author, was born in Morgan, Virginia (now West Virginia). His prime motivation for attending Annapolis came from reading James Fenimore Cooper's *History of the Navy of the United States of America* (1839). Chadwick's first naval assignment was to the U.S.S. *Constitution* in 1861. After the Civil War, Chadwick served mostly in a series of sea assignments and was regularly promoted. He had opportunity to study European naval systems in 1879, and in 1880 he published a report on British and French naval training that was very well received. Encouraged, Chadwick continued to exercise his mind and to write. He spoke French and Spanish and was a skilled draftsman; because of these skills, he was appointed naval attaché to Great Britain* as part of the Office of Naval Intelligence.* Chadwick continued to observe and to write. He wrote on shipbuilding and made studies on armaments and warship design—valuable studies that increased his visibility within the small community of U.S. naval officers.

Shortly before the Spanish American War, Chadwick was posted to Washington, DC, as chief of the Bureau of Equipment. As such, Chadwick became a valued confidant to Theodore Roosevelt.* Indeed, Chadwick visited Spain in late 1897 for a month of intelligence-gathering; he duly reported all intelligence to Roosevelt.

On 15 February 1898, the U.S.S. *Maine** exploded in Havana.* Chadwick was appointed by Admiral Montgomery Sicard* to the U.S. Naval Board of Inquiry. Chadwick performed the duties of the board professionally and impartially. Privately, however, he longed to be at war with Spain, and in missives to Roosevelt, he outlined scenarios for forthcoming engagements.

When Sicard was replaced by William T. Sampson* as commander of the North Atlantic Squadron,* Sampson, who had presided at the *Maine* inquiry, chose Chadwick as his chief of staff. As such, Chadwick knew the inside workings of the fleet, the developing Sampson-Schley Controversy* (in which he took Sampson's part), and the Battle of Santiago.*

After the war, Chadwick continued his scholarly interests and writing. He was president of the Naval War College* in 1900, commander in chief of the South Atlantic Squadron in 1903, and later promoted to rear admiral. He retired from the navy in 1906 and died early in 1919 of pneumonia after suffering a paralyzing stroke.

REFERENCE: Paolo E. Coletta, *French Ensor Chadwick, Scholarly Warrior* (Lanham, MD: University Press of America, 1980).

CHAFFEE, ADNA ROMANZA
(1842–1914)

Adna Romanza Chaffee served in the Civil War and achieved distinction in combat. He was promoted from first sergeant to second lieutenant. After the war, he served in the Southwest, fighting Indians in numerous battles. In May 1898 he was promoted to brigadier general of volunteers and served under General Henry Lawton.* Chaffee commanded the Third Brigade, Second Division of Fifth Corps.* An active participant in the land battles in Cuba, Chaffee provided on-the-ground reconnaissance work from El Pozo and its environs prior to the battle of El Caney.* He commanded his brigade at El Caney—the leading brigade in that engagement. Chaffee maneuvered his brigade through the night of 30 June and 1 July 1898 so that dawn of 1 July found Chaffee uniquely positioned. Fittingly, it was Chaffee's command that began the fighting at El Caney. Chaffee's brigade took enfilading fire from Spanish snipers on their left as they advance. Spanish fire from their defensive positions slowed the advance instantly into a deadly stalement. Finally, about 3 P.M., the artillery battery got the range of the fort, El Viso, and began to have effect. Chaffee got the Twelfth Infantry up and charged, dislodging the Spanish from their defenses. The battle continued for two more hours as the village of El Caney was secured.

The next day Lawton commanded Chaffee's brigade to march to San Juan Hill* and take a position to the right of General Wheeler's* division. Chaffee was promoted to major general of volunteers after these battles.

After the war, Chaffee returned to Cuba in late 1898 as chief of staff under General Leonard Wood.* He also commanded in the relief expedition during the Boxer Rebellion in China in 1900. Later, in 1902, he served in the Philippines as governor and military commander.

REFERENCES: Herbert H. Sargent, *The Campaign of Santiago de Cuba,* 3 vols. (Chicago: A. C. McClurg, 1914); Thomas J. Vivian, *The Fall of Santiago* (New York: R. F. Fenno, 1898).

CHARLESTON (ship)

The U.S.S. *Charleston,* a protected cruiser, was 312 feet in length and displaced 4,040 tons. She was capable of over 18 knots. Originally armed with ten 6-inch guns (plus smaller calibers), she entered the Spanish American War with two 8-inch and six 6-inch guns. *Charleston* was commissioned 26 December 1889.

After George Dewey's* squadron defeated the Spanish at Manila Bay,* one of the first requests Dewey made of his superiors was for more ammunition* and troops to secure the forts in the Philippines.* Dewey feared that the rumors of an advancing Spanish fleet the Spanish Eastern Squadron* or even Admiral Pascual Cervera's* fleet might be grounded in some reality. On 18 May 1898 *Charleston* steamed from San Francisco* with ammunition for Dewey. She was joined at Honolulu on 28 May by the transports *City of Peking,* Australia,* and *City of Sydney,* which carried 2,500 soldiers. En route, this small expedition seized Guam* in the Ladrones. The convoy reached its destination, after meeting *Baltimore*,* on 30 June. Although all the transports were top-of-the-line passenger liners, the convoy was slowed by Secretary of the Navy John D. Long's* orders to take Guam and by the slowness of *Charleston,* which could not keep pace with the liners. *Charleston* wrecked on a reef in the Philippines in 1899.

REFERENCES: John D. Alden, *The American Steel Navy* (Annapolis, MD: Naval Institute Press, 1972); David F. Trask, *The War with Spain in 1898* (New York: Macmillan Publishing Co., 1981).

CHARLESTON, SOUTH CAROLINA

Charleston, South Carolina, played a minor role in the Spanish American War, although to the Charlestonians, it may not have seemed so at the time. The expeditionary force to Puerto Rico* marshalled in part at Charleston. Several thousand men accumulated there for loading on transports for this combat zone. Major General James H. Wilson* sailed from Charleston on 20 July 1898 with about 3,000 troops bound for Fajardo.*

Earlier Charleston had figured in unrealized Spanish plans for harassing the eastern seaboard. Ramón Auñón y Villalón* proposed in May 1898 that Admiral Manuel de la Cámara* divide the Spanish home fleet into three and that one attack Charleston. The South Carolina city was a railhead and port. Through espionage efforts, a version of this plan fell into the hands of Lieutenant Williams S. Sims,* who forwarded it to the Navy Department.

REFERENCE: David F. Trask, *The War with Spain in 1898* (New York: Macmillan Publishing Co., 1981).

CHICHESTER, EDWARD
(1849–1906)

Commodore George Dewey,* commander of the U.S. Asiatic Squadron,* found himself in a stressful situation after defeating the Spanish fleet in Manila Bay.* While waiting for resupply and reinforcements in order to begin a land assault and anxiously watching for signs of Admiral Manuel de la Cámara's* fleet from Spain, Dewey also had to contend with the German Asiatic Squadron,* the Japanese, the French, the Austro-Hungarians, and the British.

Under the command of Captain Edward Chichester, the contingent from Great Britain* at Manila consisted of the gunboat *Linnet,* the armored cruiser *Immortalité,* and three other gunboats. During most of the month of May and some of June 1989, Britain was the strongest neutral force at Manila, not surprising due to that country's heavy investment in the Philippines. Dewey welcomed the British presence, for the British were rivals of the Germans and were amicably disposed to the Americans both in Hong Kong* before the outbreak of hostilities and subsequently. While outwardly maintaining a strict neutrality, Chichester made it known that his sympathies and his nation's sympathies resided with the Americans. Chichester maintained extremely cordial relations with Dewey, and rumors circulated among the neutrals that if the friction evident between Dewey and the Germans grew hotter, Great Britain would side with Dewey against the Germans. The German commander also complained to his superiors that Chichester actively promulgated anti-German rumors that found their way into numerous Asiatic newspapers and became grist for American newspapers as well.

On 13 August 1898, Dewey's fleet began a bombardment of Manila. The British *Immortalité* and *Iphigenia* moved to a position behind Dewey's fleet and between the Americans and the Germans. Later interpretation of this event dramatized it as a bold move by Chichester to strengthen the U.S. fleet against the Germans, who were supposedly ready to attack. Thomas A. Bailey has shown conclusively that this interpretation has no evidential support: Neither the American nor the German logs mentioned Chichester's movements. The British did not clear for action and, in fact, anchored upon taking up station. Clearly, the British commander was merely looking for a better view of the bombardment. Nevertheless, this erroneous interpretation continues to find adherents. There can be no doubt, however, that Chichester did favor the American interests. After the fall of Manila, Chichester maneuvered his ships to an earlier anchorage and the *Immortalité* fired a twenty-one-gun salute to the American flag then flying over Manila—the only ship to do so.

REFERENCE: Thomas A. Bailey, "Dewey and the Germans at Manila Bay," *The American Historical Review* 45 (October 1939): 59–81.

CHINA

Except for Commodore George Dewey's* use of Mirs Bay* as an assembly area for his Asiatic Squadron,* China's direct role in the hostilities of the Spanish American War was minimal. Indirectly, however, the role of China in the events of the war loomed large on the Asiatic horizon. On the eve of hostilities in 1898, the United States had important commercial interests in China enduring for over a century. While most American citizens developed impressions of China from the nation's reactions to Chinese immigration and subsequent stereotyping, keener minds saw through the fog of prejudice and perceived opportunity, potential wealth, and an unused playing field upon which to practice American ideals of democracy, economic initiative, and humanism. Alfred Thayer Mahan,* Theodore Roosevelt,* Henry Cabot Lodge,* Brooks Adams,* and others, while disagreeing in particulars, agreed that China was a ripe opportunity as a demonstration area for moral as well as material advancement. The commercial opportunities of trade, industrial development, and markets were obvious, but also important were nascent notions of the U.S. role in the world. China could become another missionary effort aimed now at the gospels of American nationalism, American potential for world leadership, and future American economic abundance. Among many U.S. national and political leaders, China became the focus for an emerging national policy in the Pacific. The acquisitions of Hawaii,* the Philippines,* and Samoa,* among other Pacific annexations, ex post facto became the stepping stones to China. Thus, as David L. Anderson observed, the Philippines became the American Hong Kong—an Asian outpost from which the United States could pursue its commercial and moral interests in Asia. Even the eventual completion of the Panama Canal strategically reinforced this national interest in the Orient by providing both commerce and navy with easy access to the Pacific.

In promulgating these desires, the United States pursued a longstanding policy of the ''open door,'' that is, of equal access by all to the markets of Asia. In this policy, the United States was actively supported by Great Britain.* Lord Salisbury,* in particular, was instrumental in allying U.S. and British interests in China and the Philippines. The ''open door'' was Britain's policy as well, and it is doubtful that the United States could have retained the Philippines in the face of European opposition without the aid and support of Great Britain.

Tactically, however, the capture of Manila* was initially perceived by American planners as a distraction to the Spanish (a way of dividing forces) and as a subsequent bargaining chip in peace negotiations.* Strategic thinkers like Roosevelt and Mahan perceived the utility of the Philippines for its commercial possibilities in China and also as a curb or sentry for Japan's expansive designs in Asia. The latter carries Roosevelt's foreboding into the twentieth century.

Thus China's principal role during the war was as a target for U.S. designs and policies in the Orient. China became a focal point of the debate about whether to retain the Philippines and an idealized objective in the rapidly evolving foreign policies during and after the war.

REFERENCES: David L. Anderson, *Imperialism and Idealism* (Bloomington: Indiana University Press, 1985); Philip Joseph, *Foreign Diplomacy in China, 1894–1900* (New York: Octagon Books, 1971); Robert McClellan, *The Heathen Chinese* (NP: Ohio State University Press, 1971).

CHRISTY, HOWARD CHANDLER
(1873–1952)

Photography being slow and cumbersome, publishers relied heavily on artists to illustrate the drama and action of the Spanish American War. Frederic Remington,* Rufus F. Zogbaum,* and others joined Howard Chandler Christy as artists attempting to describe the action and also to sell, thereby, newspapers or journals. Christy was present at El Pozo in the land battle before Santiago de Cuba.* He was an eyewitness to the attacks of 1 July 1898.

Christy used his effort to advantage. After the war, Christy became one of the most celebrated arbiters of style among fashionable young women. His "Christy girls" became household words.

REFERENCE: Howard Chandler Christy, "An Artist at El Pozo," *Scribner's Magazine* 24 (1898): 283–284.

CHURCHILL, WINSTON SPENCER
(1874–1965)

In 1895, Lieutenant Winston Spencer Churchill had only recently received his commission. The British military had not seen much action in recent years, and Churchill was eager to witness combat first-hand; he arranged to visit Cuba in November and December as a guest of the Spanish. While being escorted on a Spanish march through the interior, Churchill witnessed skirmishes between General Suárez Váldez and insurgent forces east of Sancti Spíritus. His description and military analysis of the engagement were related in a dispatch published in the New York *World* under the headline "Churchill in Battle," where he commented that the rebels were bad shots and were inclined to avoid direct confrontations with the Spanish. Churchill showed an awareness of the tactics of guerrilla warfare and a realization that the Spanish might be bogged down for a lengthy period. "Europeans' methods of warfare are almost out of the question in a wild country where an enemy operates cavalry, as infantry is useless except for marching."

REFERENCES: Charles H. Brown, *The Correspondents' War* (New York: Scribner's, 1967); Winston Churchill, *My Early Life: A Roving Commission* (New York: Scribner's, 1930).

MARK A. THOMAS

CIENFUEGOS, CUBA

Located on a fine, sheltered bay (Cienfuegos or sometimes Jagua Bay), Cienfuegos lies about 140 miles east-southeast of Havana.

Cienfuegos first entered the lexicon of the Spanish American War as part of prewar planning. Assistant Secretary of the Navy Theodore Roosevelt* made war preparations planning before 1897. The Naval War College* in Newport, Rhode Island, used a hypothetical war with Spain as a training problem in 1894, and subsequently both the Naval War College and Roosevelt assumed a naval blockade* of the most important ports of Cuba, Cienfuegos among them. Some of the plans emphasized the early seizure of Cienfuegos. The reasons for the early identification of the strategic importance of Cienfuegos included its port and facilities as well as good rail connections between Havana* and Cienfuegos. Clearly, a blockade only of the northern coast would be ineffectual. Cienfuegos would have to be included. Such was the case when the actual blockade began. While the northern blockade continued, attention was also given to the southern ports of Cienfuegos, Manzanillo,* and Santiago.* Lack of coaling facilities and a dearth of colliers kept the southern blockade somewhat tentative; Cienfuegos, however, had a relatively effective blockade by Admiral William T. Sampson's* vessels commencing 27 April 1898.

On 29 April the protected cruiser *Marblehead** and the auxiliary *Eagle** exchanged fire with the Spanish *Satélite, Lince,* and *Gaviota,* small launches or gunboats. This action lasted some thirty minutes until the Spanish vessels retired.

On 2 May the elderly Spanish gunboat *Alcedo* and the launches *Almendores* and *Gaviota* escorted eight other ships and transports out of Cienfuegos, delivering over 3,000 men and 800 horses and mules to Casilda.

On 11 May boats from *Marblehead* and the gunboat *Nashville** attempted to cut the three cables linking Cienfuegos to Madrid. They succeeded in cutting two of the three cables only. This action resulted in the first American combat fatalities.

On 19 May Commodore Winfield S. Schley* left Key West,* Florida, for Cienfuegos inasmuch as it was thought that Cervera's* squadron was heading for Cienfuegos. When rumors and later reports surfaced that Cervera was actually at Santiago, Sampson sent orders to Schley's Flying Squadron* on 23 May that he vacate Cienfuegos for Santiago. Instead, Schley dallied at Cienfuegos until the evening of 24 May. Thus began the famous Sampson-Schley Controversy.*

On 1 June Cienfuegos was used as a ruse to confuse the Spanish about the possible landing site of the U.S. Army. Naval attaché Lieutenant William S. Sims* intentionally leaked a false report that elements of the American army and navy were in disagreement over whether to land at Cienfuegos, the supposed position of the army, or at Matanzas,* ostensibly the site favored by the navy.

Also on 1 June, two groups of Spanish blockade runners successfully negotiated the blockade. *Diego Velásquez* escorted a convoy into the harbor, and the 5,611-ton transport *María Cristina* also successfully entered the port of Cienfuegos.

The last naval action near Cienfuegos occurred on 13 June between the auxiliary cruiser *Yankee** (6,888 tons) and the Spanish *Diego Velásquez* (200 tons).

Further military considerations included those of land forces. Spain had divided Cuba into five corps, one of which headquartered in Cienfuegos. It will also be remembered that Cienfuegos remained a supply source for Havana. For these reasons Cuban general Máximo Gómez* urged that General William Shafter's troops be sent to Cienfuegos. Such a plan, however, was not to Shafter's nor Washington's liking and was never implemented.

REFERENCE: David F. Trask, *The War with Spain in 1898* (New York: Macmillan Publishing Co., 1981).

CINCINNATI (ship)

The U.S.S. *Cincinnati* was one of two ships of her class, *Raleigh** being the other, authorized on 7 September 1888 and commissioned in 1894. These ships were 3,213-ton, 300-foot-long, twin-screw, protected deck cruisers. Each was armed with four torpedo tubes, a 6-inch gun, ten 5-inch guns, and fourteen other guns of smaller caliber. Both *Cincinnati* and *Raleigh* were sold out of the U.S. Navy on 5 August 1921.

The design of these sister-ships emphasized speed over everything else, and the large engines and crowded boilers combined with poor ventilation meant that temperatures of 200 degrees or more were not unusual below decks. As a result, the class was far from popular with officers or crew. Both *Cincinnati* and *Raleigh* were re-engined after the Spanish American War.

Initially, *Cincinnati* was assigned to Admiral William T. Sampson's* blockade fleet for duty in Cuban waters. On 27 April 1898 *Cincinnati* participated in the bombardment of Matanzas.* In early May, Sampson decided to divide his fleet in the hope of successfully finding the Spanish fleet. *Cincinnati* was detailed to a squadron off Havana* under the overall command of Commodore John C. Watson.* In the search for Admiral Cervera's* fleet, numerous false reports, rumors, and strategies developed: *Cincinnati* and *Vesuvius** were sent to Cape San Antonio to watch for the Spanish fleet. This scouting mission lasted for several weeks as the two ships patrolled the Yucatan Passage.

Cincinnati also convoyed the expeditionary force to Puerto Rico* during late July. On 2 August, while supporting General Nelson Miles,* *Cincinnati* and *St. Louis** shelled the hills and beaches between Arroyo* and Guayama.*

REFERENCE: John D. Alden, *The American Steel Navy* (Annapolis, MD: Naval Institute Press, 1972).

CISNEROS, EVANGELINA

In the months immediately before the Spanish American War, there were a series of events that escalated tensions between Spain and the United States. Some of these were real, some imagined, but in most cases the cumulative effect of these events was more powerful than any single incident by itself. Nevertheless, some of these incidents achieved celebrity status on their own. One such concerned the daughter of a suspected insurgent* collaborator in Cuba, Evangelina Cisneros. Her father was serving a term of detainment on the Isle of Pines,* and Evangelina chose to accompany him. The story would have ended there, but it was 1897 and William R. Hearst's* reporters smelled a story too good to leave alone. When Cisneros resisted the advances of a Spanish officer, she was herself arrested. This story then became the cause célèbre of Hearst's *Journal,* and the yellow press (*see* The Press and The War*) had a field day. The *Journal* began a petition campaign enlisting thousands of prominent American and British women. Sensational charges became front-page headlines, and to heighten the drama, Hearst sent reporter Karl Decker* to rescue the girl, a feat that proved simplicity itself. Decker simply broke a window and lifted her out. She was smuggled to the United States, where immense public receptions for her were held in Madison Square Garden and Washington, DC. Decker became a hero while the Spanish minister, Enrique Dupuy de Lôme,* fumed, unable to control the propagandist damage.

Although the incident itself seems minor enough, in a time when Americans were being bombarded daily with atrocious stories about the harsh regime of General Valeriano Weyler,* the plight of the *reconcentrados,*️ and Spanish duplicity, the story of the girl martyr Evangelina Cisneros had the effect of spraying gasoline on a flame.

REFERENCE: Walter Millis, *The Martial Spirit* (Boston: Houghton Mifflin, 1931).

CITY OF PEKING (ship)

In 1872, the U.S. government doubled the mail subsidy for mail service across the Pacific Ocean. The Pacific Mail Steamship Company was required by the terms of its contract to build iron-screw steamers. As a result, the *City of Peking* was launched in 1874 and made her maiden voyage in 1875. At 5,080 tons, she was the largest American ship upon her launch.

The U.S. Army* needed transports in the Caribbean and the Pacific. Upon Commodore George Dewey's* success at the battle of Manila Bay,* that need became acute. The army quickly chartered several liners: *City of Peking, City of Rio de Janeiro, China,* and *Peru. City of Peking* sailed with U.S.S. *Charleston*️ and others ferrying supplies and 2,500 troops to continue the war effort in the Philippines.* *City of Peking* was chartered by the War Department* from May 1898 through January 1900 and then scrapped in 1910.

REFERENCE: Frederick E. Emmons, *American Passenger Ships* (Newark: University of Delaware Press, 1985).

CITY OF WASHINGTON (ship)

City of Washington was built for the Alexandre Line for the New York–Havana* run. Launched in 1877 and displacing 2,683 tons, she was purchased by the Ward Line in 1888.

City of Washington was moored close to U.S.S. *Maine*️ on 24 February 1898, the night of the explosion. Wounded sailors were sheltered aboard the liner, and Captain Charles D. Sigsbee,* of the *Maine,* quartered on *City of Washington* after the blast.

Chartered as an Army transport from April to September 1898, *City of Washington* went out of service in 1908, was converted to a coal barge in 1911, and ultimately wrecked in Florida in 1917.

REFERENCE: Frederick E. Emmons, *American Passenger Ships* (Newark: University of Delaware Press, 1985).

CLEVELAND, GROVER
(1837–1908)

Democrat Grover Cleveland tried to moderate the growing tensions surrounding Cuba during his second term as president. Elected in 1892, he adopted a policy of deliberate inaction in the face of a groundswell of U.S. sympathy toward Cuba. It was a difficult policy to pursue: Valeriano Weyler's* reconcentration policy* aroused significant anti-Spanish feelings in the United States, and numerous pro-Cuban or pro-insurrectionist rallies and fairs sharpened the cleavage. Filibustering* by United States citizens challenged the president's policies. In the face of these challenges, Cleveland and his secretary of state, Richard Olney,* attempted to mediate between Spain* and the Cuban insurgents.* On 12 June 1895, Cleveland issued a proclamation of neutrality and studiously avoided showing sympathy for the insurgents.

Meanwhile, in Congress* leaders of both parties crossed party lines in an attempt to embarrass the administration out of its policy of strict neutrality. Every congressional session from 1895 until the beginning of hostilities witnessed pro-Cuban resolutions in both houses. In an attempt to turn up the volume of sympathy for the Cuban cause, the Cuban junta* sent Gonzalo de Quesada to Washington, DC, to lobby for U.S. recognition of Cuban belligerency.*

The administration could not ignore the pressure indefinitely. On 7 April 1896 Olney revealed that the administration would not surrender to public pressure, but would, instead, present a pacification plan. After conversations with Spanish ambassador Enrique Dupuy de Lôme,* the administration presented a plan to mediate between Spain and the Cuban rebels: It provided for continued Spanish sovereignty over Cuba, but the Cubans would gain a degree of self-government. The administration hoped the plan would defuse the rising explosive public opinion against Spain. Significantly, however, Spain had its own public opinion problems. Congress's belligerency resolution had included much debate critical of Spain, which had been reported in the Spanish press. In the face of violent anti-American demonstrations in Spain, Spanish foreign minister Carlos O'Donnell y Abreu* and his superior, Prime Minister Antonio Cánovas del Castillo,* saw the communiqué for what it was: an attempt by the Cleveland administration to mollify American opinion. They temporized for two months before replying with a strong defense of the status quo and a rejection of proposed reforms.

Alarmed at the rebuff, Cleveland worried that Spain's obstinacy would soon precipitate a war. The election debates of 1896 centered on domestic issues, however.

During his last months in office, Cleveland seemed to alter his views somewhat by recognizing that because of investment and proximity the United States had a stake in the stability of Cuba and that the optimal solution might be some form of Cuban autonomy. The most important of such comments occurred on 7 December 1896 when Cleveland stated that the United States might have to take action if Spain failed to resolve the issue. The U.S. envoy to Madrid, Hannis

Taylor,* proposed Cuban autonomy to Cánovas without any response from Spain.

Thus, at the end of his term, Cleveland had moved from strict neutrality to mention the threat of intervention.

REFERENCES: John F. Marzalek, *Grover Cleveland: A Bibliography* (Westport, CT: Meckler, 1988); Richard E. Welch, *The Presidencies of Grover Cleveland* (Lawrence: University Press of Kansas, 1988).

COAL AND COALING

Coal was one of the currencies of the Industrial Revolution that still captured the vital interests of the naval establishments in 1898. Virtually all the ships on both sides burned coal in the Spanish American War. Providing coal for a world-wide fleet or even a one-ocean fleet required a significant array of bases* and a large auxiliary naval force* of colliers and other merchant ships to maintain steam in the naval boilers. Coal varies in quality, moreover, and some burns better and cleaner than other types. This is not an insignificant matter inasmuch as bunkers full of hard Chesapeake anthracite provided greater range and less smoke than Japanese coal, for example. Both the greater range and the diminished smoke had definite tactical implications, and the act of coaling itself, or refueling, was an essential activity that dominated ship life in the nineteenth century. Not only was it a filthy necessity, but in an open roadstead on blockade* or at sea, it was a time-consuming, dangerous necessity. The transfer of sacks or buckets of coal from the heaving hull of one ship to the gyrating bunkers of another required seamanship, engineering skills, and courage of a high order. The availability of coal and its quality often dictated the tactical flexibility of naval forces. The establishment of coaling bases for their naval forces figured significantly in the strategies employed by both the United States and Spain. The need for fuel was a logistical reality that became solvable only with the conversion to oil-fired boilers in the twentieth century.

REFERENCE: John D. Alden, *The American Steel Navy* (Annapolis, MD: Naval Institute Press, 1972).

COAMO, PUERTO RICO

The town of Coamo in Puerto Rico lies in the south-central portion of the island in the foothills about 17 miles east-northeast of Ponce* on the way to Aibonito.*

Major General James H. Wilson* departed Charleston,* South Carolina, for Puerto Rico on 20 July 1898 with over 3,500 troops. Wilson's command included the First Brigade, First Division, First Corps under Brigadier General Oswald H. Ernst.* During Wilson's advance from Ponce to Aibonito, Wilson ordered Ernst on 9 August to move one regiment behind Coamo to attack Spanish troops in the town and a nearby blockhouse simultaneously. A spirited action ensued, the first serious engagement of the Puerto Rican campaign, and Coamo was carried. The Spanish losses included the Spanish commander Rafael Martínez Illescas, who raised himself in his saddle to encourage his troops and was shot through the heart. Another officer and four Spanish riflemen were killed, with thirty-odd wounded. Six of Wilson's command were wounded in the engagement, which opened the road to Aibonito.

REFERENCES: French Ensor Chadwick, *The Relations of the United Stated and Spain* (New York: Russell & Russell, 1911); Ángel Rivero Méndez, *Crónica de la Guerra Hispano Americana en Puerto Rico* (New York: Plus Ultra, 1973),

COAST DEFENSE, U.S.

Coast defense in the Spanish American War concerned itself not with repelling invasions but with defending major ports from harassing tactics or raids such as those perpetrated by the British in the Chesapeake during the War of 1812. Plans instituted by A. T. Mahan* and others relied not upon stone and brick forts but upon concrete emplacements with modern artillery, mined waterways, and speedy torpedo boats. Coast defense, for example, got a large share of the Fifty Million Bill.* Nevertheless, there was insufficient action on the existing plans. Of the intended 2,000 artillery pieces planned, only 151 were mounted by 1 April 1898. Coastal defense occupied great effort and cost, and although never used in anger, coast defense was to last through the next fifty years.

REFERENCE: Graham A. Cosmas, *An Army for Empire* (Columbia: University of Missouri, 1971).

COLLAZO TEJADA, ENRIQUE
(1848–1921)

Like Máximo Gómez,* Enrique Collazo Tejada fought in the Ten Years' War* as a troop commander. At the commencement of renewed hostilities in 1895, he once again led insurgent forces. In May 1898, he was appointed a brigade commander of the Mayarí brigade; as such he enjoyed the rank of brigadier general. He was also a graduate of the artillery school in Segovia, Spain.

Collazo achieved renown as the guide and companion of lieutenant Andrew S. Rowan* in his effort to carry the ''message to [Calixto] García.''*

REFERENCE: Mario Riera Hernández, *Ejército Libertador de Cuba, 1895–1898* (Miami: NP, 1985).

COLUMBIA (ship)

Two ships by the name *Columbia* were engaged in the American war effort. The first was the protected cruiser U.S.S. *Columbia* of 7,375 tons, armed with one 8-inch gun, two 6-inch guns, eight 4-inch guns, and miscellaneous smaller-caliber weapons. She was considered for Commodore Winfield Scott Schley's* Flying Squadron,* but the cruiser spent most of the war on coastal defense patrol near New York. *Columbia* was a fast cruiser, almost 23 knots, when commissioned in 1894 and was intended for commerce raiding.

The second *Columbia* was a 2,722-ton transport chartered by the War Department.* She engaged in operations with *Yale** and *Harvard,** transporting troops to Cuba.*

REFERENCES: John D. Alden, *The American Steel Navy* (Annapolis, MD: Naval Institute Press, 1972); Frederick E. Emmons, *American Passenger Ships* (Newark: University of Delaware Press, 1985).

COLWELL, JOHN CHARLES
(1856–?)

Lieutenant John Charles Colwell ran the most extensive network of spies and informers during the Spanish American War. A temperamental but brilliant intriguer, Colwell established an elaborate web of agents operating in Madrid, Antwerp, London, Paris, and Egypt. Concerned that he might be upstaged by his rival U.S. agent, William S. Sims,* Colwell also paid agents to inform him of Sims's activities. Colwell spent over $27,000 on spies during the brief war. Colwell and Sims were most successful tracking Admiral Manuel de la Cámara's* Manila-bound squadron, ferreting out Spanish strategic initiatives, and sowing false information to mislead the Spanish.

REFERENCE: Jeffery M. Dorwart, *The Office of Naval Intelligence* (Annapolis, MD: Naval Institute Press, 1979).

COMMAND SYSTEMS

Upon the outbreak of the Spanish American War, the U.S. military had not fought a major war for over thirty years. Over the years there had developed conflicts of authority of which many were aware but none could resolve. In the absence of wartime urgency, perhaps too few were introspective enough to decipher a future source of conflict within the system. At its heart, the conflict was one of authority between the commanding general (a line military officer) and the secretary of war (a political appointee). The politician had the ear of the president and could and did give direct orders to commanders in the field without going through the military chain of command. This situation was possible because the commanding general nominally had command only of troops in the field, whereas the secretary controlled fiscal and supply matters. Each was supposed to act independently of the other. In reality, however, with neither staff nor control over supplies, the commanding general was impotent not only in planning but frequently in execution. Not only was the secretary independent of the commanding general, but each of the bureaus also often failed to act in concert. Although the adjutant general had an advantage in these internecine squabbles, he could challenge and was challenged by the inspector general.

Such confusion was not limited to the U.S. Army. The U.S. Navy's role vis-à-vis troop and supply transport was also confused and left much room for improvisation. Although the navy had trained for landing operations, the actual transports were under the aegis of the army but escorted and protected by the navy. Communication and control was improvised, and, as might be expected, it occasionally broke down. There had been unilateral naval amphibious training before 1898, but nothing resembling a joint operation had been attempted since the Civil War. Under the circumstances, it is a wonder that U.S. forces were effective at all. The entire system relied upon informal cooperation between departments and services.

President McKinley* employed a war council consisting of Secretary of War Russell Alger,* Secretary of the Navy John D. Long,* and bureau chiefs and other staff. Long created the Naval War Board* to systematize planning, and Alger and Long coordinated to forge harmony from army and navy plans. The tactical commanders were given a free hand, however, which explains why General W. R. Shafter* fought El Caney* and San Juan Hill* in the siege of Santiago de Cuba* with minimal supporting artillery fires from the battleships of Admiral William T. Sampson.* These frustrations manifested themselves after the war in serious efforts at reform.

The Spanish used a similar nineteenth-century division of responsibility between navy and army, but with sharper lines drawn. Their army commanders had geographic responsibility under the governor-general. The minister of the marine commanded the navy upon the high seas, and strategically. In the tactical environment of Cuba or the Philippines, with changing environments, there was flexibility. Both Admiral Pascual Cervera* and Admiral Patricio Montojo* utilized councils of war with senior captains and also consulted with the governor-general. Cervera, in fact, was placed under the governor-general's command in part because of communication difficulties.

REFERENCES: Graham A. Cosmas, *An Army for Empire* (Columbia: University of Missouri Press, 1971); Graham A. Cosmas, "Joint Operations in the Spanish American War," in James C. Bradford, ed., *Crucible of Empire* (Annapolis, MD: Naval Institute Press, 1993).

COMPETITOR (ship)

Competitor was a small schooner captured in 1896 by Spain. The schooner was on a filibustering* expedition in Cuba with arms and men. Among those captured were two Americans aboard *Competitor* and two others ashore who were also from the schooner. All were released from Spanish prisons, to the relief of many on both sides, but the *Competitor* incident, like the earlier *Virginius* affair,* was a palpable strain to Spanish American relations.

REFERENCE: John Offuer, *An Unwanted War* (Chapel Hill: University of North Carolina Press, 1992).

CONCAS Y PALAU, VÍCTOR MARÍA (1845–1916)

Captain Víctor María Concas y Palau was one of the lucid Spanish chroniclers of the sea battle at Santiago de Cuba.* Concas examined American and Spanish sources, and since he commanded *Infanta María Teresa,** which was lost in the battle, and also served as Admiral Pascual Cervera's* chief of staff, he was able to combine others' eyewitness accounts with his own. Although defensive at times, Concas's discussions of strategy and Spanish tactics are essential reading. REFERENCE: Víctor M. Concas y Palau, *The Squadron of Admiral Cervera* (Washington, DC: Government Printing Office, 1900).

CONCORD (ship)

The U.S.S. *Concord* was a *Yorktown*-class gunboat, like *Bennington,** commissioned in 1891 and of identical specification. *Concord* was ordered to reinforce Commodore George Dewey* in the Asiatic Squadron.* In April 1898, the gunboat accompanied *Boston** to Subic Bay* on reconnaissance. The ship was also in Dewey's line entering Manila Bay* following *Raleigh** and just ahead of *Boston. Concord* engaged the battery on El Fraile. When the battle resumed, *Boston* exchanged places with *Concord,* and both steamed further into the bay. *Concord* engaged the Spanish steamer *Mindanao* in Bacoor Bay.* The *Mindanao* was burned.

On 7 July *Concord* steamed with *Raleigh* to Subic Bay in support of Emilio Aguinaldo,* who was being inhibited there by the German cruiser *Irene.**

On 13 August, during the land Battle of Manila,* *Concord* held station at the mouth of the Pasig River.*

The ship was sold by the navy in 1929 after serving many years as a quarantine vessel on the Columbia River. REFERENCE: David F. Trask, *The War with Spain in 1898* (New York: Macmillan Publishing Co., 1981).

CONDE DE VENADITO (ship)

The *Conde de Venadito* was an old Spanish gunboat of 1,190 tons. Sistership to *Velasco,** *Don Juan de Austria,** and *Don Antonio de Ulloa,** among others, she was built between 1879 and 1881 at the Thames Iron Works, Blackwall, England. New, she was capable of 14 knots, but by the time of the Spanish American War that speed had diminished to 10 knots or less. The *Venadito* was built of iron and had a three-masted schooner rig augmenting her compound steam engines. Unarmored, and with four 5-inch guns on sponsons, *Venadito* served in the Spanish squadron at Havana.* On 14 May 1898, *Venadito* and *Nueva España* sallied against the blockading U.S. forces, but without serious intent or effect. REFERENCE: Alfredo Aguilera, *Buques de guerra españoles, 1885–1971* (Madrid: Librería Editorial San Martín, 1972).

CONGRESS, U.S.

By definition, it is and has been difficult for such a large body as the U.S. Congress, or either house thereof, to exercise leadership in domestic or foreign affairs. Nevertheless, Congress played an important supportive role in the war initiatives and provided necessary funding and not so necessary rhetoric in the national debate before, during, and after the Spanish American War. A large number of Senate bills were introduced in January 1896 reflecting interest in the cause of Cuban liberty. Ostensibly for national defense, these bills plainly intended to arm and rearm the United States for potential conflict. Resolutions calling for U.S. intervention fluttered about in the Senate and in the House, and inflammatory debate and oratory became the rule. Much, if not all, of this debate had as its aim the embarrassment of President Grover Cleveland,* who strove to walk a tortuous line of neutrality and peace. He was the natural target of the political opposition. On 6 April 1896, Congress overwhelmingly passed the Morgan-Cameron Resolution,* which called for the recognition of a state of war in Cuba regarding which the United States should maintain a strict neutrality. Senators John T. Morgan (D-Alabama) and Donald Cameron (R-Pennsylvania) also stipulated that "the friendly offices of the United States should be offered by the president to the Spanish government for the recognition of the independence of Cuba." The resolution had no force of law; it nevertheless made clear the will of Congress regarding the Cuban crisis. This issue diminished in importance or grew over the next two years depending on the fervor, or lack thereof, of politicians and journalists. Leading the debate, of course, was the Foreign Relations Committee of the Senate. The Spanish also provided fuel for these flames as reports about General Valeriano Weyler's* reconcentration policy* and official pronouncements from Práxides Mateo Sagasta* seemed to confirm the dissolution of order in Cuba.

Under the leadership of Joseph G. Cannon,* early in 1898 Congress passed the Fifty Million Bill,* which initiated the fiscal underpinnings of the impending conflict. In response to the president's 11 April message to Congress, on 13 April the House authorized President McKinley* to intervene in Cuba to establish peace and a stable government. The Senate's report was more belligerent and resolved on 16 April to recognize the Cuban Republic and to authorize the president to use force. To this resolution, Senator Henry M. Teller offered the Teller Amendment,* which eschewed interest in acquiring Cuba for the United States.

On 22 April, Congress authorized the president to increase the size of the U.S. Army through volunteers, and the next day McKinley issued his first call for 125,000 men. Then on 25 April, McKinley asked Congress for a joint resolution declaring a state of war with Spain.

Other interests for which Congress provided deliberative forum included the annexation of the Hawaiian Islands* and, of course, the Treaty of Paris.* After the war, Congress immersed itself in debate on colonial policy, the beef controversy,* and the diseases* and scandal surrounding the camps* run by the War Department.

REFERENCE: Walter Millis, *The Martial Spirit* (Boston: Houghton Mifflin, 1931).

CONSULTATIVE ASSEMBLY OF MANILA

The Spanish defense at Manila* concerned itself with more than the movements of troops and guns and Admiral Patricio Montojo's* efforts at readying his feeble squadron. Spanish governor-general Basilio Augustín Dávila* also attempted to enlist the flagging loyalties of significant Filipinos. Augustín invited several prominent locals to participate in the governance of Manila, including Pedro A. Paterno,* Cayetano Arellano, Máximo Paterno, Abrosio Rianzares Bautista, Trinidad H. Pardo de Tavera, Manuel Genato, Gregorio Araneta, Juan Rodríguez, Bonifacio Arevalo, Aristón Bautista, José Luna, José Lozada, Ricardo Esteban Baretto, T. González, Pantaleon García, Padro Serrano Laktaw. These met with Augustín on 28 May 1898. The handwriting was already on the wall: Spain would lose and these efforts smelled of weakness. The Assembly sputtered for a few weeks and died from lack of interest.

REFERENCE: Gregorio F. Zaide, *The Philippine Revolution* (Manila: Modern Book Co., 1968).

CONVERSE, GEORGE ALBERT
(1844–1909)

Commander George Albert Converse was called to the board of inquiry on the tragic explosion and sinking of the U.S.S. *Maine.** By 6 March 1898 the court had finished with testimony of survivors and then entertained expert testimony on the wreck itself. Converse, on paper, seemed expert. At the time of the court, Converse commanded the *Montgomery,** then in Havana,* and he had much experience with underwater explosions during his career. He had instructed at the torpedo station at Newport, Rhode Island, served with the Bureau of Ordnance, and spent four years in charge of the torpedo station.

Converse testified that he believed there had been two explosions. He did not believe an internal explosion alone caused the structural damage to the *Maine.* Since Converse's testimony carried enormous weight, it elevated the emotional content of the Spanish American rift. Subsequent scholarship judges Converse to have been incorrect in some of his conclusions—most significantly, that there was an external explosion, and therefore Spanish culpability. Contemporary analyses by John T. Bucknill of the Royal Engineers disputed much of Converse's testimony but was not published until June of 1898—well after hostilities had already commenced.

REFERENCE: H. G. Rickover, *How the Battleship* Maine *Was Destroyed* (Washington, DC: Naval History Division, Department of the Navy, 1976).

COOK, FRANCIS AUGUSTUS
(1843–1916)

Eventually a rear admiral, Captain Francis Augustus Cook commanded U.S.S. *Brooklyn** in the sea battle against Spanish Admiral Pascual Cervera,* who tried to sortie from Santiago de Cuba.*

Cook was born in Massachusetts, the son of a general. A graduate of the

Naval Academy in 1863, he served in the Western Gulf Blockading Squadron. After the Civil War he served in both the Atlantic and the Pacific with a variety of commands. He also served in administrative posts with the Bureau of Navigation for three years before commanding *Brooklyn* from 1896 until 1899. On 3 July 1898, Cook ordered a turn upon the exit of the Spanish *Infanta María Teresa** and *Cristóbal Colon.** Commodore Winfield S. Schley* took considerable criticism after the war for this maneuver, inasmuch as some claimed *Brooklyn* almost collided with *Texas.** The turn was initiated by Cook, however.

REFERENCE: *Record of Proceedings of a Court of Inquiry in the Case of Rear-Admiral Winfield S. Schley, U.S. Navy: Convened at the Navy Yard, Washington, DC, September 12, 1901* (Washington, DC: Navy Department, 1902).

COPPINGER, JOHN JOSEPH
(1834–1909)

Major General John Joseph Coppinger was born in County Cork, Ireland, and served with the Rowan army, earning a chevalier for gallantry in 1860. Immigrating to the United States in 1861, he fought on the Union side during the Civil War, serving in several volunteer units. He fought at Trevillian Station, Virginia, and Cedar Creek and was brevetted a major. After the war, he married a daughter of James G. Blaine and served with the army in the West and elsewhere.

During the Spanish American War, Coppinger commanded Fourth Corps* at Mobile* and was slated to serve under General Nelson Miles* in the expedition to Puerto Rico.* Although elements of Fourth Corps did go with Miles to Puerto Rico, Coppinger did not.

CORBIN, HENRY CLARK
(1842–1909)

Henry Clark Corbin was born in Ohio and studied law until the Civil War drew him in. He joined an Ohio volunteer unit but became commander of a black regiment, the Fourteenth United States Coloured Infantry. By September 1865, Corbin had risen to the rank of brigadier general of volunteers. After the war, he served as a company commander on the Mexican border fighting Apaches. He made the acquaintance of fellow Ohioan Rutherford B. Hayes, presidential nominee, and through political influence served in a variety of staff positions with considerable distinction. He organized the veterans' parades at the dedication of Grant's Tomb and served as advisor to Presidents Hayes, Garfield, and Arthur. Successful at these tasks, Corbin was appointed to the Adjutant General's Office in 1880, where he rose steadily. In February 1898, he became adjutant general of the army with the rank of brigadier general. Not only experienced and skilled, Corbin was politically adept and diplomatic. He was to become one of the most influential generals of the turn of the century largely because of his personal integrity, capacity for hard work, and ability.

Corbin was instrumental in effecting troop replacements, supporting the idea of an expansible army, preparing bills for Congress,* and promoting officers to command. He acted as President William McKinley's* legislative agent in pressing for the Hull Bill, for example. Corbin's prestige rose as he successfully managed the assignment and transfer of officers in the army. As the president began to lose confidence in General Nelson Miles* and in Secretary Russell A. Alger*, Corbin's influence increased dramatically and he became, in effect, not just the adjutant general but the president's adjutant and, later, the de facto commanding general. Corbin organized Eighth Corps and chose its officers; as adjutant, he also provided for cooperation between bureaus. Such influence naturally earned him enemies, among them Miles, who in inquiries after the war accused Corbin and Alger of plotting against him to frustrate Miles's effectiveness.

Corbin died in 1909 a lieutenant general, one of the most revered army officers of his time. He published nothing before 1898 and never did publish on tactical or combat issues. His *Legislative History of the General Staff of the Army of the United States (Its Organization, Duties, Pay, and Allowances), from 1775–1901* represents his interests well.

REFERENCE: "Henry Clark Corbin, Lieutenant General, United States Army," *Army and Navy Life* 9 (September 1906): 5–8.

CORMORAN (ship)

After the battle of Manila Bay,* the American naval commander George Dewey* was understandably nervous about the persistent arrival of foreign warships—German ships in particular. Germany* and its motives were suspect. A slight misunderstanding occurred when the German navy's *Cormoran,* a third-class cruiser, entered the harbor and failed to communicate with the Americans until U.S.S. *Raleigh** fired three shots across *Cormoran*'s bow. This assertion comes from Commodore George Dewey, but others have observed that there is no corroboration for Dewey's remark in the logs of the concerned vessels.

Cormoran remained through August 1898, shepherding four steamers of German refugees in the Philippines.*

REFERENCES: Thomas A. Bailey, "Dewey and the Germans at Manila Bay," *The American Historical Review* 45 (October 1939): 59–81; William Reynolds Braisted, *The United States Navy in the Pacific, 1897–1909* (Austin: University of Texas Press, 1958).

CORPS, U.S. ARMY

Eight corps were mobilized in the U.S. Army for service in the Spanish American War. First Corps was created in May 1898 and assembled at Chickamauga, later Camp Thomas.* Part of the First Corps participated in engagements in Puerto Rico.* Second Corps assembled at Camp Alger*; parts of Second Corps also went to Puerto Rico. Third Corps, like First Corps, assembled at Chickamauga. Fourth Corps headquartered at Mobile* and assembled troops at gulf ports. Fourth Corps became a miscellaneous assemblage of units at Tampa* and elsewhere that did not go with the first wave to Cuba. Some of these accompanied General Nelson Miles* to Puerto Rico. Later, in July and August, elements of the Fourth Corps were shifted in an attempt to diminish disease. Fifth Corps,* composed mostly of regulars, was the corps sent to Cuba to fight at El Caney* and San Juan Hill.* It assembled at Tampa, from where it embarked for Cuba. Sixth Corps also assembled at Chickamauga. Seventh Corps had headquarters at Tampa with Fifth Corps. Seventh Corps later moved to Jacksonville,* where it became a model of a well-run force. Seventh Corps was slated to lead the expeditionary force to Puerto Rico. Eighth Corps assembled at San Francisco* and became the elements that sailed to Manila* to force the Spanish capitulation there.

REFERENCE: Graham A. Cosmas, *An Army for Empire* (Columbia: University of Missouri Press, 1971).

CORREA, MIGUEL
(1830–1900)

Miguel Correa served for a half century in the Spanish army (artillery) when appointed by Práxides Mateo Sagasta* as minister of war. As such, Correa served on the council that decided Spanish strategy and attempted to influence public opinion about the war. Correa also received cable traffic from the governor-general of Cuba, Ramón Blanco y Erenas,* and the governor-general of the Philippines, Basilio Augustín Dávila. Correa somewhat resented the Spanish navy, as he felt it was too vulnerable. Knowing it was ill matched against U.S. squadrons, Correa felt the loss of morale upon losing Spanish ships would be mortal to public opinion. He had confidence in Spain's defensive army positions, however. After the debacle with Admiral Pascual Cervera y Topete's* sortie, he pleaded with Blanco to hold Spanish troops in Cuba firm. Confident in the Army, Correa ordered General Manuel Macías y Casado* to resist in Puerto Rico* partly to improve future peace negotiations.

Correa did not long survive the war; he died in Madrid in 1900.

CORREGIDOR, PHILIPPINES

A key strategic island located at the mouth of Manila Bay,* Corregidor provided the Spanish with a number of opportunities for protecting their fleet and damaging the U.S. squadron. None of these opportunities were seized, however.

Owing to lack of preparation in the waters surrounding Subic Bay,* Admiral Patricio Montojo y Pasarón,* commander of the Spanish squadron protecting the Philippines, prepared to fight Commodore George Dewey's* U.S. squadron near Manila* in late April 1898. Montojo preferred a battle in the vicinity of Corregidor in order to take advantage of the island's guns. However, the captains of the vessels in Montojo's squadron objected to his plan, in particular because the depth of the area waters would lead to high casualties in the event vessels had to be evacuated. Additionally, Spain had failed to deploy either sufficient guns on the island or mines in the area waters; thus, the Spanish fleet moved inside Manila Bay to the area near Cavite.*

Corregidor represented a threat to Dewey's plan to enter Manila Bay under cover of night on May 1, 1898. However, only minor fire was directed at the U.S. squadron as it entered the harbor, and it was believed to be from the nearby island of El Fraile, not Corregidor.

REFERENCE: Davis F. Trask, *The War with Spain in 1898* (New York: Macmillan Publishing Co., 1981).

ALAN CORNISH

CORTELYOU, GEORGE BRUCE
(1862–1940)

George Bruce Cortelyou was born in New York and studied law. He served as a school principal and reporter before entering public service in 1889. He served in various posts as private secretary, including stints as President Cleveland's* stenographer and President William McKinley's* secretary for two years (1898–1900). He was later secretary of the treasury under Theodore Roosevelt* and became the director of several large corporations.

Cortelyou's chief significance to the Spanish American War lies in his much-cited diary, which provides insight into McKinley's moods, trials, and work.

REFERENCE: Charles S. Olcott, *The Life of William McKinley,* 2 vols. (Boston: Houghton, Mifflin, 1916).

CRANE, STEPHEN
(1871–1900)

Novelist, poet, and newspaper correspondent, Stephen Crane was born in Newark, New Jersey, in 1871, the son of a Methodist minister, and was raised in small towns in New York and New Jersey. In 1888, Crane attended the Claverack College and Hudson River Institute, in Claverack, New York, transferring for fall 1890 to Lafayette College in Eaton, Pennsylvania, and finally attempting a final semester of higher education in spring 1891 at Syracuse University. His grades had never been good, although he had been a decent baseball player. After college, he devoted his life to writing and became widely known after the publication of his Civil War novel *The Red Badge of Courage* in 1895.

In November 1896 Crane was sent to Jacksonville* by the Bacheller Syndicate, a news group headed by Irving Bacheller, for which Crane had been working. From Florida, Crane was to travel to Cuba as a "special correspondent" on one of the filibustering ships then supplying the Cuban insurgents.* While waiting in Jacksonville to gain passage on a filibuster,* he met Cora Taylor; she would later use the title Mrs. Crane when they lived together in England, although they never married.

Crane finally secured passage on the *Commodore,* signing on as a seaman at $20 a month; it sailed from Jacksonville on New Year's Eve. The ship, carrying men, arms, and ammunition destined for Cuba, was damaged after grounding on sandbars in the St. John's River before heading out for the open ocean. The crew did not realize the extent of the damage until the engine room was found to be flooding.

Abandoning the vessel, Crane, the ship's captain, and two others ended up in a small dinghy; others had already boarded three larger lifeboats. The dinghy was tossed about in the ocean for another day before being grounded on Daytona Beach on 3 January; one of its four occupants died of injuries.

Although Crane stayed in Jacksonville recuperating from his ordeal and still venturing to get to Cuba, after a month he gave up and returned to New York. The gold he had worn in a money belt to pay his way in Cuba had been lost on the *Commodore,* and the Bacheller Syndicate had no desire to sponsor him further. He signed on as a correspondent with William Randolph Hearst's* *New York Journal* and headed for Greece to cover the Greco-Turkish war in spring 1897. Although deciding to settle in England with Cora Taylor, who had also worked in Greece as a correspondent for the *Journal,* news of impending hostilities with Spain excited him into returning to the United States in April 1898.

After being rejected for service in the U.S. Navy, having failed the physical, he traveled to Cuba as a correspondent for Joseph Pulitzer's* *New York World.* Through his friendship with fellow correspondent Sylvester Scovel,* he gained passage on Admiral William T. Sampson's* flagship, the *New York,* shortly before it bombarded the shore at Cabañas* west of Havana* in late April. To allay charges of favoritism toward some papers, the navy banned correspondents from its vessels shortly thereafter.

In May, Crane traveled aboard the *World*'s dispatch boat the *Three Friends* and later the *Somers N. Smith* in unsuccessful attempts to locate Admiral Pascual Cervera y Topete's* Spanish fleet. He was also aboard the *Three Friends* on a swing down to Haiti and Puerto Rico when, on the first night out of Key West on 14 May, the small tug was nearly broadsided by the U.S.S. *Machias,* the incident related in his dispatch ''Narrow Escape of the *Three Friends.''* When military action on land finally began, Crane landed on 7 June with the U.S. Marines at Guantánamo* and stayed in the midst of the operations. He seemed to have a fatalistic urge to witness military action closely, to the point of being described as reckless.

Leaving for the Santiago area* on 17 June, he and Scovel scouted out the position of Cervera's fleet in Santiago Harbor, reporting back to Admiral Sampson. He landed again at Daiquirí* on 22 June, witnessing the buildup of U.S. forces near Santiago and engagements such as the battle for San Juan Hill.* It was during the Santiago campaign, at Siboney,* that Crane filed a dispatch for the *Journal*'s wounded reporter Edward Marshall, an act that later helped cost him his assignment for the *World.*

The *World*'s publisher, Joseph Pulitzer,* was also embarrassed by an unsigned article, often attributed to Crane and published in the *World* on 16 July, that accused officers of the Seventy-first New York Regiment of panic in the actions leading up to Battle of San Juan Hill. Circumstantial evidence, however, indicates that Crane could not have filed the controversial dispatch; it was probably written by his friend Scovel. Pulitzer's major competitor, William Randolph Hearst of the *Journal,* made much of the article's supposed slander of heroic soldiers, accusing the *World* of lacking patriotism.

After returning briefly to the United States and learning of his dismissal from the *World,* Crane was hired by the *Journal* and went to cover the Puerto Rican campaign at the end of July 1898. He arrived shortly after the Americans occupied Ponce.* After hostilities ended, Crane slipped into Havana for several months to recuperate from illness and to write, including short stories based on his Spanish American War experiences (collected in *Wounds in the Rain*).

When returning to New York in November, Crane found himself still being harassed by the police as a result of his strong criticism of them during investigative reporting back in 1896. This had also cost him the good graces of Theodore Roosevelt,* police commissioner in 1896, who never acknowledged Crane's service in the thick of action during the war. Crane set sail for England on 31 December. He died of tuberculosis at Badenweiler, Germany, in June 1900, at the age of twenty-eight.

REFERENCES: Stephen Crane, *Wounds in the Rain: War Stories* (New York: Frederick A. Stokes, 1900); R. W. Stallman, *Stephen Crane: A Biography* (New York: George Braziller, 1968); R. W. Stallman and E. R. Hagemann, eds., *The War Dispatches of Stephen Crane* (New York: New York University Press, 1964); Ames W. Williams, "Stephen Crane: War Correspondent," *The New Colophon* 1, pt. 2 (1948): 113–123.

                                                                MARK A. THOMAS

CRISTÓBAL COLÓN (ship)

Cristóbal Colón was a Spanish armored cruiser of 6,840 tons with a maximum speed of 20 knots. *Colón* was arguably the finest ship Admiral Pascual Cervera* had in his squadron, having been finished hurriedly at Barcelona* in 1898. She was designed and built in Italy and was to have been armed with two 10-inch Armstrong guns. Owing to the press of time, these guns had not been fitted, so she went to sea without armor-piercing weapons, a decided disadvantage. *Colón* did mount ten 6-inch Armstrong guns (five per side) and also six 5-inch guns. Possessed also of a nickel steel armor belt, she should have outclassed every American ship. However, without her big guns and with a new and not well trained crew, her advantages did not avail her. In fact, *Colón* was unable to participate in target practice because she lacked sufficient ammunition.

Colón sailed with the rest of Cervera's squadron from the Cape Verde Islands.* In an attempt to conserve fuel, the larger vessels towed smaller vessels; thus *Colón* towed *Furor** and necessarily made slow time toward the Caribbean. Once the squadron arrived in the West Indies, the Spanish admiral steamed from port to port seeking coal, mostly without success. One month after leaving the Cape Verdes, *Colón,* along with the rest of Cervera's ships, was at Santiago de Cuba* subject to blockade* by the U.S. Flying Squadron.* The day following the first of the blockade, 29 May 1898, *Colón* was guarding the channel at Santiago and opened fire on the American ships without effect.

Cristóbal Colón was the third vessel to exit Santiago on 3 July, the day of Cervera's attempted sortie. Because the U.S. fleet was already engaged with *Colón*'s predecessors, *Colón* ran the gauntlet at the channel mouth more successfully than her sister-ships and steaming at 17 knots, hoped to outrun the U.S. squadron. Doubtless the losses of *Vizcaya,** *Infanta María Teresa,** and *Almirante Oquendo** were intimidating to *Colón,* for when *Brooklyn** and *Oregon** got within range at about 1 P.M., with *Texas** and *New York** steaming close behind, *Colón* turned in to the shore and hoisted a white flag while her crew opened seacocks to sink the ship. Thus *Colón* escaped with only one killed and sixteen wounded—the fewest casualties of the Spanish ships. Subsequently, *Colón* capsized while *New York* was trying to nudge her into shallow water.

REFERENCES: Alfredo Aguilera, *Buques de guerra españoles, 1885–1971* (Madrid: Librería Editorial San Martín, 1972); H. W. Wilson, *The Downfall of Spain* (New York: Burt Franklin, 1971).

CROWNINSHIELD, ARENT SCHUYLER
(1843–1908)

Rear Admiral Arent Schuyler Crowninshield came from a famous seafaring family. Born in New York, he graduated from the Naval Academy in 1863. He fought in the Civil War and later served in a variety of commands, including that of the U.S.S. *Maine** from 1895 until 1897, and in the New York Navy Yard. From 1897 until 1902 he was chief of the Bureau of Navigation of those senior officers appointed to a Naval War Board* to make plans for an impending conflict with Spain. This board served in an advisory capacity to the secretary of the navy.

Crowninshield died in 1908 in Maine.

LAS CRUCES, CUBA

Located about a mile south of Santiago,* Las Cruces lay on the bay of Santiago de Cuba. General Arsenio Linares,* the Spanish army commander at Santiago, established a lengthy defensive perimeter that began over a mile northwest of Santiago at a small village called Dos Caminos, which lay at the juncture of Cobre Road and the road to Bayamo. The perimeter snaked to the east from Dos Caminos through a series of forts and block houses to San Juan* Heights and then back to the southern terminus at Las Cruces on the bay.

REFERENCE: French Ensor Chadwick, *The Relations of the United States and Spain* (New York: Russell & Russell, 1911).

CUBAN DEBT

In the inevitable wrangle that accompanied the negotiations that led to the Treaty of Paris,* one of the most frequently gnawed bones of contention was the Cuban public debt. This debt consisted of expenses incurred from the Spanish governing of Cuba and amounted to $455,710,000 in addition to interest. Compromises and counterproposals were exchanged until 25 October 1898,

when President McKinley* issued instructions to Secretary of State John Milton Hay* not to accept any proposal for the assumption of Cuban debt by either the United States or Cuba. On 27 October, Spain accepted the American position.
REFERENCE: Philip S. Foner, *The Spanish-Cuban-American War and the Birth of American Imperialism* (New York: Monthly Review Press, 1972).

CUBAN INSURRECTION

The so-called Cuban Insurrection was the culmination of a longstanding dissatisfaction with Spanish rule on the part of much of the Cuban populace. The Ten Years' War* (1868–1878) was an earlier revolutionary conflict that wrung from the Spanish concessions of reform in its colonial government system. Failing to honor its commitments, Spain found itself facing another conflict in 1895 led by veterans of the Ten Years' War and supplied and encouraged by filibustering North Americans. Citizens in the United States provided money, guns, supplies, and encouragement.

The insurrection itself engendered a strong emotional reaction in the United States. The reaction came, in part, because of American ideals of liberty and a natural sympathy for those desiring to free themselves from European domination. The American reaction came also from the disruption of a very lucrative trade and the possible destruction of significant American assets in Cuba.

The specter of Spanish cruelty, real or manufactured, inflamed American public opinion to the extent that there were efforts—political, rhetorical, and more substantive—that argued for American intervention to free the Cubans as a vital link in the future of any Central American canal. Thus, the Cuban Insurrection ignited not just the Cubans but also a variety of U.S. interests in the island.
REFERENCES: Philip S. Foner, *The Spanish-Cuban-American War and the Birth of American Imperialism* (New York: Monthly Review Press, 1972); Hugh Thomas, *Cuba: The Pursuit of Freedom* (New York: Harper & Row, 1971).

CUBAN JUNTA

As the Cuban Insurrection* gained momentum in the mid-1890s, it became evident to Cuban leaders that they needed to develop a civil government in Cuba. Disagreements and confusion were such that the junta in Cuba continued to be a military one. Junta leadership was also aware that it needed political support and a presence in the United States. To this end, a Cuban junta (and sometimes juntas) was encouraged to support the insurgency and to campaign for U.S. recognition of Cuban belligerency. First appointed in September 1895 the junta was authorized to pursue diplomatic relations with other countries. The members of the junta were mostly nationalized Cubans and, while technically subordinate to the revolutionary government in Cuba, actually acted very independently. Their chief policy exponent was Tomás Estrada Palma.*
REFERENCE: Philip S. Foner, *The Spanish-Cuban-American War and the Birth of American Imperialism* (New York: Monthly Review Press, 1972).

CUBAN REVOLUTIONARY ARMY

In the Cuban war for independence that commenced in 1895, José Martí* realized that although he could organize the political revolution, he needed a military commander. He called upon General Máximo Gómez* to lead the Cuban army. The policy decided upon by Gómez, Martí, and Antonio Maceo,* was a scorched earth–guerrilla war conducted to economically cripple Spain's interests in Cuba. Veteran of the Ten Years' War,* Gómez knew his forces could not succeed against Spain as a regular army, but an economic destroyer could be just as potent. The Cuban Revolutionary Army employed small units in hit-and-run tactics that required flexibility and mobility. Although the army never mustered more than 40,000, and frequently only 25,000, the army succeeded in wresting the countryside away from the Spanish, who could only maintain cities and especially vulnerable locations. The Cuban army had the benefits of excellent intelligence, mobility, and widespread support from the populace. Because the Cuban army could and did deny access to the interior, the Spanish army was particularly vulnerable by sea. For this reason, American planners conceived of a war with Spain in Cuba as primarily a naval problem; denied resupply from the sea and from the interior, the Spanish army would capitulate. It was the Cuban *insurrecto* that made that planning a reality.

During the actual invasion of Cuba by the United States, Cuban army units participated very little. The U.S. commanders discounted their effectiveness, although they used Cuban intelligence.

REFERENCES: Graham A. Cosmas, *An Army for Empire* (Columbia: University of Missouri Press, 1971); Philip S. Foner, *The Spanish-Cuban-American War* (New York: Monthly Review Press, 1972).

CUBAN REVOLUTIONARY PARTY

On 5 January 1892 José Martí* established El Partido Revolucionario Cubano, which had as its object the independence of Cuba and the promotion of the democratic process. At its heart, the party was a loosely federated group of clubs of expatriated Cubans, like Martí himself, and sympathizers. It was organized first in New York and Philadelphia and soon spread to Tampa* and Key West.* This party became the political base in the United States from which support, organization, funding, and propaganda could emanate. Linking itself with Máximo Gómez,* Antonio Maceo,* and others, the party served as the springboard to launch the Cuban revolution. It sustained that effort until December 1898, when the party was dissolved, having accomplished its work.

REFERENCES: Richard B. Gray, *José Martí, Cuban Patriot* (Gainesville: University of Florida Press, 1962); Hugh Thomas, *Cuba: The Pursuit of Freedom* (New York: Harper & Row, 1971).

CUSHING (ship)

The U.S.S. *Cushing,* the first real torpedo boat, was commissioned on 22 April 1890. Built of galvanized steel and displacing 105 tons, *Cushing* was capable of 22 knots and set the pattern for future torpedo boats. She had three tubes that could be aimed and three 1-pounder guns.

During the war, *Cushing* served in the blockade* of Cuba but, like most of her sister-ships, was too small to have any effect. Naval historians have concluded that as originally designed, the torpedo boats failed as a design, although they did provide valuable experience and developmental insight.

REFERENCE: John D. Alden, *The American Steel Navy* (Annapolis, MD: Naval Institute Press, 1972).

D

DAIQUIRÍ, CUBA

Daiquirí is a small village about 14 miles east of Santiago de Cuba.* General Arsenio Linares y Pomba,* the Spanish defender at Santiago, prepared an outer line of defense from Daiquirí to Siboney,* anticipating American landings in that area. Linares was correct, and in the planning meeting held on 20 June 1898 between Admiral William T. Sampson,* General William Rufus Shafter,* and General Calixto García,* the latter proposed a landing at Daiquirí. Shafter would initiate a naval barrage at Daiquirí; García's Cuban army would attack Spanish positions, and in a secret move, American ships would transport elements of Cuban forces to Cabañas,* thereby cutting off communications and supply. The Spanish at Santiago would be isolated and trapped: Admiral Pascual Cervera's* squadron would be bottled in the harbor and the Fifth Army Corps* would advance on Santiago.

On the planned day of the landing, 22 June, Sampson shelled Daiquirí, and the 300 or so Spanish defenders left the scene. The landing was unopposed. Some 16,000 troops commenced landing in a highly disorganized fashion. The diversion at Cabañas was highly effective, however. Fortunately for the unprepared U.S. troops, the Spanish withdrew before the landings, so the chief difficulties were mechanical: How to get men and material ashore. Daiquirí had neither wharves nor port facilities. Everything had to go ashore through the surf. Nevertheless, some 6,000 men landed in the first two days, and Shafter added Siboney as a landing site. Daiquirí continued to be a depot until Santiago was secured.

REFERENCE: David F. Trask, *The War with Spain in 1898* (New York: Macmillan Publishing Co., 1981).

DALY, WILLIAM HUDSON
(1842–1912)

A Pittsburgh physician, William Hudson Daly was appointed major and chief surgeon of volunteers at the outbreak of the Spanish American War. He was assigned to the staff of General Nelson A. Miles,* a longtime friend. Daly was among the first to suspect that the canned beef rations may have been tainted. He claimed to have tested the rations in Puerto Rico and to have found traces of acid in it. The subsequent beef controversy* got its start with Daly's suspicions.

REFERENCES: Graham A. Cosmas, *An Army for Empire* (Columbia: University of Missouri Press, 1971); *Food Furnished by the Subsistence Department to Troops in the Field* (Washington, DC: Government Printing Office, 1899–1900).

DANA, CHARLES ANDERSON
(1819–1897)

Born in Hinsdale, New Hampshire, Charles Anderson Dana briefly attended Harvard College before spending five years as a young man living at the utopian socialist community of Brook Farm. After this, he spent a short term as assistant editor of the *Boston Daily Chromotype* before moving on to Horace Greeley's *New York Tribune,* where he worked from 1847 to 1862, becoming managing editor in 1849. During the latter years of the Civil War, he served as a military observer for the federal government, eventually becoming an assistant secretary of war. He returned to newspaper publishing after the war and in 1868 purchased the *New York Sun.*

The Ten Years' War* in Cuba was just beginning when Dana first took over the *Sun.* While at the *Tribune* he had favored Cuban independence; now he opposed the pro-Spanish policy of the Grant administration. Although he had admired Grant during the Civil War and the *Sun* had supported Grant's candidacy, Dana came to dislike both the president and his secretary of state, Hamilton Fish.* It was Dana who coined the phrase "Turn the rascals out," in reference to the Grant administration.

Although the U.S. government would not support the insurgents, Dana encouraged the Cuban junta* and filibustering* expeditions to the island and invited Cuban exile José Martí,* living in New York, to contribute to the *Sun.* When Martí was killed in 1895, Dana personally wrote his obituary, published in the *Sun* on 23 May.

As early as 1888, Dana had advocated U.S. purchase of Cuba from Spain; when the second Cuban insurrection began in 1895, he still championed U.S. annexation. Although generally supportive of U.S. overseas expansion, the antislavery Dana had opposed annexation before the Civil War, when he was with the *Tribune,* because he feared Cuba would become a slave state. When Dana died in October 1897, the Council of the Cuban Revolutionary party issued a statement that his death was a national loss to Cuba. Dana was well known on that island, so much so that the city of Camagüey in 1899 renamed a plaza in his honor in appreciation of his enduring and vocal support for Cuban independence.

REFERENCES: Janet E. Steele, *The Sun Shines for All: Journalism and Ideology in the Life of Charles A. Dana* (Syracuse, NY: Syracuse University Press, c. 1993); Candance Stone, *Dana and the Sun* (New York: Dodd, Mead & Co., 1938).

MARK A. THOMAS

DAUNTLESS.
See O'BRIEN, "DYNAMITE JOHNNY."

DAVIS, CHARLES HENRY
(1845–1921)

Rear Admiral Charles Henry Davis, a captain in the Spanish American War, graduated from Annapolis in 1864. A noted navigator, Davis worked with submarine telegraph cables. He also enjoyed command at sea and from 1897 to 1898 commanded U.S.S. *Dixie.** During the war, he led a naval attacking force in the capture of Ponce,* Puerto Rico.* Davis was Henry Cabot Lodge's* father-in-law and was instrumental in getting Theodore Roosevelt* appointed assistant secretary of the navy. Perhaps because of these connections, Davis was able to influence Admiral William T. Sampson* favorably in a plan in early August to seize San Juan* with naval might alone. A. T. Mahan* argued Davis's plan along with Sampson. However, when General Nelson Miles* learned of it, it became another element of interservice contention.

Davis served a distinguished career and authored technical works as well as a biography of his father, also a rear admiral.

REFERENCE: French Ensor Chadwick, *The Relations of the United States and Spain* (New York: Russell & Russell, 1911).

DAVIS, RICHARD HARDING
(1864–1916)

Journalist and author Richard Harding Davis was born in Philadelphia in 1864, the son of novelist Rebecca Harding Davis and a newspaper editor. After attending college at Lehigh and Johns Hopkins, he entered into a newspaper career in 1886. His first involvement with troubles in Cuba occurred when he was sent there in late 1896 to cover the insurrection of 1895* for *Harper's Weekly* and William Randolph Hearst's* *New York Journal.*

With illustrator Frederick Remington,* Davis attempted to sneak into Cuba aboard Hearst's dispatch boat the *Vamoose.** Due to a hesitant crew and bad weather, they were never able to leave Key West* and eventually traveled to Cuba via a regular passenger ship, the *Olivette,** obtaining an official Spanish pass instead of sneaking behind insurgent lines. It was on this trip that Davis witnessed the Spanish execution of a young Cuban prisoner, about which he wrote one of his more famous articles, "The Death of Rodríguez."* *

In February 1897 the *Journal* published an article, based on one of Davis's dispatches, about a young Cuban woman, sympathetic with the insurgents, being stripped and searched aboard the *Olivette* after being exiled from Cuba. Accompanied by a lurid illustration by Remington, the article claimed that male Cuban officers performed the search—an embellishment of Davis's nebulous dispatch—when in fact female matrons had done so. Davis was outraged by the misrepresentation of his dispatch; he angrily explained himself in a published letter to Hearst's archrival, Joseph Pulitzer's* *New York World,* and refused to work for Hearst for the remainder of his life.

After several assignments in Europe for various papers and magazines, Davis was back the United States in early 1898 to cover the Spanish American War for the *New York Herald,* the *Times* of London, and *Scribner's Magazine.* He had turned down the opportunity for a commission as a captain in order to cover the war; he later regretted this decision, although many would attest to his value as a correspondent.

After arriving in Florida, he talked himself aboard the U.S. Navy flagship *New York,** from which he witnessed the naval bombardment of Mantanzas* and gave the *Herald* an early scoop in the war. Subsequently, the navy adopted a policy forbidding reporters on its ships. Thus, he was forced to await the beginning of hostilities along with other correspondents in Tampa.* Davis christened this place, where correspondents and military officers spent hours lounging on the verandas of the ornate Tampa Bay Hotel,* as "the rocking-chair period" of the war.

After hostilities started, Davis was in the midst of action during the Santiago* campaign. A personal favorite of Theodore Roosevelt,* he helped to build the legend surrounding Roosevelt's Rough Riders.* Despite praising those in battle, Davis did not hesitate to criticize some of the U.S. military leadership during the actions in Cuba. After conclusion of hostilities in Cuba, he covered the brief campaign in Puerto Rico.*

The patriotic Davis enthusiastically supported U.S. imperialist goals and the cause of a democratic Cuba free from Spain. Other more cynical correspondents often viewed him with disdain for his seeming naiveté and his obvious aloof attitude toward them. He was a well-dressed dandy with patrician airs who wrote for literary publications as well as for newspapers; this set him apart from many other journalists but gave him a romantic appeal that made him quite popular with the reading public in his time.

REFERENCES: Charles H. Brown, *The Correspondents' War* (New York: Scribner's, 1967); Charles Belmont Davis, ed., *Adventures and Letters of Richard Harding Davis* (New York: Scribner's, 1918); Richard Harding Davis, *Cuba in War-Time* (New York: R. H. Russell, 1897); Richard Harding Davis, *The Cuban and Puerto Rican Campaigns* (New York: Charles Scribner's Sons, 1898).

MARK A. THOMAS

DAWES, CHARLES GATES
(1865–1951)

Banker, lawyer, politician, and prominent Republican, Charles Gates Dawes was born in Marieta, Ohio. He received his law degree from the Cincinnati Law

School in 1886. He moved to Lincoln, Nebraska, after graduation and practiced law until 1894. The Panic of 1893 nearly destroyed him financially. He looked to other fields of interests in other parts of the country, involving himself with two utility companies in Wisconsin and Illinois and eventually gaining majority control of them. By 1895, he was an important player in Republican politics. Barely thirty years old, Dawes immersed himself in Illinois politics, especially Chicago machine politics, having moved to Chicago in January 1895. He had met William McKinley* in Ohio in 1894 and backed him for the presidency. Working with McKinley's right-hand man, Marcus Alonzo Hanna,* Dawes was able to give the important Illinois support to the McKinley camp that virtually locked up the election. President-elect McKinley rewarded Dawes with the position of comptroller of the currency, which he held until 1901. Dawes was very knowledgeable in fiscal matters, including banking regulations. However, he was fiscally at odds with his friend William Jennings Bryan,* especially on the issue of "free and unlimited coinage of silver to cure the Nation's ills." He wrote a book entitled *The Banking System of the United States and Its Relation to the Money and Business of the Country,* which was to set his financial philosophy for the rest of his life.

Dawes held a variety of public and banking positions over the next thirty years of his life, including vice-president of the United States (1925–1929). He died on 23 April 1951 in Evanston, Illinois.

REFERENCE: Bascom N. Timmons, *Portrait of an American: Charles G. Dawes* (New York: Henry Holt & Co., 1953).

RICHARD W. PEUSER

DAY, WILLIAM RUFUS
(1849–1923)

Born in Ravenna, Ohio, William Rufus Day read law and became a somewhat noted jurist. In March 1897, he was appointed assistant secretary of state under President William McKinley.* He succeeded John Sherman* on 26 April 1898 to become secretary of state but was in turn succeeded by John Hay* the following September.

Senator Sherman was old and infirm, and McKinley's desire to appoint him to the cabinet came from a wish to free a Senate seat for McKinley's friend Marcus Hanna.* McKinley never intended that Sherman act in the office; Day was the shadow secretary. Demonstration of this fact occurs in the exchanges between Enrique Dupuy de Lôme* and Assistant Secretary of State Day in January of 1898. Subsequently, Day became particularly involved in the negotiations over the Philippines.* Day was forthright in stopping negotiations with Emilio Aguinaldo,* and McKinley often spoke through Day to Great Britain,* Germany,* and France.

McKinley replaced Day so that Day could serve on the Peace Commission,* which Day was only too glad to do. Day's personal feelings on the Philippines balked at taking the whole archipelago, but he was in the minority.

REFERENCES: Lewis L. Gould, *The Spanish American War and President McKinley* (Lawrence: University of Kansas Press, 1982); Joseph Erigina McLean, *William Rufus Day, Supreme Court Justice from Ohio* (Baltimore: Johns Hopkins University Press, 1946).

"DEATH OF RODRÍGUEZ"

"Death of Rodríguez" is the title of an article Richard Harding Davis* wrote describing the execution of Cuban rebel Adolfo Rodríguez. In January 1897, Davis was in Cuba with Frederick Remington* covering the rebellion for the *New York Journal.* On the nineteenth, Davis witnessed the execution of Rodríguez by a Spanish firing squad. Rodríguez, the twenty-year-old only son of a Cuban farmer, had joined the insurgents, and after being captured by the Spanish, he was found guilty of bearing arms against the government. Davis's sympathetic portrayal of the young man helped strengthen anti-Spanish sentiment in the United States.

REFERENCE: Richard Harding Davis, *Cuba in War-Time* (New York: R. H. Russell, 1897).

MARK A. THOMAS

DECKER, KARL
(1868–1941)

A correspondent for the *New York Journal,* Karl Decker was instrumental in providing grist for William R. Hearst's* sensational newspaper. Decker rescued the "Cuban Girl Martyr," Evangelina Cisneros,* from a prison on the Isle of Pines* and, in the process, became a hero. The rescue began late in August 1897 when Decker initiated planning, at Hearst's behest, to identify the whereabouts of Evangelina. On 8 October news came that she had been rescued.

Decker continued to serve Hearst as a correspondent during the prelude to the war and later. He was rumored to be leading a military intervention in Cuba in December 1897 when Spanish authorities stopped one of Hearst's yachts, the *Buccaneer,* in an effort to seize the troublesome correspondent.

REFERENCE: Charles Henry Brown, *The Correspondents' War* (New York: Scribner's, 1967).

DECLARATION OF WAR

On 11 April 1898 President William McKinley* asked Congress* for authority to use U.S. military force to end Spanish rule in Cuba. On 22 April actual hostilities commenced when the president's order to blockade* Cuba became an actuality. The declaration itself was not requested until 25 April, when McKinley sent a request to Congress. Congress readily agreed, backdating the conflict to 21 April. Spain had already declared a state of war on 23 December. The precise declarations came tardily to the political arena, inasmuch as Congress on 19 April had already declared that Spanish rule in Cuba must end and hostilities commenced with orders to blockade Cuba on 21 April.

REFERENCE: Henry Cabot Lodge, *The War with Spain* (New York: Arno Press, 1970); Walter Millis, *The Marial Spirit* (Boston: Houghton Mifflin, 1931).

DEPARTMENT OF WAR.
See WAR DEPARTMENT.

DERBY, GEORGE MCCLELLAN
(1856–1948)

George McClellan Derby was born at sea in 1856. Educated privately in Paris, Dresden, and Switzerland, he graduated from West Point in 1878 and joined the Corps of Engineers. Before his retirement in 1907, he was promoted to colonel. During the Spanish American War, Derby was the chief engineer of Fifth Corps* at Santiago de Cuba* and later chief engineer of Second Corps. With Fifth Corps, Derby and a picked group of associates daily scouted between Daiquirí* and Santiago* for General William R. Shafter.* Derby's group created the first detailed topographic maps of the Santiago area, identified Spanish positions, and located a tactically significant mountain trail of which the Spanish were ignorant. His reconnaissance was excellent.

Derby also utilized balloon* ascents for tactical intelligence. Although much information was obtained, the balloon caused serious casualties, inasmuch as the Spanish used it as a firing marker.

REFERENCE: Joseph Wheeler, *The Santiago Campaign, 1898* (New York: Drexel Biddle, 1899).

DETROIT (ship)

The U.S.S. *Detroit* was one of the *Montgomery**-class unprotected cruisers of 2,094 tons armed with two 6-inch, eight 5-inch, and ten other guns. *Detroit* also possessed three torpedo tubes and had a speed of 19 knots. Commissioned in 1893, *Detroit* was found to be unstable, and her armament was altered. Little better than a gunboat, this class of vessel was actually intended for peacetime cruising.

With her sister-ship *Montgomery, Detroit* steamed in the squadron commanded by Admiral William T. Sampson* that attacked San Juan, Puerto Rico,* on 12 May 1898. *Detroit* bombarded defenses while receiving no hits. The cruiser also convoyed troopships to Santiago de Cuba.*

Detroit served in the North Atlantic after the war and was stricken from the navy list in 1910.

REFERENCE: John D. Alden, *The American Steel Navy* (Annapolis, MD: Naval Institute Press, 1972).

DEWEY, GEORGE
(1837–1917)

Born on 26 December 1837, in Montpelier, Vermont, George Dewey studied at Norwich University before entering the U.S. Naval Academy in 1854. He graduated from Annapolis in 1857 and received his first commission as lieutenant in 1861. During the Civil War he served with Admiral Farragut in operations against New Orleans and, later, as part of the Atlantic blockade. He held various ship and shore assignments over the next ten years, attaining the rank of commander in 1872, captain in 1884, and commodore in 1896.

During the period between 1871 and 1896, Dewey served a wide variety of positions and duty stations, including naval secretary to the Lighthouse Board (1878), chief of the Bureau of Equipment (1899), and president of the Board of Inspection and Survey (1895). He also became commander of the Asiatic Squadron* in 1897, a position gained by strong political ties. Dewey was often criticized by his peers and other line officers for using political patronage at a time when promotions were slow. Dewey nonetheless cultivated the backing and friendship of very influential people, including Assistant Secretary of the Navy Theodore Roosevelt.*

Dewey took command of the prestigious Asiatic Squadron from Acting Rear Admiral Frederick G. McNair in Japan in November 1897. He was well aware of the situation in Cuba and the consequences if war developed. So keen was his knowledge of that rapidly developing situation that with the help of Roosevelt he managed to obtain guns, ammunition, and other badly needed supplies for his Asiatic Squadron just before he left Washington, DC for the Far East.

As war grew imminent with Spain, Dewey continued readying his squadron for action. He openly disregarded China's neutrality by coaling his fleet at Mirs Bay* without consulting the Navy Department. Although Dewey worried about not having enough ammunition for his fleet, he never wavered in his confidence in its ability to wage war. On 22 April 1898, Dewey was told to leave Hong Kong* by the governor of Hong Kong, General Wilsone Black.* On the same day, U.S.S. *Baltimore*￼ arrived from Honolulu with ammunition after setting sail in march. With his flagship U.S.S. *Olympia*￼ leading the way, Dewey and the Asiatic Squadron left Hong Kong on 25 April.

Dewey's orders were to proceed to the Philippines* to capture or destroy the Spanish naval force in Philippine waters, thereby breaking Spain's defenses of the islands. In doing this, the U.S. Navy was neutralizing Spain's overseas territories so they would never be a factor.

The Spanish squadron under the command of Admiral Patricio Montojo* was at best a motley collection of ten ragtag, ill-equipped ships, most of which were slow and outdated. Lack of ordnance and ammunition made the Spanish situation worse. Montojo settled on Manila Bay* for defensive posture after little or no progress was made on protecting and defending Subic Bay.* At a point called Cavite* within Manila Bay, the Spanish squadron waited for the American invaders.

Guiding his fleet past mines and firing shore batteries, Dewey's force sailed in single column into Manila Bay seeking the enemy. On 1 May he found them prepared to fight. The battle proved to be one-sided as the U.S. squadron devastated the Spanish force, inflicting high casualties. Dewey seized the land batteries that had peppered his ships as they arrived in the bay and claimed the then-emptied garrison as an American base of operation. He was to occupy the bay area and land in and around Manila without diplomatic or army assistance for several months until General Wesley Merritt's* land forces relieved him in August.

When news of the American victory reached President McKinley on 7 May, celebrations broke out all over the country. Dewey became a national hero. Congress promoted him to rear admiral and gave citations to the men of his fleet. He served as president of the newly created General Board in 1900 and briefly entertained notions of running for president of the United States. Dewey was a prolific writer in his later years, publishing his accounts of the battle of Manila Bay for a variety of newspapers and magazines. He also published his autobiography in 1913. He died on 16 January 1917 in Washington, DC.

REFERENCES: Michael Blow, *A Ship to Remember: The* Maine *and the Spanish-American War* (New York: William Morrow & Co., 1992); Ronald Spector, *Admiral of the New Empire* (Baton Rouge: Louisiana State University Press, 1974); David F. Trask, *The War with Spain in 1898* (New York: Macmillan Publishing Co., 1981).

RICHARD W. PEUSER

DÍAZ MOLINA, PEDRO
(1850–1924)

Pedro Díaz Molina was a Cuban commander in the Ten Years' War* and was promoted to colonel. He replaced Pancho Carillo in the brigade at Remedios and jointed Antonio Maceo's* column in 1895. He was named chief of the Western Division and commander of the insurgents* in Pinar del Río Province. It was Díaz who notified Máximo Gómez* of the death of Gómez's son, Panchito, at the side of Maceo in December 1896. Gómez promoted Díaz to the rank of major general and placed him in command of the Sixth Corps in Pinar del Río.

As it did with other Cuban commanders who had been fighting for years, the actual war in 1898 almost passed him by. Nevertheless, the Cuban insurgents were exceptionally skilled at hit-and-run tactics and were able to tie down large numbers of Spanish troops all over the island.

REFERENCE: Mario Riera Hernández, *Ejército Libertador de Cuba, 1895–1898* (Miami, FL: NP, 1985).

DIEDERICHS, OTTO VON
(1843–1918)

After President McKinley's* Declaration of War,* Commodore George Dewey* sailed almost immediately with the U.S. Asiatic Squadron* and steamed toward Manila Bay.* Completely destroying the Spanish fleet there on 1 May 1898, Dewey settled down to await the arrival of troops. Dewey controlled the sea approaches to Manila, but the land fortifications and Spanish garrisons were out of his reach until 30 June 1898, when a troopship arrived with soldiers and replenishment stores. Therefore, during this two-month period of time, Dewey attempted to maintain a blockade to deny the Spanish succor and to protect American interests. In the meantime, Admiral Manuel de la Cámara* sailed from Spain with a superior fleet on 16 June 1898 to engage Dewey's squadron. During the intervening weeks British, Japanese, French, German, and Austro-Hungarian warships came and went to Manila—augmenting the complexity and tensions considerably. It is against this backdrop of international tension that Vice Admiral Otto von Diederichs, the German Asiatic Squadron* he commanded, and the role of the nation of Germany* in the Spanish American War took the stage.

Initially, German warships steamed to the Philippines to protect German nationals and German economic interests in the archipelago. These economic interests were substantial: Germany ranked sixth among foreign importers from the Philippines and second in exports behind Great Britain,* who was first also in imports. In addition, Prince Bernhard von Bülow,* the German foreign secretary, heard rumors that the Filipino insurgents might welcome a German protectorate in the Philippines. On 2 June 1898, Diederichs received orders while in Nagasaki, Japan,* refitting, to steam to the Philippines. He was not to challenge the United States but to strengthen the German presence in the event that the United States chose not to acquire the Philippines.

Diederichs, who outranked Dewey, arrived on the *Kaiserin Augusta** on 12 June 1898. His arrival created comment throughout the international community at anchor in Manila. The Spaniards, in particular, welcomed the Germans and even proposed to Diederichs that the neutral powers assume control of Manila—but Diederichs refused.

The tension on Dewey and his squadron was acute. Short of men and ammunition and facing a rapidly approaching and stronger Spanish fleet, Dewey assumed the worst of intentions on the part of the Germans. The subsequent arrivals of two additional German cruisers, the *Kaiser* (18 June 1898) and the *Prinzess Wilhelm* (20 June 1898) increased the tensions dramatically. With the arrival of these two cruisers, the German fleet was perhaps 20 percent stronger than Dewey's squadron and possessed the only ship of the armored class in either fleet. Although subsequent investigation revealed that the German intentions were mostly innocent, Diederichs did insist on his rights (as he perceived them) during blockade.

Captain Edward Chichester,* ranking British naval officer, maintained an outwardly strict neutrality while simultaneously cultivating very cordial and personally supportive relationships with Dewey. The British interests paralleled the American—to the dismay of the Germans. Under these circumstances, misunderstandings were virtually inevitable and innocent events were invested with sinister meaning. These tensions increased with two subsequent incidents that occurred on the German cruiser *Irene,** and the surreptitious evacuation of the Spanish governor-general, Basilio Augustín Dávila* on the cruiser *Kaiserin Au-*

gusta (5 August 1898). Diederichs may have been trying to maintain good relations with the Americans, but he failed to do so; Dewey felt that Diederichs attempted to flout the blockade and to insult the Americans.

Diederichs's role in Manila later became the subject of much controversy, ultimately leading to renewals of German-American friction. One of these controversies, though untrue, became legendary. First published by Henry Cabot Lodge,* the gist of the narrative concerns events on 13 August 1898, while Dewey's ships bombarded Spanish positions in preparation for a landing. Lodge's account emphasized that the Germans were going to attack Dewey, but Chichester steamed between the American and German ships, clearly aligning with the Americans. The account concludes that the Germans, nonplussed by the British support of the American cause, retired. The British saved Dewey. The problems with the story are many. Although the British did move two ships between the U.S. squadron and the German ships, it was merely to gain a better vantage point from which to watch the bombardment. The Germans had no intentions of attacking. The story, nevertheless, gained wide currency and was reiterated for at least two decades whenever propaganda required German perfidy and British loyalty.

Thus, the frictions caused by Diederichs and his fleet were a series of misunderstandings brought about by Dewey's sensitivity to his precarious position, the large size and power of Diederichs's fleet, which spoke louder than his claim to noninterference, and his insistence upon his rights during the blockade. In contrast to Chichester's supportive and friendly posture, the German admiral unwittingly created a fertile environment for mistrust and friction.

REFERENCE: Thomas A. Baily, ''Dewey and the Germans at Manila Bay,'' *The American Historical Review* 45 (October 1939): 59–81.

DISASTER OF '98

From the Spanish point of view, the unwelcome news of naval losses and the failure of Spanish soldiery was not just bad news, but a ''disaster.'' Patriotic fervor had flamed fantasies of success in the Spanish mind. Those fantasies were rudely destroyed with the debacles at Santiago de Cuba* and Manila* and a pending debacle in Puerto Rico.* The reversal of fortunes spiked a deepening Spanish pessimism that wondered aloud if Spain and its institutions had a right even to exist. Initial reactions were isolationism, Europeanization, and regionalism. But as this self-examination continued, the disaster of '98 also became an important reform movement and literary movement. It bound Spain and Spanish America in a mutual distrust and dislike of the United States. It fostered inward-looking social analysis and outward-looking resolutions. Conservatives desired to bring back the centrality of Christianity and Catholicism, in particular, into Iberian life. Liberals, such as Miguel de Unamuno, challenged the tenets of conservatives and argued that freedom of religion and intellectual freedoms would lead Spain out of its darkened forest of despair. The Generation of '98, as some of these reformers came to be labeled, sought to intellectualize the rebirth or regeneration of Spain through the essayists Ángel Ganivet, José Ortega y Gasset, and others; poets Ramón Jiménez and Antonio Machado; musicians such as Manuel de Falla and Isaac Albéniz; the historian Rafael Altamira y Crevea; and, of course, Miguel de Unamuno. It became a movement in society, philosophy, history, music, literature, and education.

REFERENCE: Frederick B. Pike, *Hispanismo, 1898–1936* (Notre Dame, IN: University of Notre Dame, 1971).

DISEASE

Until recent times, disease always marched in column with battling armies. The Four Horsemen—war, famine, death, and pestilence—were not casual visitors to battle but intrinsic in war's prosecution. Generals planned for pestilential losses. The Spanish American War followed the same pattern.

Although often confused, typhus and typhoid are distinct. Typhus is spread by lice in the winter—a disease of camps when there is crowding. Typhoid is carried by filth (fecal material, dirty hands, linens) and is suspended in water, milk, and so on or is spread by flies on food after contamination elsewhere. Yellow fever* came by way of mosquitos. Typhoid is controllable through proper hygiene and sanitation practices. Because it can be controlled, some commanders who wanted to avoid censure or even scandal encouraged medical personnel to list typhoid as mumps, measles, chicken pox, or indigestion. Because there were cases of indigestion, measles, and the rest, it is difficult to distinguish actual statistics. The real problems in the camps* came from sanitation. The American buildup for the Spanish American War happened so quickly that many ordinary sanitation practices were ignored and others were unknown, particularly among the volunteer units. The medical officer corps, never large and operating in an advisory capacity only, was unable to address the public health challenges that faced the troops. At Camps Alger,* Thomas,* Meade, and Wikoff,* at Tampa* and Jacksonville,* and in Santiago* and Puerto Rico,* 20,738 typhoid cases were reported, with 1,500 fatalities. Worse, it was estimated that this may have been only half the actual number. Compared with the number wounded in the Spanish American War (1,581), it can be seen that for U.S. troops, disease was a much more formidable enemy. The fevers traveled with the troops. Every American regiment of the First, Second, Third, Fourth, Fifth, and Seventh Army Corps developed typhoid. More than 90 percent of the volunteer regiments developed typhoid within eight weeks of arrival at camp. Over 86 percent of total deaths were from typhoid. The toll in the Philippines was a pittance by comparison: Only fourteen died of typhoid.

Yellow fever was the source of principal alarm for U.S. military planners and a festering evil among the Spanish troops. Many Cubans, it was reported, viewed yellow fever benignly, inasmuch as it killed Spaniards but not Cubans, who were often immune.

The immediate results of these epidemics were profound. U.S. Army Medical Corps personnel eradicated yellow fever in Havana within a few years. The

Dodge Commission* shined a light on the sanitary shortcomings of the army, which led to the creation of the Veterinary Medical Corps in the U.S. Army, food inspection, and more rigorous sanitary measures.
REFERENCE: P. M. Ashburn, *A History of the Medical Department of the United States Army* (New York: Houghton Mifflin, 1929).

DIXIE (ship)

Dixie (formerly *El Sud*) was a 6,114-ton transport purchased for the Spanish American War by the U.S. Navy. Capable of 15 knots and fitted with ten 5-inch guns, she served as an auxiliary cruiser in the Flying Squadron* with the intent of cruising the Spanish coast. The defeat of Admiral Pascual Cervera's* fleet at Santiago de Cuba* changed the mission of the *Dixie.* The surrender of Spanish authority in Cuba freed *Dixie,* along with *Oregon,* *Iowa,* *Newark,* *Yankee,* *Yosemite,* and *Badger,* under the command of Commodore John C. Watson* to steam east through the Suez Canal* to provide assistance to George Dewey's* effort in the Philippines. However, General Nelson Miles* requested a strong naval convoy to protect and assist in the expedition to Puerto Rico.* Thus on 21 July 1898, *Dixie, Gloucester,* and *Massachusetts* convoyed about a dozen transports from Guantánamo* to Puerto Rico.

After the war, *Dixie* served as a training platform for fleet exercises and landing exercises—the forerunner of the amphibious U.S. Marine forces known today.
REFERENCE: H. W. Wilson, *The Downfall of Spain* (New York: Burt Franklin, 1971).

DODGE, GRENVILLE MELLEN
(1831–1916)

General Grenville Mellen Dodge is better known to historians as the chief engineer and builder of the Union Pacific Railroad and chief engineer of the Texas and Pacific Railroad than for anything else, perhaps. Nevertheless, Dodge played a key role in the last days of 1898 as head of the Dodge Commission.*

Born in Massachusetts, Dodge studied engineering at Norwich University and in the early 1850s surveyed railroads in Illinois. Dodge was commissioned during the Civil War and was wounded multiple times. He was promoted to major general of volunteers. From 1866 to 1869 he directed the construction of the Union Pacific and continued survey and engineering work for a variety of railroads in diverse locales, the last being in Cuba in 1903.

As the tensions developed with Spain over Cuba, Dodge—who was a friend of both President William McKinley* and Russell A. Alger*—urged both to keep the peace. He felt that much of the Cuban discord was fanned by the United States, and that if left alone, the insurrection* in Cuba would reach its own peaceful solution. Despite his feelings, Dodge was offered the senior major generalship of the First Corps.* After consultation with Alger and McKinley, he decided instead to tend to his many business affairs.

Nevertheless, General Dodge took a keen interest in the professional aspects of the prosecution of the war. Dodge carried on armchair strategy by letter with McKinley and Alger. He was genuinely excited at the fall of Santiago de Cuba.*

General Nelson Miles,* desirous of making political capital at the end of the war, introduced issues about the suitability of some of the foodstuffs issued to troops. The beef controversy,* as it came to be called, was one—but only one—of the scandals played out in the popular press at war's close. McKinley appointed a commission of nine to investigate Miles's charges as well as other charges. Dodge, whose views were well-known, was reluctant to serve; McKinley was persuasive, however, and Dodge agreed. When the commission met, he was elected chairman. He plunged into the work of what inevitably became known as the Dodge Commission.* The commission traveled extensively to camps,* where they interviewed 495 witnesses over four months. Miles sent beef samples to chemists at Yale University and elsewhere. The results of these and other studies exonerated the War Department* of corruption and found that Miles's charges were without foundation in fact.

Dodge became aware that Miles's attack had little to do with beef: It was an attack on the administration. Yet Dodge and the commission issued a restrained report that recommended no action against Miles.

REFERENCE: Stanley P. Hirshon, *Grenville M. Dodge* (Bloomington: Indiana University Press, 1967).

DODGE COMMISSION

On 26 September 1898, President William McKinley* formed a commission to inquire into several charges of War Department* mismanagement. The commission chose General Grenville M. Dodge* to chair its proceedings and became popularly known as the Dodge Commission. The Dodge Commission investigated general administration as well as the so-called beef controversy,* which had been inflamed by General Nelson Miles* and others. The commission listened to close to 500 witnesses, made numerous site visits, and paid for its own chemical tests to ascertain the truth of various charges. After these lengthy and extensive hearings, the commission reported on 9 February 1899 that it found no corruption nor intent to neglect duty; it observed further that the War Department was not sufficiently aware of problems as they developed. In addition, the commission found that the charges "embalmed beef" were without foundation.

The work of this commission and its impact far exceeded the purview of the Spanish American War. From some of the commission's findings there developed a stimulus toward reform in the U.S. Army, much of it initiated by Elihu Root.* A series of laws were passed in the first years of the century that regulated training and militias and created a Veterinary Corps in the U.S. Army for animal inspection and meat inspection.

REFERENCE: *Report of the Commission Appointed by the President to Investigate the Conduct of the War Department in the War with Spain,* 8 vols., Senate Doc. 221, 56th Cong., 1st sess. (Washington, DC: Government Printing Office, 1900).

DOLPHIN (ship)

The U.S.S. *Dolphin* was a 1,485-ton dispatch vessel armed with two 4-inch guns and eight smaller-caliber guns. Commissioned in 1885, *Dolphin* served in Admiral William T. Sampson's* blockade* of Cuba and in the search for Admiral Pascual Cervera y Topete's* Spanish fleet. On 6 June 1898, in company with *Suwanee** and *Vixen,** *Dolphin* began to bombard the forts at the mouth of Santiago* harbor. Later, *Dolphin* joined the eastern van (*New York,** *Iowa,** *Oregon,** and *Yankee**), slowly cruising into the harbor firing on the Spanish batteries of Socapa* and at moored Spanish warships.

On 14 June, *Dolphin* supported a battalion of U.S. Marines at Caimanera* with fire. On 15 June, *Marblehead,** *Suwanee, Texas,** and *Dolphin* attacked and destroyed a Spanish fort at Cay del Tor.

After the war, *Dolphin* served in the North Atlantic. In 1922, the Mexican navy purchased *Dolphin* and renamed her *Plan de Guadalupe.* She was scrapped three years later.

REFERENCE: H. W. Wilson, *The Downfall of Spain* (New York: Burt Franklin, 1971).

DON ANTONIO DE ULLOA (ship)

Sister-ship to *Conde de Venadito** and others, *Don Antonio de Ulloa,* built in 1887, was a copy of a British design, albeit slightly smaller at 1,150 tons. The *Ulloa* fought and sank in the Battle of Manila Bay,* receiving over thirty hits with the loss of eight killed and ten wounded.

DON JUAN DE AUSTRIA (ship)

Launched on 23 January 1887, *Don Juan de Austria* was an unarmed gunboat of 1,150 tons. The *Austria* fought at Manila* and was shelled, burned, and sunk, suffering twenty-two wounded. She was later refloated by the U.S. Navy, repaired, and rearmed to serve in China* waters for some years. The U.S. Navy retained the Spanish name of the ship.

DORST, JOSEPH HADDOX
(1852–1915)

Joseph Haddox Dorst graduated from the U.S. Military Academy in 1873. He became immersed in Indian campaigns in the West against Comanche, Kiowa, Utes, and Apache (particularly Geronimo's band). He was promoted to captain in 1898. The War Department* issued orders to Dorst to attempt to supply Cuban insurgents.* Dorst left Tampa* on 10 May 1898 to attempt resupply along the north coast of Cuba. With him, Dorst had 120 men of the First Infantry. Unfortunately for Dorst, newspapers got wind of the expedition, and it was trumpeted far in advance of Dorst's arrival in the wooden side wheeler *Gussie,* which was well known in Cuba. Chased by Spanish cavalry along the shore, *Gussie* steamed looking for *insurrectos.* Dorst never found any, and after an abortive landing, he returned to Tampa, embarrassed. Dorst left again in *Florida,* a more appropriate form of transport, and in secrecy. He landed an insurgent general, 400 troops, 7,500 Springfield rifles,* ammunition, clothing, and other supplies.

Dorst fought also in the Philippine Insurrection* (1899–1900) before returning to the States in 1911.

REFERENCES: R. A. Alger, *The Spanish American War* (New York: Harper & Brothers, 1901); Frank Freidel, *The Splendid Little War* (Boston: Little, Brown & Co., 1958).

DOS CAMINOS, CUBA

A village about 12 miles north of Santiago de Cuba,* Dos Caminos was one of the strong points upon which General Arsenio Linares* placed his Spanish troops in anticipation of an American attack. Linares's fortification stretched from Dos Caminos to Punta Blanca. This line was reinforced by General José Toral* with 5,500 troops. Dos Caminos lies on the road to Manzanillo,* and General William R. Shafter* requested General Calixto García* to block the road to Manzanillo. However, García lacked the troops to effect the block. General García was finally able to occupy Dos Caminos on 10 July 1898.

DUFFIELD, HENRY MARTYN
(1842–1912)

Brigadier General Henry Martyn Duffield commanded some of the few volunteer troops in Fifth Corps.* Duffield led a brigade of 2,500 Michigan volunteers. They arrived in Cuban waters on the *Yale** on 27 June 1898 and disembarked at Siboney.*

Duffield was given the task of making a ''demonstration'' or diversion on 1 July at Aguadores with the assistance of the U.S. Navy while General William R. Shafter* and the main body of troops attacked El Caney* and San Juan Hill.* The purpose of the diversion was to keep Spanish general Arsenio Linares* from reinforcing El Caney and San Juan Hill. Desultory fire from the Spanish and *New York,** *Suwanee,** and *Gloucester** characterized the action. There is no evidence that the purpose of the demonstration was achieved.

On 2 July, Duffield's brigade joined General John C. Bates's* independent brigade.

In civilian life Duffield was a lawyer who had earned an officer's commission in the Civil War.

REFERENCES: R. A. Alger, *The Spanish American War* (New York: Harper & Brothers, 1901); David F. Trask, *The War with Spain in 1898* (New York: Macmillan Publishing Co., 1981).

DU PONT (ship)

The U.S.S. *Du Pont,* a torpedo boat capable of 28 knots, displaced a mere 165 tons. Commissioned in 1897, *Du Pont* showed herself a very dependable boat in 1898 cruising on blockade* duty more than 9,000 miles without mechanical failure. While on blockade, she also served as a dispatch boat. *Du Pont* joined Commodore Winfield Scott Schley's* squadron on 20 May 1898 and did reconnaissance at Cienfuegos.*

After the war *Du Pont* served at Newport.

REFERENCE: John D. Alden, *The American Steel Navy* (Annapolis, MD: Naval Institute Press, 1972).

DUPUY DE LÔME, ENRIQUE
(1851–1904)

Of French parentage, Enrique Dupuy de Lôme served in the difficult position of Spanish ambassador to the United States from 1892 until February 1898, shortly before the Spanish American War began. He served during a time of increasing tensions.

President Grover Cleveland's* policy of neutrality halted not only the U.S. Navy's drills in southern waters—lest they be construed as ''shows of force''— but also the customary courtesy visits of U.S. warships to Havana.* When William McKinley* became president, he desired to resume these courtesy visits as a gesture of friendliness to Spain, but the interruption left an awkward taste in both American and Spanish mouths; the gesture might be interpreted as hostile instead of friendly.

Due to further disturbances in Cuba, the McKinley administration felt that a reversal of Cleveland's policy was necessary. McKinley decided to send the battleship *Maine,*** resplendent in glistening white paint, to Havana as a symbol of the new U.S. Navy and to protect American interests in Cuba. Secretary of State William R. Day* approached Dupuy de Lôme with the president's proposal to send the *Maine* as a gesture of friendliness. Dupuy de Lôme agreed. No sooner was the minister's assent assured than orders were given for the *Maine* to sail.

As a patriot of Spain, Dupuy de Lôme found himself in the distasteful position of supporting the autonomous government of Cuba, an agreement of trade reciprocity between Spain and the United States, and other initiatives he held in contempt. But it was not just the initiatives he held in contempt—he had little respect for President McKinley, as well. A consummate diplomat, Dupuy de Lôme performed his ambassadorial duties faithfully even though often distasteful to him. Singled out at McKinley's first diplomatic dinner, the Spanish ambassador received a very cordial reception by McKinley. Unfortunately, Dupuy de Lôme had sent a letter to a Spanish friend, José Canalejas,* who was living in Havana. The letter was critical of McKinley. Dated December 1897, the letter characterized McKinley as a weak and waffling politician and noted that further negotiations with the insurgents would be a waste of time. This letter, intended for Canalejas, somehow found its way into the hands of the Cuban junta.*

The junta ensured that the letter also found its way into William R. Day's* hands on 9 February. Seeking confirmation of its authenticity, Day called upon Dupuy de Lôme, who acknowledged the letter as his own. Dupuy de Lôme had already cabled his resignation to Madrid. Even as Day and Dupuy de Lôme spoke, Hearst's* *New York Journal* was on the streets with an English translation of the letter under the headline, "The Worst Insult to the United States in Its History." By the end of the day, newspapers across the country were running the same type of story. Immense national indignation followed, and McKinley demanded an apology from the Spanish government.

Inasmuch as the letter represented personal, not official, opinion and surfaced as the result of a theft, many perhaps wondered at the virulent reaction. Spain, nevertheless, apologized, but not until 14 February, only two days before an explosion sent the *Maine* to the bottom of Havana harbor.

REFERENCES: Margaret Leech, *In the Days of McKinley* (New York: Harper & Row, 1959); H. Wayne Morgan, *William McKinley and His America* (Syracuse, NY: Syracuse University Press, 1963).

E

EAGAN, CHARLES PATRICK
(1841–1919)

Charles Patrick Eagan left his native Ireland at an early age and traveled to California. There he wed and joined the Washington Territorial Infantry, serving in frontier units in California and the territory of Washington. On 11 March 1898, Eagan was promoted to brigadier and commissary general, reflecting years of service in U.S. Army commissary duties.

As commissary general, Eagan proved an able administrator who struggled to improve rations to the troops. That is not to say he was an innovator—he was not. With the exception of adding canned salmon to the staples, Eagan left the rations as they had been for years, but he attempted to improve distribution and quality. Eagan's chief change was to substitute freshly slaughtered beef, which was impractical in Cuba and the Philippines, with boiled, tinned beef— a product in the army's rations inventory for over twenty years. The technology was not new, and Eagan expected it to be an economical and portable ration. He was wrong. Reports from the field indicated that some of the beef sent to Cuba could not be eaten without cooking, a process not always possible.

After the war the beef controversy* became a front-page scandal. Fueled in part by General Nelson Miles's* personal grievances and political agenda, the controversy revolved primarily around Eagan's commissary decisions. A man of volatile temper, Eagan took personally Miles's lurid charges and called Miles a liar and, in so many words, likened him to the enemies of the country. Eagan's verbal assault on the commanding general ruined the commissary general's career. The ensuing court martial verdict found Eagan guilty of insubordination. President William McKinley* decided to suspend Eagan from duty for six years but kept him on full pay. These six years lasted until Eagan's retirement.

REFERENCE: Margaret Leech, *In the Days of McKinley* (New York: Harper & Row, 1959).

EAGLE (ship)

The U.S.S. *Eagle,* like *Gloucester,* Vixen,* Mayflower,** and others, was a yacht* purchased by or loaned to the U.S. Navy for auxiliary duty in the Spanish American War. These yachts were intended as tenders to the blockade* ships, for picket duty, and for harbor patrol.

Eagle joined Admiral William T. Sampson's* blockade. On 29 April 1898, a brief skirmish at Cienfuegos* between U.S. vessels *Eagle* and *Marblehead** and the Spanish gunboats *Galicia** and *Vasco Núñez de Balboa* occurred. This engagement resulted in damage to the *Galicia*'s boilers by a 6-pounder shot from *Eagle. Eagle* also served as dispatch boat bringing orders from Admiral Sampson to Commodore Winfield S. Schley.* In fact, *Eagle* was very active in chasing wisps of smoke on the horizon and had at least two encounters with Spanish vessels: *Alfonso XIII* on 4 July and *Santo Domingo* on 12 July.

REFERENCE: H. W. Wilson, *The Downfall of Spain* (New York: Burt Franklin, 1971).

EASTERN SQUADRON

The destruction of the Spanish squadron in Manila Bay* on 1 May 1898 by the U.S. Asiatic Squadron* set in motion a series of events. Spanish Admiral Manuel de la Cámara* left Spain on 16 June with the battleship *Pelayo,** armored cruiser *Carlos V,** two auxiliary cruisers, and three destroyers. The purpose of Cámara's squadron was to relieve Manila.

Apprised the next day of Cámara's sailing, the U.S. Navy Department proposed the creation of another naval squadron, the Eastern Squadron, to sail to Spain to harass Spanish ports, combat Cámara's squadron, and eventually strengthen Commodore George Dewey* at Manila. The squadron would be composed of armored vessels from Admiral William T. Sampson's* blockade* (*Iowa,* Oregon,** and *Brooklyn**) in addition to auxiliary vessels. Secretary of the Navy John D. Long* ordered Sampson to prepare this squadron. Command was given to Commodore John C. Watson.*

At the same time, the Navy Department* leaked the existence of the Eastern Squadron with the intent that Spain would recall Cámara.

Waiting off Cuba for the arrival of General William R. Shafter's* troops, Sampson naturally argued against the formation of the Eastern Squadron. He believed it would weaken the blockade and diminish the force necessary to contend with Admiral Pascual Cervera's* squadron. Long nonetheless attempted to urge Sampson forward. With Cervera's defeat at Santiago de Cuba,* which eliminated the Caribbean threat, Sampson wanted the ships reassigned to the campaign in Puerto Rico.* Cervera's defeat and the Eastern Squadron's threat to the remaining Spanish fleet determined the recall of Cámara's squadron to Spain. Nevertheless, the Eastern Squadron remained an object of discussion until hostilities ended. Its proposed mission was to augment Dewey's power against a supposed assault on the Philippines by Germany.* Because of Sampson's delaying tactics, however, the squadron never left the Caribbean.

REFERENCE: French Ensor Chadwick, *The Relations of the United States and Spain* (New York: Russell & Russell, 1911).

ECKERT, THOMAS THOMPSON
(1825–1910)

Thomas Thompson Eckert, chairman of the board of Western Union, understood better than most people the significance of communication during war. Eckert served in numerous capacities during the Civil War as a superintendent of military telegraph. He was promoted several times, in 1865 brevetted to brigadier general of volunteers. Eckert's efforts during the Spanish American War were notable because he encouraged and enabled employee M. L. Hellings* to establish an eminently useful intelligence operation* utilizing Western Union cable operators in Havana.*

REFERENCE: G.J.A. O'Toole, *The Spanish War* (New York: W. W. Norton & Co., 1984).

EIGHTH ARMY CORPS, U.S.

One of only two U.S. Army corps* to go overseas, Eighth Corps was initiated on 3 May 1898 by a request from Secretary of War Russell A. Alger* to General Nelson Miles* for a force of 5,000 to go to Manila.* To be created from regular and volunteer units on the West Coast, the force was to be assembled at the Presidio in San Francisco.* Because of Alger's 11 May, order the planned size of the already assembling force doubled, and on 12 May General Wesley Merritt* took command of what would later (21 June) become Eighth Corps. Over 10,000 troops had assembled at San Francisco by the end of May. Eventually, Eighth Corps was to consist of 20,000 men.

In contrast to General Shafter's* Fifth Corps embarkation from Tampa,* the corps left in an organized and orderly fashion. Merritt had orders to ignore the Filipino insurrectionists, and so the reduction of Manila became an effort to defeat the Spanish through the combined efforts of Admiral George Dewey* and Merritt, denying any role to Emilio Aguinaldo* and his supporters in the Philippine Insurrection.* The first to sail were three transports containing 2,500 men under Brigadier General Thomas M. Anderson.* This contingent arrived at Manila on 30 June 1898. By the time Merritt reached Manila on 25 July, another 8,300 men had arrived. By late July, Merritt felt he was ready to attack Manila. He negotiated directly with the insurgent elements that ringed Manila, thus avoiding discussion with Aguinaldo. From 30 July until 7 August, the Spaniards nightly engaged in rifle and artillery fires, causing 12 Americans killed and numerous wounded. At Merritt's request, Dewey threatened to shell the town, which threat effectively stopped Spanish fire. Through the mediation of Edouard André,* Belgian consul, Merritt and Dewey negotiated with the Spanish commander Fermín Jáudenes* for the surrender of the city. Jáudenes was concerned about censure from Madrid and so insisted upon a token resistance. The battle commenced on 13 August and was over before lunch. The next day, on 14 August, Jáudenes signed articles of surrender.

Eighth Corps found itself in the midst of what became known as the Philippine Insurrection early in 1899.

REFERENCES: *Correspondence Relating to the War with Spain* (Washington, DC: Government Printing Office, 1902); William Thaddeus Sexton, *Soldiers the Sun* (Harrisburg, PA: Military Service Publishing Co. 1939).

ELECTIONS OF 1896

The focus of the presidential election of 1896, according to historian Gilbert C. Fite, was upon domestic issues; most importantly, the issue of order. In this respect, the 1896 election resembled other national elections during the Gilded Age. The most significant specific issue was the currency issue.

The election demonstrated, above all, that despite Grover Cleveland's* two terms as president, the Republican party was still the nation's majority party and held vast organizational and financial advantages over the Democratic party. These advantages were used to build William McKinley's prestige and discredit Bryan and the doctrine of free silver.

Foreign policy issues did not play a significant role in the presidential election. However, historian Paul Glad noted that the election was significant in one respect: the establishment of William Jennings Bryan as leader of the opposition to the coming Republican administrations. This opposition eventually extended to the issue of imperialism.

The November results gave McKinley a strong victory over Bryan: McKinley led Bryan by over 7 million popular votes, winning by a margin of 271 to 176 in the electoral college. In the congressional races, wins by Democrats and Populists cut the large Republican delegation in the U.S. House of Representatives from 244 to 204 members, but the Republican party still maintained solid control over both houses of Congress.

REFERENCES: Paul Glad, *McKinley, Bryan, and the People* (Philadelphia: Lippincott, 1964); Arthur M. Schlesinger, ed., *History of American Presidential Elections, 1789–1968* (New York: Chelsea House Publishers, 1971).

ALAN CORNISH

ELECTIONS OF 1898

Historian Walter LaFeber noted that ''the 1898 elections gave Democrats some substantial victories,'' gaining some twenty-seven seats in the U.S. House of Representatives. However, debate on U.S. participation in the Spanish American War or on postwar policy with regard to Puerto Rico* and the Philippines was not a significant factor in Democratic gains.

One important result of the elections of 1898 was the election of Theodore Roosevelt* to high political office. Roosevelt was given the Republican gubernatorial nomination in New York based upon his exploits in the Cuban campaign. As biographer Henry Pringle noted, throughout his campaign Roosevelt emphasized national issues, particularly expansionism. He frequently made public appearances with uniformed Rough Riders.* Roosevelt won a narrow victory, setting the stage for his selection as William McKinley's* vice-presidential candidate just two years later.

REFERENCES: Henry F. Pringle, *Theodore Roosevelt: A Biography* (New York: Harcourt, Brace & World, 1931, 1956); Arthur M. Schlesinger, ed., *History of American Presidential Elections, 1789–1968* (New York: Chelsea House Publishers, 1971).

ALAN CORNISH

ELECTIONS OF 1900

Issues raised by the Spanish American War, in particular those relating to the role of the United States as an expanding world power, played a significant part in the presidential election of 1900. In mid-1900, both presidential candidates, incumbent President William McKinley* and Democratic challenger William Jennings Bryan,* had privately stated that issues related to imperialism would dominate the coming campaign. As historian Walter LaFeber notes, the subsequent campaign reflected McKinley's skill of using his power as president to shape foreign policy debate advantageously.

Those Americans opposing the expanding U.S. world role faced limited options with the McKinley-Bryan race. Philip Foner and Richard Winchester noted that "the presidential election of 1900 confronted the anti-imperialist movement with a difficult political decision. Republican in political orientation and orthodox on the currency question, most of the leadership was unhappy with the choice of either Bryan or McKinley." Bryan had volunteered and served as a colonel during the Spanish American War, although he saw no combat. Additionally, he played a key role in securing passage of the Treaty of Paris* in early 1899 by influencing key Democratic senators to vote for the agreement. Certain acts, such as Bryan's statement upon receiving his party's nomination on 8 August 1900, strongly supported his view that silver and currency-related issues were more significant to victory than was the peace issue.

In November 1900, McKinley defeated William Jennings Bryan by a larger margin that he had attained in 1896. Additionally, the Democratic party fared poorly in congressional races, with their representation in the U.S. House falling from 161 to 151 members.

REFERENCES: Philip S. Foner and Richard C. Winchester, eds., *The Anti-Imperialist Reader: A Documentary History of Anti-Imperialism in the United States* (New York: Holmes & Meier, 1984); Arthur M. Schlesinger, ed., *History of American Presidential Elections, 1789–1968* (New York: Chelsea House Publishers, 1971).

ALAN CORNISH

ENDICOTT REPORT

Report of the Board on Fortifications and Other Defenses Appointed by the President (House Doc. 49, 49th Cong., 1st sess., 1886) was the result of a planning board headed by the then–secretary of war, William C. Endicott. Becoming known as the Endicott Report, it seized the attention of Congress* to the extent that an army gun factory was established and a plan put in place for restructuring and rebuilding coast defenses* and fortifications. Although Endicott's plans were never adequately funded, enough infrastructure and planning existed to commence defensive efforts quickly. Curiously, public alarm over the possibility of Spanish raids on the East Coast caused demand for coast defenses in excess of the Endicott Report's findings.

ENGINEERS, U.S. ARMY

The Corps of Engineers of the U.S. Army was one of those branches requiring special skills and education. Accordingly, the engineers had their own schools of higher education. In addition, the engineers fielded a 500-man battalion especially trained in construction work and mechanical arts. In 1897, Brigadier General James Moulder Wilson* was made chief of the Corps of Engineers. The Fifty Million Bill* provided a tremendous boost to coastal fortifications. Twenty-five construction projects were soon underway, with thirty more approved. Coast defense* also demanded the mining of harbors, which was handled by the Corps of Engineers. Although the mines had to be cleared after the war, the fortification program continued well into the next century.

Tactically, engineers accompanied combat troops, just as did the Signal Corps,* to provide combat support.

REFERENCES: Graham A. Cosmas, *An Army for Empire* (Columbia: University of Missouri Press, 1971); *The History of the U.S. Army Corps of Engineers* (Washington, DC: The Corps, 1986).

EQUIPMENT SHORTAGES

A fact and factor in war is the enormous logistical challenge that is thrust suddenly on armies, navies, and national resources. The Spanish American War was no exception. The Spanish colonial entities in which the conflicts occurred are all thousands of miles from Spain. General Ramón Blanco,* governor-general of Cuba, and Admiral Pascual Cervera,* along with General Basilio Augustín* and Admiral Patricio Montojo* of the Philippines were forced to fight with only that which they possessed on hand. Cervera sailed with insufficient ammunition, and what he did have was defective. One of his ships did not even have its guns mounted. What torpedoes were used for defense of the harbors were often ineffective and too few to matter. Nor did Cervera always have ready access to colliers. Montojo faced similar and even greater challenges because of the great distance from Spain to Manila and Manila's relative isolation. The industrial base of Spain was, however, unequal to the equipment challenge even had there been a means of delivering equipment.

The advantage the Spanish possessed, if it can be called an advantage, was their defensive positions on land. Routines had been established, and garrison life possessed some regularity. Even if that regularity was one of paucity and lack, it was an expected paucity and lack.

The U.S. Army faced a different challenge that had political ramifications: as the army swelled with recruits, there were expectations, both societal and individual, that went unfulfilled. Production of guns, butter, tentage, uniforms, and every other imaginable article doubled, then tripled, and increased further. The peacetime army maintained stocks and equipment for approximately 25,000 troops. The initial calls for volunteers of 125,000 could not be met, for although the men rapidly arrived at camps, everything from food and clothing to medical care and materials took longer. Neither the armories nor the private plants employed to augment the system could keep up with demand in the first months of the war. Utilizing funds from the Fifty Million Bill,* the quartermaster's Department, as well as the Ordnance Department, among others, instituted a contract system from private suppliers for everything from beef rations to artillery shells. Nevertheless, since there had been no stockpiles of materials, improper or substandard equipment was first issued to volunteer units. Understandably, charges of corruption were exchanged. The real culprit, however, was the rapidity of the buildup and the inability of the peacetime systems to change quickly enough to a wartime production pace. The beef controversy* was born of the same urgency to increase stocks rapidly. The absence of smokeless powder was also a result. In addition, the supply system required requisitions; that is, commanders had to request needed supplies rather than expect the various bureaus and departments to provide the needed equipment and supplies as a matter of routine. The requisition system slowed communication and ensured late delivery of goods. In fact, the Subsistence Department was the most successful of these departments partly because Commissary General Charles Eagan* scrapped the requisition system and employed camp commissary depots that were much more responsive to the needs of the units. One reason regulars were sent into combat first was that they were already equipped. Infrastructure such as warehouses and railroad sidings naturally had to wait for construction equipment and materials. However, the railroads* responded quickly, and by late May and early June 1898, the American supply problems manifested themselves in large traffic snarls and huge numbers of goods.

REFERENCE: Graham A. Cosmas, *An Army for Empire* (Columbia: University of Missouri Press, 1971).

ERICSSON (ship)

Like the *Du Pont,** the U.S.S. *Ericsson* was a small steel torpedo boat (120 tons) commissioned in 1897. Unlike *DuPont,* however, her machinery was somewhat unreliable. Nevertheless, *Ericsson* was the only U.S. torpedo boat present at the battle off Santiago de Cuba.* She distinguished herself by rescuing over 100 Spanish sailors from sinking and burning ships. By 1900 *Ericsson* was out of commission.

REFERENCE: John D. Alden, *The American Steel Navy* (Annapolis, MD: Naval Institute Press, 1972).

ERNST, OSWALD HERBERT
(1842–1926)

A graduate of the U.S. Military Academy at West Point in 1864, Oswald Herbert Ernst was an engineer officer who served during the Civil War and was brevetted captain. Ernst served in succession on the Pacific coast, in Spain, again at West Point, in the West, and at Galveston and on the Texas coast, and from 1893 to 1898 he served as superintendent at West Point.

Ernst went to Puerto Rico* in July 1898 as commander of the First Division, First Corps.* On 9 August he commanded the action at Coamo.*

After the war Ernst served on the Isthmian Canal Commission. He retired, a major general, in 1906.

REFERENCE: *Annual Report of the War Department,* (Washington, DC: Government Printing Office, 1898).

ESCARIO, FEDERICO
(1854–?)

Colonel (later General) Federico Escario led a Spanish relief column from Manzanillo* to Santiago de Cuba,* arriving the night of 3 July 1898. Escario passed through a gap in General William R. Shafter's* line, skirmished with General Calixto García's* Cuban insurgents, and marched into Santiago. Escario led 3,500 men, fewer than necessary to lift Shafter's siege. In effect, he added to the burdens of the defending force.

There was considerable consternation and some recrimination because the relief column, harassed by insurgents all the way from Manzanillo, was able to march into Santiago.

Escario served as a Spanish commissioner to negotiate the surrender of Santiago eleven days after his arrival in the city.

REFERENCE: Severo Gómez Núñez, *La Guerra Hispano-Americana,* 5 vols. (Madrid: Imprimería del Cuerpo de Artillería, 1899–1902).

ESTRADA PALMA, TOMÁS
(1835–1908)

Born in Oriente Province close to Bayamo, Cuba, Tomás Estrada Palma received his education in Havana* and also at the University of Seville, in Spain. At the commencement of the Ten Years' War* (1868–1878) Estrada Palma took the part of the rebels. Two years before the war's conclusion, the Cuban insurgents elected him president of the provisional government. Captured the next year, he spent the remainder of the war a prisoner in Spain.

After the war, Estrada Palma traveled extensively and briefly held the office of postmaster or director of postal service in Honduras, where he met his wife. Traveling again to New York, he opened a school for boys. There, in 1895, he was approached by José Martí* about rejoining the Cuban revolutionary movement. He accepted and led the Cuban junta* in New York. As leader of the junta, Estrada Palma actively worked for Cuban independence and served as

Cuban delegate to the United States. He opposed the autonomy* movement and was instrumental in ensuring the publication of the Dupuy de Lôme* letter in the *New York Journal.* Estrada Palma labored tirelessly to achieve Cuban aims.

After the war, he was the first elected president of Cuba, and it was he who leased Guantánamo to the U.S. Navy.

REFERENCES: Russell Humke Fitzgibbon, *Cuba and the United States, 1900–1935* (New York: Russell & Russell, 1964); Allan Reed Millett, *The Politics of Intervention* (Columbus: Ohio State University, 1968).

EVANS, ROBLEY DUNGLISON
(1846–1912)

Captain Robley Dunglison Evans was a graduate of the U.S. Naval Academy (1863) and was wounded in attacks on Ft. Fisher in 1865. "Fighting Bob," as he came to be known, commanded *Yorktown* at Valparaiso during frictions between the United States and Chile in 1891. He succeeded William T. Sampson* as commander of *Iowa** and fought Admiral Pascual Cervera's* fleet off Santiago de Cuba* on 3 July 1898. He also served under William S. Schley* in the Flying Squadron.*

Promoted to rear admiral in 1901, he served as commander in chief, Asiatic Station and then commander in chief, Atlantic Fleet; he also commanded the Great White Fleet on its round-the-world-cruise in 1907–1908.

REFERENCES: Robley D. Evans, *A Sailor's Log* (New York: D. Appleton & Co., 1901); Richard W. Turk, "Robley D. Evans: Master of Pugnacity," in James C. Bradford, ed., *Admirals of the New Steel Navy* (Annapolis, MD: Naval Institute Press, 1990).

EXPANSIBLE ARMY

In 1878 Brevet Major General Emory Upton* published a book of great significance that explored U.S. military policy and contrasted America's experience with that of Europe. Upton planted seeds of reform by proposing a national volunteer military force, closely linked to the regular army, similar to a federal national reserve. This national reserve, distinct from the state militia, underwent numerous variations in reaction to the political peregrinations of the time. The need for a rapidly expansible army was evident, however. Originally, planners thought that in the coming conflict with Spain, the U.S. Navy would play the major role and the U.S. Army very much a subordinate one. As a general observation, that remained true, but the degree of U.S. involvement in the conflict surpassed expectations, and some variants of Upton's ideas directly conflicted with the state militias' popular desire to get involved in the conflict.

Representative John A. T. Hull* sponsored what became known as the Hull Bill to legislate a permanent solution to the problem of how to expand the army effectively. The bill proposed increasing the regular army from less than 30,000 to over 100,000 troops. However, a coalition of Populists, who feared the use of federal troops in labor disputes, and southern Democrats, smarting yet from Reconstruction, joined with pro-state militia or National Guard forces to defeat the bill. The National Guard* rightly believed that had the Hull Bill passed, they would have been excluded from the conflict. The pressures from the National Guard and its allies foisted a larger volunteer force on the army than it wanted or required. Although the army did get an expansible regular army, it came too late to accomplish its goals of having a force of regulars and a trained reserve for rapid mobilization. Further hampering the effort was congressional stinginess, which resulted in insufficient equipment for the troops thus mobilized.

REFERENCE: Graham A. Cosmas, "From Order to Chaos: The War Department, the National Guard, and Military Policy, 1898," *Military Affairs* 29 (Summer 1965): 105–121.

EXPANSIONISM

Expansionism has a tattered and soiled reputation today (and among many it did in 1898, as well), but it was once a heady, robust world view. Like a second installment of Manifest Destiny, expansionists like Theodore Roosevelt,* brothers Henry and Brooks Adams,* John Hay,* and Rudyard Kipling* expounded an American assertiveness mingled with Anglo-Saxon virtues and Darwin's natural selection that urged not just an expansion of America's power, influence, and commerce but also the sowing of the seeds of American notions of order, liberty, and democracy. Expansionism for the believers was not just increased power and commercial advantage, although it was certainly that; it was also a duty approached with missionarylike zeal. In their writings and pronouncements, the expansionists appealed to American ideals. Roosevelt was perhaps their most well known spokesman, but others' influences were even more potent. President McKinley* explained the annexation of the Philippines in the gospel jargon of the expansionists. Expansionism pulsated healthily until World War I, when it began to acquire the rancid taste of rapacity and pain.

REFERENCES: Walter LeFeber, *The New Empire* (Ithaca, NY: Cornell University Press, 1963); Ephraim K. Smith, "William McKiley's Enduring Legacy: The Historiographical Debate on the Taking of the Philippine Islands," in James C. Bradford, ed., *Crucible of Empire* (Annapolis, MD: Naval Institute Press, 1993).

F

FAJARDO, PUERTO RICO

Fajardo was the original destination of General Nelson Miles's* expeditionary force. However, en route Miles received intelligence that the Spanish expected his landing at Fajardo, so he landed at Guánica* instead. Word of this change did not reach Generals James H. Wilson* and Theodore Schwan* until 26 July 1898. Wilson and his transports then steamed to Guánica.

Fajardo is about 30 miles east of San Juan* in the northeast of the island.

FIFTH ARMY CORPS, U.S.

As the U.S. Army prepared and then developed plans during the war, eight corps were created in the first weeks of May 1898. Fifth Corps, with headquarters at Tampa,* was charged specifically with preparing for the invasion of Cuba. For this reason, it was composed largely of regulars. General William R. Shafter* commanded, and his mission, which he received in a series of orders given the last week in May, was to capture or destroy the Spanish garrison at Santiago* and aid in the defeat of Admiral Pascual Cervera's* squadron. The orders arrived only hours before departure, resulting in such confusion that much-needed equipment remained on the docks.

Composed of infantry regulars plus volunteer units like the Rough Riders,* Fifth Corps troops were all generally well trained and well led. Nevertheless, none had ever participated in such a large-scale effort. Mistakes were made, but the troops learned quickly. Thirty-one transports, most small, conveyed the expeditionary force to Cuban waters with naval escort. Landing with no Spanish resistance at Siboney* and Daiquirí,* the Fifth Corps fought successively and successfully at Las Guásimas,* El Caney,* San Juan Hill,* and Aguadores and engaged in sundry smaller actions in the environs of Santiago.

Equipment shortages* and supply shortages created self-imposed hardships. Much of the difficulty lay in inadequate transport. Rations, stoves, tentage, and artillery sat on the beach or in steamers' holds without means of distribution. Some failures represent planning omissions in the War Department.

Las Guásimas was fought on 24 June, El Caney on 1 July, San Juan on 1–3 July, and Aguadores on 1–2 July. Santiago was formally occupied by Fifth Corps on 17 July. Besides fighting the Spanish, Fifth Corps also battled diseases* like yellow fever.* By the end of July, Fifth Corps's death rate to disease reached fifteen casualties per day. Fifth Corps officially disbanded 3 October 1898.

REFERENCE: Graham A. Cosmas, *An Army for Empire* (Columbia: University of Missouri Press, 1971).

FIFTY MILLION BILL

By 6 March 1898 President William McKinley* faced a dilemma. He wanted peace with Spain, but the rising martial spirit of American citizens and their elected representatives as a result of the destruction of the *Maine,*￼ the revelation of the Dupuy de Lôme* letter, and the inflammation of public sympathy for perceived sufferings of Cuba under the yoke of Spain made war a likelihood. McKinley felt that to prepare for war would be to precipitate it, whereas not to prepare would mean disaster should war come. He concluded that the United States must arm itself and on 6 March sent for Representative Joseph G. Cannon,* chairman of the House Appropriations Committee.

McKinley explained to Cannon the need for extraordinary funding to prepare for war. Cannon suggested that he send a message to Congress asking for $50 million. McKinley liked the amount and the idea of the appropriation, but he balked at initiating the action himself. The president was concerned that his sponsorship might color his efforts at peace. Cannon then volunteered to assure the passage of the bill.

Cannon had anticipated such a request and had already determined that monies in the amount of $50 million were available without resorting to additional taxes or bonds. McKinley liked Cannon's idea; in particular, he like the message it sent to the European powers—that the United States had money to spare for such purposes.

Introduced on 8 March, the bill came up for a vote on 9 March, when it passed the House 313 to 0 (44 abstentions). There had been over seventy speeches in its favor. The Senate voted 76 to 0 with far fewer speeches, however. Stewart L. Woodford,* U.S. minister to Spain, reported from Madrid that the Spanish were "simply stunned" by the one-sidedness of the vote. The Fifty Million Bill did indeed send a message to Europe.

The passage of the Fifty Million Bill created an almost instantaneous impact. Telegrams had already been sent in search of warships a-building and auxiliaries.* Some $18 million was spent on ship purchases, and over $29 million from the bill was spent by the U.S. Navy. The bill was somewhat confining, however, in that it specified that the War Department was to expend the money for defensive measures; at least, Secretary Russell A. Alger* interpreted the bill thus.

This interpretation hurt the army in that surplus stocks of arms and equipment were initially insufficient for the U.S. offensive action.

REFERENCES: Lewis L. Gould, *The Spanish American War and President McKinley* (Lawrence: University of Kansas Press, 1982); William Rea Gwinn, *Uncle Joe Cannon, Archfoe of Insurgency* (NP: Bookman Associates, 1957); David F. Trask, *The War with Spain in 1898* (New York: Macmillan Publishing Co., 1981).

FILIBUSTERS AND FILIBUSTERING

Filibusters, by definition, are individuals or groups that illegally take part in military expeditions on foreign soil. Cuban insurgents* welcomed financial aid and munitions from the United States, and from 1850 through the war in 1898, various American-financed but not government-sanctioned expeditions journeyed or tried to journey to Cuba to provide both aid and arms. Some were merely gun runners, but others consisted of large contingents of armed troops. The *Virginius* affair* of 1873 was a particularly inflammatory example. Another was "Dynamite Johnny" O'Brien,* who aboard *Dauntless* had been an agent in several expeditions in Cuba and also Panama.

For Cuban leadership, filibustering was a dilemma. The Cubans wanted and needed the aid, but their leaders were wary that filibustering might lead to intervention.

REFERENCE: Philip S. Foner, *The Spanish-Cuban-American War and the Birth of American Imperialism, 1895–1902* (New York: Monthly Review Press, 1972).

FIRES, IN SHIPS

All conflicts present technological lessons as well as geopolitical ones. In 1898, many ships were still in a transitional phase between earlier nineteenth-century notions and practice and later twentieth-century theories of damage control design. In many Spanish vessels wooden cabinetry, deckhouses, fittings, and decks prevailed. American shells splintered these combustible materials and ignited them, creating conflagrations that wreaked great damage in *Infanta María Teresa,* *Vizcaya,* and *Almirante Oquendo.* These lessons were not lost on numerous naval observers from Germany and France and, of course, on the combatants themselves.

REFERENCE: H. W. Wilson, *The Downfall of Spain* (New York: Burt Franklin, 1971).

FIRST U.S. VOLUNTEER CAVALRY.
See ROUGH RIDERS.

FISH, HAMILTON
(1808–1893)

Politician and statesman Hamilton Fish was born in New York. He graduated from Columbia College in 1827 and studied law in the office of Peter A. Jay. Fish ran for the New York State Assembly unsuccessfully as a Whig in 1834. He was elected to one term in Congress in 1842 and was elected governor of

New York in 1848, serving one term. His progressive administration saw the expansion of roads, the development of the canal system, and the advent of public education. Fish then served as a senator, from 1852 until 1858. He transferred his allegiance to the newly formed Republican party after the demise of the Whigs and backed Abraham Lincoln throughout the Civil War. Fish served reluctantly as President Ulysses Grant's secretary of state through both terms, from 1869 until 1877. He was good at managing the business of the Department of State and in time became the steady, moderate influence lacking in other areas of the Grant administration.

One thorn in the side of Secretary of State Fish was Spain. In November 1873 the steamer *Virginius,* under American registry and flying the American flag, was taken prisoner by a Spanish gunboat somewhere between Cuba and Jamaica. The ship belonged to a pro-Cuban revolutionary committee out of New York City and, when seized, was attempting to show support for Cuban revolutionaries (an insurrection had broken out in Cuba in 1868). Its captain and crew—fifty-four in all, mostly American—were summarily executed. Tensions grew as Fish demanded justice, and through a set of ultimatums, war was almost declared. It came so close that the U.S. minister to Madrid, Daniel Sickles, had already asked for his papers to return to Washington. President Grant assembled a small naval flotilla at Key West* for possible action. In February 1874, the new minister to Spain, Caleb Cushing, secured the indemnity claims for the loss of *Virginius* by recognizing the new Spanish government headed by Alphonso XII.

Secretary of State Fish also wanted the issue of Cuba settled. If Spain wanted good relations with United States, the pacification of Cuba was important. These instructions were passively received by the Spanish government, and little was accomplished. Fish finally asked for reforms within the Spanish government of Cuba leading to home rule and the "effective abolition of slavery." Again, the Spanish government vacillated on these issues, at the same time sending huge amounts of military aid to successfully crush the rebellion by late 1876. Fish was able to gain some satisfaction in settling claims for the loss of *Virginius,* however. On the larger issue of Cuban autonomy, he was less successful: It would take twenty more years, with the culmination of the war with Spain, to free Cuba.

Curiously, Fish's grandson, also named Hamilton, was the first Rough Rider* casualty in Cuba.

REFERENCE: Allan Nevins, "Hamilton Fish," *The Inner History of the Grant Administration* (New York: Dodd, Meade & Co., 1936).

RICHARD W. PEUSER

FLAGLER, DANIEL WEBSTER
(1835–1899)

Brigadier General Daniel Webster Flagler was a West Pointer who served his entire career in the technical bowels of the Ordnance Department. He had commanded virtually every arsenal in the United States and had weighty expertise in the highly technical specialty of ordnance. Because of his acknowledged abilities, he was promoted over more senior colonels to become chief of ordnance in 1891.

Flagler worked indefatigably with engineers to design and build the coast defense system.* He was also instrumental in the development of rapid response for weapons of all calibers. Without any advance warning at all, Flagler negotiated contracts for rifles, ammunition, and artillery. He expressed dissatisfaction with the higher costs associated with private contractors, and after the war, he urged a greater reliance on increased-capacity government arsenals. One of his chief frustrations was the failure to secure smokeless powder.

REFERENCE: Graham A. Cosmas, *An Army for Empire* (Columbia: University of Missouri Press, 1971).

FLEET-IN-BEING.
See MAHAN, ALFRED THAYER.

FLYING SQUADRON

Initially, in planning and strategy, U.S. naval forces were disposed to blockade* Cuba and to protect U.S. territory. The concern expressed in a 15 March 1898 meeting of a board of defense composed of Theodore Roosevelt* and several senior naval officers was that the limited capital resources of the U.S. Navy might be used only defensively on the eastern seaboard, not offensively. Concern about the Spanish *Pelayo** and *Carlos V** heightened the inherent conflict between offense and defense. Naval strategists argued for an aggressive offense. Politicians and others nervously counted possible lost votes if a Spanish raiding squadron should bombard the coast. The result of these tensions was a compromise strategy—at least initially—in which the U.S. Army units such as Coast Artillery and coast defense forces* would protect U.S. harbors in the east. In addition, the naval forces would be split into two: a blockading force and a Flying Squadron. The latter created in orders of 17 March would be based at Hampton Roads, Virginia.* The commander of the Flying Squadron was Commodore Winfield Scott Schley,* and the squadron originally counted *Brooklyn,** *Massachusetts,** *Texas,** and *New Orleans** among other smaller vessels. Orders dictated that the squadron was to patrol from Maine to the Delaware Capes.

The fears motivating the origins of the Flying Squadron quickly passed, and two months later, on 15 May, the squadron was ordered to Charleston, South Carolina, to reinforce the Cuban blockade or, if need arose, to protect Key West.*

When Admiral Pascual Cervera* began to steam toward the Antilles, the conservative naval strategy seemed less useful and Schley was ordered south to protect transports converging on Tampa* for the expeditionary force; he was also to locate Cervera's squadron. Schley's ships then participated in the search for the Spanish combatant at Cienfuegos* and later at Santiago de Cuba.* When the Spanish were finally located at Santiago, the Flying Squadron merged with Admiral William T. Sampson's squadron.

Schley's slowness and unexplained hesitancy at Cienfuegos and the voyage to Santiago precipitated some of the conflict later evident in the Sampson-Schley Controversy.*
REFERENCES: French Ensor Chadwick, *The Relations of the United States and Spain* (New York: Russell & Russell, 1911); H. W. Wilson, *The Downfall of Spain* (New York: Burt Franklin, 1971).

FOOTE (ship)

The U.S.S. *Foote* of 142 tons was a torpedo boat that served with *Du Pont*,* *Ericsson*,* and others in the blockade* of Cuba. *Foote* was also launched in 1897, and Admiral William T. Sampson's* orders were for *Foote* to attempt to torpedo the enemy—an event that never occurred. *Foote* was out of commission in 1900.

FORAKER, JOSEPH BENSON
(1846–1917)

Senator Joseph Benson Foraker came from agrarian Ohio roots and enlisted at age sixteen as a private in the 89th Ohio Infantry. By war's end, he had risen to brevet captain. He studied law and gravitated to politics, at first local and then national, becoming a senator and serving as such from 1897 to 1903. Foraker twice presented William McKinley's* name in nomination for the presidency: 1896 and 1900.

Foraker was a hawk, but he was also a proponent of the Cuban Republic and wrote an amendment to McKinley's intervention resolution submitted on 13 April 1898, and passed three days later, that recognized the Cuban Republic. Although an expansionist, Foraker had scruples. The Foraker Amendment of February 1899, tacked onto an army appropriations bill, was designed, like the Teller Amendment, to restrain American avarice and economic activity in Cuba.
REFERENCE: Joseph B. Foraker, *Notes of a Busy Life* (Cincinnati: Stewart & Kidd, 1916).

FORT SAN ANTONIO, PHILIPPINES

In the Spanish defense of Manila,* Fort San Antonio received a buildup of artillery because Governor-General Basilio Augustín Dávila* perceived the fort as a prime point of attack. The fort was south of Manila along a string of entrenchments and fortifications called the Zapote line. The fort was on the waterside, and fortifications stretched westward to Blockhouse 14. Filipino and American pressures at the fort justified Augustín's concerns. On the night of 29 July 1898, Americans occupied positions between Augustín's anchor at the fort and blockhouse 14.

Over the next few weeks, U.S. naval commander George Dewey,* General

Wesley Merritt,* and Fermín Jáudenes* worked out a scenario for a somewhat staged defense of Manila with token bombardments, the fort being one of these targets. On 13 August, General Francis V. Greene* led the attack on the fort following a naval bombardment. When U.S. troops assaulted the fort, they found it vacant.

REFERENCE: *Annual Report of the War Department, 1898* (Washington, DC: Government Printing Office, 1898).

FORTS VERSUS SHIPS

One of the strategic challenges facing any amphibious attempt to land troops or to force a harbor is to assess the strength of harbor fortifications and potential artillery. Ships were expensive and vulnerable to fire from forts. Much of the impetus to the coast defense* of the United States came from these strategic concerns, which, of course, affected tactics. It was one thing to be able to silence a fort's guns, but something else again to destroy a fort. Superior fire can silence a fort, but only accurate fire, actually destroying guns and mounts, can destroy a fort. Destruction of forts in the nineteenth century by seaborne artillery was difficult. Indeed, one of the chief reasons Havana* was not chosen as a primary naval objective was the effective presence of fortress artillery. The operant word is effective, for had the Spanish been able to be more effective in the placement and utilization of batteries at the entrances to Manila Bay,* a very different outcome might have been realized.

The Spanish also had smokeless powder that did not give away the location of their batteries and thus in a sense hid the batteries from gunners on American ships. At Matanzas,* for example, well-directed fire from shore proved deadly. Other small engagements demonstrated that a modern, well-served artillery battery in a fortification was not only very effective against naval forces but an effective deterrent as well.

REFERENCE: H. W. Wilson, *The Downfall of Spain* (New York: Burt Franklin, 1971).

FORUM.

See ADAMS, BROOKS.

FRANCE

France played a low-key diplomatic role in the crisis of 1898. Because France possessed American colonies, Madrid thought that the monarchial principle would bind France to its cause, as it would Russia and Germany.* Germany, however, wanted France to lead European diplomatic intervention. Tensions between Great Britain* and the other European powers as well as concerns about the American intentions suggested caution. Distrust between Russia and Great Britain and Germany and rising apprehensions in the United States encouraged France to be dilatory. French ministers opposed the creation of another naval power in the Pacific, and while Berlin awaited an initiative from Paris, Paris,

St. Petersburg, and Rome looked to Berlin for leadership. Germany found no sure footing for intervention, and so nothing happened.

During the peace process, France was discussed as a possible custodian of some of Spain's former possessions.

REFERENCE: J. Fred Rippy, "The European Powers and the Spanish American War," *James Sprunt Historical Studies* 19 (1927): 22–52.

FRY, JOSEPH
(1826–1873)

Born in Tampa* around 1828, Joseph Fry joined the U.S. Navy in 1841. Promoted to lieutenant in 1855, he was unable to secure a commission with the Confederate navy and so opted for a command in the army.

After the war, Fry became an adventurer, with his most notable and last fling the command of *Virginius*. The voyage was a filibuster* to supply munitions and soldiers to Cuban insurgents.* Fry gathered a crew for *Virginius* and sailed on 23 October 1873. The ship ran afoul of the Spanish gunboat *Tornado* and the filibustering Fry hove to and surrendered. The Spanish tried Fry and the *Virginius* crew as pirates, and on 7 November, Fry and thirty-six others were placed before a firing squad.

The effects of the seizure and executions were strong. Of course, there was a legal issue—were the captain and crew of *Virginius* pirates? But the larger issue was the developing rift in Spanish American relations that erupted into the Spanish American War twenty-five years later, which had a brief rehearsal in the *Virginius* affair.* Reconstruction, race, republicanism in Spain, and a moderation of public opinion played an important role in 1873 to defuse the conflict. Many of these same issues had an opposite effect in 1898.

In 1875 the Spanish government paid an indemnity of $80,000 because of the *Virginius*.

REFERENCE: Richard H. Bradford, *The Virginius Affair* (Boulder: Colorado Associated University Press, 1980).

FRYE, WILLIAM PIERCE
(1831–1911)

Born in Maine, William Pierce Frye studied law at Bowdoin and became a member of Congress in 1871. Elected senator ten years later, he served as president *pro tempore* from 1896 to 1901.

Frye came from one of the foremost maritime states in the union and represented well his state's trading and shipbuilding concerns. Partly because of this interest, Frye was an ardent expansionist who argued for the annexation of Hawaii.* He also served on President William McKinley's Peace Commission,* along with William R. Day,* Cushman Davis, Whitelaw Reid,* and George Gray.* True to form, Frye, Davis, and Reid pushed for the annexation of the Philippines. It was Frye who suggested to McKinley on 30 October 1898 that a concessionary payment be made to Spain to secure the Philippines.

REFERENCE: Whitelaw Reid, *Making Peace with Spain: The Diary of Whitelaw Reid* (Austin: University of Texas Press, 1965).

FUNSTON, FREDERICK
(1865–1917)

Another Ohio army officer, Frederick Funston actually grew up in Kansas. He was on the Death Valley Expedition as a special agent of the Department of Agriculture in 1890, and he traveled down the Yukon River alone by canoe in 1893–1894.

In 1896 Funston joined the Cuban insurgents* as a captain of artillery. He was rapidly promoted to major and participated in a variety of campaigns with Generals Máximo Gómez* and Calixto García.*

Upon the outbreak of the Spanish American War, Funston returned to the United States, where he was placed in command of the Twentieth Kansas Volunteer Infantry, which was sent to the Philippines. There he fought in the campaign of General Arthur MacArthur* in northern Luzon. Promoted to brigadier general in 1899, he participated in the Philippine Insurrection,* where he distinguished himself through bravery and initiative. He was awarded the Congressional Medal of Honor in 1900.

Funston later served as commander of U.S. troops on the Mexican border in pursuit of Pancho Villa.

REFERENCES: Thomas W. Crouch, *A Leader of Volunteers: Frederick Funston and the 20th Kansas in the Philippines, 1898–1899* (Lawrence, KS: Coronado Press, 1984); Thomas W. Crouch, *A Yankee Guerrillero: Frederick Funston and the Cuban Insurrection, 1896–1897* (Memphis: Memphis State University Press, 1975); Frederick Funston, *Memories of Two Wars: Cuban and Philippine Experiences* (New York: Scribner's, 1911).

FUROR (ship)

The Spanish destroyer *Furor,* built 1896 and displacing 370 tons, was of the *Terror** class and sailed across the Atlantic Ocean with Admiral Cervera's* fleet in 1898. The others in this small fleet included *Infanta María Teresa,* *Vizcaya,* *Cristóbal Colón,* *Almirante Oquendo,* and *Plutón.** Used by Admiral Cervera for intelligence and scout work during May, *Furor* barely escaped a scrap with *Harvard** in Martinique.*

During the naval battle of 3 July 1898 off Santiago de Cuba,* *Furor* and *Plutón* emerged last from the harbor entrance at the tailend of Cervera's fleet. Almost immediately, they became the targets of *Texas,* *Iowa,* *Indiana,* and *Brooklyn** simultaneously. *Furor*'s real nemesis, however, was the converted yacht *Gloucester** commanded by Lieutenant Commander Richard Wainwright.* *Gloucester* pummeled *Furor,* crippling her machinery and decimating her crew, while receiving no hits in return. *Furor* surrendered, aflame with her crew in the water mangled by the still-spinning screws. After a series of explosions, *Furor* sank.

REFERENCE: Christian de Saint Hubert and Carlos Alfaro Zaforteza, ''The Spanish Navy of 1898,'' *Warship International* 7 (1980): 39–59, 110–119.

G

GALICIA (ship)

The Spanish torpedo boat *Galicia,* of 530 tons, was launched in 1891 and had a speed of 18 knots. *Galicia* was stationed in Cuba at Cienfuegos* Cuba when on 29 April 1898 the U.S.S. *Marblehead** and *Eagle** attacked the Spanish naval forces. *Galicia*'s boilers were hit by *Eagle,* causing much damage.

On 12 June U.S.S. *Yankee** tangled with *Galicia* off Cienfuegos, but the latter escaped with the help of shore batteries and the *Vasco Núñez de Balboa.*
REFERENCE: Augustín Rodríguez González, *"Operaciones menores en Cuba, 1898,"* *Revista de Historia Naval* 3, no. 9 (1985): 125–146.

GARCÍA DE POLAVIEJA Y CASTILLO, CAMILO (1838–1914)

General Camilo García de Polavieja y Castillo rose through the ranks of the Spanish army through merit. Polavieja served twice in Cuba and was distinguished for his military acumen. In December 1896, Polavieja was named governor-general of the Philippines. He executed José Rizal* in December and by February had destroyed the Filipino military capabilities in almost sixty battles. Conventional warfare was not an option for the insurgents. Polavieja returned to Spain in April 1897.
REFERENCE: Gregorio F. Zaide, *The Philippine Revolution* (Manila: Modern Book Company, 1968).

GARCÍA ÍÑIGUEZ, CALIXTO (1839–1898)

Calixto García Íñiguez was the Cuban insurgent who perhaps had greatest impact on the Spanish American War as it was fought by the American army—some of it unintentional.

First, Calixto was the "García" of Andrew Rowan's* message. The Military

Information Division* sent Rowan to García for intelligence, at which the Cubans excelled. When Elbert Hubbard published Rowan's story it became a bestseller, and García became one of the best-known participants of the war. García also provided maps and information about the Spanish and sent officers with Rowan to aid in coordination and strategy.

Second, García was essential to the planning efforts of General William R. Shafter,* who needed intelligence on terrain and avenues of approach. García was able to provide much of this information and was instrumental in the planned assault on Santiago.* It was García who suggested the landing at Daiquirí,* for example, which occurred on 22 June 1898.

Third, García and his army were to provide valuable aid in the battle of El Caney* and at Santiago. García's men were to keep Spanish reinforcements out of the battle. Unfortunately, García was unable to interdict Colonel Federico Escario and a relief column of Spanish troops and supplies. Shafter blamed García with negligence. García, in his defense to Máximo Gómez,* pointed out that by obeying orders to maintain contact with the Americans, he was unable to interdict Escario.* García offered to send General Jesús Rabí with a force of insurgents to stop Escario, but Shafter, concerned about the pending attack on Santiago, refused to weaken the attacking force.

García was embroiled in the forefront of developing Cuban American friction. Motivated by racial tensions, Shafter and other commanders deliberately ignored the insurrectionists, minimized their contributions, and, in general, snubbed the Cubans. In fairness to Shafter, he also had great difficulty working with the U.S. Navy; it could be said that he lacked an effective mechanism to operate jointly with any other command. The frictions came to a head when Shafter disallowed García and his army any participation in the capitulation of Santiago. In frustration, García protested Shafter's treatment by resigning. Leonard Wood* was able to smooth the relationship somewhat, and García agreed to visit the United States late in 1898. He visited with President William McKinley,* attended public functions, and then died suddenly on 11 December 1898 in Washington, D.C.

REFERENCES: Philip S. Foner, *The Spanish-Cuban-American War and the Birth of American Imperialism, 1895–1902* (New York: Monthly Review Press, 1972); José Antonio Medel, *The Spanish American War and Its Results* (Havana: P. Fernández & Co., 1932); David F. Trask, *The War with Spain in 1898* (New York: Macmillan Publishing Co., 1981).

GARRETSON, GEORGE ARMSTRONG
(1844–1916)

Born in Ohio, Brigadier General George Armstrong Garretson graduated from the U.S. Military Academy in 1867 and served in a variety of locales until resigning in 1870. He then served in the Ohio National Guard. By profession, he was a banker.

During the Spanish American War he was promoted to brigadier general of volunteers on 27 May 1898. He was honorably discharged on 30 November. Garretson commanded U.S. forces during the campaign in Puerto Rico.* On 26 July 1898, he led the attack against Yauco,* the first engagement in Puerto Rico. United States forces were able to occupy the town on 28 July. After the attack, Garretson was to have marched a column north to Adjuntas* and ultimately Arecibo.*

REFERENCE: *Correspondence Relating to the War with Spain,* 2 vols. (Washington, DC: Government Printing Office, 1902).

GATLING GUN

Invented by Doctor Richard Jordan Gatling in 1862, the Gatling gun was used as a close support machine gun for the first time during the Spanish American War. Captain John H. Parker organized a gatling gun detachment to be included in Brigadier General William R. Shafter's* Fifth Army Corps.* About 150 Gatling guns were in the service of the War Department* at the outbreak of the war, and of those, a consignment of 15 was sent to Tampa* for the expedition to Santiago,* Cuba.

During the fighting at El Caney,* Parker's men engaged four Gatlings, each carrying 10,000 rounds of ammunition on its carriage. At a distance of 600 to 800 yards, the guns fired 500 shots a minute upon the Spanish blockhouses at San Juan Hill.* With the assistance of the Tenth Calvary and Roosevelt's Rough Riders,* the Gatlings flushed the Spaniards from their trenches. By the end of the day, the ground was riddled with fallen enemy who could not avoid the machine gunfire.

During the siege of Santiago, the Gatlings were used successfully in conjunction with two automatic guns and a dynamite gun.

After the war, the Gatling gun received enormous praise for the important role it played in the conflict. General Shafter stated in his official report on the assault on San Juan Hill that "in this part of the field most efficient service was rendered by . . . the Gatling Gun Detachment." Theodore Roosevelt* praised Parker as deserving "more credit than any other one man in the campaign. . . . He had the rare good judgment and foresight to see the possibilities of the machine guns."

REFERENCES: Fairfax Downey, *Sound of the Guns* (New York: D. McKay, 1956); Paul Wahl and Donald R. Toppel, *The Gatling Gun* (New York: Arco, 1965).

MITCHELL YOCKELSON

GEIER (ship)

A light cruiser in the navy of Germany,* *Geier* was launched in 1894 with an 1,888-ton displacement. *Geier* sailed for the West Indies from Kiel on 9 December 1897, arriving at Port-au-Prince, Haiti, on 7 January 1898 in the wake of the incarceration of Emile Lüders, a German national in Haiti.* The intent of *Geier*'s voyage was to enforce German demands of an indemnity. However, the voyage of the *Geier* augmented tensions in the Caribbean because it was known that Germany desired a coaling station in the West Indies and was more favorably inclined toward Spain* than the United States in the controversy over Cuba. Of course, Germany had designs in China* and the Pacific as well. Fitzhugh Lee,* consul general at Havana,* advised President William McKinley* that the *Geier*'s visit to Havana would provide an excellent pretext for sending a U.S. warship there. The *Geier,* therefore, provided the pretext for sending the U.S.S. *Maine*** to Havana. *Geier* was captured by the U.S. Navy in 1917 and sunk 1918.

REFERENCE: G.J.A. O'Toole, *The Spanish War* (New York: W. W. Norton & Co., 1984).

GERMAN ASIATIC SQUADRON

Under the command of Vice Admiral Otto von Diederichs,* the German Asiatic Squadron assembled piecemeal at Manila* from May 1898 through the month of June. When all five ships arrived, they represented a stronger force than that available to Commodore George Dewey* until the arrivals of the monitors *Monterey*** and *Monadnock*** on 4 August and 16 August, respectively. The unnecessary strength of the German Squadron and Diederichs's insistence upon what he perceived were his rights under Dewey's blockade caused potentially serious misunderstandings that still echoed three decades later. These misunderstandings continued to be a source of friction between the United States and Germany.*

The German Squadron consisted of *Kaiser, Irene,*** Cormoran,*** Kaiserin Augusta,*** and *Prinzess Wilhelm.* The squadron's mission was to protect German citizens and German economic interests as well as to ensure Germany's share in any dismemberment of the Spanish empire.

REFERENCE: Thomas A. Baily, "Dewey and the Germans at Manila Bay," *The American Historical Review* 45 (October 1939): 59–81.

GERMANY

European nonbelligerents jostled each other during the Spanish American War not only about competing interests in the two geographic arenas—Cuba and the Caribbean and the Philippines and the Pacific—but also within larger spheres of political ambition. The balance of power precariously teetered, and in doing so gave the advantage to the United States in a succession of diplomatic initiatives and communiqués. Germany was integral to the balancing act of the Europeans.

Essentially, Germany wished to conserve the principle of monarchy. The evident instability of the Spanish monarchy and the potentially threatening transatlantic power of the United States combined to sound warnings in European capitals. In Germany, these warnings could have led to precipitate actions had it not also been for the economic and political realities. Germany's trade with the United States exceeded that of any other European nation excepting only Great Britain.* The recently enacted Dingley Tariff authorized the president to lower duties on a nation's goods upon the principle of reciprocal concessions. Thus Germany labored to maintain its monarchial and colonial desires without the economic unpleasantness of offending the United States. In spring 1898, Spain took the lead in asking Germany to head a European demonstration of support for the principles of monarchy. Bernhard von Bülow,* German foreign secretary, sought consensus among the nations of Austria-Hungary,* France,* and Germany. The initiative stalled when none of these nations would take the first step. Germany next considered papal arbitration as plausible, but Spain rejected arbitration as a basis for surrendering Cuba. Afraid of angering the United States openly and wary of the motives of Great Britain, Germany hesitated. The emperor suggested the possibility of intervention, but he backed away from his own suggestion in favor of mediation.

The tensions in the Philippines* added heat to the stew. Vice Admiral Otto von Diederichs,* commander of the German Asiatic Squadron,* caused Commodore George Dewey* to be apprehensive about German intentions. Dewey's apprehensions, ostensibly justified, proved groundless. Spain suggested that Germany, France, and Russia assume control over Manila.* Bülow found St. Petersburg and Paris uninterested. German diplomats, however, also came to the conclusion that any solution forthcoming must be made through an understanding with the United States, and so these German initiatives also came to naught. Great Britain complicated these negotiations through a propaganda campaign and clever rumors intended to sympathize with the Americans while painting Germany as the American nemesis. These British efforts had the effect of encouraging Germany to reach an understanding with the United States. Neither temptations proffered by Spain nor the Filipino insurgents induced Germany to adventure in the Philippines. Instead, Germany seemed more interested in coaling* stations and spoils from the breakup of the Spanish empire. There was an accommodation with the United States so that both would profit from Spain's colonial dismemberment.

Therefore, Germany's involvement in the Spanish American War followed two phases. First, there were early attempts to contain the United States and protect the status quo. International alliances and joint statements were considered to head off the United States and to protect the monarchic principles. The lack of cooperation of the other European powers frustrated this goal. The second phase was Germany's efforts to acquire more coaling stations and cable stations as a colonial and maritime power. On 4 February 1899, Germany agreed to pay Spain twenty-five million pesetas for the Caroline, Pelew, and Ladrone islands (minus Guam).

REFERENCES: J. Fred Rippy, "The European Powers and the Spanish American War," *James Sprunt Historical Studies* 19, no. 2 (1927): 22–52; Lester B. Shippee, "Germany and the Spanish American War," *The American Historical Review* 30 (July 1925): 754–777.

GIBRALTAR

Gibraltar—the rock and the straits—served two minor functions in the Spanish American War. As an English possession, Gibraltar was used by U.S. intelligence operations* to ferry agents in and out of Europe. Its second role was strategic: One of the naval plans for prosecuting the war involved sending a U.S. naval squadron into Spanish waters to harass the Spanish coast. Such a squadron in a third theater would require sufficient strength to negotiate Gibraltar if a Spanish contingent should find it there.

GLASS, HENRY
(1844–1908)

Henry Glass first saw the light of day in Hopkinsville, Kentucky. He graduated from the U.S. Naval Academy in 1863 and saw action from 1863 until 1865. After the Civil War, he progressed through the ranks to command various ships and naval yards, mostly in the Pacific. In May 1898 he took command of the *Charleston** and, en route to Manila,* captured the Ladrone Islands (Guam*). Glass was port captain of Manila from August through October 1898. He was promoted to rear admiral in 1901 and commanded the Pacific Station in 1903–1904.

REFERENCE: L. W. Walker, "Guam's Seizure by the United States in 1898," *Pacific Historical Review* 14 (March 1945): 1–12.

GLOUCESTER (ship)

On 9 March 1898 the U.S. Congress passed a $50 million defense measure, almost $30 million of which went to increase the size of the U.S. Navy. By the end of the war, 102 vessels had been purchased. Among these was J. Pierpont Morgan's yacht,* the lovely *Corsair*. Converted into the armed yacht *Gloucester, Corsair* participated heroically in the Battle of Santiago* on 3 July 1898 by plunging into the fray and vigorously attacking the Spanish destroyers *Plutón** and *Furor.** *Gloucester* attacked in spite of being unarmored and with significantly less fire power than either Spanish vessel. As a result, the *Gloucester*'s commander, Richard Wainwright,* became an overnight hero in the wartime press.

Gloucester, 786 tons, was armed with four 6-pounders, four 3-pounders, and two Colt automatic machine guns. The ship subsequently participated in the capture of Guánica,* Puerto Rico, on 25 July 1898 and Arroyo,* Puerto Rico, on 1 August 1898.

REFERENCE: *Log of the U.S. Gunboat Gloucester* (Annapolis, MD: U.S. Naval Institute, 1899).

GÓMEZ BAEZ, MÁXIMO
(1836–1905)

Major General Máximo Gómez Baez was the Spanish commander of reserve forces in Santo Domingo, his birthplace. He traveled to Cuba in 1865. Working with a variety of insurrectionists, Gómez was an early supporter and participant in the Ten Years' War, which he came to view as pointless. After the war he retired to his plantations and watched Cuba from afar.

Traveling to the United States, Gómez visited with Cuban expatriates and linked himself with José Martí* and other expatriates. Between the two men was a gap of thirty years as well as fundamental differences in outlook. Martí was something of an idealist, whereas Gómez was a soldier, comfortable in the military mode. To Gómez, revolution was not an ideological process but a military one. When the Cuban expatriates did not seem supportive of Gómez's plans, he returned to Santo Domingo.

In 1895 Martí asked Gómez to be the military leader of the new revolution. Gómez accepted and began insurgent actions against the Spanish in the eastern provinces of Cuba. Many of Gómez's guerrilla tactics of hit and run and plantation burning relied on rapid mobility, the kind the Spanish army under General Valeriano Weyler* could not match. Weyler responded with the *trocha,* a fortified ditch to contain the forces of Gómez and General Antonio Maceo.*

This second revolution possessed another new element: the civil revolutionary Cuban civil government headed by Salvador Cisneros* Betancourt. Cisneros was of the same age as Gómez, but once again Gómez's autocratic demeanor served him poorly. Cisneros issued orders to replace José Maceo and to cease support of Antonio Maceo. Gómez refused the orders, and Cisneros discharged Gómez as commanding general. Gómez's plea to Antonio Maceo to come to his aid precipitated Maceo's death on 7 December 1896.

Despite *trochas,* 160,000 Spanish soldiers under Weyler, and dwindling logistical support, Gómez fought on. When the Spanish prime minister Antonio Cánovas del Castillo* launched a plan for Cuban autonomy* as a measure to disarm the insurrection, he did not reckon on Gómez, who refused to consider such a compromise. Gómez's study defiance in the face of Weyler's *reconcentrado* program and the augmentation of Spanish forces, in addition to his refusal to be deterred by the autonomy plan, gave Gómez credibility in the United States. When the war began in 1898, U.S. forces arranged to supply Gómez's forces. Informed of these plans by American agents operating in Cuba, Gómez instructed General Calixto García to detach his forces for campaigns to aid in the downfall of the Spanish. For some time, Gómez had been operating in the central and eastern provinces and had found plenty of Spanish soldiers with whom to skirmish. However, for a host of reasons, the expected joint operations between Cuban insurgents and U.S. troops failed to materialize. Fighting styles, equipment, and command structure were different. In addition, the U.S. forces did not seem to want the help of the Cubans under Gómez.

At the conclusion of hostilities, Gómez was an old man of seventy-five. More than half his life had been spent in the cause of a free Cuba. He died in Havana* in 1906.

REFERENCES: Grover Flint, *Marching with Gómez* (Boston: Lanson, Wolffe & Co., 1898); Hugh Thomas, *Cuba* (New York: Harper & Row, 1971).

GOODRICH, CASPAR FREDERICK
(1847–1925)

Captain Caspar Frederick Goodrich graduated from the U.S. Naval Academy in 1864 and progressed through the officer ranks. He was promoted to captain on 16 September 1897.

Goodrich commanded *St. Louis** and was in charge of naval aspects of the landing at Daiquirí.* He had earlier run sweeps looking for Admiral Pascual Cervera* in the Pacific. On 12 August, with an accompanying force that included *Newark,** *Suwanee,** *Hist,** *Osceola, Alvarado,** and *Resolute,** Goodrich took Manzanillo.* Goodrich and *St. Louis* also cut cables near Santiago.*

Goodrich was critical of the army. From his position as naval liaison to General William R. Shafter,* he had occasion to view its shortcomings, which in his view transcended the usual interservice friction. Goodrich was promoted to rear admiral in 1904.

REFERENCE: Caspar F. Goodrich, *Rope Yarns from the Old Navy* (New York: Naval History Society, 1931).

GORMAN, ARTHUR PUE
(1839–1906)

Senator Arthur Pue Gorman (D-Maryland) attempted a coalition of liberals and conservative Democrats to defeat the ratification of the peace treaty (transmitted 4 July 1899) with Spain. Gorman counted loose votes and reckoned that he had enough to reject the treaty. In addition, Gorman hoped to secure leadership of his party. He worked through January in an attempt for success.

Revolt on Luzon, the beginnings of the Philippine Insurrection,* commenced on 4 February 1899 as fighting erupted between Americans and Filipinos. This crisis lent greater urgency to the Republican expansionist efforts, for without a ratified treaty, the United States would lose credibility among the world powers. Indeed, without a treaty, the United States could not effectively prosecute the Philippine war. The treaty was ratified by only one vote.

Gorman took his defeat out on the War Department* by skimming the army appropriations bill. He left the Senate, defeated, on 4 March.

REFERENCE: Margaret Leech, *In the Days of McKinley* (New York: Harper & Row, 1959).

GRAY, GEORGE
(1849–1925)

Judge George Gray was born in Delaware and studied law at Harvard. Elected Senator, he served from 1885 until 1899. A Democrat and the senior minority member of the Foreign Relations Committee, Gray was an anti-imperialist who was appointed by President McKinley* to the Peace Commission.* Gray opposed the annexation of the Philippines for a host of reasons, including the need for an increased navy, the immorality of war, anti-Catholicism, and fear of an influx of cheap immigrant Asian labor. However, when McKinley sent word to

the commission on 26 October 1898 that he desired the annexation, Gray felt honorbound to support the president. Again, on 13 November, while wrangling over the debt and Kusaie,* Gray acceded to McKinley's wishes.
REFERENCE: David F. Trask, *The War with Spain in 1898* (New York: Macmillan Publishing, Co., 1981).

GREAT BRITAIN

The diplomatic role Great Britain enjoyed in the 1890s must be cast against the backdrop of broader European issues. Britain's emerging rival, Germany,* with its Triple Alliance of Germany, Austria, and Italy, provided much of the stimulus for British actions and reactions. Concern over the intentions of Germany and its colonial aspirations pushed Britain toward the United States. In August 1896 Spain sought diplomatic support from the other European powers against the threat of American intervention. Great Britain leaked to the U.S. minister to Spain, Hannis Taylor,* a memorandum about Spain's efforts to gain European support. The leak effectively sabotaged Spain's desires. This incident of 9 August 1896 was followed later in the year by a note sent jointly by France,* Germany, and Britain, urging Spain to accept an American offer of meditation.

Although Britain maintained strict neutrality once the conflict commenced, there was substantial tacit support for the United States, particularly in the Far East. Commodore George Dewey's* squadron was allowed to complete preparations at Hong Kong* with British connivance, and the English at Manila* proved a psychological bolster during Dewey's postbattle tension. In all its actions, Great Britain was perceived as an American supporter, though that support was more perception that substance. Nevertheless, so positive were feelings in the United States that an Anglo-American League was formed in July 1898. Great Britain seemingly welcomed the new American colonialism as much as it feared German colonialism. For American interests, it was useful to have an overseas ally in the new business of foreign enterprise and government. A developing Anglo-American alliance that has endured for almost a century got its start in the world politics of the 1890s coincident to the Spanish American War.
REFERENCE: Marshall Bertram, *The Birth of Anglo-American Friendship* (New York: University Press of America, 1992).

GREAT CUBAN-AMERICAN FAIR

Americans sympathetic to the Cuban cause and plight included labor organizations, business leaders, Cuban American clubs, veterans groups, patriotic societies, and many dignitaries. Some of these had nursed pro-Cuban sympathies since the *Virginius* affair* of 1873. In a great outpouring of nationalistic fervor and genuine sympathy bathed in democratic ideals, New York's Madison Square Garden hosted the Great Cuban-American Fair during the last week of May 1896. General Daniel E. Sickles, former ambassador to Spain, was a notable guest. Present also was a young Frederick Funston,* who, along with the throng, was stirred by the excitement and promise of adventure. The fair focused national attention on Spain's perceived misrule in Cuba and increased visibility for those seeking an end to that rule.

REFERENCE: G.J.A. O'Toole, *The Spanish War* (New York: W. W. Norton & Co., 1984).

GREENE, FRANCIS VINTON
(1850–1921)

Major General (of Volunteers) Francis Vinton Greene was born in Rhode Island. Graduated first in his class at West Point in 1870, he was commissioned into the artillery but did a branch transfer to the Corps of Engineers.* He served on the international commission that surveyed the northern boundary of the United States, and in 1877 he became the military attaché to St. Petersburg. In that capacity he was a keen observer of the Russian army and accompanied the Russians on campaigns in Turkey, writing *The Russian Army and Its Campaigns in Turkey in 1877–78*. Greene resigned from the regular army in 1886 and began an engineering practice; nevertheless, he served as a colonel in the 71st New York Volunteers. When his regiment was called up in 1898, he went with it to Florida. He was promoted to brigadier general of volunteers on 27 May 1898, and to major general on 13 August. Meanwhile, he was made a brigade commander in Eighth Corps* and left San Francisco for the Philippines in the second contingent. Departing on 15 June in three transports with 3,586 men, Greene and his troops landed at Camp Dewey on 17 July.

In preparing for the assault on Manila,* General Wesley Merritt,* for political reasons, did not wish to deal directly with Filipino troops allied with Emilio Aguinaldo.* Fortunately, General Greene had already developed sufficient rapport with the Filipinos to enable Greene to negotiate without involving Aguinaldo.

In the assault on Manila, Greene commanded the left of the American line with orders to assault Fort San Antonio.* Orders were given on 12 August, and the attack commenced at 9:30 A.M. the next day. Two hours later it was over. Ignoring Merritt's effort to keep them out of the fray, Philippine insurgents,* competed with Greene in a race to the suburbs of Manila. The Spanish held their line long enough for the Americans to arrive, affording Greene success in his objectives.

In early 1899, Greene again resigned to work in civilian life; he directed power companies and worked as police commissioner of New York City. Greene also wrote several books on military policy. He died in New York in 1921.

REFERENCE: *Correspondence Relating to the War with Spain,* 2 vols. (Washington, DC: Government Printing Office, 1902).

GRIGSBY'S COWBOYS

The Rough Riders* of Theodore Roosevelt* and Leonard Wood* were not the only cowboy volunteer units. Two others, Grigsby's Cowboys and Torrey's

Rocky Mountain Riders, were also organized. Jay L. Torrey was to recruit men from the Northwest. Wood recruited in the Southwest (the Rough Riders), and Melvin Grigsby, of Sioux Falls, South Dakota, was to recruit in Maryland and the District of Columbia. Only the Rough Riders went to Cuba, and thus only the Rough Riders had opportunity to gain fame. Grigsby's Cowboys languished in Florida.

REFERENCE: Clifford P. Westermeir, *Who Rush to Glory* (Caldwell, IA: Caxton Printers, 1958).

GRIMES, GEORGE SIMON
(1846–1920)

George Simon Grimes, born in England, enlisted into the Union caused during the Civil War and fought with the ninety-third U.S. Colored Infantry. Commissioned in 1865, he rose to the rank of captain by 1887 and commanded artillery batteries. In this last capacity, Grimes commanded the artillery battery at El Pozo* on 1 July 1898 and also at San Juan Hill.* Grimes survived to be promoted to major in 1899, lieutenant colonel, colonel, brigadier general in 1901, 1903, and 1907, respectively.

GRITO DE BAIRE

On 24 February 1895 in a village about 25 miles from Santiago de Cuba,* the Cuban Insurrection* officially commenced with the "cry" of Baire. Juan Gualberto Gómez led the revolt. Lamentably for the Cubans, the Spanish learned of the uprising and quelled it on the very same day.

Nevertheless, on 29 March Antonio Maceo* landed; on 11 April Máximo Gómez* and José Martí* also landed and the insurrection began in earnest.

REFERENCE: Philip S. Foner, *The Spanish-Cuban-American War and the Birth of American Imperialism, 1895–1902* (New York: Monthly Review Press, 1972).

GUAM

On 22 May 1898 the U.S.S. *Charleston,** Captain Henry Glass* commanding, steamed from San Francisco toward the Philippines. Three days later, three transports carrying the first expeditionary force, almost 2,500 officers and men, also sailed for the Philippines. Secretary of the Navy John D. Long* had issued orders to Glass on 10 May to capture Guam (an island in the Ladrone group, now called the Marianas) on the way to Manila. The *Charleston* with her three transports arrived at Guam on 20 June. Glass first fired at a fort, which proved to be unoccupied. Thinking Glass's fire was a salute, Spanish authorities came alongside *Charleston* to apologize for their inability to return the salute. Glass then informed them that Spain and the United States were at war and arranged for the island's surrender. Thus was opened the strategic route that linked the United States with the far Pacific for many decades to come.

REFERENCE: F. Portusach, "History of the Capture of Guam by the United States

Man-of-War *Charleston* and Its Transports,'' *United States Naval Institute Proceedings* 43 (April 1917): 707–718.

GUÁNICA, PUERTO RICO

Guánica lies on the southwest coast of Puerto Rico about 20 miles west of Ponce.* On 21 July 1898, General Nelson Miles* sailed with 3,415 men in an expeditionary force to Puerto Rico. Ten transports were convoyed by *Massachusetts,* * *Columbia,* * *Yale,* * *Dixie,* * and *Gloucester,* * under the naval command of Captain Francis J. Higginson. On 25 July, the squadron landed a small force at Guánica and a minor action ensued in which twenty-eight marines under the command of Lieutenant H. P. Huse fought ten men under the command of Lieutenant Enrique Méndez. The fight was unequal in every respect, and after Méndez and two others were wounded, Spanish resistance evaporated. This was the first U.S. action in Puerto Rico.

REFERENCE: Ángel Rivero Méndez, *Crónica de la Guerra Hispano Americana en Puerto Rico* (New York: Plus Ultra, 1973).

GUANTÁNAMO, CUBA

Guantánamo lies on a bay of the same name about 40 miles east of Santiago de Cuba.* Guantánamo had long been considered a useful coaling station* for the U.S. Navy, and plans were instituted early in the war for its seizure. Late in May 1898, Captain Caspar F. Goodrich* of *St. Louis* * cut submarine telegraph cables. On 7 June, *Marblehead* * and *Yankee* * left the blockade* and entered the bay, meeting no serious resistance. On 10 June, a battalion of U.S. Marines under the command of Lieutenant Colonel Robert W. Huntington came ashore and occupied a hill on the east side of the harbor entrance. On 11 June, the Spanish commenced a three-day attack on the marine position. Despite the 6,000 Spanish troops in the area, Spanish resistance ceased by 15 June. No more fighting occurred at Guantánamo. This was the first permanent American foothold in Cuba.

Guantánamo further served as an assembly area for the expedition to Puerto Rico.* It sailed from that port on 21 July.

LAS GUÁSIMAS, CUBA

Las Guásimas was a village about 3 miles north of Siboney* on the road to Santiago de Cuba.* As soon as the Fifth Corps* had sufficient strength ashore at the 22 June 1898 landing site of Daiquirí,* General William R. Shafter* began the march toward Santiago. General Henry W. Lawton's* division was ordered to advance toward Siboney, and Lawton advanced on 22 June, the same day as the landing. The Spanish left Siboney before the arrival of U.S. forces, so Lawton was able to report to Shafter on the morning of 23 June that Siboney was in American hands.

General Joseph Wheeler,* commanding the Cavalry Division, received information from Cuban general Demetrio Castillo that about 2,000 Spaniards were at Las Guásimas. In an obvious effort to bypass Lawton and draw first blood, Wheeler chose to misinterpret Shafter's orders and sent General Samuel B. M. Young* on a reconnaissance in force to initiate action at Las Guásimas. Young commanded one of Wheeler's brigades composed of the First U.S. Cavalry, Tenth U.S. Cavalry,* and First U.S. Volunteer Cavalry—the Rough Riders.* Wheeler's initiative interrupted Shafter's original plans for at least a rational disembarkation and deployment, if not an orderly one.

On 24 June Young's brigade advanced down the road, which diminished into a path, and had no communication until they fortuitously arrived in a rough line-abreast formation at the approach to the Spanish-held ridges at Las Guásimas. General Antero Rubín,* the Spanish commander, had orders to retire to Santiago to avoid being cut off. General Castillo knew of these orders and had so informed the Americans. Covered with a dense growth of trees and brush, the terrain was very difficult to traverse. The density of the brush also afforded excellent concealment and some cover to the advancing brigade, however. The regulars were on the right and center; the Tenth U.S. Cavalry, in the middle, including Lieutenant John J. Pershing*; and the Rough Riders of Colonel Leonard Wood,* on the left. The action lasted about two hours, whereupon Rubín began his planned withdrawal and Young's brigade carried the ridges.

Militarily unimportant, the battle and "victory" at Las Guásimas made marvelous newspaper copy, but the battle could very easily have gone the other way. None of the American commanders seemed to have realized that the Spanish executed a planned withdrawal, despite Castillo's intelligence on the matter. Whereas U.S. forces suffered sixteen killed and wounded, Spanish losses, depending upon who is consulted, ranged from seven to eleven fatalities. Whichever number is accurate, Spanish casualties were fewer than those suffered by U.S. forces.

REFERENCES: Jack Cameron Dierks, *A Leap to Arms* (Philadelphia: J. B. Lippincott, 1970); Severo Gómez Núñez, *La Guerra Hispano-Americana,* 5 vols. (Madrid: Imprimería del Cuerpo de Artillería, 1899–1902); Joseph Wheeler, *The Santiago Campaign, 1898* (New York: Drexel Biddle, 1899).

GUAYAMA, PUERTO RICO

Guayama lies about 30 miles south of San Juan. There were two slight skirmishes at Guayama with contingents of General John R. Brooke's* command. Guayama was captured on 5 August 1898 after desultory firing in and around the town. Three Americans were wounded; one Spaniard killed, and two wounded.

On the date of 8 August another skirmish resulted in five casualties to Brooke's men. This engagement occurred about 8 miles north of Guayama on the road to Cayey.*

REFERENCE: *Correspondence Relating to the War with Spain,* 2 vols. (Washington, DC: Government Printing Office, 1902).

GUNBOATS

A virtually unwritten chapter in the Spanish American War is the work done by gunboats in estuaries and small bays and on picket duty. Some gunboats, like *Concord** and *Petrel,** were in Commodore George Dewey's* battle line. Most, however, especially the Spanish gunboats, served anonymously at Cárdenas,* Caibarien, Nuevitas,* Nipe,* Cienfuegos,* and Manzanillo.*

Although slow, gunboats were also used for dispatch work. They were hot, cramped, and unarmored. They possessed only two virtues: shallow draft and expendability. However, those two virtues meant that the gunboats saw more action than any ships in the fleet.

REFERENCE: John D. Alden, *The American Steel Navy* (Annapolis, MD: Naval Institute Press, 1972).

GUNNERY, NAVAL

During the sea battle off Santiago,* U.S. ships fired 9,429 rounds, achieving 120 hits on Spanish vessels. American 4-inch guns achieved a 5.1 percent hit rate—the best among American guns. At Manila,* firing 4,230 rounds, the Americans scored 141 hits compared to less than 15 for the Spanish gunners. The weight of broadside in both battles significantly favored the U.S. forces. These lopsided figures represent differences not in design effectiveness but in training. Several U.S. ships in Admiral William T. Sampson's* command could achieve 70 percent or higher hit rate in practice—and they regularly performed gunnery practice. Spanish gunnery practice was infrequent; and its ammunition, according to Cervera, was often defective.

REFERENCE: H. W. Wilson, *The Downfall of Spain* (New York: Burt Franklin, 1971).

H

HAITI

Haiti played a very secondary part in the American conflict with Spain. German intrusions, demands, and swaggering in regard to Haiti made American politicians and military leaders nervous and helped drive American sentiment toward the British.

General William R. Shafter* utilized cables routed through Haiti to report on operations at Santiago.* This latter communication interface became an important command and control function.

HAMPTON ROADS, VIRGINIA

Besides providing useful anchorage, Hampton Roads's central location provided rapid naval response north or south along the eastern coast of the United States. For this reason, the U.S. Flying Squadron's* base was initially at Hampton Roads and several vessels that participated in Admiral William T. Sampson's blockade* of Cuba originated from this port. The Flying Squadron remained in a defensive posture at Hampton Roads until the disposition of Admiral Pascual Cervera's* squadron was ascertained, at which point the Flying Squadron sailed to join the North Atlantic Squadron.*

HANNA, MARCUS ALONZO
(1837–1904)

Businessman, politician, and millionaire, Marcus Alonzo Hanna was born in New Lisbon, Ohio. His family moved to Cleveland in 1852 for better economic opportunities. He went to Case Western Reserve University, where he was brought up on disciplinary charges for a prank. Hanna left the college after only two months and plunged into his father's wholesale grocery business in 1858. The business prospered immensely from the shipping trade on the Great Lakes and the settling of Wisconsin and Minnesota. In 1862, Hanna became a partner in the company, taking his father's place when he became ill. Hanna loved to play cards and dance, and he was well known among Cleveland social circles. He served in a limited capacity in the Civil War. By 1885 he had become one of the wealthiest men in the country. He expanded the business, taking on new clients such as the Pennsylvania Railroad and the Cambria Iron Company. He also supported the arts in the Cleveland area and owned the Cleveland Opera House. Politics also became a passion. Hanna never strayed from the Republican party and took an active interest in it. In 1880, Hanna campaigned hard for Republican nominee James A. Garfield and was rewarded with membership in the Republican State Committee.

National politics seemed the next logical step for him. Hanna supported Ohio native and favorite son John Sherman for the Republican nomination in 1888. Qualifications and an impressive public record, as well as being an Ohio native, made him all the more attractive to Hanna. Backroom negotiations, behind-the-scenes intrigue, and poor organizational support led to the eventual defeat of the Sherman candidacy. It also left an indelible mark on Mark Hanna. The rupture of his friendship with Joseph B. Foraker,* another Ohio senator, as well as his new alliance and friendship with William McKinley,* can be traced back to the Republican Convention of 1888, which marked a new political direction for Hanna: the election of William McKinley of Ohio for president.

Hanna took an active role in selling McKinley. Spending large amounts of money, including his own, Hanna devoted most of this time to grooming McKinley for the presidency. His organizational skills as well as his knack for raising money made him an excellent choice for chairman of the Republican National Committee. On 18 June 1896 McKinley was nominated on the first ballot.

Hanna was appointed senator when President McKinley chose John Sherman as secretary of state. He was reelected in 1897 in a bitter contest. A strong opponent of intervention in Cuba, Hanna wanted to avoid war with Spain at all costs. Public opinion went against him on this issue, however, and like McKinley, he caught the spirit of war that was sweeping the country. He reversed his stance and became an ardent imperialist, promoting the expansion of the United States in the newly acquired territories gained from the war with Spain.

Hanna remained active in Republican politics after the war, raising money for the local candidates in Ohio. He maintained a lesser role of presidential advisor to President Theodore Roosevelt* upon the death of McKinley in 1901. Many in the Republican party supported Senator Hanna for president even though he denied any such aspirations. He died on 15 February 1904.

REFERENCE: Herbert David Croly, *Marcus Alonzo Hanna: His Life and Work* (New York: The Macmillan Company, 1912).

RICHARD W. PEUSER

HARVARD (ship)

The U.S.S. *Harvard* was built for the British Inman Line and launched in 1888 as *City of New York.* Registered in the United States in 1893 as *New York,* she became part of the American Line, making regular passages between New

York and Southampton. Displacing 10,508 tons and capable of 20 knots, the liner was taken over by the U.S. Navy as a scout cruiser from April through October 1898 and renamed *Harvard.*

By the middle of April 1898, *Harvard* was a reinforcing component of Admiral William T. Sampson's* fleet. Sampson used the armed liners *Harvard, Yale,** and *St. Louis** as scouts, transports, and dispatch vessels because of their speed. During the first week of May, *Harvard* cruised in and around Puerto Rico,* St. Thomas, and Martinique.* In Martinique, *Harvard* learned of the presence of Admiral Pascual Cervera's* fleet in the West Indies and communicated this intelligence to Sampson.

Harvard was away unloading stores during the battle of Santiago de Cuba* and so missed the action. On 5 July, Spanish prisoners of the defeated *Vizcaya** attempted to resist their American guards aboard *Harvard.* The Americans fired upon the Spaniards, killing seven and wounding others. No one is sure whether a mistake on either side precipitated this incident.

After the war *Harvard* was refitted and renamed *New York* to resume her career as a liner. The U.S. Navy took her over again as a transport during World War I, after which she made a few more passenger voyages before being scrapped at Genoa in the early 1920s.

REFERENCES: Frederick E. Emmons, *American Passenger Ships* (Newark: University of Delaware Press, 1985); H. W. Wilson, *The Downfall of Spain* (New York: Burt Franklin, 1971).

HAVANA, CUBA

Close to the United States and the seat of Spanish government in Cuba, Havana was naturally an object of early U.S. military planning. The most effective of these plans was the naval blockade* that kept Havana ill supplied. One strategy was to starve the Spanish into surrender. Another was to land a powerful land force to attack Havana. The city boasted most of the Spanish forces and infrastructure; its defeat would mean the success of American arms. The location and intentions of the Spanish fleet under Admiral Pascual Cervera* and fears of disease* in Havana caused American planners to vacillate on whether to attack Havana. Everyone agreed that sea power would be the deciding factor.

Havana was also a stage upon which intelligence operations* flourished. Spanish intelligence failed to detect that Cuban revolution sympathizers were telegraphing events to the United States from Havana.

Most important, it was in Havana that the U.S.S. *Maine** exploded on 15 February 1898, a precipitating crisis that led to hostilities.

HAWAII

The annexation of Hawaii in 1898 was an event coincident with the Spanish American War; the war speeded the effort for annexation that had been building for some time. The most recent attempt had been the previous year, 1897. A treaty of annexation gathered dust in the U.S. Senate until war's outbreak, at which time the strategic significance of a Pacific base on the route to the Philippines and the Far East came sharply to the fore. On 4 May 1898 a joint resolution was introduced into the House of Representatives with the support of President McKinley.* It passed the House on 15 June, the Senate on 6 July, and by 7 July when McKinley signed it, it became a fact.

The annexation of Hawaii provided grist to a rising conflict with Japan.* Japanese were the largest ethnic group in the islands. Frictions over immigration policy reflected only surface foam of a much deeper conflict that would boil over in 1941: who would control the Pacific. In the 1897 annexation attempt, Japan was very vocal in its opposition. By 1898, the environment had changed.

Several nations perceived that an independent Hawaii posed a threat to peace in the Pacific. Annexation relieved much of that threat. Great Britain* supported the United States in the annexation, but Germany,* perhaps the most likely opponent, intimated that it might demand some form of compensation for perceived losses in the Pacific. On 12 July the U.S. minister in Berlin received warning that Germany viewed the continued growth of American power and possessions in the Pacific with alarm. Further, the developing Anglo-American diplomatic partnership was viewed as a source of consternation not just to Germany but other European nations as well.

REFERENCE: Sylvester K. Stevens, *American Expansion in Hawaii, 1842–1989* (Harrisburg: Archives Publishing Co. of Pennsylvania, 1945).

HAWK (ship)

U.S.S. *Hawk* was another yacht* purchased for the Spanish American War. She served in the blockade* of Havana.* Admiral William T. Sampson* sent *Hawk* to Commodore Winfield S. Schley,* informing him that Admiral Pascual Cervera's* fleet was probably at Santiago de Cuba,* and that if the Spanish fleet was not at Cienfuegos,* Schley was to blockade the fleet at Santiago. These orders were dispatched on 22 May 1898. Schley, however, disbelieved Sampson's message, instead believing that Cervera was at Cienfuegos.

Hawk was built as the steam yacht *Hermione* in 1891 at Paisley, Scotland, and displaced 375 tons. Her main armament consisted of a pair of 6-pounders—one forward and one aft—and a few small-caliber Colts.

Hawk served off and on as a training vessel until the eve of World War II.

REFERENCE: William P. Stephens, ''The Steam Yacht as a Naval Auxiliary,'' *Transactions of the Society of Naval Architects and Marine Engineers* 6 (1898): 89–113.

HAWKINS, HAMILTON SMITH
(1834–1910)

Hamilton Smith Hawkins was a forty-year veteran of the U.S. Army by the year 1898. He had attended West Point from 1852 until 1855. A Civil War veteran, he was promoted to brigadier general of volunteers on 4 May 1898.

Hawkins led the First Brigade in General J. F. Kent's* First Division at the battle of San Juan Hill.* Hawkins's brigade clawed its way to the front of the assault, but the seventy-first New York Volunteers recoiled at the heavy Spanish fire and failed to resume the attack. However, the Sixth and the Sixteenth Infantry advanced on the left, leading the assault under Gatling gun* covering fire in a confused action. Hawkins was slightly wounded in the foot.

Hawkins was promoted to major general and retired on 4 October 1898.

REFERENCE: French Ensor Chadwick, *The Relations of the United States and Spain,* 2 vols. (New York: Russell & Russell, 1911).

HAY, JOHN MILTON
(1838–1905)

Born in Salem, Indiana, the young future poet and statesman John Milton Hay grew up in the river town of Warsaw, Illinois, just downstream from Nauvoo and across the river from Keokuk. Studying law in his youth, he found it a useful preparation for public life. He was educated at Brown University, but more significantly, through his own reading, observation, and experience. Hay was able to hear much great debate by such political luminaries as Stephen Douglas and Abraham Lincoln. Through these associations, Hay became a secretary of Lincoln's, and from 1861 until Lincoln's murder in 1865, the young Hay had daily interaction with the president.

In March 1865 Hay was appointed secretary to the U.S. legation at Paris. A two-year seminar of social and diplomatic practice followed in which Hay, a keen observer, learned much. After Paris, Hay served as the chargé d'affaires at Vienna, where he took opportunity to travel in Turkey, Poland, and Spain. Returning to the United States, Hay took up journalism in 1870 and worked under Whitelaw Reid.* Hay also married Clara Stone and came reluctantly under the influence of his father-in-law, moving to Cleveland. As soon as practical after Amasa Stone's death, he left Cleveland.

As a journalist, Hay's literary abilities blossomed into narrative, novel, and poetry. He became one of the leading literary figures of the 1880s and 1890s. He also wrote a biography of Lincoln, with John Nicolay, who had also been one of Lincoln's secretaries.

In 1878, Hay had become assistant secretary of state and formed lasting friendships with Henry Adams,* Henry Cabot Lodge,* and others. In and out of politics, he continued journalism and learned much through numerous trips abroad.

A longtime associate of William McKinley,* Hay worked diligently for the Republican nominee in 1896 and was rewarded with the ambassadorship to Great Britain in 1897. Hay's lifetime preparation came to focus as he negotiated through a series of ticklish challenges in Great Britain: the tension aroused by the Venezuelan boundary dispute and the increasing tensions with Spain. Hay was able to secure a positive working relationship with the British—the British came to realize that their national interests coincided with U.S. imperialism—and as a result Great Britain proved to be America's most consistent supporter.

As ambassador, Hay kept McKinley informed on developing European attitudes and initiatives and offered timely advice and intelligence. Because of Hay's experience and early training, as well as the age in which he lived, he interpreted events and issues through the monocles of Europe. China, the Philippines, and the Far East were issues generally interpreted through a European perspective. As a supporter of the president, Hay followed his leader. Originally, Hay felt that the United States should acquire only a part in the Philippines. However, as the political winds changed direction, Hay became as imperialistic as necessary. His success with Great Britain left him vulnerable to charges that he was an Anglophile—a charge with which he had to contend until the end of his career.

In August 1898, Hay was asked to become secretary of state; he took office the following month. Hay expressed the president's wishes to the Peace Commission* and was, of course, very interested in both the process and its outcome.

Hay's work in diplomacy and international issues transcended the Spanish American War. He became known chiefly for his open door policy in China and the accords over the Isthmian canal.

REFERENCES: Alfred L. P. Dennis, *Adventures in American Diplomacy, 1896–1906* (New York: E. P. Dutton & Co., 1928); William Roscoe, *The Life and Letters of John Thayer Hay,* 2 vols. (Boston: Houghton Mifflin, 1915).

HEARST, WILLIAM RANDOLPH
(1863–1951)

Born in San Francisco, William Randolph Hearst was the only child of U.S. Senator George Hearst and Phoebe Apperson Hearst. While attending Harvard, he worked with the Harvard *Lampoon;* later he apprenticed with Joseph Pulitzer's* *New York World,* the flamboyant style of which he later used as the model for his own papers. He took over operation of the *San Francisco Examiner* as a gift from his father in 1887, financed by his family's great mining fortune. Hearst hired top creative talents, and the *Examiner* under him engaged in flashy self-promotion; this cost him dearly, but circulation rose enough for the paper to make a profit. He then set his sights on the New York market.

Hearst purchased the *New York Journal* in late 1895 and immediately entered into intense competition with the *World,* hiring away several top writers and managers from Pulitzer. He tried to outdo other New York papers with the *Journal'*s splashy articles, often publishing distorted stories and sponsoring self-promotion exploits to boost circulation.

The Cuban Insurrection* in the 1890s provided much raw material for Hearst's sensationalistic style. The *Journal* came out strongly on the side of the insurgents, constantly urging U.S. intervention, and depicted the Spanish authorities as brutal monsters (the standard term used by the *Journal* when referring to Cuban governor Valeriano Weyler* was ''the butcher Weyler''). Hearst's populist stories were written to gain the favor of the less-educated members of the voting public, and his portrayal of himself as a knight in shining armor out

to expose corruption and evil is often interpreted as a part of his personal political goals.

One of the *Journal*'s most notable schemes was its campaign to release Evangelina Cisneros* from prison in Cuba. She had been imprisoned for trying to
help her father, a revolutionary, escape from prison. The *Journal* embarked on
a major international publicity campaign on her behalf, claiming that this "Cuban Joan of Arc" was imprisoned merely for defending her own chastity from
lecherous Spanish guards and for reporting the conditions of her imprisonment
as far more brutal than they really were. Fearing the Spanish might soon release
her, Hearst sent Karl Decker* to rescue her from the Recojidas prison in Havana
through a combination of cloak-and-dagger antics and bribery of the guards.

As part of his publicity to aid the Cubans, in 1897 Hearst commissioned a
$2,000 jewel-encrusted sword to be presented to rebel leader Máximo Gómez.*
The first person given the assignment to smuggle the sword into Cuba was Ralph
W. Paine; after several failed filibustering* expeditions, he had to give up. Next
with the assignment was Granville Fortescue, who likewise never made it to
Cuba. The sword was not presented to Gómez until after the end of the war;
Gómez was said to have been unappreciative of the expense of something so
showy when the money could have helped his forces in more practical ways.

Another infamous *Journal* scoop was their story of Clemencia Arango,* a
Cuban woman who, according to the *Journal,* had been strip-searched by Spanish officers while en route to New York on *Olivette,* a U.S. flagged vessel.
The story had been based on a misleading dispatch from *Journal* correspondent
Richard Harding Davis* and featured a prominent illustration by Frederic Remington* of Spanish officers leering at the disrobed señorita Arango. Davis was
furious at Hearst for misrepresenting his dispatch (women matrons had actually
conducted the search), refusing to work for him again and exposing the *Journal*
article as false in the pages of Pulitzer's competing *World.*

In June 1898 Hearst undertook the gimmick of traveling to Cuba as a war
correspondent and publishing a "Cuban Edition" of the *Journal-Examiner.* He
chartered *Sylvia* from the Baltimore Fruit Company and arrived at Santiago*
during Admiral William T. Sampson's* blockade of the Spanish fleet in the
harbor. Hearst did land and did personally witness fighting, writing reports on
the action for his papers; *Sylvia* was sent to Port Antonio, Jamaica, several times
to cable the dispatches to New York.

After the war, Hearst sponsored flamboyant celebrations of American victory.
He also did not hesitate to continue publicizing scandal such as the supposedly
wretched conditions among the returning troops at the army reception center at
Montauk Point, Long Island, and he viciously attacked the secretary of war,
Russell A. Alger.*

Hearst is often given credit for almost single-handedly creating the war with
Spain. An unsubstantiated part of the Hearst legend is that shortly before the
hostilities, illustrator Frederic Remington was growing bored with the lack of
action in Cuba. He cabled Hearst, "Everything is quiet. There is no trouble.

There will be no war. I wish to return.'' Hearst supposedly replied, ''Please remain. You furnish the pictures and I'll furnish the war.'' The extent to which the public or the U.S. government was actually manipulated by a deceptive press—in the words of the age, ''yellow journalism''*—or by any one individual remains debatable, however. Regardless of credit due him, Hearst remained proud of his role in the war and was quick to credit himself for helping end Spanish colonial rule.

REFERENCE: W. A. Swanberg, *Citizen Hearst: A Biography of William Randolph Hearst* (New York: Scribner's, 1961).

MARK A. THOMAS

HELLINGS, MARTIN LUTHER
(1841–1908)

Martin Luther Hellings was a Civil War veteran wounded at Antietam. He learned telegraphy after the war and was hired by Western Union Telegraph Company. Successful at his new employment, he was promoted to manager of the Ocean Telegraph Company, a Western Union subsidiary based in Key West,* Florida.

Hellings married well and moved in significant circles. He knew Charles D. Sigsbee,* captain of the U.S.S. *Maine,* and began his brief but useful career in intelligence operations* by arranging for confidential messages to be sent on Plant System* ships. Hellings also maintained contacts in Havana* with Domingo Villaverde,* who would wire information to Hellings about Cuban operations. In addition, Hellings was commissioned a captain in the Army Signal Corps.* As such, he would forward the information to American authorities. It was from Villaverde via Hellings that Washington learned of the arrival of Admiral Pascual Cervera's* squadron at Santiago.* Admiral William Sampson's* squadron was then able to blockade Cervera's ships and eventually neutralize them.

REFERENCE: G.J.A. O'Toole, *The Spanish War* (New York: W. W. Norton & Co., 1984).

HENRY, GUY VERNOR
(1839–1899)

Brigadier General Guy Vernor Henry graduated from West Point in 1861 and fought through the Civil War. After the war, he served in the West and was shot in the face at Rose Bud, Montana.

General Henry was at Camp Alger* in 1898 when he received orders to prepare to move several regiments to Cuba and send the rest to South Carolina. Henry's men, about 10,000 troops, never went to war in Cuba, however; they were originally to go to Puerto Rico,* which did become their eventual destination. Ordered to Santiago de Cuba* on 5 July, Henry arrived at Siboney* aboard *St. Paul** on 10 July. General William Shafter* intended to use Henry in the reduction of Santiago. Henry arrived at Shafter's headquarters on 12 July, and Santiago surrendered on 17 July. General Henry's brigade, comprised of some 3,300 men, next sailed for Puerto Rico on 21 July. They steamed with the artillery aboard *Comanche* and by 24 July were ashore and engaged in reconnoitering the environs of Guánica,* about 15 miles east of Ponce.* On the next day, Henry's men encountered fire on the road to Yauco.*

On 6 August, Henry's regiments were ordered to march from Ponce toward Arecibo* and Adjuntas.* On 13 August, Henry had passed Adjuntas on the way to Utuado. In spite of the peace protocol signed the previous day, Henry continued to advance and occupied Lares.

Henry was promoted to major general of volunteers in December. Also in December, Henry became the first military governor of Puerto Rico.

REFERENCE: Ángel Rivero Méndez, *Crónica de la Guerra Hispano Americana en Puerto Rico* (New York: Plus Ultra, 1973).

HIST (ship)

On 28 June 1898, President McKinley* extended the Cuban blockade* to Manzanillo.* On 30 June, *Hist,* an American armed yacht* of 472 tons, in company with the armed auxiliary *Hornet* and the tug *Wompatuck* began a reconnaissance of the coastal areas near Manzanillo with the intent to blockade Manzanillo and to prevent Spanish land forces at Santiago* from receiving provisions via Manzanillo. Two actions ensued: one on the thirtieth in Niquero Bay between *Hornet* and *Hist* and a Spanish launch of 30 tons, the *Centinela;* the other, the same day in the afternoon at Manzanillo. In the first encounter, the *Centinela* was completely outgunned and outclassed and therefore retired after receiving twenty-five balls, damage to machinery, and the death of a fireman. She subsequently sank. *Hist* and consorts did not follow *Centinela* in flight but proceeded to Manzanillo, where the three American ships found several Spanish gunboats, armed pontoons, and transports. A vigorous battle ensued in which *Hist* was struck eleven times from vessels in the harbor and a shore battery. *Hist* retired with the rest of the little squadron until they could be reinforced. On 18 July, *Hist,* along with six other vessels, destroyed or immobilized all the ships in Manzanillo.

REFERENCE: Augustín Rodríguez González, "Operaciones menores en Cuba, 1898," *Revista de Historia Naval* 3, no. 9 (1985): 125–146.

HOAR, GEORGE FRISBIE
(1826–1904)

Like his friend Edward Atkinson,* George Frisbie Hoar, senator, was an ardent disciple of free trade and anti-imperialism. Hoar voted for the annexation of Hawaii* in 1898 but opposed the acquisition of the Philippines.* An early opponent of the developing diplomatic battle with Spain, Hoar stood with an interesting array of capitalists who saw a war with Spain as disruptive to trade and destabilizing to economic conditions. Nevertheless, as events transpired—especially the sinking of the *Maine**—Hoar's confidence that the nation could and should avoid war eroded badly. Hoar quickly supported and praised the resolution by Representative Henry M. Teller* that disavowed any idea of acquiring Cuba. Thus with a conscience free of any dark acquisitive motives, Hoar urged Congress to cease its divisiveness and support the Spanish American War.

Hoar's concern for the impact of the provisions of the Treaty of Paris* on American institutions led him to oppose the treaty. While no toady, Hoar was very loyal to President William McKinley,* and the latter's obvious expansionist plans caused consternation to the senator. Hoar was invited to join the Anti-Imperialist League* but refused, fearing further disharmony with his Republican brethren. Hoar was anti-imperialist, but he saw solutions within the Republican ranks rather than through the league, or, worse, through a third party, as some members of the league urged. Hoar maintained a correspondence with Edward Atkinson, Charles Francis Adams, Jr., and Erving Winslow, all prominent and vocal anti-imperialists; but Hoar found the anti-imperialists too heterogeneous for his Republican sensibilities.

The essence of Hoar's argument against Philippine annexation was that it was unconstitutional, in this case, the government would not derive its just powers from the consent of the governed. Hoar also believed it was "wicked," that it violated traditional political ideals as he interpreted them. Hoar's opposition to the Treaty of Paris made him one of the most well known politicians of his day.
REFERENCE: Richard E. Welch, Jr., *George Frisbie Hoar and the Half-Breed Republicans* (Cambridge: Harvard University Press, 1971).

HOBSON, RICHMOND PEARSON
(1870–1937)

Born on 17 August 1870 in Alabama, Richmond Pearson Hobson was the second of seven children. Early in his life his parents instilled in him a fierce desire to succeed, which was to derive Hobson throughout his life. Hobson decided that he wanted to attend the Naval Academy in Annapolis. Nomination to the Naval Academy was determined by competitive exam. At the age of fourteen Hobson placed first out of all applicants in his congressional district. While in the Naval Academy he never stood lower than third academically and in 1889 graduated first in his class.

After his midshipman's cruise aboard U.S.S. *Chicago,* Hobson spent three years in France studying naval architecture. Upon returning to the United States, Hobson served with the Navy Department in Washington, D.C., specifically with the Bureau of Construction and Repair. In 1895 Hobson was detailed to the armored cruiser U.S.S. *New York.**

Hobson was aboard *New York* when war was declared on 21 April 1898. *New York* was Rear Admiral William T. Sampson's* flagship of the North Atlantic Squadron.* On 22 April, Admiral Sampson's fleet sailed to establish the blockade* of Havana* and lesser ports to the east and west of the capital.

Admiral Pascual Cervera's* Spanish squadron headed for Santiago de Cuba,* one of the few ports not blockaded by the Americans. Admiral Sampson would have preferred to storm the harbor when he located Cervera's ships, but he correctly suspected that there were mines in the channel. Sampson developed a plan to sink the collier *Merrimac** in the entrance of the harbor, thereby temporarily containing Cervera until the U.S. Army arrived: The army could capture the harbor's fortifications, the *Merrimac* could be removed from the channel, and the fleet could enter to defeat Cervera. Hobson was placed in charge of developing plans for the navigation of the *Merrimac* and the method to sink her quickly and efficiently. It was decided to send the ship in alone by moonlight on Thursday, 2 June, at 3:30 A.M. The *Merrimac* would enter the channel with a lifeboat in tow. Secured on the port side would be ten torpedoes that would sink the ship quickly upon detonation. The crew would use the lifeboat to rendezvous with the remainder of the squadron.

After several delays, the *Merrimac* set off on its mission with Hobson as the commanding officer. Admiral Sampson, however, felt was too much light and recalled the *Merrimac*. The next night they set off again. As they edged into the channel, they were spotted by the Spanish and heavy firing began. Both the rudder and the steering gear were rendered useless. As the ship began to head in the wrong direction, Hobson ordered the crew to detonate the torpedoes and abandon ship. However, only two of the original ten torpedoes exploded. Because the ship did not immediately sink, it was caught in the tide and dragged off course before sinking. Richmond Hobson and the entire crew were captured. Almost a month later Hobson and his men were exchanged for some Spanish prisoners.

Although the operation had been a complete failure from start to finish, Hobson became a national hero. The media praised Hobson for his heroic efforts and his display of ''American'' daring and magnificent courage.

Hobson resigned from the U.S. Navy in 1903 to promote causes such as U.S. naval supremacy and the prohibition of alcohol. He served as a member of Congress form 1907 until 1915. In 1933 Congress awarded Hobson the Medal of Honor for his war exploits.

REFERENCE: Richmond Pearson Hobson, *The Sinking of the* Merrimac: *A Personal Narrative* (Annapolis, MD: Naval Institute Press, 1988).

HOLGUÍN, CUBA

Holguín was an insurgent center in both the Ten Years' War* and the 1895–1898 Cuban Insurrection.* It lies about 65 miles north of Santiago.* Because of its location and history, Holguín possessed a Spanish garrison that had a defensive posture. Some 12,000 Spaniards in the vicinity of Holguín were ''surrounded'' by 3,000 insurrectionists. The plan was to prevent the Spanish at Holguín from aiding the garrison at Santiago.

Holguín was also considered as a retreat objective. On 2 July 1898 Governor-General Ramón Blanco y Erenas* ordered the commander at Santiago, General José Toral,* to fall back to Manzanillo* or Holguín if he could not hold Santiago. This general idea was reiterated six days later when Toral, negotiating surrender with General William Shafter,* offered to vacate Santiago if the Americans would allow Toral's troops to march without hindrance to Holguín. A Cuban report of a relief column assembling at Holguín caused Shafter to press Toral for surrender and to accelerate the attack on Santiago.

REFERENCE: David F. Trask, *The War with Spain in 1898* (New York: Macmillan Publishing Co., 1981).

HONG KONG

In one sense, at least, the relationship of Hong Kong to the Spanish American War could be subsumed in the larger issue of the U.S. designs and plans for China.* However, Hong Kong itself, and specifically the government of Great Britain as represented by acting governor Sir Wilsone Black,* had a direct and interesting impact on the prosecution of Commodore George Dewey's* Manila campaign.* For four years Great Britain* had been negotiating the ninety-nine year lease of the New Territories. The agreements were reached in 1898, with formal British possession of the New Territories scheduled for 17 April 1898.

While Great Britain contemplated taking over the New Territories, Dewey assembled his Asiatic Squadron* in Hong Kong. Black received notification of the commencement of hostilities and informed Dewey that he must leave under the laws of neutrality. Anticipating hostilities and this very eventuality, Dewey removed the squadron to Mirs Bay,* some 30 miles from Hong Kong, but still within the New Territories, as configured in the lease between China and Great Britain. Thus, technically, Dewey had moved his squadron to neutral Chinese territory (the neutrality of China, apparently, could be violated with impunity). However, Great Britain delayed taking possession of the New Territories so that Dewey would have a base for the imminent Philippine campaign. British colonial minister Joseph Chamberlain* also hoped for a U.S. alliance and even hinted at British support of the United States in the Spanish American War.

Courtesy of the British government, Hong Kong provided a staging area for Dewey's squadron and the eventual Battle of Manila Bay.*

REFERENCES: Philip Joseph, *Foreign Diplomacy in China, 1894–1900* (New York: Octagon Books, 1971); Peter Wesley-Smith, *Unequal Treaty, 1898–1997* (Hong Kong: Oxford University Press, 1980).

HOSPITALS

Within the U.S. Army Medical Department,* which included surgeons as well as hospital stores, there existed the Hospital Corps. Founded in 1887, the corps was comprised of soldiers especially trained in nursing and first aid, stretcher bearers, and ambulance service. In early 1898 the Hospital Corps mustered only some 791 men. With the rapid increase to almost 6,000 men by 31 August 1898, the Corps lacked sufficiently trained personnel necessary to carry out its mission. Surgeon General George M. Sternberg* introduced female nurses into military hospitals—the first females so utilized—and brought Doctor Anita Newcomb McGee into his office as chief of nurses.

Sternberg oversaw a hospital system that dated from the Civil War. The assembly camps had multiple hospitals run by each regiment. As the division and eventually the corps were organized, these regimental hospitals were to be consolidated into larger, more effective divisional or corps hospitals. In addition, the *Relief,* a well-equipped hospital ship, served in the Caribbean. The rapidity of the buildup and resulting shortages of everything from doctors to pillows combined to corrupt the hospital system in the camps* overseas and at home. The volunteer units, most of which maintained a geographic identity, resisted the consolidation of regimental hospitals to a division or corps. The results were chaotic: poorly trained personnel working without adequate supplies or equipment. Sanitation suffered; disease* spread. Sternberg, a researcher, did not grasp the bureaucratic necessities of his office. The breakdown in the Inspector General's Office abetted the Medical Department's problems. Surgeons worked heroically, but with rising sickness and without the wherewithal to function, some hospitals reached total paralysis.

By August and September many of the sick had been transferred to other camps like Camp Wikoff,* for example, and then sent to civilian hospitals for treatment. Unfortunately, press stories and the "Round Robin"* turned Camp Wikoff into a synonym for neglect and maltreatment. Overcrowding, filth, and poor or lacking equipment also characterized other camps. However, once Sternberg became aware of the magnitude of the problems, he labored diligently and energetically to find solutions and to plan against future epidemics. Major Walter Reed* and the typhoid board nevertheless concluded that none of these remedies actually made much difference. Mortality decreased simply because the disease had run its course.

From the ashes of this administrative disaster, the army learned much. Necessary reforms and administrative improvements did not, however, remove the stigma for some time.

REFERENCE: Graham A. Cosmas, *An Army for Empire* (Columbia: University of Missouri Press, 1971).

HOTEL INGLATERRA

On the ocean front of Havana, the elegant Hotel Inglaterra was a favorite hangout for American correspondents, many of whom never left Havana to see action during the Cuban Insurrection* but gathered their information by trading gossip at the hotel's bar.

REFERENCE: G.J.A. O'Toole, *The Spanish War* (New York: W.W. Norton and Co., 1984).

MARK A. THOMAS

HOWELL, JOHN ADAMS
(1840–1918)

Commodore John Adams Howell graduated from Annapolis in 1858. He served during the Civil War, taking part in the Battle of Mobile Bay. Howell rose through the ranks to commodore. In September 1897, Senator William E. Chandler lobbied for Howell to become the future commander of the Asiatic Squadron,* but Theodore Roosevelt* intercepted Secretary of the Navy John D. Long's* recommendation of Howell to President McKinley.* Roosevelt's opinion of Howell was not as flattering as Long's: he favored George Dewey.* Soliciting the aid of Senator Redfield Proctor,* Roosevelt and Dewey combined to get to McKinley first, so that through their maneuvering Dewey became the squadron commander.

By April 1898 Howell commanded the Northern Patrol Squadron* and patrolled from Delaware to Maine. A few months later he was named second in command of the North Atlantic Squadron.* Then on 11 July Howell was ordered to command one of the squadrons off Cuba. He was promoted to rear admiral in August 1898.

Howell is also known as the originator of gyroscopically steering torpedoes.
REFERENCE: Richard S. West, Jr., *Admirals of American Empire* (Indianapolis: Bobbs-Merrill Co., 1948).

HUBBARD, ELBERT
(1859–1915)

A self-made businessman and dilettante, Elbert Hubbard was editor of the *Philistine* and dabbled in the arts and crafts movement with his Roycroft shop and publications. Hubbard took Lieutenant Andrew S. Rowan's* effort to contact the Cuban insurgent forces led by Calixto García* and turned it into a sermon on initiative and pluck entitled ''A Message to García.'' Hubbard's version was not particularly accurate, and it turned a modest adventure into a sermonizing lesson; but it did become a bestseller and went into numerous reprintings. Schoolchildren were required to read it for decades, and ''Message'' acquired a life of its own.
REFERENCE: Donald Pizer, ed., *American Thought and Writing: The 1890s* (New York: Houghton Mifflin, 1972).

HUDSON (ship)

The U.S.S. *Hudson* was a small revenue cutter built 1893 and armed with two 6-pounders. On 11 May 1898, *Hudson,* in company with *Winslow,* *Wilmington,* and *Machias,* entered Cárdenas.* Because of her shallow draft, *Winslow* was sent to investigate a Spanish gunboat. A hidden Spanish battery commenced fire on *Winslow,* disabling steering gear and boilers and wounding or killing ten of her twenty-five crew. *Hudson* dashed in to the disabled *Winslow,* secured a towing hawser, and pulled the unlucky ship from the action.
REFERENCE: H. W. Wilson, *The Downfall of Spain* (New York: Burt Franklin, 1971).

HULL, JOHN ALBERT TIFFIN
(1841–1928)

Born in Ohio but raised in Iowa, John Albert Tiffin Hull served in the Union army in the Civil War and pursued agricultural and banking interests in Iowa after the war. In 1872 he embarked on a political career, first in Iowa state politics, then twenty years in Congress,* commencing in 1891. He was chairman of the House Committee on Military Affairs before and during the Spanish American War. On 17 March 1898, Hull sponsored a bill that attempted to legislate a plan for an expansible army.* Developed in concert with the War Department,* the Hull Bill intended to establish a new order of things in the army rather than just address the crisis with Spain. In sum, Hull and his backers wanted a federal reserve force that could be quickly mobilized in time of war. The bill created three battalions in each regiment, the third a skeleton that could be expanded. By keeping this third battalion unmanned except during war, the army skirted the issue of a large peacetime force. Nevertheless, the regular army would almost quadruple to 104,000 officers and men. However, the Hull Bill also meant a diminished role for the National Guard.* Indeed, several prominent officers and politicians viewed the regulars as the offensive arm and the National Guard as a coast defense force. Once the guard mobilized to defeat the Hull Bill, Hull himself had to spend all his time defending the bill. It was defeated on 7 April by a decisive vote of 155 to 61. To some extent, the success of the National Guard forced the McKinley* administration, and the War Department in particular, to pursue a politicized enlistment system fraught with inefficiencies.

The failure of the Hull Bill revealed not just the power of the National Guard but also an element of distrust in its principal authors: Russell Alger,* Henry Corbin,* and to a lesser degree Hull himself.

REFERENCE: Graham A. Cosmas, *An Army for Empire* (Columbia: University of Missouri Press, 1971).

I

IMMUNES

Volunteer infantry regiments were created in the first two weeks of May 1898 to supplement and expand the regular army. Among these volunteer regiments were four regiments of "immunes" composed largely of blacks from the South. It was erroneously believed that African Americans were immune to yellow fever* and other tropical diseases, hence the name. The units were commanded by regular officers and were the Seventh, Eighth, Ninth, and Tenth U.S. Volunteer Infantry. One of these units, the Ninth, was ordered to Santiago de Cuba,* but not to fight. Like most of their white counterparts, the volunteer units had little opportunity to see action. Instead they performed garrison duty in order for nonimmune units to be moved out to hospitals, for example.

REFERENCES: Graham A. Cosmas, *An Army for Empire* (Columbia: University of Missouri Press, 1971), Bernard C. Nalty, *Strength for the Fight: A History of Black Americans in the Military* (New York: Free Press, 1986).

INDEPENDENCE

In Cuba, Puerto Rico,* and the Philippines* there existed desires and movements for self-determination antedating the Spanish American War. The Cuban movement for independence had a long history. Woven into that history was sympathy from the United States, which manifested itself in numerous attempts at filibustering.* The Cuban Insurrection of 1895* utilized U.S. soil as a staging ground for fundraising and for political and diplomatic support on issues such as autonomy* and belligerency.* The Cuban junta,* Cuban Revolutionary Army,* and the Cuban Insurrection first grew supportive and fiscal roots in the United States and then moved to the island. One of the advantages the Cubans possessed over the Filipinos and Puerto Ricans was that U.S. objectives in Cuba were clearly defined and well articulated. They had been rehearsed in Congress* and in the press (*see* The Press and the War*) and had a well-developed documentary history. Independence for Cuba was a primary objective. Although U.S. diplomatic and executive practice often fell short of stated objectives, and in spite of subsequent U.S. occupation forces, independence remained not just a Cuban initiative but a U.S. initiative as well.

Puerto Rico presented a different face to the waning power and influence of Spain. Jarred by the strife in Cuba, Puerto Rico's local leadership took a more moderate course. Although there was considerable desire for independence, there was also vocal desire for union with the United States—a conflict that persists on the island. A middle road of autonomy was developed by Spanish prime minister Antonio Cánovas de Castillo* and later implemented by his successor, Práxides Mateo Sagasta,* in 1897. The independence movement remained alive, however. Doctor José Julio Henna, speaking for Puerto Rican patriots to President McKinley* on 21 March 1898, said that the Puerto Rico's complaint against Spain was the same as Cuba's and should result in the same consequence, namely, independence. The autonomous charter had barely been implemented when Puerto Rico was invaded by U.S. forces. Soon its people realized that they had neither the protection of the autonomous constitution nor the U.S. Constitution of 1789. Yet Puerto Ricans aided U.S. forces, not the Spanish, during the campaigns waged by General Nelson Miles.* Divided economic, political, and religious interests continued to keep the island under U.S. sovereignty, but an independence movement persisted.

The Philippines provided yet another variation on the theme. Emilio Aguinaldo* and the Grito de Baire* announced a revolution that predated the Spanish American War. Commodore George Dewey's* and General Wesley Merritt's* exclusion of Emilio Aguinaldo from the campaign at Manila* signaled the McKinley administration's developing motives in the Philippines. Annexation was a byproduct of the war, for the islands were annexed for strategic and economic reasons rather than for political ones. The independence movement flamed in the so-called Philippine Insurrection.*

REFERENCES: Edward J. Berbusse, *The United States in Puerto Rico, 1898–1900* (Chapel Hill: University of North Carolina Press, 1966); Garel A. Grunder and William E. Livezey, *The Philippines and the United States* (Norman: University of Oklahoma Press, 1951); Teodoro M. Kalaw, *The Philippine Revolution* (Quezon City: University of the Philippines Press, 1969); Hugh Thomas, *Cuba: The Pursuit of Freedom* (New York: Harper & Row, 1971).

INDIANA (ship)

The U.S.S. *Indiana* was commissioned 20 November 1895. Designated as a coast battleship, *Indiana,* like her sister-ships *Oregon** and *Massachusetts,** was given a small coal capacity. As such, she had limited range and endurance. With a displacement of 10,288 tons, *Indiana*-class battleships were the first U.S. battleships to carry hull numbers; *Indiana* was BB-1. Her armament consisted of four 13-inch guns, eight 8-inch guns, four 6-inch guns, six torpedo tubes, and thirty smaller-caliber weapons. She had a speed of 15.5 knots and an armor belt

of 18 inches. Because of low freeboard, the *Indiana*-class battleships, reminiscent of monitors,* were usually awash in any kind of heavy seas. This characteristic limited the use of the 13-inch turret guns. In addition, when trained
abeam, the main battery guns caused a list to the extent that the armor belt was
completely submerged on one side. This instability hampered effective gunnery
and seaworthiness.

Indiana was part of Admiral William T. Sampson's* fleet in Cuban waters
sent to blockade* that island and also to locate Admiral Pascual Cervera's*
Spanish fleet. *Indiana* suffered several mechanical breakdowns but was nevertheless able to keep station. Later *Indiana* bombarded San Juan,* Puerto Rico,
on 12 May 1898. Throughout May and early June *Indiana* performed fleet and
convoy duties in the Caribbean. On 2 July *Indiana* arrived off Santiago de Cuba*
with such a foul bottom that she could make only 10 knots. On 3 July, when
Cervera's fleet sailed from Santiago, *Indiana* was east of the mouth of the bay.
She opened fire on the Spanish *Infanta María Teresa** at about 9:40 A.M. As
the Spanish ships exited Santiago, *Indiana* and her consorts fired upon them.
One shell from *Indiana* struck *Plutón** amidships, killing everyone in the engine
room. *Indiana* also claimed many hits on *Vizcaya,** *Almirante Oquendo,** and
the two Spanish destroyers. During the Battle of Santiago, *Indiana* was hit twice
without injury. *Indiana* expended 1,876 rounds.

Subsequent to the naval battle, *Indiana* shelled the town of Santiago (10 July)
and was part of Sampson's planned fleet to travel to Europe to harass the Spanish coasts. General Nelson Miles's* request for armed convoy to Puerto Rico
interrupted that mission.

Indiana was sunk as an experiment in aerial bombing in Chesapeake Bay in
1920.

REFERENCE: John C. Reilly, Jr., and Robert L. Scheina, *American Battleships, 1886–
1923* (Annapolis, MD: Naval Institute Press, 1980).

INFANTA MARÍA TERESA (ship)

The Spanish *Infanta María Teresa* and her sister-ships *Almirante Oquendo**
and *Vizcaya** were armored cruisers launched in 1890–1891. Displacing about
7,000 tons, the cruisers had a speed of 20 knots and carried two 11-inch guns
fore and aft and ten 5.5-inch guns in company with smaller-caliber guns and
eight torpedo tubes. Detracting from this armament was a great amount of combustible material, mostly wood, in staterooms and cabins, as well as twin un-
shielded ammunition hoists that led directly to the 5.5-inch magazines.

Infanta had represented Spain in 1897 at New York for the inauguration of
the monument to U.S. Grant. However, *Infanta María Teresa* met her end in
Cuba at the battle of Santiago.* Admiral Pascual Cervera* led his fleet to Santiago, with each of the cruisers except *Vizcaya* towing a destroyer. Several mechanical breakdowns slowed the progress of the fleet. The first ship reached
anchorage in Santiago around 8:00 A.M., on 19 May 1898. On the day of the
battle, *Infanta María Teresa* led the Spanish fleet from the harbor. *Texas,**

Iowa,* Indiana,* and *Brooklyn** together fired on *Teresa* almost simultaneously and she caught fire. *Teresa* returned fire, but much of it was poorly aimed "overs." In addition to these woes, *Teresa*'s ammunition was often defective. A series of 8-inch hits on *Teresa* killed and disabled many of her crew, wrecked two of the 5.5-inch guns, and holed the hull, setting it ablaze. With the *Teresa*'s captain wounded, Admiral Cervera turned the ship into Nima-Nima Cove, where it grounded. *Gloucester** steamed in to rescue survivors, including Admiral Cervera.

In September 1898 a salvage company got the cruiser afloat and began the tow to Norfolk, Virginia. A storm parted the hawser, and *Infanta María Teresa* was lost.

REFERENCE: Alfredo Aguilera, *Buques de guerra españoles, 1885–1971* (Madrid: Librería Editorial San Martín, 1972).

INSURGENTS.
See CUBAN INSURRECTION; INSURRECTION OF 1895; PHILIPPINE INSURRECTION.

INSURRECTION OF 1895
The Ten Years' War* assuaged little of the revolutionary fervor of Cuba. Promised political reforms were not fulfilled, and many had been driven from Cuba by want and repression. The resurgence of the revolution depended upon the leadership of many of these expatriates: Máximo Gómez,* Antonio Maceo,* José Martí,* and others lived in Central America, Mexico, Venezuela, and, most significantly, in New York and other cities of the United States. New York possessed Cubans of influence and wealth; but importantly, they also enjoyed sympathy from various allies in the press* and from influential organizations. Their goal was independence,* and to achieve independence required another war. This war commenced inauspiciously the night of 10 April 1895 when Gómez and Martí and four others rowed ashore from a German freighter on a storm-lashed sea. Neither Gómez, Maceo, nor Martí expected to win the war through pitched battles; it was a guerrilla war in which the Cubans committed to ruin Cuba economically for Spain. Gómez ordered that all plantations be destroyed. He further ordered that any Cuban aiding in a sugar factory was a traitor to be summarily shot. From April to January, Gómez burned one end of Cuba to the other. Arsenio Martínez Campos,* the governor-general who had also arrived in April 1895, was unable, because of scruple and a dearth of effective forces, to halt the insurrection's destruction. Oddly, it was Martínez who outlined what was to become the *reconcentrado** policy. Martínez, however, did not have the stomach to implement it. Spanish prime minister Antonio Cánovas del Castillo* chose General Valeriano Weyler y Nicolau* to effect the reconcentration. It became a brutally effective policy; unintentionally, it also hastened the Spanish American War.

The Cuban junta,* the Cuban liberation army, and the Cuban League of the

United States found the grist of propaganda in ''Butcher'' Weyler, as he was called, and the suffering and death of thousands of Cubans. The Cuban Insurrection* was the source of repeated sparks that eventually inflamed U.S. public opinion, leading to war.
REFERENCE: Philip S. Foner, *The Spanish-Cuban-American War and the Birth of American Imperialism, 1895–1902* (New York: Monthly Review Press, 1972).

INTELLIGENCE OPERATIONS

During the years 1894–1897 the Naval War College* and the Office of Naval Intelligence* jointly prepared a series of contingency plans in the event of war with Spain. After the declaration of war on 22 April 1898, these plans were implemented with the U.S. North Atlantic Squadron* attempting a blockade* of Cuba. The Asiatic Squadron* also moved to destroy Spanish naval forces in the Philippines*; this was accomplished on 1 May. Meanwhile, in Florida and at San Francisco the U.S. Army assembled expeditionary forces destined for Cuba; these troops were under the command of General William R. Shafter.* Major General Wesley Merritt* commanded the Philippines-destined units.

For their part, the naval forces of Spain presented two distinct threats: First, Admiral Manuel de la Cámara* had assembled transports and naval vessels at Cádiz (Spain) to attack the Asiatic Squadron at Manila.* Second, Admiral Pascual Cervera y Topete's* squadron had left the Cape Verde Islands* steaming for the Americas. These two fleets and their movements became targets of the Office of Naval Intelligence. Another intelligence target was the Spanish army in Cuba; the Office of Naval intelligence pursued information about the Cuban countryside, Spanish movements there, and coordination with Cuba insurgents.*

The Office of Naval Intelligence did well in its first mission, that of providing timely intelligence on Cámara's squadron.

The second, regarding the movements of Cervera, was much less successful. Navy intelligence operated from two navy-run networks and benefited from the U.S. Army Signal Corps* network as well. The two navy networks were run by Lieutenant John C. Colwell* and Lieutenant William S. Sims,* both of whom planted agents, sowed disinformation, and established networks of informers as far away as Suez. As mentioned, the efforts directed at Cámara worked well; but Cervera was able to sail, destination unknown. The intelligence thread regarding Cervera was picked up by Martin L. Hellings,* a former manager of Western Union at Key West,* who had a network of telegraphers still operating in Cuba. It was Hellings, now an officer in the Signal Corps, who learned of Cervera's arrival at Santiago.*

The U.S. Army's Military Information Division* carried out army operations in Cuba and in Puerto Rico.* Lieutenant Andrew S. Rowan,* of ''message to García''* fame, and navy lieutenant Victor Blue* maintained a liaison with Cuban insurgents such as General Calixto García.* Lieutenant Henry H. Whitney* carried out covert operations in Puerto Rico for the Military Information Division under the guise of a merchant marine officer from Great Britain.* What

U.S. intelligence lacked in professionalism it surely made up in adventuresome spirit.

On the Spanish side, what little intelligence gathering occurred was largely ineffectual. Spanish naval lieutenant Ramón Carranza* attempted to run an operation in Montreal, but it was quickly compromised.

Elements of British intelligence were acquired by U.S. agents in Montreal and Hong Kong* and from Spanish sources. All these operations were covert to negate any breach of neutrality on the part of Great Britain.

REFERENCES: Graham A. Cosmas, *An Army for Empire* (Columbia: University of Missouri Press, 1971); G.J.A. O'Toole, *The Spanish War* (New York: W. W. Norton & Co. 1984).

IOWA (ship)

The U.S.S. *Iowa,* commissioned on 16 June 1897, displaced 11,340 tons. *Iowa*'s armament included four 12-inch guns, eight 8-inch guns, six 4-inch, and over thirty smaller-caliber weapons. Four torpedo tubes were fitted as well. *Iowa* boasted an armor belt of 14-inch thickness and had a speed of 17 knots. *Iowa* was a marked improvement over the *Indiana*-class* battleships, with greater freeboard, speed, and range, although the main battery diminished from 13 to 12 inches. *Indiana, Massachusetts,* *Oregon,* and *Iowa,* respectively BB-1 through BB-4, were the backbone of the blockade* of Cuba during the Spanish American War. From time to time Admiral William T. Sampson* shifted his flag to *Iowa;* thus *Iowa* was the first ship to fire on San Juan, Puerto Rico,* on 12 May 1898. Return fire from the shore battery hit *Iowa,* wounding three.

Iowa also participated in the June bombardments of Santiago de Cuba.* On 3 July, the day of Admiral Pascual Cervera's* attempted escape from Santiago, *Iowa* was stationed outside the harbor. Smoke was sighted inside the harbor, and *Iowa* signaled the rest of the fleet. Right at the mouth of the harbor, *Iowa* had the best view of the Spanish fleet as it steamed for the harbor mouth. *Iowa* engaged the first ship, *Infanta María Teresa,* then *Almirante Oquendo,* *Vizcaya,* and the destroyers *Plutón* and *Furor.* Later, upon recognizing that the Spanish had abandoned the fight, *Iowa* sent her boats to rescue Spanish seamen. Men of the *Iowa* reported often on the courage and dignity of the Spanish: Indeed, as a token of his respect, Captain Robley D. Evans of the *Iowa* would not accept the sword of the captain of *Vizcaya.*

Iowa was a good ship at sea, but the rapid pace of battleship development overtook her quickly. Shortly after the turn of the century, she served in menial tasks, ending her career as a radio-controlled gunnery target ship in 1920. Finally, in 1923 the *Mississippi* sank *Iowa* with her guns near the Gulf of Panama.

REFERENCES: John C. Reilly, Jr., and Robert L. Scheina, *American Battleships, 1886–1923* (Annapolis, MD: Naval Institute Press, 1980); H. W. Wilson, *The Downfall of Spain* (New York: Burt Franklin, 1971).

IRELAND, JOHN
(1838–1918)

John Ireland, archbishop of St. Paul, Minnesota, was a widely published author of political as well as religious subjects and an avid supporter of President William McKinley.* The Vatican utilized Ireland as an agent in the Cuban crisis immediately before the declaration of war. The pope wanted to intervene between Spain and the United States, hoping to arrange an armistice and the withdrawal of the North Atlantic Squadron* from Key West.* For political reasons— much of the country was anti-Catholic—McKinley could not seriously entertain a papal-arranged armistice, so nothing came of it.

REFERENCE: James H. Moynihan, *The Life of Archbishop John Ireland* (New York: Harper, 1953).

IRENE (ship)

The German-protected cruiser *Irene* (4,947 tons) arrived at Manila*, on 6 May 1898, steaming into the bay and ignoring *Olympia** and Commodore (later Admiral) George Dewey.* Although this was a breach of blockade etiquette, Dewey did not make an issue of it. Nevertheless, this minor incident rankled sufficiently that when another cruiser from Germany* (*Cormoran**) ignored a hail from a U.S. steam launch, the U.S.S. *Raleigh** fired a shot across *Cormoran*'s bow, thus punctuating the tensions between Germany and the United States in Eastern waters.

ISLA DE CUBA (ship)

Isla de Cuba was a large-sized gunboat of 1,045 tons with a two-masted schooner rig and four guns in the main battery. Like her sister-ship *Isla de Luzón,** *Cuba* was built in England in 1890. During the engagement at Manila,* *Cuba* was scuttled and burned; she suffered two wounded.

After the hostilities, *Cuba* was refloated by the Americans and sent to Hong Kong* to be refitted. She served in the U.S. Navy for a number of years and was finally sold to Venezuela and renamed *Mariscal Sucre*.

REFERENCE: Alfredo Aguilera, *Buques de guerra españoles, 1885–1971* (Madrid: Librería Editorial San Martín, 1972).

ISLA DE LUZÓN (ship)

Sister-ship to the *Isla de Cuba** and *Marqués de la Ensenada*, *Luzón* fought with them at the Battle of Manila.* As lighter gunboats, they stayed out of the heat of the action but nevertheless suffered six wounded. *Luzón,* like *Cuba,* was scuttled, and *Petrel** fired the ships.

Admiral George Dewey* criticized Admiral Patricio Montojo y Pasarón* for the latter's conduct during the battle, particularly since both *Cuba* and *Luzón* had torpedo tubes, yet neither was ordered into action.

Luzón, like *Cuba,* was refloated and entered the U.S. Navy under her original name. She survived until after World War I.

ISLE OF PINES (ISLA DE PINOS)

Part of the nation of Cuba, the Isle of Pines lies 30 miles to the southwest across the Gulf of Batabanó. Its role in the Spanish American war was minimal. The Naval War College* developed three plans in 1895 in case of war with Spain. These plans included the seizure of the Isle of Pines as a naval base— the only proposed annexation in prewar planning. It was suggested that this annexation would be in compensation for ridding Cuba of Spain.

On 1 July 1898 General Nelson Miles* proposed using the Isle of Pines as a base for cavalry action on the larger island, as well as for hospitals, supply depots, and entrepôt for the expedition to Puerto Rico.* Secretary of War Russell A. Alger* rejected the plan.

The island was omitted from the Platt Amendment,* and many Americans went to settle there believing it was indeed U.S. territory. A series of flawed treaties and judgments confused the issue further. In 1907 the U.S. Supreme Court ruled that the island was de facto part of Cuba, but the Senate did not ratify a treaty to that effect until 1925. As late as 1919, 25 percent of the population were U.S. citizens living in their own towns (one was named Mc-Kinley).

REFERENCE: Hugh Thomas, *Cuba: The Pursuit of Freedom* (New York: Harper & Row, 1971).

ITALY

A delicate balancing act was practiced among the European powers before, during, and, of course, after the Spanish American War. The need was to balance the power and influence of France,* Great Britain,* and especially Germany.* After the Franco-Prussian War, Germany had become the pivotal European power. (This balance of power changed in World War I, but the stresses and strains remained for many years.) Italy desired to enjoy support from both Great Britain and Germany for its own overseas ambitions—an increasingly difficult desire to fulfill. Italy had been repulsed in North Africa but still entertained aspirations for Ethiopia and possibly other foreign conquest.

The inchoate friction between Spain and the United States over Cuba caused nervous ripples in a variety of European council chambers, including Italy's. Spain teetered in its affection between France and the Triple Alliance. As another Mediterranean power, Italy struggled with the same balance. The threat to overseas expansion the American demands seemed to make of Spain alarmed many Italians, who had sympathy for Spain. As late as 27 March 1898, Visconti Venosta, Italian minister of foreign affairs, cabled Paris, London, St. Petersburg, Vienna, Berlin, Madrid, and Washington that Italy "guaranteed" its friendship with Spain. The Italian government also sought to mediate via Pope Leo XII in an attempt to avoid war and to continue negotiations. On 9 April 1898 representatives in Spain from Italy, Russia, Great Britain, and Austria-Hungary met to unite behind some joint action. The effort came to naught, however. At this point Rome considered further negotiations useless.

Thus the actions of Italy followed two paths: a diplomatic initiative to negotiate peace and an effort to keep Spain from leaning toward France.

REFERENCE: Fernando García Sáenz, "El contexto internacional de la guerra de Cuba: la percepción italiana del "98" español," *Estudios de Historia Social* 1–4 (1988): 295–310.

J

JACKSONVILLE, FLORIDA

Jacksonville served as an overflow camp for Fifth Corps.* General William R. Shafter* opened Jacksonville as an additional camp when Tampa* became too crowded. Major General Fitzhugh Lee* took command of Seventh Corps at Camp Cuba Libre* near Jacksonville, and it became one of the better-run camps of the war. Seventh Corps was to attack Havana,* but it never left Florida.

REFERENCE: *Correspondence Relating to the War with Spain,* 2 vols. (Washington, DC: Government Printing Office, 1902).

JAPAN

Like Great Britain* and Germany,* Japan played an important secondary role in the Spanish American War's Pacific theater. There was considerable tension in Washington and in Tokyo over Japanese immigration to Hawaii* and California. In March 1897 the Hawaiian government refused admittance to a boatload of Japanese. Sabers rattled as Japanese pronouncements increased in volume. The American navy prepared a war plan against Japan and at the same time increased its presence in Hawaii. John W. Foster, former secretary of state, drafted an annexation treaty that President William McKinley* received before the end of May. The impulse to annex Hawaii came from a desire to beat Japan at is own game. That the islands were not in fact annexed until the height of the Spanish American War reveals the additional strategic value of the islands as the Pacific conflict developed.

With growing nationalism and developing militarism, Japan also viewed events in the Philippines with more than casual interest. Not quite the spoiler that Germany tried to be, Japan made it plain that a native government at Manila* would be unacceptable. The restoration of Spanish rule could not succeed. If the United States withdrew from the Philippines, those islands would face threats from both Germany and Japan. Therefore, as a reasonable compromise Japan supported U.S. sovereignty.

REFERENCE: Lewis L. Gould, *The Spanish American War and President McKinley* (Lawrence: University Press of Kansas, 1982).

JÁUDENES Y ÁLVAREZ, FERMÍN

After the naval battle of Manila,* Commodore George Dewey* awaited reinforcements of land and sea forces. These reinforcements were complete by 6 August 1898.

The Spanish commander of the Spanish forces in the Philippines* was General Basilio Augustín Dávila,* who early recognized the futility of his position. In dispatches to Spain he repeatedly enumerated the hopelessness of his situation and through the British consul, E. H. Rawson-Walker, attempted to surrender to Dewey shortly after the American victory of 1 May. Sensing Dávila's desire to surrender, Spain replaced him with General Fermín Jáudenes y Álvarez, who became Spanish governor-general and also inherited a hopeless situation. Given insurgents and U.S. troops, he was outnumbered, and inasmuch as he was also surrounded, he could neither escape nor retreat into the countryside. Water had been cut off and rations exhausted, thus increasing the sickness of Spanish soldiers and civilians alike. There was no hope of a relief force from Spain, and in any event, Jáudenes no longer had communication links with Spain, Asia, or even the rest of the Philippines. After Rawson-Walker's sickness and death, Belgian consul Edouard André* carried on the diplomatic exchanges between Dewey, General Wesley Merritt,* and Jáudenes. Through these diplomatic exchanges, early in August Jáudenes began to discuss the possibility of surrender to the Americans after a token resistance to appease his Spanish superiors. This was, in fact, accomplished on 13 August 1898, when General Merritt received the surrender of Manila. Don Fermín Jáudenes was censured publicly, which fact angered many American officers familiar with the Spanish situation in Manila.

REFERENCE: Ignacio Salinas y Angulo, *Defensa del General Jáudenes* (Madrid: NP, 1899).

K

KAISERIN AUGUSTA (ship)

Kaiserin Augusta was Admiral Otto von Diedrichs's* flagship, a 6,218-ton cruiser launched in 1892. The arrival of the *Kaiserin Augusta* caused consternation to Commodore George Dewey,* who was holding Manila Bay* pending the arrival of Eighth Corps* and reinforcements. Diedrichs's arrival increased tensions significantly between Germany* and the United States.

KATAHDIN (ship)

Built by the Bath Iron Works of Bath, Maine, for the U.S. Navy, *Katahdin,* of 2,155 tons, was a ship built with one aim in mind: to ram enemy vessels. Antiquated in concept by the time of her commissioning on 20 February 1896, *Katahdin* was intended for harbor defense. Although the idea of ramming may have been questionable, *Katahdin* furthered several ideas that came to be associated with another type of vessel, the submarine.

The ram, to do its work, had to strike an enemy below the water line. *Katahdin* only had five feet of freeboard anyway, but to lower her dish-shaped hull more, the ram employed a double bottom that could be flooded to lower even further the ship's silhouette and ram strike point. As a result of this low profile, in any sea heavier than a calm backwater, *Katahdin* had to be kept sealed like a submarine. Poor ventilation smothered the crew in 110° F. heat in the wardroom; the engineering spaces were almost uninhabitable. After a fitful year she was decommissioned.

The Spanish American War resuscitated the ram as a putative defense against Spanish marauders on the eastern seaboard. Late in June 1898 *Katahdin* received orders to join the blockade* in Cuba, but before the ram arrived on station, Admiral Pascual Cervera's* fleet was destroyed.

Decommissioned immediately after the war, *Katahdin* survived until September 1909, when she was sunk as a gunnery target in Virginia.

REFERENCE: David Potter, " 'Old Half-Seas Under': Experiences in the U.S. Ram *Katahdin* during the War with Spain," *U.S. Naval Institute Proceedings* 68 (January 1942): 57–69.

KATIPUNAN

The Katipunan was an organization dedicated to the violent end of Spanish rule in the Philippines. Loosely based on Masonic rites and principles, the Katipunan was headed by Andrés Bonifacio,* who along with many other frustrated Filipinos sought a more radical organization than the Liga Filipina.* Bonifacio assumed leadership on 1 January 1896 and organized armed resistance and terrorist assassinations. The Katipunan operated as a shadow Filipino government with a president and various officers such as secretaries of state, war, justice interior, and finance. It attempted to ignite nationalistic fervor among the Philippine poor, and several of its leaders took inspiration from the French Revolution.

The Katipunan was only four years old when Bonifacio took over. Spanish authorities were generally unaware of the organization's existence and objectives until August 1896, when an Augustinian monk named Mariano Gil obtained information from a *katipuñero,* Teodoro Patiño, about an impending uprising. The Grito de Balintawak* sounded the Philippine revolution and bloodshed began. Philippine patriots tore into pieces their citizenship and tax cards and fighting broke out all over Luzon. Emilio Jacinto led Katipunan armies against Spanish forces. These were hard-fought engagements with serious losses to both sides.

Emilio Aguinaldo,* as president of the revolutionary government, in one sense represented a rival organization to the Katipunan. José Rizal,* soon-to-be martyr of the Liga Filipina was also too pacific for Bonifacio and Jacinto, although Rizal was held in great esteem by the Katipuñeros.

The Katipunan revolution generated considerable alarm among the Spanish and their native supporters. The Katipunan made overtures to Japan* for arms and support, but even without such support the Katipuñeros wrought havoc. The Spanish responded with some 4,000 arrests and exiles. There were numerous executions, which also hardened the resolve of many revolutionaries. On 3 December 1896 General Camilo de Polavieja* arrived in Manila as the new Spanish military governor. Polavieja, like his counterpart Valeriano Weyler* in Cuba, instituted harsh reconcentration* measures to control the population. Polavieja ordered the execution of Rizal. Eleven more were executed on 4 January 1897, including two priests. A week later another thirteen were executed.

Bonifacio's early successes were followed by a string of defeats, and the rising influence of Aguinaldo hastened the absorption of the Katipunan into Aguinaldo's American-inspired revolution. At the Tejeros Convention in March 1897, the representatives of several revolutionary factions voted to form a new revolutionary government. The Katipunan ended.

After the American arrival and during the Philippine Insurrection,* the Katipunan was revived briefly commencing in January 1900.

REFERENCES: Teodoro M. Kalaw, *The Philippine Revolution* (Kawilihan, P.I.: Jorge B. Vargas Filipiniana Foundation, 1969); Gregorio F. Zaide, *The Philippine Revolution* (Manila: Modern Book Company, 1968).

KENNAN, GEORGE
(1845–1924)

In early 1898 George Kennan was sent by the editors of *Outlook,* a weekly journal, to report on the war in general and the role of the American National Red Cross* specifically.

Kennan's reporting from the field in Cuba was extremely critical of the U.S. Army's leadership in terms of its planning for the invasion. Reporting that appeared in *Outlook* in early August 1898, for example, noted that troops at the front were suffering from short rations because of the inability to establish a safe landing point on the beach and the army's failure to bring sufficient wagons and mules to ensure the delivery of supplies within Cuba. Kennan's 30 July 1898 *Outlook* article, "The Wounded before Santiago," tied the suffering of the wounded to inadequate medical supplies and a shortage of trained medical personnel.

Following the war Kennan published *Campaigning in Cuba,* a book in which he strongly criticized the U.S. Army's failure to prevent loss of life among its troops due to disease. The most direct target of Kennan's criticism was Major General William R. Shafter,* the U.S. commander of the invasion force, whom Kennan depicted as a poor military strategist and a poor planner of medical care on the ground in Cuba.

Kennan's 1899 book also provides an interesting perspective on the news coverage of the war: "Few things impressed me more forcibly . . . than the costly, far-sighted, and far-reaching preparations made by the great newspapers of the country to report the war."

REFERENCES: George Kennan, *Campaigning in Cuba* (Port Washington: Kennikat Press, 1971 [reprint of the 1899 ed.]); George Kennan, "The Santiago Campaign: The Wrecking of the Army by Sickness," *Outlook,* October 22, 1898, pp. 471–476; George Kennan, "At the Front and in Siboney," *Outlook,* August 6, 1898, pp. 821–824; George Kennan, "The Wounded before Santiago," *Outlook,* August 6, 1898, pp. 769–774.

ALAN CORNISH

KENT, JACOB FORD
(1835–1918)

Born in Philadelphia, Jacob Ford Kent graduated from the U.S. Military Academy at West Point in 1861 and served in the infantry. In recognition of his gallantry, Kent was promoted in 1864 to captain of regulars and simultaneously brevetted to colonel of volunteers. After the war, he served on the American frontier, in 1895 commanding the 24th Infantry Regiment. Promoted to brigadier general of volunteers in May 1898, he commanded the First Infantry Division in General William Shafter's* Fifth Corps.* Kent's Division was at the left of the line before Santiago.* In the battle for San Juan Hill,* it was Kent's division that carried the hill on 1 July 1898. His lost 89 dead and 489 wounded.

Kent later served briefly in the Philippines. He had been promoted to major general of volunteers in July 1898. Promoted to brigadier general of regulars in October 1898, he retired the same month.

REFERENCE: French Ensor Chadwick, *The Relations of the United States and Spain* (New York: Russell & Russell, 1911).

KETTLE HILL, CUBA

To the right of the road from Siboney* to Santiago* and to the west of San Juan Hill lay Kettle Hill. Kettle Hill was positioned with a lagoon or pond between it and San Juan; a small stream flowed from the north on the west side of the hill. Kettle Hill therefore lay in the advance to San Juan Heights: It was the first objective.

Originally the Spanish had 137 trooper defending the hill, but the number was later increased. Against these forces Brigadier General H. S. Hawkins* led the Ninth and Tenth Cavalry* and the Rough Riders.* Once the crest was gained, Rough Rider Theodore Roosevelt* asked Brigadier S. S. Sumner* for permission to splash through the pond to seize the San Juan Heights. Doing so, Roosevelt became one of the immortals of the war. He later claimed that the action on Kettle Hill was the most important event in his life.

REFERENCES: Walter Millis, *The Martial Spirit* (Boston: Houghton Mifflin, 1931); Theodore Roosevelt, *The Rough Riders* (New York: Charles Scribner's Sons, 1899).

KEY WEST, FLORIDA

Key West, only 100 miles from Havana,* Cuba, was a natural springboard for military operations in the Caribbean. The United States kept a naval base at Key West, and the North Atlantic Squadron* used it for winter exercises in December 1897. In addition, Key West served as the advance naval base, and during the war dispatch boats and colliers traveled constantly in order to sustain the blockade* of Cuba. The North Atlantic Squadron and later the Flying Squadron* enforced the blockade.

Key West also served as the cable terminus for an intelligence operation* run out of Havana. Martin Luther Hellings* provided intelligence from insurgent sources in Cuba.

General Nelson A. Miles* wanted to use Key West as a staging area for the invasion of Puerto Rico,* but Secretary of War Russell A. Alger* overruled him. Nevertheless, some 4,000 men did embark on transports at Key West. Miles had previously ordered General William R. Shafter* to disperse troops at Tampa* to other locations in order to relieve the congestion.

For the Spanish, Key West was a target for destruction. Segismundo Bermejo*

sent Admiral Pascual Cervera* orders and an outline of plans for the reduction of Key West, but given U.S. naval superiority, nothing came of the plan.
REFERENCE: David F. Trask, *The War with Spain in 1898* (New York: Macmillan Publishing Co., 1981).

KIAOCHOW, CHINA

Germany's Vice Admiral Otto von Diedrichs* arrived at Kiaochow Bay on 14 November 1897, landed several hundred marines, and seized the bay in response to incidents between Chinese mobs. As a pretext for a German presence in China the incidents were wonderfully convenient. Within a few weeks over 4,500 German troops had invaded Kiaochow. Germany* was able to exact a lease of ninety-nine years and ensure economic predominance for Germany in Shantung Province. Rapidly, Kiaochow also became a naval base and cable terminus.

Kiaochow's significance in the Spanish American War occurred during peace negotiations. Possessing Kiaochow, the Germans also wanted coaling stations on navigation routes to the proposed Isthmian canal and elsewhere. The disputes over the Carolines and German Samoa resulted from these events.

Kiaochow was seized by Japan* in 1914 and returned to China in 1922.
REFERENCE: Alfred L. P. Dennis, *Adventures in American Diplomacy, 1896–1906* (New York: E. P. Dutton & Co., 1969).

KIMBALL, WILLIAM WARREN
(1848–1930)

A downeaster, William Warren Kimball graduated from the Naval Academy at Annapolis in 1869. He developed significant skills with torpedoes and was among the first to study them in depth and to write professionally on torpedoes and ordnance. In the late 1880s he became the friend of John Holland and worked to develop submarines as a tactical reality within the U.S. Navy.

During 1894–1897 Kimball was the intelligence officer on the staff of the Naval War College.* As such, he began a strategic study of the implications of a war with Spain after his superior, Lieutenant Commander Richard Wainwright,* urged him to do so. Kimball's plan (he had assistance from others, too) was primarily an operation to free Cuba through naval action: blockade,* attacks on Manila,* and attacks on the Spanish Mediterranean coast. Under constant review from 1896 until the outbreak of hostilities, this plan outlined the fundamental U.S. strategy during the war.

Kimball served in various commands, but during the Spanish American War he organized and commanded the Atlantic Torpedo Boat Flotilla. He retired in 1910 a rear admiral.
REFERENCE: John A. S. Grenville and George Berkeley Young, *Politics, Strategy, and American Diplomacy* (New Haven, CT: Yale University Press, 1966).

KIPLING, RUDYARD
(1865–1936)

The debate in the United States over whether to pursue an imperialist and colonial policy heated significantly with the discussion over the status of the Philippines.* The Anti–Imperialist League* became active in opposition to the annexation of overseas territories. Support for an American empire came from England in the unlikely form of a poem. Rudyard Kipling published ''The White Man's Burden''* in February 1899 in more than a half dozen places. Some versions sported the subtitle ''The United States and the Philippine Islands,'' and others, ''An address to the United States.'' Kipling's encouragement of the United States to follow Great Britain on a romantic crusade ''to take up the white man's burden'' became a contemporary call to Anglo-Saxon and Christian duty and subsequently became an epithet for racism.

Curiously, the U.S. copyright edition of ''The White Man's Burden'' was first published as a pamphlet by the Anti-Imperialist League* on 18 February 1899. Why the league should publish Kipling's poem remains a mystery.

REFERENCE: James McG. Stewart, *Rudyard Kipling: A Bibliographical Catalogue* (Toronto: Dalhousie University Press, 1959).

KRAG-JÖRGENSEN RIFLE

In 1893, after ten years of exhaustive testing, the U.S. Army received its first magazine, bolt-action, .30-caliber general issue rifle, the Krag-Jörgensen, named for its Norwegian designers. After the rifle had been exhaustively tested and modified, production began in the Springfield Armory in 1894. Equal to or better than any European military rifle, the Krag, as it was known, remained the U.S. Army rifle until 1903, undergoing numerous modifications during its tenure. Utilizing smokeless powder, the Krag became the standard issue for the army regulars. In fact, at the outbreak of the Spanish American War only the regulars had Krags. The volunteer units and National Guard* units had none. In the confusion of the rapid buildup, the decision to equip the regulars first had implications in deciding which units would be the first to fight. The arsenals did not have sufficient equipment, and the federal armories could not produce Krags. Without licensing, private armories could not produce them.

In actual combat, the differences were often slight between the Krag and the older Springfield. The Krag was fired as a single-loader in combat, which nullified its magazine. Volume of fire was less important than accuracy, and the effective range of both weapons was about the same. The Krag possessed only two real advantages: a flatter trajectory and smokeless powder.

REFERENCES: William S. Brophy, *The Krag Rifle* (North Hollywood, CA: Beinfeld Publishing, 1980); Graham A. Cosmas, *An Army for Empire* (Columbia: University of Missouri Press, 1971).

KUSAIE, CAROLINES

The easternmost island of the Carolines and only 8 miles in diameter, Kusaie became a pawn in the peace negotiations* at the end of the Spanish American

War. Kusaie, Yap, and Ponape had been secretly ceded to Germany* provided that Spain achieved her aims in the process. Spain also later tried to use Kusaie as a bargaining chip with the United States. Nevertheless, Germany acquired all the Carolines for a price; the treaty concluded on 10 February 1899 was ratified in June of the same year.

REFERENCES: H. Wayne Morgan, *Making Peace with Spain: The Diary of Whitelaw Reid* (Austin: University of Texas Press, 1965); Harold H. Sprout and Margaret T. Sprout, *The Rise of American Naval Power, 1776–1918* (Princeton, NJ: Princeton University Press, 1939); Harold H. Sprout and Margaret T. Sprout, *Toward a New Order of Sea Power* (Princeton, NJ: Princeton University Press, 1939).

L

LAKELAND, FLORIDA

As the Fifth Corps* of the U.S. Army swelled in numbers during May 1898, additional camps were used to relieve congestion at Tampa.* One of these was at Lakeland, Florida; another was at Jacksonville.* Lakeland was the scene of some minor and not so minor racial incidents. The camp was vacated when the expeditionary force sailed for Cuba in June.

LANDING CRAFT

Despite the experience of the U.S. Marines and the U.S. Navy in occasional amphibious training operations before the Spanish American War, the services were caught wholly unprepared for the logistical demands of the army in its expedition to Cuba. Transports were in short supply and had to be commandeered. Many of these ships were without adequate ventilation, storage, or quarters. Landing craft per se were still a dream of the future. Lifeboats, naval launches, tugs, barges, and steam lighters were pressed into duty to ferry troops, provisions, munitions, and transport through the surf to the shore. Chaos was the result, and it speaks well for the initiative of the commanders that the landing was successful at all.

The Eighth Corps* in the Philippines used lifeboats and steam launches also. These were supplemented by native craft pressed into onerous duty to transport troops ashore. By the very nature of such transport, numerous accidents occurred, causing loss of life and casualties.

REFERENCE: Graham A. Cosmas, *An Army for Empire* (Columbia: University of Missouri Press, 1971).

LAWTON, HENRY WARE
(1843–1899)

Henry Ware Lawton left his Ohio birthplace at a tender age and grew up in Indiana. Enlisting in the Civil War in 1861, he was commissioned first lieutenant. He fought at Shiloh, Murfreesboro, and Chickamauga. By war's end he had been brevetted to colonel and awarded the Medal of Honor for an action near Atlanta.

Briefly studying law at Harvard after the war, Lawton accepted a commission with regulars and served in Texas, Indian Territory, and Arizona under Ranald MacKenzie and Nelson Miles.* It was Lawton who captured Geronimo after a lengthy pursuit.

Promoted to brigadier general of volunteers in May 1898, Lawton was placed in command of General William R. Shafter's* Second Division within the Fifth Corps.* Upon landing at Daiquirí,* Shafter ordered Lawton to advance toward Siboney* with the intent to provide support and protection for additional landings. Brigadier General John C. Bates's* Independent Brigade was to support Lawton.

Meanwhile, General Joseph Wheeler,* commander of the dismounted cavalry division, maneuvered to bypass Lawton in what became a successful effort to draw first blood at Las Guásimas.* Lawton attempted to inform Shafter of Wheeler's initiative, but Shafter was still offshore.

Lawton's division next prepared for the attack on El Caney,* which straddled the road from Santiago* to Guantánamo.* Concerned that El Caney might serve as a source of flanking attacks, Shafter fingered the community as one of two secondary targets on the way to San Juan Hill* and Santiago. Accordingly, Lawton and Generals Adna R. Chaffee* and Joseph Wheeler spent 28 and 29 June 1898 reconnoitering El Caney. Wheeler discovered that General Joaquín Vara del Rey* commanded about 500 Spanish troops there. After the seemingly easy victory at Las Guásimas, U.S. leaders felt that El Caney would fall with little or no pressure. In this supposition the Americans erred. Because of El Caney's tactical utility for the Spanish, Shafter would not attack San Juan Hill until El Caney had been seized.

Lawton was ready to attack at 7 A.M. on 1 July. For thirty minutes there had been an artillery barrage—without Spanish reply, for Vara de Rey had no artillery—and then Lawton's 5,400-man division attacked a Spanish force one-tenth its size, and for eight hours of full-scale attack, the Spanish held their ground. Lawton was forced to commit his reserve. Only when the American artillery battery found the range on the stone fort at El Viso did the battle turn. Even so, the Spanish did not retreat but continued to fight until only approximately eighty men remained. American losses included 81 killed, and 360 wounded.

Lawton was later made military governor of Santiago, but he developed a drinking problem in Cuba and was soon replaced. On 10 March 1899 Lawton arrived in the Philippines to serve under General Elwell S. Otis* in what became known as the Philippine Insurrection.* Lawton was killed in action in December 1899.

REFERENCES: French Ensor Chadwick, *The Relations of the United States and Spain*, 2 vols. (New York: Russell & Russell, 1911); George Kennan, *Campaigning in Cuba*

(Port Washington: Kennikat Press, 1971); William Thaddeus Sexton, *Soldiers in the Sun* (Harrisburg, PA: Military Service Publishing, 1939); Joseph Wheeler, *The Santiago Campaign, 1989* (New York: Drexel Biddle, 1899).

LEE, FITZHUGH
(1835–1905)

A U.S. Army officer and a Confederate army officer, Fitzhugh Lee was born in Fairfax County, Virginia, the grandson of Henry "Light-Horse Harry" Lee and the nephew of Robert E. Lee. He graduated from West Point in 1856 and was commissioned in the cavalry. Lee served as instructor at both Carlisle Barracks, Pennsylvania, and West Point, New York. He resigned his commission with the U.S. Army when hostilities started and joined the Confederate army. During the Civil War, Lee served with distinction in cavalry forces of the army of Northern Virginia, rising through the ranks and becoming major general in September 1863.

Lee was active for the next twenty years in various Confederate veterans' organizations and worked hard writing, promoting, and teaching the history of the South during the Civil War. He was influential in working for the reconciliation and rehabilitation of the South during Reconstruction. He became interested in politics, especially the Democratic party, and was elected governor of Virginia in 1885, serving one term. In 1893 he lost an election for the U.S. Senate. In 1896 President Grover Cleveland* appointed him consul general in Havana,* Cuba. President McKinley* retained him after his election to the presidency in 1897.

Cuba was in chaos by 1897. The liberal Spanish government, headed by Práxides Mateo Sagasta,* attempted to pacify the rebels by offering home rule to Puerto Rico* as well as to Cuba. Lee monitored the situation and gathered as much information as was available by holding meetings and acting as a peace mediator. He was at first sympathetic to the rebel insurgents and pressed for American intervention. McKinley wanted the Spanish government to work out the problems without American interference. This diplomatic approach troubled Lee terribly, and his reports to the State Department recounted horrible tales of mass murder in a Cuba struggling with an inept Spanish government in a fight for survival.

Lee reexamined his views on the intervention of the United States into the conflict and adopted a more conservative approach. President McKinley had already ordered the U.S.S. *Maine** into Havana Harbor on 24 January to protect American interests after the Havana riots on 12 January 1897. It was only a few hours later that Consul General Lee cabled Washington not to send a warship, albeit too late. Eventually Lee saw the battleship's presence in Havana Harbor as a means of maintaining the status quo in Cuba. He became convinced that Cuban autonomy would fail due to the lack of reforms promised and the misery suffered by the Cuban people.

The sinking of the U.S.S. *Maine* and the declaration of war ended Lee's tenure as consul general in Havana. He returned to Washington on 12 April 1898. His tenure as consul general in Havana was at a time of considerable controversy and political upheaval, which he handled relatively well. His reports and information were crucial in the shaping of policies adopted by the McKinley administration. On 5 May 1898, Lee was commissioned a major general in the U.S. Army and given command of the Seventh Army Corps.* He never participated in combat during the war, although his Seventh Corps trained intensely in Jacksonville,* Florida, for the possible invasion of Havana.

In January 1899 Lee and the Seventh Corps were sent as an occupational force to establish order in Havana. On 12 April 1899 to 2 March 1901, Lee was made brigadier general of volunteers by the Volunteer Services Act of 2 March 1899. During this period he also commanded the Department of the Missouri. He retired from military service on 2 March 1901.

In 1894, Lee wrote a biography of his uncle, Robert E. Lee; he also wrote *Cuba's Struggle,* a massive work about Cuba's 400-year struggle with Spain. Lee wore many hats, including those of soldier, farmer, diplomat, historian, and businessman. At the time of his death, Lee was involved in the planning for the Jamestown Exposition of 1907. He died on 28 April 1905 in Washington, D.C.
REFERENCES: Michael Blow, *A Ship to Remember: The* Maine *and the Spanish American War* (New York: William Morrow & Co., 1992); James L. Nichols, *General Fitzhugh Lee: A Biography* (Lynchburg, VA: H. E. Howard, 1989); David F. Trask, *The War with Spain in 1898* (New York: Macmillan Publishing Co., 1981).

RICHARD W. PEUSER

LEGAZPI (ship)

Legazpi was an iron-hulled freighter built at Sunderland, England, in 1874 as the British *Formosa.* Displacing 1,024 tons, the steamer was bought by Spain in Hong Kong* in 1880 and used in the Far East for several years as part of the naval forces in the Philippines.* Spain armed her with small 3.5-inch Hontoria guns and later with Nordenfelt machine guns. In 1884 *Legazpi* left Manila* for Spain, where she engaged in transport duties between Spain and the African colonies. Then in the 1890s *Legazpi* steamed to Cuba,* where she was lost on 13 November 1898 at Cape Gavilán.

Legazpi and *Alfonso XII* were moored 200 yards to starboard of the U.S.S. *Maine** on 15 February 1898, when the latter exploded in Havana.*
REFERENCE: Alfredo Aguilera, *Buques de guerra españoles, 1885–1971* (Madrid: Librería Editorial San Martín, 1972).

LEO XIII, POPE
(1810–1903)

Gioachino Vincenzo Pecci served as pope from 1878 until his death. As Pope Leo XIII, he offered to mediate the escalating crisis between the United States and Spain over the rebellion in Cuba. This offer was made in late March and early April 1898, at a time when the U.S. position was hardened toward war with Spain barring unilateral concession that provided a clear path to Cuban independence. The pontiff's offer of mediation was communicated by Spanish foreign minister Pío Gullón to Stewart Woodford,* the U.S. ambassador to Spain. The offer was rejected primarily because of insistence upon the withdrawal of U.S. naval forces from the vicinity of Cuba. As Secretary of State William R. Day* noted in a communication with Woodford, "The disposition of our naval forces must be left to us." The U.S. government thus rejected the pontiff's mediation offer.

However, Minister Gullón erroneously reported to Woodford that President William McKinley* had accepted the pope as a mediator. Woodford knew the message had been garbled, and so he clarified the situation in Madrid: Spain and the pope believed papal mediation meant McKinley would back away from his position on Cuba. Woodford explained that an armistice would mean that Cuba would either be ceded to the United States, or granted autonomy.

REFERENCE: Ernest R. May, *Imperial Democracy* (New York: Harcourt, Brace & World, 1961).

ALAN CORNISH

LEÓN Y CASTILLO, FERNANDO DE
(1842–1918)

Fernando de León y Castillo was by training a lawyer, but he enjoyed a distinguished political career under Práxides Mateo Sagasta.* León also served as Spain's ambassador to Paris (1887, 1892, and 1897–1910). In this latter capacity León attempted to negotiate a joint resolution by several European powers during the crisis surrounding the destruction of the U.S.S. *Maine.** He failed in this attempt when Great Britain* would not comply and it became evident that neither would Germany.*

Later, on 18 July 1898, on the instructions of the Spanish foreign minister, el Duque de Almodóvar del Río,* León approached the French about the possibility of a ceasefire or an armistice. The Spanish government had already lost its Atlantic Squadron under Admiral Pascual Cervera,* and Santiago de Cuba* had surrendered on 17 July. Manila* was sure to follow. Various communiqués between the Spanish and the French then precipitated French overtures to the United States. A series of delays held up the process, but the French minister entrusted with the mission, Jules Cambon,* labored diligently. Meanwhile on 25 July U.S. forces landed in Puerto Rico.* León's role in these early feelers was primarily that of envoy.

Later in September León participated with the Peace Commission* in Paris. He comprehended Spain's poor bargaining position and worked unstintingly in his nation's interest, at one point plaintively entreating Whitelaw Reid* to endorse France's proposals.

REFERENCES: H. Wayne Morgan, ed., *Making Peace with Spain: The Diary of Whitelaw Reid* (Austin: University of Texas Press, 1965); David F. Trask, *The War with Spain in 1898* (New York: Macmillan Publishing Co., 1981).

LEYDEN (ship)

U.S.S. *Leyden* was an armed tug or towboat fitted with 6-pounders, 3-pounders, and machine guns. On 21 July 1898, in company with *Annapolis,* Topeka,** and *Wasp, Leyden* attacked the Spanish battery at Nipe Bay* and the Spanish gunboat *Jorge Juan. Jorge Juan* sank, bow first, but her crew escaped in boats by rowing ashore. The attacking force either threaded its way through thirteen Spanish mines at the mouth of Nipe Bay or luckily missed them. Also sunk in the attack was the small Spanish gunboat *Baracoa.* American sources claim there were over thirty mines, but the Spanish count of thirteen must be more credible.

REFERENCE: Augustín Rodríguez González, "Operaciones menores en Cuba, 1898," *Revista de Historia Naval* 3 (1985): 125–146.

LIGA FILIPINA

Founded by José Rizal* on 3 July 1892, the Liga Filipina was a Philippine reform organization that sought to unite the peoples of the archipelago, encourage education and commerce, and promote reform. Rizal appealed to the upper classes in Philippine society and while not openly revolutionary nor anti-Catholic, Rizal was anticlerical and argued strenuously for reform. Rizal was not successful and was, in fact, deported. Nevertheless, the Liga Filipina served as a catalyst for the more militant Katipunan,* which led the revolution that swept through the islands.

REFERENCE: Teodoro M. Kalaw, *The Philippine Revolution* (Kawilihan, P.I.: Jorge B. Vargas Filipiniana Foundation, 1969).

LINARES Y POMBA, ARSENIO
(1848–1914)

General Arsenio Linares y Pomba was made a lieutenant in 1868. He received promotions regularly thereafter for service in conflicts in Cuba, against the Carlists in Spain, and in the Philippines. He returned to Cuba as division general and the governor of Santiago de Cuba.* It was Linares who organized the defenses of Santiago against U.S. troops.

The governor-general of Cuba, Ramón Blanco y Erenas* had notified Linares in April 1898 that Santiago was the American objective. Linares had under his command over 35,000 men, but they were dispersed throughout the district as various garrisons. By 20 June Linares commanded over 9,400 men at Santiago. The addition of Admiral Pascual Cervera's* sailors increased the complement by over 1,000 men. Many have criticized, perhaps justly, Linares's failure to concentrate the total of his forces at Santiago to repulse the Americans. In hindsight, it was an easy criticism to make. However, Linares was engaged in a war not just with U.S. forces but also with Cuban insurrectionists,* who ranged the countryside. Movement of troops would have exposed them to severe harassing fires and ambushes. Movement by water was impossible. Additionally, the political implications of abandoning Spanish loyalists in cities like Baracoa,

Guantánamo,* Holguín,* or Manzanillo* must have loomed darkly before Linares. If these reasons proved insufficient, the last was most compelling: There were insufficient supplies for the Spanish force at Santiago, so that an additional 25,000 men would have meant disaster.

Linares positioned his men in a perimeter, but it was obvious that the cause was lost before it began. Without the possibility of resupply or reinforcement from sea or land, all Linares could do was await the inevitable attack by the Americans.

Linares bravely defended Santiago, personally leading his men at San Juan Hill,* where he was seriously wounded in the arm on 1 July 1898.

REFERENCES: José Müller y Tejeiro, *Battles and Capitulation of Santiago de Cuba* (Washington, DC: Government Printing Office, 1899); Severo Gómez Núñez, *La Guerra Hispano-Americana* (Madrid: Imprimería del Cuerpo de Artillería, 1899–1902).

LODGE, HENRY CABOT
(1850–1924)

Not only was Henry Cabot Lodge born in Boston in 1850, but he was also born *into* Boston society. Across the street lived George Bancroft, the Republic's premier historian. Family friends included Senator Rufus Choate, abolitionist Charles Sumner, writers Henry Wadsworth Longfellow and Francis Parkman, and others of similar wealth, rank, and intellectual achievement. Lodge's own family listed grandfather George Cabot, a senator, who was an intimate of numerous Revolutionary figures, including George Washington, Alexander Hamilton, John Adams, and others. Lodge's education included a significant dose of patriotism ingested during the Civil War. Although he was too young to fight, the passions stirred by the conflict abided his entire life. Lodge also toured Europe in the grand manner: First in 1866 and again in 1871, the latter a honeymoon interspersed with Harvard attendance. Lodge became among the first three Ph.D.'s minted in 1876 from Harvard. He taught history at Harvard for three more years and began a publishing regimen that served him well. Lodge quite naturally also became intrigued with politics. He became a confidant of Theodore Roosevelt* and other political aspirants in the Republican cause. In Congress, Lodge sat next to William McKinley.* Lodge began a campaign in the early 1890s to obtain a seat in the Senate. Since he was not one to wait for office to come to him, he campaigned vigorously in pursuit of office and became a senator in 1893.

As a senator, Lodge viewed himself as a pragmatic politician. Foreign affairs were important to him as a competitive arena in which access to raw materials, markets, and national prestige were the stakes. He shared this sentiment with Theodore Roosevelt.* Expansionism, for Lodge, was a necessity driven by a complex appeal to idealism, patriotism, economic advantage, and the possibility of developing transportation and communication facilities. Lodge reveled in A. T. Mahan's* doctrines and was committed to arming for defense. In this Lodge and Roosevelt were allies, although Lodge did not collude with Roosevelt in drafting orders to Commodore George Dewey* to prepare to attack the Philippines, as has been frequently reported. A member of the Foreign Relations Committee, Lodge watched events in Cuba closely. He deliberately kept silent after the explosion of the U.S.S. *Maine** in Havana,* awaiting the results of the inquiry. Realizing that the mood of Congress was warlike, Lodge worked closely with President McKinley and Congress to draft a joint resolution. The resolution, done at the behest and initiative of the president, desired that Spain be expelled from Cuba. Once the McKinley initiative was passed (19 April 1898), Lodge ended his silence and voiced his ardent nationalism.

Lodge supported the war with more than rhetoric. He turned his house at Nahant, Massachusetts, over to the U.S. Army as a signal station. One of his sons served on *Dixie** and saw action off Cuba. His son-in-law also saw action. Lodge also arranged events to cement greater unity within the nation. In 1861 the Sixth Massachusetts had marched through Baltimore accompanied by hurled stones, boos, and violence. Lodge arranged for the same unit to march through Baltimore on 20 May playing "Dixie." The result was cheers, flags, and warm patriotic feeling.

The American victory filled Lodge with pride and also ambition. He lobbied to be a member of the Peace Commission.* President McKinley, however, felt he was too expansionist for the commission and too junior on the Foreign Relations Committee.

Lodge labored incessantly to acquire the Philippines. He cared little what happened in the Caribbean so long as Spain was evicted, but the Philippines represented an opportunity not to be missed. In addition to trade and economic arguments for the acquisition of a Far East base was a moral one: Lodge felt it repugnant to leave the insurgents to the Spanish. He played a key role in the debate over the Philippines and introduced clever parliamentary initiatives to further his aims. Along with several others, Lodge claimed credit for the Senate approval of the treaty with Spain.

Lodge continued to work for a developing American expansionism and to support his friend Roosevelt, now a war hero.

REFERENCES: John A. Garraty, *Henry Cabot Lodge: A Biography* (New York: Alfred A. Knopf, 1953); Henry Cabot Lodge, *The War with Spain* (New York: Arno Press, 1970), William C. Widenor, *Henry Cabot Lodge and the Search for an American Foreign Policy* (Berkeley: University of California Press, 1980).

LONG, JOHN DAVIS
(1838–1915)

John Davis Long, who later became governor of Massachusetts and secretary of the navy, grew up near his birthplace in Maine. Although none of his family were politicians, Long enjoyed his family's keen interest in public affairs. Educated at Harvard, Long's first employment was as a teacher, a career he pursued for two years. In fall 1859 he began to read law in Boston; he was admitted to the bar in January 1861. The same year, Long became interested in politics and made speeches. From this tentative beginning Long developed a vocation in 1871, when he ran for the state legislature. He was elected speaker in 1876, testimony of his oratorical prowess. Two years later Long became lieutenant governor, and by 1880, governor of the state of Massachusetts. By 1883 he was serving in Congress. During the 1880s and while in Congress, Long seized the attention of several politicians, including William McKinley.* In Fall 1891 President-elect McKinley asked Long to serve on his cabinet as secretary of the navy.

As the wartime secretary of the navy, Long pushed ahead with characteristic steadiness and probity. Some of Long's insights into co-workers are interesting. He praised his assistant Theodore Roosevelt* as full of boundless energy and thoroughly honest, but occasionally lacking in judgment. He felt Russell A. Alger* was unprepared, but full of bluster. Long took great pride in the thoroughness with which the new American navy was equipped and armed. Yet Long appreciated economy and felt that he ran an economical bureau through superior administration. Long's forte was as politician and as a manager. For example, he supported William T. Sampson* in his controversy with Winfield S. Schley.* He believed the United States should not keep the Philippines but felt the risks and responsibilities of expansion were exaggerated. He accepted the expansionists reluctantly.

Long did not cooperate well with the War Department (or vice versa), but lack of cooperation was pervasive at all levels. Interservice squabbling was a frustrating experience for all.

Long left the cabinet in 1902 and began work on a history of the U.S. Navy. He also published some of his own poetry. Long died in 1915.

REFERENCES: John D. Long, *America of Yesterday as Reflected in the Journal of John Davis Long* (Boston: Atlantic Monthly Press, 1923); John D. Long, *The New American Navy,* 2 vols. (New York: Outlook Co., 1903).

LUDINGTON, MARSHALL INDEPENDENCE
(1839–1919)

Born in Pennsylvania, Marshall Independence Ludington was given his middle name after the holiday of his birth: July Fourth. Ludington served as quartermaster in various units during the Civil War and was brevetted to brigadier general of volunteers in 1865. He worked his way up the ranks, becoming brigadier and quartermaster general on 3 February 1898.

As quartermaster general, Ludington began war preparations in earnest after a 3 April 1898 meeting with the War Department. Wagons, mules, tropical uniforms—every aspect of equipping and arming the soon-to-be assembling troops fell upon the Quartermaster and Ordnance departments. Previous to the War Department meeting of 3 April, Ludington realized the strains that a rapid buildup would present to his bureau. He made plans for contracting out of his own shops, eventually delegating contracting authority to subordinates. By war's end about two-thirds of the tents and clothing procured for the troops came from sources outside the system. Ludington's system of contracts and negotiated prices was also followed by the Ordnance Department.* When it became obvious that demand for clothing and tentage would outstrip capacity, Ludington improvised with below-standard army cloth. His idea was that the soldier would prefer to have a less-than-standard issue uniform or tent than none at all. Naturally, Ludington and his bureau were heavily criticized by the press and by politicians for this perceived shortchanging of soldiers, despite the fact that other options were few or nonexistent. Ludington also attempted to raise efficiency in shipping. In cooperation with the railroads, he forwarded contents lists of individual freight cars and had each freight car carry a brief shipping manifest on its exterior.

Some of Ludington's efforts came to naught. He tried vainly to secure the lightweight cotton cloth the British called khaki, but no American mills could produce it. Other failures ascribed to Ludington, such as the failure to acquire transports and shipping lighters, were not really his failures. The War Department changed its plans without warning, creating logistical nightmares on top of the generalized and rapid buildup. Ludington showed commendable enterprise in administration during difficult times by initiating changes frequently before the need was felt. Ludington was promoted to major general in 1903, and he retired soon after.

REFERENCE: Graham A. Cosmas, *An Army for Empire* (Columbia: University of Missouri Press, 1971).

LUDLOW, WILLIAM
(1843–1901)

Born in Islip, Long Island, New York, William Ludlow graduated from West Point in 1864 and served with distinction during the Civil War. He was commissioned in the engineers and served in a variety of positions and posts. In May 1898 Ludlow was promoted to brigadier general of volunteers and commanded the First Brigade at El Caney* under Henry Lawton's* division in Cuba. He was also the ranking overseas engineer and as such charged with embarking General Calixto García's* force at Aserraderos.*

In September 1898 he was promoted to major general of volunteers, and in January 1900 his permanent rank was advanced to brigadier.

After the war Ludlow served as military governor at Havana,* where he used his engineering expertise to advantage. He also led a board of officers, later called the Ludlow Board, that recommended an Army War College in 1900. He died after a short illness in August 1901.

REFERENCE: French Ensor Chadwick, *The United States and Spain,* 2 vols. (New York: Russell & Russell, 1968).

LUZON, PHILIPPINES

Luzon is the largest and most important island in the Philippine archipelago. The principal Spanish defense centered at Manila,* the capital, and at Cavite,* also on Luzon. It was at Manila that Admiral Patricio Montojo* awaited the American squadron led by Admiral George Dewey.* It was to relieve Luzon and its environs that Admiral Manuel de la Cámara* sailed from Spain on 16 June 1898 with his Eastern Squadron.* It was also on Luzon that the Liga Filipina* and insurrectionist movement like the Katipunan* had their start and retained their strength. In short, Luzon was the principal stage for the Spanish American War in the Philippines.

Luzon also played an important role as bargaining chip in the posthostilities peace negotiations.* Expansionists in the United States wanted all the Philippines; moderates were willing to settle for only a naval base at Manila Bay. The mood of expansionism* prevailed, and Luzon, along with the rest of the Philippines, passed into U.S. possession.

REFERENCE: David F. Trask, *The War with Spain in 1898* (New York: Macmillan Publishing Co., 1981).

M

MACARTHUR, ARTHUR
(1845–1912)

Arthur MacArthur was born in Massachusetts but grew up and was educated in Milwaukee. At age seventeen MacArthur obtained a commission in the Twenty-fourth Wisconsin Infantry, and he distinguished himself repeatedly so that by the end of the Civil War, he was a colonel of volunteers but not yet twenty years of age. After the war, he entered the regular army and served on the frontier and in the Adjutant General's Department.

When the Spanish American War broke out, MacArthur was promoted to brigadier general and joined Eighth Corps* under General Wesley Merritt.* MacArthur commanded the right in the attack on Manila* on 13 August 1898. His brigade suffered five killed and thirty-eight wounded while taking the objective.

Promoted again, MacArthur commanded the forces that defeated Emilio Aguinaldo* in the Philippine Insurrection.*

REFERENCE: William Thaddeus Sexton, *Soldiers in the Sun* (Harrisburg, PA: Military Service Publishing Co., 1939).

MCCALLA, BOWMAN HENDRY
(1844–1910)

Born in New Jersey, Bowman Hendry McCalla graduated from the Naval Academy in 1864. He served in ships in both oceans and in European waters. Later he taught at the academy. While commanding *Enterprise*, McCalla struck a mutinous sailor named John Waller. He was court-martialed for striking a mutinous fireman but survived this career blow. In 1897 he was appointed commander of the U.S.S. *Marblehead,** which command he retained during the Spanish American War. Aboard *Marblehead* he commanded a division of the Cuban blockade* near Havana* and also near Cienfuegos.* In June 1898 he was sent with a U.S. Marine Corps* battalion to Guantánamo,* where he created a naval base that he also commanded.

After the war McCalla served in the Philippines and China. He was promoted to rear admiral in 1903.

REFERENCE: Paolo E. Coletta, *Bowman Hendry McCalla, Fighting Sailor* (Washington, DC: University Press of America, 1979).

MCCLERNAND, EDWARD JOHN
(1848–1926)

Son of Major General John Alexander McClernand of Civil War fame, Edward John McClernand graduated from West Point in 1870 and served in the western states against the Nez Percé. He earned the Congressional Medal of Honor in 1894. Eventually promoted to brigadier general in 1912, during the Spanish American War McClernand had served as a lieutenant colonel with General William Shafter's* Fifth Corps.* Overweight and suffering from gout, Shafter was unable to meet the field demands of a commander at Santiago.* He therefore deputized McClernand, at the time his adjutant, to be his battlefield "eyes." If was from McClernand that Admiral William T. Sampson* learned that Spain was suing for peace.

REFERENCE: John D. Miley, *In Cuba with Shafter* (New York: Charles Scribner's Sons, 1899).

MACEO GRAJALES, ANTONIO
(1845–1896)

General Antonio Maceo Grajales, along with Máximo Gómez* and José Martí,* became one of the great men of the Cuban nationalist movement. Maceo was a mulatto who strove with energy and brilliance to free the island from the Spanish as well as to free the slaves. Years of attempts to reform the Spanish system failed, and along with many others Maceo began a war of independence in 1895. He was instrumental in proposing a liberation government, which was really a loose understanding between the generals Gómez, Calixto García,* and Maceo. This war of liberation was unlike the Ten Years' War*; the Cuban Insurrection* enjoyed wide support among the Cuban populace, regardless of class. The reality of the struggle, however, pitted 8,000–10,000 Cubans against over 50,000 Spaniards. Maceo's column was atypical. Mostly of African descent, they were armed with machetes and a few rifles, but all were mounted. They were superb horsemen.

Spanish general Valeriano Weyler* relentlessly pursued Maceo partly because of racial concern, but mostly because Maceo was most efficient at destroying the sugar plantations and mills that provided profit to Spain. Maceo avoided any pitched battles but was pursued doggedly by Weyler until their cat-and-mouse manuevers became a duel of sorts. Weyler issued his reconcentration* orders, and in an attempt to rejoin Gómez, Maceo was caught and killed in December 1896.

Even in death Maceo continued to struggle. Garbled versions of Maceo's demise surfaced in the United States and caused a sensation, spawning another congressional resolution for belligerent rights for Cuba.

REFERENCES: Philip S. Foner, *Antonio Maceo* (New York: Monthly Review Press, 1977); Hugh Thomas, *Cuba: The Pursuit of Freedom* (New York: Harper & Row, 1971).

MACÍAS Y CASADO, MANUEL
(1845–?)

Spanish governor of Puerto Rico* and lieutenant general, Manuel Macías y Casado proved to be a better politician than military strategist. He left his forces dispersed throughout the island, and they fell with such ease that Spain's bargaining position eroded. Even had Macías concentrated his forces, the outcome may not have been different. Macías had virtually no naval forces to repulse an invasion, and the ground forces at his disposal were weak. Many Puerto Ricans welcomed U.S. forces and actively aided them; still more were apathetic to both sides.

Macías had previously presided over the inauguration of an autonomous charter in Puerto Rico, on 9 February 1898. On 27 March an insular assembly had been elected. However, when hostilities commenced, Macías revoked elements of the charter. He remained to cede Puerto Rico to the United States on 29–30 September 1898.

REFERENCE: Ángel Rivero Méndez, *Crónica de la Guerra Hispano Americana en Puerto Rico* (New York: Plus Ultra, 1973).

MCKINLEY, WILLIAM, JR.
(1843–1901)

The man who would be president during the war with Spain in 1898 came from Scottish and Irish ancestry. His parents lived in Ohio, and William McKinley's early schooling was in that state. He was taught that religion and life were inseparable components of the whole. Adept at recitation and debate, McKinley early earned his way as a teacher. Upon hearing of the fall of Fort Sumpter in the Civil War, McKinley volunteered for service with an Ohio regiment. His coolness under fire marked him in the eyes of the regimental commander, Rutherford B. Hayes, who saw to McKinley's promotion and eventual commission. At war's end in 1865, McKinley was a brevet major who had served as Hayes's aide-de-camp and on the staffs of several generals. The war had an important effect on young McKinley. He was not natively aggressive nor violent, and the bitterness of the conflict clashed with his own notions of Christian duty and civilized conduct.

McKinley pursued legal training and was admitted to the bar. Singular in aspect and character, McKinley had not changed in moral outlook after four years of army life: He did not drink, smoke, or swear. His Methodist upbringing forbade dancing, cards, or play-going. A demonstrated and dashing horseman, he never raced. He became a leader in the temperance movement and showed in this, and other such endeavors, a group consciousness rather than any desire for individual leadership. Consensus building became not just a natural outcome of his youthful character and personality but also a strength.

McKinley was elected to Congress in 1876 after enthusiastically supporting Hayes for the Ohio governorship. McKinley knew how to connect himself with power. He also served as governor of Ohio at age forty-nine, serving two terms. His critics in Congress and at home labeled him as a changeling and inconstant. It was, perhaps, this adaptability that merited him Republican respect as a practical politician. Such practicality earned notice from constituents and, more importantly, from the rich and power-seeking Marcus A. Hanna.* Further success in Congress and significant backing by Hanna and others led to McKinley's successful defeat of the presidential Populist challenge of William Jennings Bryan* in 1896. On 4 March 1897 McKinley was inaugurated president of the United States. One year and one month later McKinley became a war president in the conflict with Spain.

On 24 February 1895 a revolt commenced in Cuba.* The Cuban insurgents* did not fight a war of pitched battles but instead chose economic targets. By 1897 the active and vocal role of the Cuban junta* in the United States convinced Spain that the United States was not sincere in its professed neutrality. The reconcentration policy* of General Valeriano Weyler* provided ample raw material for American newspaper stories of atrocities and horror. European interest in the developing struggle added further complexity to the issue. McKinley dealt with events as they occurred, be they filibustering* or public crises. He was slow to develop attitudes toward Spain. Perhaps the initial foundational forum was a report by Assistant Secretary of State William R. Day.* Day's report revealed inhumane actions in Cuba that McKinley found repugnant. On 26 June 1897 McKinley sent his first formal message to Spain, which became one of the tenets of McKinley's slowly developing policy: The United States demanded civilized, humane methods of suppressing the revolt in Cuba and demanded the right to monitor such methods. Spain found the American position unacceptable.

Later, in September, McKinley entrusted his minister to Spain, Stewart L. Woodford,* with a set of instructions outlining McKinley's policies toward Spain and Cuba. In essence, McKinley doubted the Spanish resolve and ability to extricate itself nobly from the Cuban embroglio. McKinley further asserted that whatever happened in Cuba unavoidably affected the United States, and he hinted at some future U.S. action should peaceful resolution of the Cuban crisis not be forthcoming. The intent of all this was to nudge Spain into recognizing that some form of Cuban independence or autonomy was inevitable. In this respect, McKinley's policy diverged sharply from Grover Cleveland's.*

Responding to McKinley's concerns, the Spanish government under Práxides Mateo Sagasta* began autonomy* initiatives and severely modified the reconcentration policy. By late November 1897 autonomy plans had been announced. Spain's willingness to compromise buoyed the president, who desired that the implemented reforms be given a chance. Nevertheless, McKinley never lost sight of his goal: an independent Cuba. To this end diplomatic pressure continued. Since McKinley stopped short of supporting belligerency* status for the Cubans, radicals in the United States shouted for stronger measures. In similar fashion Spanish nationalists bristled at McKinley's hint that further actions may be required if desired results were not obtained through Spain's concessions. McKinley punctuated these statements with some ominously preparatory steps: He sent the North Atlantic Squadron* to Key West* for winter exercises (only some 90 miles from Havana*), and he had the Navy Department review war plans. On 11 January 1898 orders were given not to release sailors whose enlistments were about to terminate. The intent of these actions was to focus the Spanish government on the seriousness of the situation.

Besides concern about Cuba, McKinley also faced diplomatic challenges with Germany,* which sought bases in the Antilles and the East. Although the concern over Cuba was paramount, German depredations in Santo Domingo, Haiti,* and China* bore watching as well. Despite these pressures and a growing prowar faction in Spain, McKinley was committed to freeing Cuba by pressuring Spain to accept the loss as inevitable—and without the necessity of a public demand by the United States to that effect. His resolution on this issue was tested severely during the month of February 1898, when consecutive events ratcheted the conflict up out of the realm of diplomacy and into a grave arena. On 9 February Dupuy de Lôme's* personal and unflattering comments about McKinley were published. McKinley allowed consular correspondence on Cuba to be published, thereby inflaming the American public even more. Then on 15 February the U.S.S. *Maine** exploded in Havana harbor. Bellicose American public opinion demanded action, but McKinley determined to work for a peaceful resolution. Nevertheless, he stepped up military preparation (Senator Joseph Cannon's Fifty Million Bill,* for example). McKinley also explored several other options but found the insurgents unwilling to negotiate for anything short of independence. With dwindling options; Spain sought for a European coalition to mediate the dispute or even intervene. At last, in April 1898, all avenues of diplomacy had failed and McKinley asked Congress for authority to halt the bloodshed in Cuba.

Throughout the Spanish American War McKinley was an active commander-in-chief who used modern communications to keep in touch with his commanders in the field and also to monitor French and British cable traffic. While Theodore Roosevelt* had ordered Commodore George Dewey* to prepare for actions in the Philippines, he did so following a plan that had been extant for some time; it was the president who gave the order to attack. Similarly, it was McKinley and his advisors who planned and developed a Pacific strategy that strengthened American future interests in not only the Philippines but also the larger Pacific. McKinley used his influence to annex Hawaii,* which process commenced in May 1898 but continued in congressional debate through the summer. Further, it was McKinley's administration and leadership that recognized Emilio Aguinaldo's* leadership in the Filipino revolution and acted to ensure that the United States retained postwar options while defeating the Spanish. As president, McKinley struggled with political ramifications of the bill proposed by Senator John Hull,* that attempted to reorganize the manner in which wars were fought by diminishing the roles of volunteer forces and the National Guard.* He personally made appointments of general officers from the South such as Joseph Wheeler* and Fitzhugh Lee* to promote national unity. Similarly, he ensured that political opponent William Jennings Bryan had no opportunity for fame or glory.

McKinley also recognized the weaknesses among his staff and cabinet and made changes. That he did not change Russell A. Alger* is reflective of political judgment rather than an undue concern for efficiency. McKinley's direction of the peace negotiations* culminating in the protocol of 12 August 1898 and the eventual treaty lifted the presidency into the light of international politics.

During the war President McKinley directed the efforts that enhanced the territory and prestige of the United States manyfold. Although all was not done well, particularly the difficult and trying rapid mobilization and its attendant logistical trials, McKinley demonstrated initiative and creativity in his office. He expanded presidential power and influence in a way that led naturally into the twentieth-century notions of that office. It was not too many years past that the most frequent historical statement on William McKinley was the oft-repeated description "a kindly soul in a spineless body." Modern scholarship has revised that assessment considerably, calling him instead the first modern president, prefiguring the Roosevelts and Woodrow Wilson.

REFERENCES: Lewis L. Gould, *The Spanish American War and President McKinley* (Lawrence: University Press of Kansas, 1982); Margaret Leech, *In the Days of McKinley* (New York: Harper & Row, 1959).

MAHAN, ALFRED THAYER
(1840–1914)

Alfred Thayer Mahan was born on 27 September 1840 at West Point, New York, where his father taught military engineering. Although his father wanted him to follow his own lead into an army career, the younger Mahan was more interested in the sea. He attended Columbia College and then graduated in 1859 from the U.S. Naval Academy at Annapolis, which launched him on a forty-year career in the U.S. Navy. Mahan saw combat at sea during the Civil War and then completed several tours of duty at sea between 1865 and 1885. He then devoted himself to a teaching career, finally becoming president of the Naval War College* in 1886. Blessed with a keenly analytical mind, a prodigious memory, and intellectual ambition, Mahan specialized in military and naval history, with an emphasis on tactics.

After years of careful study and thought, Mahan began writing naval history in the 1890s. Few historians have ever had such influence on their contemporaries. Mahan's first book, *The Influence of Sea Power upon History, 1660–*

1783, was published in 1890 and received rave reviews in Great Britain* and Germany.* Two years later he wrote *The Influence of Sea Power upon the French Revolution and Empire, 1793–1812.* In 1897 he wrote *The Life of Nelson* and *The Interests of America in Seapower.* Mahan's thesis was simple but powerful: Throughout history, from the time of the Greeks, world power status had depended on commercial expansion, and commercial expansion depends on naval protection. Without a powerful navy, Mahan claimed, no modern nation can guarantee its own prosperity or become a genuine world power. As examples he cited the success of the British Empire and the failure of the French Empire. Mahan went on to describe the implications of his thesis for the United States. Increased industrial production demanded new markets overseas, but access to those markets in Asia, Africa, and Latin America depended on a large merchant marine and a powerful navy. Colonies would be needed in the Pacific and the Caribbean to exploit the vast economic opportunities of Asia. Mahan also believed that the world's only real chance for peace lay in the development of Anglo-American seapower.

Within months of the publication of Mahan's books, they were required reading by naval students in Great Britain, Germany, the United States, Russia, and Japan. Prominent American expansionists in the business, religious, and political communities picked up on Mahan's recommendations, calling for a stronger navy and overseas expansion; after the Spanish American War, when Congress debated the merits of imperialism and whether the United States should acquire a Pacific and Caribbean empire, Mahan's ideas provided the theoretical rationale to such proimperialists as Henry Cabot Lodge,* Albert Beveridge, Theodore Roosevelt,* and John Hay.* A close friend of Mahan and Republican senator from Massachusetts, Lodge remarked in 1898, "It is the sea power which is essential to the greatness of every splendid people."

Mahan retired from the navy at the end of the century but continued an active academic and public career. He served as president of the American Historical Association in 1902 and as chairman of the Commission on Naval Affairs in 1908. He consulted frequently with naval experts from around the world and continued to write history. Before his death he had written twenty books on naval history and naval policy. When World War I broke out in August 1914, Mahan confidently predicted the ultimate demise of Germany and the other Central Powers because the United States and Great Britain controlled the sea lanes. Alfred Thayer Mahan died on 1 December 1914.

REFERENCES: W. D. Puleston, *Mahan: The Life and Work of Alfred Thayer Mahan* (New Haven, CT: Yale University Press, 1939); Robert Seager, *Alfred Thayer Mahan: The Man and His Letters* (Annapolis, MD: Naval Institute Press, 1977).

JAMES S. OLSON

MAINE (ship)

On 15 February 1898 at 9:40 P.M., the U.S.S. *Maine* blew up in Havana Harbor, Cuba,* killing 266 men. The next day, large-circulation newspapers like the *New York World* filled the front pages of their 17 February editions with graphic depictions of the exploding ship, with sailors flying and dying from the blast, while large black headlines darkly hinted (or flatly stated) that the explosion was the deliberate work of ''an enemy''—which in the sensational tabloids of the United States meant an agent of Spain.

The sinking of the *Maine* did not create greater diplomatic pressure to find solutions to the Cuban embroglio but instead released pressure in the form of outbursts and demands. At the beginning of 1898, President William McKinley* had waffled between assisting the Cuban independence movement, assisting the creation of an autonomous government, or backing Spanish efforts to retain control of Cuba. Each of these courses had significant drawbacks. Spanish policy was associated with the *reconcentrado** effort and other forms of repression morally repugnant to American opinion. An autonomous government required the cooperation of Spaniards and Cubans alike—an event more hoped for than realistic. American statesmen had little confidence in the capacity of Cuba to govern itself effectively under autonomy.* With the publication of the stolen Enrique Dupuy de Lôme* letter and a violent riot in Cuba on 12 January 1898, on 24 January *Maine* was sent from Key West,* Florida, to Havana on a ''friendly'' visit. Tensions mounted.

The destruction of the *Maine* and the death of over two-thirds of her crew was a deafening thunderclap in this charged atmosphere. The press* fanned the flames of charges against Spain and her past atrocities, real and imagined. The upcoming Naval Court of Inquiry was hastily convened with Captain William T. Sampson,* president, Captain French E. Chadwick* and Lieutenant Commander William P. Potter,* members, and Lieutenant Commander Adolph Marix* as judge advocate. The captain of the *Maine,* Charles D. Sigsbee,* attended not only to serve as a witness but also to cross-examine witnesses. The court investigated and deliberated. Lost in the hyperbole of the press was an attempt by Spain to hold its own court of inquiry or to perform a joint effort with the United States. On 28 March the U.S. court issued its report: Without attaching responsibility to any persons or group, it believed the explosion was caused by a mine. With the publication of the report, Congress,* the press, and influential individuals pressed McKinley for war. On 19 April Congress passed a joint resolution recognizing Cuba's independence, though not a Cuban government, and authorizing President McKinley to compel Spain to give up Cuba.

Interestingly, recent research and reexamination by experts of the data, testimony, photographs, and files of the earlier inquiries reveal that the *Maine* blew up by accident from an *internal* explosion of a magazine most likely ignited by a fire in an adjacent coal bunker.

Maine had been commissioned as a battleship, though originally classified as an armored cruiser, on 17 September 1895. She displaced 6,682 tons and was capable of 17 knots. *Maine*'s armament consisted of four 10-inch guns, six 6-inch guns, miscellaneous smaller calibers, and four torpedo tubes. She was refloated in 1912, towed to sea, and scuttled.

REFERENCE: H. G. Rickover, *How the Battleship* Maine *Was Destroyed* (Washington, DC: Naval History Division, 1976).

MALARIA

As a disease,* malaria was both a grim reaper of soldiers and a naked threat to the potency of armies. The Spanish had firsthand experience with malaria, yellow fever,* and typhoid, diseases rampant in the tropics. United States commanders, on the other hand, had no such experience, although all were familiar with the military history of tropical areas, where whole armies succumbed to disease. According to extant statistics, malaria accounted for 5.7 percent of all American deaths, but that figure assumes accurate diagnosis. Frequently, medical officers confused yellow fever, typhoid, and malaria, so this figure is at best questionable. Although even mention of yellow fever caused the hair to stand on the backs of commanders' necks, it was the less virulent malarial fever that laid low Fifth Corps's* troops.

In the Philippines, American commanders were much more fastidious and, consequently, fever outbreaks were less violent.

REFERENCES: *Annual Report of the War Department, 1898* (Washington, DC: Government Printing Office, 1898); Graham A. Cosmas, *An Army for Empire* (Columbia: University of Missouri Press, 1971).

MALATE, PHILIPPINES

An important suburb of Manila,* Malate came under Philippine insurgent* control at the end of May 1898. Insurgents seized other neighborhoods in addition to Malate in a bid to assault Manila proper. Commodore George Dewey,* of the U.S. Navy, determined that insurgent leader Emilio Aguinaldo* lacked the forces to carry either Cavite* or Manila. In light of the growing tension between the Americans and the insurgents, the occupation of Malate was a source of possible friction. Brigadier General Thomas M. Anderson* was quite concerned about the possibility of U.S. troops engaging Filipinos in or near Malate.

In addition, Malate was the location of Fort San Antonio,* where the agreed-upon fighting "demonstration" was to take place between the Spanish and U.S. forces. Actual fighting between the U.S. and Spanish forces did occur at Malate during the battle for Manila, and Anderson's brigade lost one killed and fifty wounded.

REFERENCE: French Ensor Chadwick, *The Relations of the United States and Spain* (New York: Russell & Russell, 1968).

MANGROVE (ship)

The U.S.S. *Mangrove* (821 tons) was a lighthouse tender pressed into the service at the site of the inquiry about the explosion and sinking of the U.S.S. *Maine.** Early in the morning of 21 February 1898, *Mangrove* arrived in Havana,* and the navy's court of inquiry commenced the same day aboard *Man-*

grove and continued there until the court's deliberations sent it to Key West*
on 28 February to interview survivors.

Mangrove served in Admiral William T. Sampson's* squadron during most
of the hostilities, particularly distinguishing herself by capturing the faster, more
heavily armed Spanish liner *Panamá* on 25 April 1898. The crew of *Mangrove*
accomplished this feat without uniforms and with only one revolver among
them. Clearly these Spaniards were not whole-heartedly in the war.

Mangrove participated in the blockade of Matanzas.* Her last adventure occurred on 14 August at Caibarien, where she attacked the Spanish gunboat *Her-
nán Cortés.* The launch *Cauto* sallied under a white flag to inform *Mangrove*
that peace had been proclaimed.
REFERENCE: H. W. Wilson, *The Downfall of Spain* (New York: Burt Franklin, 1971
[1900]).

MANILA (ship)

Launched in England and built of iron, *Manila* was purchased by Spanish
interests for merchant service and renamed *Carriedo.* The Spanish navy acquired
Carriedo in 1885, named her *Manila,* and sent her to her namesake in the
Philippines.* There, *Manila* transported material and troops against various in-
surgent-reduction efforts by the Spanish. *Manila* also voyaged to the Carolines.
She was at Manila* during the American attack and was later taken over for
transport duty by U.S. forces.
REFERENCE: Alfredo Aguilera, *Buques de guerra españoles, 1885–1971* (Madrid: Li-
brería Editorial San Martín, 1972).

MANILA, PHILIPPINES

Manila, capital of the Philippines, lies on the island of Luzon* on the eastern
shore of broad Manila Bay.* As the capital, it was the seat of the Spanish
colonial power and, as such, was the focus of Filipino insurrectionary efforts.
The Philippine revolutionaries had seized all but Intramuros, the centuries-old
Spanish sections of the city, in its struggles from 1896 to 1898. After Com-
modore George Dewey* defeated Admiral Patricio Motojo* in the Battle of
Manila Bay,* the Spanish and Dewey waited two months for the arrival of
Eighth Corps,* the expeditionary force that would seize control of the rest of
the city. Difficult and ticklish political maneuvers by Dewey and General Wesley
Merritt* kept the Philippine revolutionaries of Emilio Aguinaldo* at bay while
American military commanders negotiated with Spanish counterparts for an arranged battle (to save Spanish face) and the surrender of Spain to the United
States. The surrender occurred on 13 August 1898. Ironically, this battle took
place after the peace protocol had been signed the previous day. For a while
during the peace negotiations,* moderates urged the Peace Commission* to annex Manila or Luzon only. Expansionism* won the day, however, and the entire
archipelago was acquired.
REFERENCE: *Annual Report of the War Department, 1898* (Washington, DC: Govern-

ment Printing Office, 1898); Whitelaw Reid, *Making Peace with Spain* (Austin: University of Texas Press, 1965).

MANILA BAY, PHILIPPINES

Perhaps the finest harbor in the Orient, Manila Bay lies in southwest Luzon* near the South China Sea. Dimensionally about 35 miles by 30 miles, its entrance of about 11-miles width is guarded by the island fortress Corregidor,* splitting the channel in two. Cavite* and Manila* are on the eastern shore.

The most significant event in Manila Bay was the naval battle of 1 May 1898 between Commodore George Dewey's* U.S. squadron and Admiral Patricio Montojo's* Spanish fleet. Generally, the Spanish ships were in harbor, even at anchor. Dewey steamed through a purportedly mined channel, skirmished with Spanish shore batteries, and decisively engaged the Spanish ships. Not only did the *Olympia,* *Boston,* *Baltimore,* *Raleigh,* *Concord,** and *Petrel** have the tactical advantage, they were heavier, better armed, and faster than the Spanish *María Cristina, Castilla,* *Don Antonio de Ulloa,* *Don Juan de Austria,* *Isla de Luzón,* *Isla de Cuba,* *Velasco,* *Argos,* and *General Lezo.* The encounter was a very one-sided battle in which the U.S. forces lost no ships, had none killed, and suffered only nine wounded. Dewey made five passes, and since some of the Spanish ships were, in fact, inoperable, the devastation wrought by the Asiatic Squadron* was profound. The Spanish counted 371 casualties with 161 killed and its entire squadron sunk.

Despite the overwhelming success of the American attack, largely due to Dewey's meticulous preparation, gunnery was not good at all. Only 2.5 percent of the American shells hit their targets. This ineffectiveness may have been due to range-finding difficulties, but the percentage is very low nonetheless. The Spanish were unable to mount an effective defense partly because of the lack of preparation; if adequately handled, the shore batteries might have made a better showing and thus possibly changed the outcome. However, the Spanish also labored under ammunition shortages and were undergunned.

Ships from Germany,* Great Britain,* and Japan* either were in the bay or arrived shortly after hostilities began. The array of international vessels presented complications and proved the source of some anxiety to Dewey. Particularly troublesome to him was the presence of German admiral Otto von Diederichs.*

Dewey's victory made him a hero at home, and President McKinley* made him an admiral. The victory was the first of the war, a resounding one that resulted in bringing Manila Bay under the authority of U.S. naval power. Dewey, however, possessed no soldiers to invest Manila proper until the end of June.

REFERENCES: French Ensor Chadwick, *The Relations of the United States and Spain: The Spanish American War* (New York: Russell & Russell, 1968); U.S. Office of Naval Intelligence, *Notes on the Spanish American War* (Washington, DC: Government Printing Office, 1900).

MANZANILLO, CUBA

Manzanillo, Cuba, lies in the province of Oriente near the apex of the Gulf of Guacanayabo, about 85 miles west-northwest of Santiago de Cuba* (the trip from Santiago took about 150–160 miles in 1898, however). Surrounded by malarial swamps, it was not a healthy locale. Nevertheless, it possessed strategic importance inasmuch as it was a viable overland supply route to Santiago during the American blockade.* Spanish military leadership had stationed some 6,000 troops in Manzanillo. Some writers have criticized Lieutenant General Arsenio Linares y Pomba,* commander of the Spanish armies in eastern Cuba, for dividing his forces, but the facts dispute that criticism: The countryside was under the control of Cuban insurrectionists, and the available provisions, ammunition, and medical supplies available at Santiago could not have supported the 35,000 men under Linares's command. The American forces controlled the sea lanes; the insurgents controlled the countryside. In fact, on 22 June Colonel Federico Escario* left Manzanillo with about 3,700 men to aid the forces at Santiago. This troop fought some forty skirmishes with insurgents who were under the overall command of General Calixto García.* Escario's column did not reach Santiago until the night of 2 July, after losing about 400 men to disease, exhaustion, and insurgent action. Yet upon arrival, Escario's column actually increased the difficulties of Santiago's garrison: There was little or no water, and no food. The Manzanillo column became another force trapped in Santiago.

That Escario's Manzanillo column arrived at all is due to the remarkable tenacity of Escario's troops. Major General William R. Shafter* blamed García for Escario's successful march. Regardless, García was able to slow the Spanish column enough so that it arrived after Shafter's battles on San Juan Hill* and El Caney* on 1 July.

Manzanillo and neighboring coasts also served the Spanish as an intermediary port in a substantial coasting trade. Aware of this trade and its negative impact on the U.S. blockade, Admiral William T. Sampson* noted that as soon as he obtained shallow draft vessels, Manzanillo would also be subject to blockade. The State Department announced on 28 June that the blockade would be extended to include the south coast of Cuba as well as Puerto Rico.* On 30 June the converted yacht (now gunboat) *Hist,** gunboat *Hornet,* and armed tug *Wompatuck* began a reconnaissance of the coast near Manzanillo. Passing by Niquero, this small U.S. squadron surprised the 30-ton armed launch *Centinela,* under the command of Ensign Alejandro Arias Salgado. A brisk cannonade followed in which a Spanish fireman died and the *Centinela* received engine damage and was holed at the water line. Clouds of steam obscured *Centinela* as she disengaged and subsequently sank (later to be raised and incorporated into the squadrons at Manzanillo). The American squadron moved on to Manzanillo, entering that port around 3:30 P.M. Awaiting the American squadron were the Spanish gunboats *Estrella* (Lieutenant Joaquín Rivero), *Guantánamo* (Lieutenant Bartolomé Morales), *Guardían* (Lieutenant Carlos del Camino), *Delgado Parejo* (Lieutenant Ubaldo Serís), and two old wooden gunboats, *Cuba Española* (Lieutenant Luis Pou) and the paddle-wheeler *María.* The squadron was under the command of Captain Joaquín Gómez de Barredo. Clearly, the American squadron was outgunned. The Spaniards had the additional weight of a hastily emplaced shore battery that they also used to good effect. During the ensuing battle, which lasted for an hour, *Hornet* was hit three times, resulting in a water-line hole and a shot that cut the main steam pipe, immobilizing the ship (she was towed out of danger by *Wompatuck,* which was also struck three times). *Hist* was hit eleven times. The battered U.S. squadron retired, miraculously without losing a man, although three men were scalded by steam on *Hornet.* The Spaniards sustained two dead and four wounded between *Delgado Parejo* and *María.* The town militia and citizens counted two more wounded.

Centinela, having been refloated, joined the forces of Goméz de Barredo at Manzanillo the next day, 1 July. After-action reports by *Hornet, Hist,* and *Wompatuck* greatly exaggerated the damage inflicted on the Spanish ships in the harbor as well as the type and number of ships. The Americans believed that it remained only to knock out the shore batteries. Consequently, the converted yacht *Scorpion** (850 tons, armed with four 5-inch guns and six 6-pounders) and the armed tug *Osceola** (571 tons, two 6-pounders, one 3-pounder, and one machine gun) sailed to Manzanillo to engage the batteries. A brisk twenty-minute fire against the battery caused no damage to the Spanish; the Spanish artillery hit *Scorpion* twelve times without casualty. Clearly, the reduction of Manzanillo had to be postponed until there was sufficient force. Admiral Pascual Cervera's* defeat on 3 July freed necessary naval assets for the reduction of Manzanillo. On 18 July the U.S. gunboats *Wilmington** (1,397 tons, eight 4-inch guns, four 6-pounders, four 1-pounders, and four machine guns), *Helena* (a *Wilmington*-class gunboat), the armed yachts *Scorpion, Hist,* and *Hornet,* and the armed tugs *Wompatuck* and *Osceola* steamed into Manzanillo and while staying out of range of the Spanish guns, systematically destroyed ten ships in the harbor. Unable to reply effectively and outgunned, the Spanish transferred as many guns from the ships to the shore as possible. There were no American casualties; Spanish losses included three dead and fourteen wounded.

On 12 August Captain Caspar F. Goodrich* arrived in command of a strong force to take possession of Manzanillo. Included in his small fleet was the protected cruiser *Newark,** *Suwanee,** *Hist,* and *Osceola,* the captured Spanish gunboat *Alvarado,* obtained from the fall of Santiago, and the armed transport *Resolute* with a marine battalion. Goodrich called upon the Spanish commander to surrender; he refused. Thereupon the American ships began a bombardment at 3:40 P.M. that lasted into the night. Cuban insurgents also began an attack on Manzanillo. Upon notification that the armistice* had been signed, fire ceased. The Americans had no casualties. The Spanish suffered six dead, thirty-one wounded.

REFERENCES: Augustín Rodríguez González, ''Operaciones menores en Cuba, 1898,'' *Revista de Historia Naval* 3, no. 9 (1985): 125–146; H. W. Wilson, *The Downfall of Spain* (New York: Burt Franklin, 1971 [1900]).

MARBLEHEAD (ship)

Officially listed as "unprotected cruisers," the *Montgomery*-class cruisers—
Montgomery, * *Detroit,* * and *Marblehead*—were actually large gunboats of
2,094 tons. *Marblehead* was built by City Point Works, Boston, Massachusetts,
and commissioned 2 April 1894. Despite having little or no protection, the three
vessels of this class were vigorously engaged during the Spanish American War.
Marblehead was part of the Cuban blockade.* Off of Cienfuegos,* *Marblehead*
and *Eagle** had an exchange of fire with the Spanish *Satélite, Lince,* and *Gaviota,* small gunboats or launches that displaced only 129 tons among them. This
action of 29 April 1898 was so spirited that the Americans thought they were
combatting the larger *Galicia* (500 tons) and *Vasco Núñez de Balboa* (300 tons),
and so reported in the after-action summaries. Both ships were in Cienfuegos,
but neither participated in the combat of 29 April.

With her cannons *Marblehead* also supported a cable-cutting expedition on
11 May. While marines in two steam launches ran in to sever three cables off
Cienfuegos, *Marblehead* and the gunboat *Nashville** shelled the beaches at-
tempting to suppress Spanish fire. The Americans were only partially successful
in that effort; they cut two of the three cables but suffered four killed and five
wounded among the steam launches. *Marblehead* continued the blockade of
Cienfuegos. *Marblehead* was attached to Commodore Winfield S. Schley's*
Flying Squadron* in the general blockade of Santiago.* On 2 June 1898 Admiral
William T. Sampson* issued the orders that *Marblehead* was to be part of
Schley's division along with *Brooklyn,* * *Massachusetts,* * *Texas,* * and the armed
yacht *Vixen.* * *Marblehead* participated in the shelling of Santiago on 6 June and
on 7 June shelled Caimanera* and cut the cable that ran from Caimanera to
Haiti.* *Marblehead* also supported the landing at Caimanera and destroyed a
small fort on the Cay del Tor. The cruiser continued with minor skirmishes such
as the cable cutting at Guantánamo* and a minor combat with the little Spanish
gunboat *Sandoval* on 7 June.

After the war *Marblehead* was posted to the Pacific. She was sold out of the
service in 1921.

REFERENCE: John D. Alden, *The American Steel Navy* (Annapolis, MD: Naval Institute
Press, 1972).

MARE ISLAND NAVAL STATION, CALIFORNIA

Located in the bay of San Francisco,* Mare Island served as a ship-repair
facility and entrepôt for ships headed to the Philippines. *Monterey,* * *Monadnock,* * and, of course, *Charleston** were readied at Mare Island. *Olympia,* *
Boston, * *Baltimore,* * *Petrel,* * and *Concord** had been drydocked or in other
ways received maintenance at Mare Island. *Monadnock* had in fact been built
at Mare Island in 1883. Rear Admiral W. A. Kirkland commanded at Mare
Island throughout the Spanish American War.

REFERENCE: Arnold S. Lott, *A Long Line of Ships* (Annapolis, MD: United States
Naval Institute, 1954).

MARÍA CHRISTINA OF AUSTRIA, QUEEN REGENT OF SPAIN
(1858–1929)

María Christina, of the Germanic Hapsburgs, was archduchess of Austria and served as queen regent of Spain from 1885 to 1902. She was the second wife of King Alfonso XIII. When Alfonso died in 1885, María was pregnant with the future Alfonso XII; she therefore reigned as queen regent for fifteen years during the crisis known as the Spanish American War.

On 8 August 1897 Miguel Angiolillo* assassinated Antonio Cánovas del Castillo* and María recalled Práxides Mateo Sagasta* to lead the government. María was not a passive regent but was active in international affairs through her ministers. United States minister to Spain Stewart Lyndon Woodford* conversed with her on numerous occasions and reported that she was a conservative—she wanted to conserve Cuba for Spain. Indeed, she was adamant that Spain's colonial possessions remain. In that effort, and to preserve peace, the queen sought support and counsel from other European powers in a vain attempt to find support for Spain and also in an effort to delay responding to U.S. demands. In addition, she had a potential domestic crisis on her hands. Revolutionary fervor threatened not just Cuba but also Spain, and María desired above all to preserve the throne for her son. Thus, while the queen, Sagasta, and other Spanish ministers sought peace, they opted for war as an honorable solution or diversion to the revolutionary threat.

María Christina again took control of events during the peace process. The developing Treaty of Paris* was viewed by many in Spain as dishonorable; the vote for ratification was too close for legislative success. María Christina then overrode the Cortes and ratified the treaty on 19 March 1899, using her own powers.

REFERENCE: Jerónimo Bécker, *Historia de las relaciones exteriores de España durante el siglo XIX,* vol. 3 (Madrid: J. Rates, 1926).

MARIANAS ISLANDS

The Marianas lie in the western Pacific Ocean some 1,500 miles east of the Philippines. They were discovered by Magellan, who named them the Ladrones, a name that persisted even though the Spanish renamed them Marianas in 1668. The southernmost island, and most well known, is Guam.*

After the Spanish naval defeat at Manila Bay,* President William McKinley,* upon the advice and planning of the War Department, sent a large expeditionary force to combat the Spanish garrisons in the Philippines. Part of this force included the transport *City of Peking,** two other transports, and an accompanying protected cruiser, *Charleston.** The *Charleston* captured Guam without a fight. By capturing Guam, the United States denied it to Germany* while simultaneously acquiring a useful coaling station that would fill a strategic need. During the peace negotiations, the remaining Marianas (minus Guam, which remained in U.S. hands) were spoils that secret negotiations between Spain and Germany* transferred to Germany.

REFERENCES: William Reynolds Braisted, *The United States Navy in the Pacific, 1897–1909* (Austin: University of Texas Press, 1958); J. Fred Rippy, ''The European Powers and Spanish American War,'' *James Sprunt Historical Studies* 19 (1927): 22–52.

MARIEL, CUBA

Mariel is in western Cuba less than 30 miles south and west of Havana.* Mariel was one of the initial ports targeted for the American blockade.* Early planning for the expeditionary forces' thrust into Cuba designated Havana as the objective; Mariel was to be among the first areas assaulted, and plans called for Mariel to serve as staging area for the attack on the capital. The plan to attack Havana hatched in a meeting between President William McKinley,* Secretaries Russell A. Alger* and John D. Long,* who were accompanied by General Nelson A. Miles* and Admiral Montgomery Sicard.* This plan never saw fruition. Miles proposed another assault on Havana, also using Mariel as an entrepôt for the assault. The general's concerns centered on the capital and avoiding fever-infested areas. Secretary Alger defeated this plan also.

REFERENCE: R. A. Alger, *The Spanish American War* (New York: Harper & Brothers, 1901).

MARINE CORPS, U.S.

Whereas the U.S. Navy's plan to blockade* Cuba and eventually Puerto Rico,* and to focus on Spanish outposts in the Pacific, was clearly drawn, the role of the U.S. Marine Corps was less distinct. As the blockade planning came to implementation, two battalions of marines were ordered to accompany Admiral William T. Sampson's* blockading force. Colonel Charles Heywood, marine commandant, received orders to form the battalions on 16 April 1898. Reconsideration reduced the two battalions to one, augmented by 200 men. This marine expeditionary force was commanded by Lieutenant Colonel Robert Huntington. The battalion embarked on the transport *Panther,* joined Captain Winfield S. Schley's* Flying Squadron,* and steamed to Key West,* arriving on 29 April—the same day that Spanish admiral Pascual Cervera* left the Cape Verde Islands* for the Caribbean.

Meanwhile, on 1 May Commodore George Dewey* defeated the Spanish at Manila Bay.* Without troops, however, Dewey could take Manila but could not hold it, much less command a military presence in the archipelago. However, First Lieutenant Dion Williams from the *Baltimore* secured the former Spanish naval station at Cavite.*

On 10 June the previously inactive marine battalion at Key West landed at Guantánamo* and began a series of continuing attacks against Spanish positions, which were successful. Perhaps even more important, Stephen Crane* and other news correspondents made much of the fact that the U.S. Marines were in combat while the Fifth Corps* was still at Tampa.*

On 9 August the Marine First Battalion steamed from Guantánamo to take the Isle of Pines.* En route they were to assault Manzanillo,* but the peace protocol ceased further combat.

Marines also manned some of the secondary batteries on battleships. Although claims were made by marines that the secondaries scored more hits at Santiago,* the gunnery at Manila and Santiago did not merit praise.

REFERENCE: Jack Shulimson, "Marines in the Spanish American War," in James C. Bradford, ed., *Crucible of Empire* (Annapolis, MD: Naval Institute Press, 1993).

MARIX, ADOLPH
(1848–1919)

Born in Dresden, Adolph Marix graduated from the Naval Academy at Annapolis in 1868 and rose through the ranks. As lieutenant commander he served as the judge advocate of the inquiry on the sinking of the U.S.S. *Maine.** During the Spanish American War he commanded *Scorpion** and was promoted for conspicuous bravery. He later attained the rank of rear admiral in 1908 after serving as port captain of Manila* during the turbulent era between 1901 and 1903.

REFERENCE: *Annual Report of the Navy Department, 1898* (Washington, DC: Government Printing Office, 1898).

MARQUÉS DEL DUERO (ship)

Marqués del Duero was a Spanish gunboat launched in 1875 of 492 tons. During the battle of Manila Bay,* *Duero* kept station behind the main Spanish line and therefore escaped much of the shelling, receiving only five hits. The U.S.S. *Petrel** set fire to *Duero* and sank her.

REFERENCE: H. W. Wilson, *The Downfall of Spain* (New York: Burt Franklin, 1971).

MARSHALL, JOHN R,
(1859–?)

Departing from past practice, President William McKinley* paid particular attention to African American volunteers. The Eighth Illinois Volunteers were, for example, composed of African American troops, but in a move without precedent, these volunteers were also commanded by the first black colonel in the U.S. Army: John R. Marshall. Heretofore these units always had white officers.

REFERENCE: W. T. Goode, *The Eighth Illinois* (Chicago: Blakely Printing, 1899).

MARTÍN CEREZO, SATURNINO
(1866–1945)

When a small band of Spanish soldiers held out against Philippine insurgents* for 337 days, the event became a feat of arms and tenacity that has become almost legendary. Saturnino Martín Cerezo took over command of the Spanish garrison during the Siege of Baler.* He also took on the task of maintaining vigor, health, and military discipline—indeed, Martín Cerezo executed two deserters on 1 June 1899, the day he capitulated. Out of respect for Spanish heroism, Emilio Aguinaldo* arranged for their safe conduct at the end of the siege when only thirty survivors remained. This was the last surrender of the Spanish.

REFERENCES: Saturnino Martín Cerezo, *Under the Red and Gold: Being Notes and Recollections of the Siege of Baler,* 2nd ed. (Kansas City, MO: Franklin Hudson Publishing Co., 1909); Gregorio F. Zaide, *The Philippine Revolution* (Manila: Modern Book Company 1968).

MARTÍNEZ CAMPOS, ARSENIO
(1831–1900)

Arsenio Martínez Campos had a distinguished political and military career. In 1869 Martínez Campos went to Cuba during the Ten Years' War* and waged a highly successful campaign against the insurrection.* He was promoted to brigadier general in 1874 and not only was able to produce a successful outcome but showed himself a humanitarian.

When rebellion flared again in 1895, Antonio Cánovas del Castillo,* the Conservative party leader, sent Martínez Campos again to Cuba as captain general in hopes of his performing another miracle. Martínez Campos served a year attempting to negotiate a settlement and working for Cuban autonomy.* Mistrusted by the Spanish government, he was recalled and replaced by Valeriano Weyler.*

REFERENCE: *Diccionario de historia de España* (Madrid: Revista de Occidente, 1953).

MARTINIQUE

A French island in the Windwards, Martinique served as a cable terminus, and as such American ships like *Harvard** and *St. Louis** used it as a source of cable traffic. Admiral Pascual Cervera* also used Martinique as a coaling resupply point for his fleet's journey to Cuba but was frustrated and had to travel to Curaçao.* Indeed, it was at Martinique that Cervera was detected. Because Cervera was sighted, the original plan to land U.S. troops at Mariel,* Cuba, was cancelled.

MARTÍ Y PÉREZ, JOSÉ
(1853–1895)

José Martí y Pérez was born on 28 January 1853 in Havana, Cuba.* Although, or perhaps because, his father was a professional soldier, the younger Martí questioned authority and became an early believer in democracy. One of his school teachers was Rafael María de Mendive, who opposed the Spanish Empire, praised the virtues of democracy, and called for Cubans to unite together as a single people. Mendive had an enormous intellectual impact on Martí. Martí was only fifteen years old when the Ten Years' War* erupted in 1868, but he rallied behind Carlos Manuel de Céspedes and became an ardent exponent of Cuban independence. The war also inspired Martí's budding career as a writer. Blessed with a keen intellect and a gifted pen, Martí wrote about the plight of the Cuban people. Early in 1869, in conjunction with close friend Fermín Valdés Domínguez, Martí wrote *El Diablo Cojuelo,* a satire on Spanish authority which demanded, subtly of course, freedom of speech and freedom of the press. Martí's first play, published later in the year, was not so subtle. *Abdala* called for Cuban independence and earned Martí an arrest for sedition. Martí was sentenced to six years in prison, a term which was subsequently reduced.

After two years at hard labor, Martí was paroled, and exiled, to Spain in 1871. He studied law at the University of Madrid for a year, transferred to the University of Zaragoza in 1872, and received his degree there in 1873. Martí found an intellectual home among liberal Spanish students, who rallied to his demands for Cuban independence. Martí also wrote diligently while he was in Spain—*Adultera* (1872), *Amor con Amor Se Paga* (1875), and *Amistad Funesa* (1875). In 1875 Jose Martí went to work as a journalist in Mexico City for *La Revista Universal.* When the Pact of Zanjón ended the Ten Years' War in 1878 and declared a general amnesty for all revolutionaries, Martí returned to Havana.

He immediately resumed his political activities, and late in 1878 Spanish authorities exiled him once again. Spain was still unwilling to countenance any political opposition. Martí moved to New York City, where he spent the next seventeen years raising money and promoting the cause of Cuban independence. Martí was convinced that any successful insurrection in Cuba would have to be democratically inspired and internally driven. If a successful revolution were ever to develop in Cuba, a unified revolutionary party had to be forged, one capable of attracting the loyalties of traditional, upper-class separatists as well as the larger group of socially alienated poor Cuban workers and Cuban blacks. Toward that end Martí established the Partido Revolucionario Cubano (Cuban Revolutionary party), or PRC, in 1892. Centrally organized and authoritarian, the PRC attracted the support of old-line separatists. But Martí also realized that the PRC would eventually have to attract support among the lower classes as well. The legacy of colonialism would also have to be obliterated. The Spanish system of government, with sovereignty resting in upper-class elites and power flowing down from them to other social groups, was antidemocratic and conducive to dictatorship. Only a democratic government could guarantee social justice.

In New York City, Martí emerged as the leader of the Cuban emigre community. Along with other emigres like Máximo Gómez,* Antonio Maceo,* and Gonzalo Gualberto Gómez, he planned the rebellion. When José Martí issued the call for an uprising on 24 February 1895, Cuba was ripe for insurrection. The "Crown Jewel of the Spanish Empire," the "Ever Faithful Island," was faithful no more. In April 1895 Martí made his way to Florida, and from there he crossed the Florida Strait to Cuba to fight in the revolutionary war. Martí's career as a soldier was short lived. On May 19 1895, just weeks after he had arrived on the island, Spanish soldiers ambushed his unit and killed Martí. News of his death spread among the rebels, and he became the first martyr of the revolution. José Martí remains a national hero in Cuba today.

REFERENCES: Richard B. Gray, *José Martí, Cuban Patriot* (Gainesville: University of Florida Press, 1962); John M. Kirk, *José Martí: Mentor of the Cuban Nation* (Tampa: University Presses of Florida, 1983).

JAMES S. OLSON

MASSACHUSETTS (ship)

The battleship U.S.S. *Massachusetts* was a ship of the same tonnage (10,288) and armament as her sister-ships *Indiana* and *Oregon*.* Commissioned on 10 June 1896, *Massachusetts* was less than two years old at the outbreak of the Spanish American War. In April 1898 *Massachusetts* lay at Hampton Roads,* Virginia, in the squadron commanded by Commodore Winfield S. Schley.* By 19 May the battleship had moved to Key West,* Florida, and remained in Schley's squadron during the search for Admiral Cervera's* fleet at Cienfuegos.* Once the Spanish fleet was located at Santiago de Cuba,* the battleship sailed to Santiago with the intent of giving battle. On 21 May 1898 *Massachusetts,* in company with *Iowa* and *New Orleans,* sailed near the harbor mouth to try the range on the Spanish ships and to reconnoiter the shore batteries. *Massachusetts* also participated in the blockade* and in the heavy bombardments of 6 June, during which *Massachusetts* was struck on the mast. On 3 July 1898, the day of the Battle of Santiago, *Massachusetts* steamed toward Guantánamo* to coal, thereby missing the battle. Afterward she was briefly detailed to Commodore John C. Watson's* Eastern Squadron.* When that squadron failed to materialize, a debate ensued in the Naval War Board* among Admiral Montgomery Sicard* and A. T. Mahan* over the best use of naval assets like the *Massachusetts.* One possibility was to reinforce Commodore (later Admiral) George Dewey* at Manila* in case a third power—Germany,* perhaps—tried to intervene. Another was to support and convoy an expedition to Puerto Rico.* The latter won, and *Massachusetts* convoyed 3,415 troops and General Nelson A. Miles* to Puerto Rico.

Massachusetts survived until 22 November 1920, when she was sunk while a target for shore batteries at Pensacola,* Florida.

REFERENCE: H. W. Wilson, *The Downfall of Spain* (New York: Burt Franklin, 1971).

MATANZAS, CUBA

Fifty miles east of Havana* on the northern coast of Cuba lies Matanzas on a bay of the same name. Because it is a sizable port, Matanzas figured in early military plans as a base of operations against Havana. Matanzas was also listed as a port of blockade* for the U.S. Navy. Admiral William T. Sampson* ordered the bombardment of Matanzas, which occurred on 27 April 1898. Accordingly, *New York,* *Cincinnati,* and *Puritan* were dispatched from that mission. Inasmuch as almost no damage was done by either side (the Spanish reporting

the loss of a mule), the incident would have had no significance except that it was the first occasion the American ships came under fire from the Spanish.
REFERENCE: *Annual Report of the Navy Department, 1898* (Washington, DC: Government Printing Office, 1898).

MAUSER RIFLE

The Mauser rifle was designed by Peter Paul Mauser of Obendorf, Germany, along with one of his four brothers, who served as a business partner. They are credited with developing one of the first successful metallic cartridge bolt-action rifles, the Model 71. Considered the finest military rifles in existence, Mauser based his weapon designs on careful observation of actual battlefield conditions. European battle techniques called for weapons to fire as many rounds per minute as possible. Mauser's weapons were just the answer. His bolt-action repeating rifle clip-loaded five cartridges at a time into its magazine with one push of the hand.

The United States considered adopting the Mauser as its main infantry weapon. In 1891 General Daniel Webster Flagler,* the new chief of ordnance, declared his intention to acquire a new rifle that would fire smokeless powder. The Mauser was tested at the Springfield Armory and rejected for a variety of reasons by an ordnance board tightly controlled through Flagler. The board eventually selected the Krag-Jorgensen* as the new U.S. Army rifle.

Spain first began using the Mauser rifle in 1891 and shipped the 1892 model to Cuba for use by Spanish soldiers. In 1893 a slightly modified version of the 1892 was manufactured for the Spaniards and also shipped to Cuba. A carbine version was adopted in 1895. Thirty thousand rifles and carbines were delivered to Spanish troops in Cuba and used as the main line of defense in Cuba during the Spanish American War. The weapons employed a 7-mm smokeless cartridge, were rapidly loaded by clip, and had a velocity and range far superior to the arms carried by U.S. troops.

The Spanish soldiers used the Mausers with deadly accuracy, especially in the Battle of San Juan Hill.* With only a few hundred troops defending the hill, the Spanish Army inflicted over 1,400 casualties on the attacking U.S. forces. More than 21,000 Mausers had been seized by the Americans when the war ended.
REFERENCES: William H. Hallahan, *Misfire* (New York: Scribner's, 1994); W.H.B. Smith, *Mauser Rifles and Pistols* (Harrisburg, PA: Stackpole, 1954).

MITCHELL YOCKELSON

MAXFIELD, JOSEPH EDWIN
(1860–1926)

Early in April 1898 the Signal Corps* possessed a balloon* transferred to New York to help warn of impending Spanish attacks on the East Coast. Lieutenant Colonel of Volunteers Joseph Edwin Maxfield, a captain in the regular army, was assigned to balloon service and sent to New York. The intent was to have two balloons and trains, but inasmuch as everything had to be specially made, the second balloon and train never materialized. The existing equipment was for training purposes and comprised six wagons, compressed gas tubes, a generator, a compressor, and a silk balloon. It was decided that the balloon should follow the troops, so the entire apparatus was sent to Tampa.*

Meanwhile Maxfield went to France to acquire balloon cable, hydrogen-producing materials, more balloons, generators, compressors, and so on. Maxfield wanted two balloon companies, but owing to the press of time (he did reach Tampa until 31 May), only one could be made ready, and that just barely. Maxfield could not locate his equipment in the snarled railroad yard and personally had to search through sheets of lading bills to locate the boxcars with his equipment. He obtained seventeen men to operate his equipment and sailed with the Fifth Corps* to Santiago.* While sailing to Cuba, Maxfield got the tent out of the hold for inspections and to prevent rot.

At Daiquirí* the balloon detachment was among the last to leave, disembarking on 28 June. There was only enough gas to fill the balloon one time, but once the company was ashore, the balloon was pressed into service instantly, making three ascents the first day.

Moving to El Pozo* the following day, Maxfield linked up with Colonel George Derby.* Maxfield's horse was shot out from under him. Nevertheless, Derby and Maxfield got the balloon up again. Derby wanted the balloon closer to the action at El Caney* and San Juan Hill, but in getting closer, the men in the car came under intense fire, perhaps more intense than any that day. Both Derby and Maxfield were later recommended for brevet promotions for extraordinary heroism in providing intelligence to ground commanders. However, the balloon itself became a casualty, riddled with so many holes that it would not hold gas. It had to be retired.

REFERENCE: Howard A. Giddings, *Exploits of the Signal Corps in the War with Spain* (Kansas City, MO: Hudson-Kimberly Publishing Co., 1900).

MAYAGÜEZ, PUERTO RICO

Lying in western Puerto Rico, some 70 miles west of San Juan,* is Mayagüez. Mayagüez, San Juan, and Ponce* were the three largest cities on the island at the time of the Spanish American War. Nevertheless, Mayagüez possessed no fortifications whatever and Governor-General Manuel Macías y Casado* placed a battalion at Mayagüez for defense.

Under the orders of General Nelson Miles,* Brigadier General Theodore Schwan* and the augmented Eleventh Infantry moved from Yauco* to Mayagüez. A skirmish 7 miles south of the city on 10 August 1898 resulted in approximately fifty Spanish casualties and seventeen U.S. casualties, including one killed. The Spanish withdrew from the city and Schwan's forces entered without incident.

REFERENCE: *Report of the War Department, 1898* (Washington, DC: Government Printing Office, 1898).

MAYFLOWER (ship)

Among the several yachts* purchased by the Navy Department or on loan, *Mayflower* was the largest at 2,690 tons. She was purchased for $430,000, and her lavish fittings were almost all removed (saving one of the original four solid marble bathtubs). This 273-foot vessel was armed with two 5-inch guns in the waist, a few torpedo tubes in the former dining room, a dozen 6-pounders, and four Colt automatic machine guns. Steel plates were added midship to protect engines and boilers from gunfire. *Mayflower* took part in Admiral William T. Sampson's* blockade* of Cuba and was slated to be part of the Eastern Squadron.*

Subsequent to the war *Mayflower* served a variety of missions, including service as the presidential yacht for twenty-five years. She was the longest lived of the Spanish American War yachts, surviving to serve as the *Malla* carrying Jewish refugees to Palestine as late as 1948.

REFERENCE: John G. Alden, *The American Steel Navy* (Annapolis, MD: Naval Institute Press, 1972).

MEDICAL DEPARTMENT, U.S. ARMY

The Medical Department of the U.S. Army purchased all medical supplies and hospital stores, with the exception of draft animals, wagons, and tents, which were obtained from the Quartermaster's Department,* and was responsible for treating the sick and wounded and advising commanders on health and sanitation issues. During the Spanish American War Brigadier General George Miller Sternberg* was surgeon general of the army. Under Sternberg's able direction the Medical Department sumptuously equipped expeditions with stores, including a life-saving individual first-aid kit credited with saving many lives. Transportation failure nullified much of this preparation, however, inasmuch as much equipment, hospital ambulances, furniture, and so on, was left behind at Tampa* due to lack of space on the transports. The campaign in Puerto Rico* did not suffer from transport shortage, but it did lack surgeons and nurses.

During the war the Medical Department enjoyed the services of some of the best doctors and scientists in the country. Nevertheless, Sternberg was bureaucratically and politically naive. The doctor could only advise commanders and had no means of enforcing sanitation. The very rapid mobilization placed enormous strains on the slender transportation and personnel resources available to the department; as a result of these shortages and deficiencies and the ravages of disease,* the Medical Department received considerable public abuse for its perceived role in the failure to contain public health epidemics and disease. Without the aid of the American National Red Cross,* it would have been much worse.

Camp Wikoff* on Long Island received much negative publicity from the press after the war as a singularly inept quarantine station. The scandal, added to the other scandals surrounding the U.S. Army, created a public outcry. Once aware of the problems, Sternberg moved quickly to alleviate shortages, expand the surgeon's powers, provide more facilities, and reduce crowding. He also tried to plan for future epidemics and organized a Yellow Fever Commission and other commissions to address basic research into diseases and their cause. These commissions were very successful in preventing or containing epidemics of yellow fever,* malaria,* typhoid, and at Manila,* small pox. In a great success—one of the landmarks of science—Major Walter Reed* identified in 1901 the mosquito as the source of yellow fever. These successes did much to assuage the bad images lingering from the scandals of the war. The scandals spurred greater efforts for the future.

REFERENCES: P. M. Ashburn, *A History of the Medical Department of the United States Army* (Boston: Houghton Mifflin, 1929); Graham A. Cosmas, *An Army for Empire* (Columbia: University of Missouri Press, 1971).

MELLOR, FRANK ARTHUR

Frank Arthur Mellor, a Canadian-born agent of a detective agency, was hired by Ramón Carranza,* a Spanish intelligence officer, to enlist in the U.S. Army and provide intelligence. John E. Wilkie,* head of the U.S. Secret Service, already knew of Carranza's operations in Montreal. Shortly after Mellor tried to enlist in Tampa (but was turned down), the Secret Service arrested him.

REFERENCE: Don Wilkie, *American Secret Service Agent* (New York: Stokes, 1934).

MERCHANT AND NAVAL AUXILIARIES

Besides the regularly commissioned naval vessels in both the Spanish and U.S. navies were auxiliaries of various types that were either chartered, leased, donated to the respective navies, or purchased outright. The rapid development of hostilities in early 1898 left both navies scrambling for auxiliaries for troop transport, scouting, dispatch work, colliers, resupply, and repair. On 8 April 1898 Spain acquired some merchant liners for use as armed cruisers, including the HAPAG vessels *Normannia* (renamed *Patriota*) and *Columbia* (renamed *Rápido*) followed by *Alfonso XII, Ciudad de Cádiz, Joaquín del Piélago, Buenos Aires* and *Antonio López* (on 27 May 1898) and the German *Havel* (8 June 1898). Several of these were renamed by the Spanish. Others were also acquired. Some of these vessels were given the mission to harass eastern U.S. shipping as commerce raiders, but the Philippine debacle at Manila Bay* had dramatically altered priorities. These liners, now armed cruisers, were attached to Admiral Manuel de la Cámara's* abortive effort to relieve the Philippines.*

Similar to Spanish practice, the U.S. Navy acquired *Harvard** (ex–*New York*), *Yale** (ex–*Paris*), *St. Louis,** *St. Paul,** *Yankee** (ex–*El Norte*), *Yosemite** (ex–*El Sol*), *Dixie** (ex–*El Sud*), and *Prairie* (ex–*El Río*). Some of these vessels such as the *St. Paul* and *St. Louis,* saw action. The U.S. Navy also had a history of commerce raiding that dated back to the Revolutionary War. Of particular interest were the yachts* of the wealthy that were armed and used in numerous roles.

The types of auxiliaries were almost as numerous as the vessels themselves:

tugs, lightships, tenders, Fish Commission vessels, Revenue Service cutters, survey ships, pilot boats, ferry boats, refrigerator ships and an ice boat, oil tanker (*Arethusa*, the navy's first), water distilling ships, ambulance and hospital ships, a floating forge, blacksmithy, and repair ship (*Vulcan*), as well as common freighters, big liners, and others. The origin of the numerous fleet auxiliaries of World War II and later lay in these modest beginnings.

REFERENCES: John P. Alden, *The American Steel Navy* (Annapolis, MD: Naval Institute Press, 1972); Christian de Saint Hubert and Carlos Alfaro Zaforteza, ''The Spanish Navy of 1898,'' *Warship International* 17 (1980): 110–120.

MERRIAM, HENRY CLAY
(1837–1912)

Major General Henry Clay Merriam first served in Maine volunteer regiments as an officer, rising to the rank of captain. He read law and served in a variety of military posts until promoted to major general of volunteers in 1898. He had won a Congressional Medal of Honor at Mobile in the Civil War. Merriam commanded the military departments of Columbia and then California in 1898 and as such played an important role in supporting General Wesley Merritt's* Eighth Corps.*

REFERENCE: *Report of the Commission Appointed by the President to Investigate the Conduct of the War Department in the War with Spain,* Senate Doc. No. 221, 8 vols. (Washington, DC: Government Printing Office, 1900).

MERRIMAC (ship)

On 3 June 1898 Richmond P. Hobson* and a volunteer crew tried to bottle Admiral Cervera's* fleet in Santiago* by sinking the collier *Merrimac* in the harbor channel. Hobson was unsuccessful after a gallant and courageous effort.

Merrimac was a collier originally named *Solveig* that was purchased on 12 April 1898 from T. Hogan and Sons of New York for $342,000. She sailed with Commodore Winfield S. Schley's* Flying Squadron* to Cuba, where her propensity for breaking down mechanically helped place her at the top of a short list of expendable vessels.

REFERENCE: Richmond Pearson Hobson, *The Sinking of the "Merrimac"* (Annapolis, MD: Naval Institute Press, 1987).

MERRITT, WESLEY
(1836–1910)

General Wesley Merritt graduated from West Point just in time for the Civil War. He served with the Army of the Potomac and saw action in all its battles. By the end of the war his regular rank was lieutenant colonel, but he had been brevetted major general of volunteers.

During the Spanish American War, on 12 May 1898, Merritt was appointed commander of Eighth Corps* at San Francisco* and led the American ground forces at the Battle of Manila.* Merritt had some difficulty defining the role of

the ground forces inasmuch as President William McKinley's* Philippine policy
was in embryo—although it developed rapidly. He sailed with explicit orders
not to ally the United States with Emilio Aquinaldo's* insurgent forces.

REFERENCES: Karl I. Faust, *Campaigning in the Philippines* (San Francisco: Hicks-
Judd Co., 1899); William Thaddeus Sexton, *Soldiers in the Sun* (Harrisburg, PA: Military
Service Publishing Co., 1939).

"A MESSAGE TO GARCÍA"

Elbert Hubbard wrote a somewhat fanciful account of Lieutenant Andrew
Rowan's* journey to Cuban insurgent General Calixto García.* Titled "A Message to García," the account was published by Hubbard's Roycrofters Press in
numerous printings commencing in 1899. A genuine article of Spanish American
War folklore, "A Message to García" was required reading for generations of
students and certain company employees. Hubbard's work emphasized a type
of masculine duty that was revered and emphasized.

REFERENCE: Elbert Hubbard, *A Message to García: Being a Preachment* (East Aurora,
NY: Roycrofters, 1905 [1899]).

MEXICO

Mexico as a nation involved itself hardly at all in the brewing crisis that
culminated in the Spanish American War. Oddly, Mexico was often more sympathetic to Spain (because of Spanish economic interests) than to the resurgent
Cuban insurrection. Mexico became a source of blockade runners once hostilities
commenced after 22 April 1898. Ships departed from Mexico for ports such as
Havana* or Santiago.* Admiral William T. Sampson's blockade* intercepted
many such ships.

MIANTONOMAH (ship)

During the Spanish American War the U.S.S. *Miantonomah* served in the
blockade* of Cuba and in bombardment duties. *Miantonomah,* a monitor,* left
Key West* for Havana* on 29 May 1898. Slow, low in the water, limited in
fuel supply, and very poorly ventilated, *Miantonomah* and her sister-ships *Amphitrite,* *Monadnock,** and *Terror** were never designed for serious sea duty
and were often towed by other warships.

Armed with 10-inch guns, plus smaller calibers, and displacing 3,990 tons,
Miantonomah was laid down in 1874 as a repair order for an older ship—a
devious practice employed after the Civil War to get money out of Congress
because it was not forthcoming any other way. She ended her days as a gunnery
target.

REFERENCE: John D. Alden, *The American Steel Navy* (Annapolis, MD: Naval Institute
Press, 1972).

MILES, NELSON APPLETON
(1839–1925)

Nelson Appleton Miles was born on 21 April 1839 to devout Baptist parents
on a Massachusetts farm. Raised in a strong abolitionist environment, his mil-

itary career began when he enlisted in the Union army after the Battle of First Manassas (Bull Run). Organizing and equipping a company of seventy men, Miles entered the army a lieutenant in the 22nd Massachusetts Volunteer Infantry Regiment. Having been present at almost every engagement of the Army of the Potomac and wounded twice, his bravery earned him promotions that concluded with the rank of brigadier general at the age of twenty-five during the latter part of the war. Miles received the Medal of Honor in 1892 for his actions at the Battle of Chancellorsville.

After the Civil War Miles gained notoriety as the commandant at Fort Monroe, Virginia, and the custodian of the imprisoned former Confederate president Jefferson Davis. Miles insisted upon keeping Davis shackled in his cell, drawing severe public criticism in both the North and South. In 1868 Miles married the niece of famed general William T. Sherman and a member of a powerful Ohio Republican family. This connection would prove beneficial in fostering his military career. A year later he was appointed commander of the 5th U.S. Infantry and sent to fight Indians on the western frontier. During his high-profile career on the plains, Miles earned notice for enticing the Apache chief Geronimo to surrender, restoring U.S. control over the Native Americans at Wounded Knee, and suppressing the Pullman strikers in Chicago. Because of his senior military status, Miles became the general-in-chief of the army in 1895.

When the prospect of war with Spain appeared on the horizon, Miles announced designs on how the U.S. Army should be mobilized. His ideas clashed with the plans of Secretary of War Russell A. Alger.* The secretary proposed to assemble, train, and equip a small force of about 80,000 for an invasion of Havana* with almost all troops from the regular army. Miles, on the other hand, suggested the War Department concentrate the troops at Chickamauga Park, Georgia, for extensive training before embarking on Cuba.

He bypassed Alger and reasoned to President McKinley* that it was unhealthy to land in Cuba during the rainy season. In addition, Miles claimed that an attack on Havana was the wrong military strategy. Reminding the president about the unsuccessful frontal attacks of the Civil War, Miles favored an attack on Spain's weakest positions at Puerto Rico* and the eastern portion of Cuba— a plan Miles claimed would destroy the Spanish forces with a minimal amount of American losses. However, President McKinley and Secretary of War Alger felt the press of public pressure to avenge the sinking of the *Maine** and ignored Miles by mobilizing the regular army along with the volunteers for immediate descent to Cuba.

Alger and Miles would clash a number of times during the war. Because Miles was appointed to his position of commanding general entirely on the basis of rank, he could hold the post until retirement. The secretary of war could neither fire nor transfer him. Both wished that the other would go away, but this would never materialize. Throughout the planning of the Santiago* campaign, Miles constantly interfered and promoted his own campaign to invade Puerto Rico.* After the surrender of Santiago in July, Miles landed his expeditionary force at Guánica,* Puerto Rico, and by the middle of August the Americans were in complete control. The success of the campaign played a significant role in encouraging the Spanish government to seek an early peace and helped redeem Miles for his sometimes erratic and irresponsible behavior. Miles was also given credit for suggesting that the army select a different camp-site on a daily basis and move inland to the mountains, which helped prevent the spread of yellow fever.*

After the fighting in Cuba ceased, Miles became embroiled in a controversy over the meat that was issued to the troops. He had charged that the War Department* had supplied troops canned beef injected with toxic chemicals. A commission headed by retired General Grenville Dodge* was appointed to study this issue and eventually rejected Miles's accusation. Miles faced further scrutiny after the war when he publicly criticized the conduct of certain U.S. officers during the fighting in Cuba and later in the Philippines.

Although his role during the Spanish American War was mostly administrative in nature, Miles proved his ability as an able officer during the invasion of Puerto Rico. However, his critics would charge that he failed to advise President McKinley correctly in organizing the army and the volunteers, which stifled the War Department plans.

REFERENCES: G.J.A. O'Toole, *The Spanish War* (New York: W. W. Norton and Co., 1984); Robert Wooster, *Nelson A. Miles and the Twilight of the Frontier Army* (Lincoln: University of Nebraska Press, 1993).

MITCHELL YOCKELSON

MILITARY INFORMATION DIVISION, U.S. ARMY

It was not until 1885 that efforts were made to create a separate entity in the War Department* to gather military information. The Military Information Division, like the Office of Naval Intelligence,* was developed under the Adjutant General's Office* to address the needs of information gathering and assessment. Both the army and the navy initially used attachés in various American legations abroad to gather military information and forward it to Washington. Within four years the division had officers operating in London, Paris, Vienna, Berlin, and St. Petersburg. By 1898 that number had been increased to sixteen, significantly including Japan,* Spain,* and several countries in Latin America. Equally significant, the number did not include any officers operating in the Philippines.*

The prospects of war with Spain naturally brought heightened interest to the division. Captain (later General) Tasker H. Bliss,* military attaché in Madrid, sent regular reports early in 1898 allowing the War Department to gauge the forces of Spain in Cuba. Lieutenant Andrew S. Rowan* and his celebrated clandestine insertion into Cuba was a division initiative, as was also the intelligence operation* of Henry H. Whitney* in Puerto Rico* in anticipation of General Nelson Miles's* landing on that island. Each of these bore positive fruit: Miles benefited from Whitney's reconnaissance of Puerto Rico, and Rowan's famous trek provided needed information to General William R. Shafter* and his expeditionary force in Cuba, as well as precipitating a meeting between Shafter and insurgent General Calixto García* at Daiquirí.* The most consistently successful intelligence work was done under the direction of Martin Luther Hellings* of the Signal Corps,* who maintained a network of telegraph informers in Havana.* Despite these successes, military commanders such as General Wesley Merritt* in the Philippines, Shafter in Cuba, and Miles in Puerto Rico, as well as subordinate commanders, consistently complained of the lack of reliable information or usable intelligence. After the war the demands of quelling the Philippine Insurrection* and the Boxer Rebellion in China,* in addition to other foreign commitments, underlined the need for greater and more accurate intelligence; military reform, however, drove the postwar changes.

REFERENCE: Bruce W. Bidwell, *History of the Military Intelligence Division, Department of the Army General Staff, 1775–1941* (Frederick, MD: University Publications of America, 1986).

MILITIA ACT OF 1903

As crises often do, the Spanish American War uncovered flawed thinking and practice. The war created sensational scandals that were investigated in the immediate postwar years. One of these scandals that had substance to it revolved around the War Department,* Secretary Russell A. Alger,* and the organization and command structure of the U.S. Army. The ensuing investigations led to a variety of changes, one of which was the Militia Act passed by Congress on 21 January 1903. The act attempted to define better the relative authority of the commanding general and the secretary of war and to strengthen the training and preparations for war. It became part of the reforms of Elihu Root.*

MINDANAO, PHILIPPINES

Mindanao is the next largest island after Luzon* in the Philippine archipelago. It is located at the southern end of the islands.

Mindanao was the destination of Admiral Manuel de la Cámara's* Eastern Squadron.* From that island, Cámara hoped to be able to plan to relieve Manila Bay* from Commodore George Dewey's* victorious squadron.

Mindanao also became a bargaining chip in the developing peace process* after hostilities ceased. Germany* evidenced an interest in Mindanao, and so did the Americans. For a time it was thought that Mindanao might be returned to Spain in exchange for an American base in the Caroline Islands, such as Kusaie.*

In addition, Mindanao was the scene of much fighting by Emilio Aguinaldo's* insurrectionary forces.

MINES

Universally dreaded submarine mines were ineffectively used in the Spanish American War. The United States mined New York harbor, but nothing else.

It was erroneously thought that a mine caused the explosion of the U.S.S.

Maine* in Havana.* The U.S. Naval Court of Inquiry decided that a mine had caused the ship's destruction, but subsequent, more thorough research has revealed otherwise.

In the Philippines the Spanish mined the approaches to Manila Bay* with contact mines and controlled mines. Lacking the expertise and the wherewithal to mine the channels effectively, the Spanish efforts were wasted in the Philippines.

Mining of Santiago,* however, kept Admiral William Sampson* from forcing the Cuban harbor and thus led to a land battle. Mining of Cienfuegos,* Nipe,* and other smaller ports in Cuba had no tactical effect.

REFERENCE: Tamara Moser Melia, *"Damn the Torpedoes": A Short History of U.S. Naval Mine Counter Measures, 1977–1991* (Washington, DC: Naval Historical Center, 1991).

MINNEAPOLIS (ship)

The U.S.S. *Minneapolis,* like the *Columbia,** was a lightly armed and armored cruiser built to destroy commerce and little else. Laid down in 1891 and commissioned in 1894, *Minneapolis* displaced 7,375 tons and had a speed of 21 knots, although on her trials she made a little over 23 knots. Twin 6-inch guns faced forward, one 8-inch faced aft, and in sponsons, four 4-inch guns per side comprised the main battery of *Minneapolis.*

Minneapolis joined the European Squadron in 1895 until summer 1897, when she was placed in reserve at Philadelphia. With the outbreak of war with Spain, *Minneapolis* joined Commodore W. S. Schley's* Flying Squadron* and served coastal patrol duty in the North Atlantic. Initially in the war there was considerable concern about the possibility of Spanish raids or bombardments on the American seaboard. As these fears diminished, *Minneapolis* joined the search for Admiral Pascual Cervera's* squadron and performed scout work in the Caribbean.

After the war *Minneapolis* oscillated between training duty and showing the flag until decommissioned in 1906. World War I caused her to be recommissioned, and she was assigned convoy duty. Decommissioned again in 1921, she was sold the same year.

REFERENCE: *Dictionary of American Naval Fighting Ships* (Washington, DC: Navy Department, 1969).

MIRS BAY, CHINA

Just east of the New Territories, Hong Kong, lies Mirs Bay, which was leased by China to Great Britain* late in 1898. George Dewey,* commander of the U.S. Asiatic Squadron,* anticipated hostilities with Spain and moved the squadron from Hong Kong* to Mirs Bay. Major General Wilsone Black,* the governor of the British enclave, notified Dewey of the outbreak of hostilities on 25 April 1898 and that Great Britain would remain neutral. Sensing that the Chinese would be less exacting in their adherence to the laws of neutrality, Dewey took advantage of the Chinese ambivalence and removed his squadron the 30 miles to Mirs Bay. At 2:00 P.M. on 27 April, Dewey's squadron sailed for Manila.*

MIX, TOM
(1880–1940)

Born Thomas Hezikiah Mix in Mix Run, Cameron County, Pennsylvania, Tom Mix joined the army on 26 April 1898, the day after the United States declared war with Spain.

He was assigned to Battery M of the 4th Artillery, which was assigned to guard several posts in Delaware for the duration of the war. In September 1899 Mix was promoted from private to corporal. He remained with Battery M until 17 April 1899, when he was promoted to sergeant and transferred to Battery O of the 4th Artillery. He was then stationed at Fort Monroe, Virginia, an artillery training center that had been a receiving station for wounded during the war. During his duty at Fort Monroe the Philippine Insurrection* began, but Mix's unit remained busy in the United States. Battery O was transferred to Fort Hancock, New Jersey, in June 1900, and Mix was promoted to first sergeant in November.

After an honorable discharge in April 1901, he immediately reenlisted for another three-year period. He apparently served at Fort Hancock over the next year, but on failing to return to the fort after a furlough, he was officially listed as a deserter in November 1902. The army seems not to have pursued the matter further; however, Mix's subsequent move to Oklahoma may have been an attempt on his part to distance himself from the authorities. Also, out of disdain for Mix's desertion, his father-in-law arranged to have Mix's marriage to his daughter, whom he had married while in the army, annulled.

Mix later worked as a cowboy and performed in traveling Wild West shows before gaining fame as a star in western movies. Long before becoming a motion picture celebrity, he seems to have embellished, changed, or ignored facts about his own past. For instance, upon enlistment Mix gave his middle name as Edwin (his father's name), which he used for the remainder of his life, and he gave the year of his birth as 1877 rather than 1880. Rumors about his military career that are apparently false include that he served with the 1st U.S. Volunteer Cavalry—Teddy Roosevelt's Rough Riders*—that he served in the Philippines during the Philippine Insurrection,* that he received a decoration while serving in China during the Boxer Rebellion, and even that he volunteered for duty in the Boer War. No records indicate any military service outside the United States.

In 1927, however, Mix applied for and was granted a life membership in the United Spanish War Veterans, Joe Wheeler Camp No. 5, Prescott, Arizona. The film star's army desertion appears to have been ignored or rationalized on the basis that it was believed he had left to be a mercenary in Africa. After he died in an automobile accident near Florence, Arizona, in 1940, the question of his desertion arose again when the Veterans Association at first refused to give his estate an American flag to drape over the casket at his funeral. The film director John Ford intervened to obtain the flag.

REFERENCE: Paul E. Mix, *The Life and Legend of Tom Mix* (South Brunswick, NJ: A. S. Barnes, 1972).

MARK A. THOMAS

MOBILE, ALABAMA

Mobile was a U.S. Army assembly area for the buildup for an expedition to Cuba. Brigadier John J. Coppinger* commanded at Mobile. Other assembly areas were Tampa* and New Orleans. In the second week of May 1898, all regular army units left for these three assembly areas. General William R. Shafter* then assembled troops that were to form the expeditionary force to Cuba at Tampa from Chickamauga, Mobile, and New Orleans. This was done the first week of June. Later, as the Puerto Rico expeditionary force developed, Brigadier General Theodore Schwan's* division, which was at Mobile, was included in the force.

MÔLE ST. NICOLAS, HAITI

Môle St. Nicolas is a coastal town in the northwest quadrant of Haiti.* It was an important cable connection utilized by the U.S. Navy and also a port heavily used during the search for Admiral Pascual Cervera's* squadron. Washington maintained direct cable communication with the Môle, from where U.S. forces laid a cable to Guantánamo,* Cuba, thus affording close and direct communication between Fifth Corps* and Washington. Spanish cables near the Môle were cut by U.S.S. *St. Louis** in May 1898.

REFERENCE: David F. Trask, *The War with Spain in 1898* (New York: Macmillan Publishing Co., 1981).

MONADNOCK (ship)

The U.S.S. *Monadnock* was one of the *Amphitrite*-class monitors,* but built in California. Laid down the same year as her sister-ship *Miantonomah** and under the same conditions, *Monadnock* was not commissioned until 1896.

On 1 May 1898 Commodore George Dewey* defeated Admiral Patricio Montojo y Pasarón,* Spanish commander of naval forces at Manila Bay.* The navy reinforced Dewey against possible foreign intervention and the threat of Spanish retribution from Admiral Manuel de la Cámara's* fleet by sending three ships: the cruiser *Charleston** and the monitors *Monterey** and *Monadnock. Monadnock* was sent to the Philippines* in late May 1898, but owing to the slowness of the monitor, she did not arrive until 16 August 1898, where her four 10-inch and two 4-inch guns made an effective defensive statement.

Monadnock served in the Far East for some years before being sold in 1923.

REFERENCE: William Reynolds Braisted, *The United States Navy in the Pacific, 1897–1909* (Austin: University of Texas Press, 1958).

MONITORS

What was a brilliant idea conceived by John Ericsson and executed well during the Civil War had become, thirty years later, a tired old design rouged up for the press but functionally without much of a point. Monitors were trumpeted by their advocates as powerful defensive weapons, proof against invasion through coastal defense. By 1898, monitors were no longer considered line ships but auxiliaries. Admiral William T. Sampson* did not seem to think they were useful even as auxiliaries, however. The monitor's low freeboard meant it shipped seas in all weather. Monitors rolled so quickly that they were poor gun platforms. Their slow speed of 6 to 8 knots and poor fuel capacity meant they were often coaling at sea—a task all sailors loathed—or they were towed by other ships. They could not keep up with newer warships. They had heavy primary guns but insufficient secondary batteries, making them easy targets for torpedo boats.* Low freeboard meant they were very wet ships in any seaway, hazardous to crew and of marginal utility in fleet action. Ventilation was so poor that in tropical climates speeds would drop below 5 knots because the below-deck temperatures rose to over 200 degrees, so that the crew could not sustain operations.

During the Spanish American War the monitors *Puritan,* *Amphitrite,* *Miantonomah,* and *Terror* served in Cuban waters primarily as auxiliary forces in the blockade* and for bombardment. *Monterey* and *Monadnock* journeyed from California to the Philippines to augment Commodore George Dewey's squadron.

REFERENCES: John G. Alden, *The American Steel Navy* (Annapolis, MD: Naval Institute Press, 1972); Francis J. Allen, "The U.S. Monitors," in John Roberts, ed., *Warship,* vol. 7, (Annapolis, MD: Naval Institute Press, 1983).

MONTEREY (ship)

The 4,130-ton U.S.S. *Monterey* had two 12-inch and two 10-inch guns and was capable of 13 knots, which was relatively speedy compared to other monitors.* As a class monitors were defensive, heavy, slow, and wet. Also, by design they had very low fuel capacity.

Like *Monadnock,* *Monterey* was sent to Manila* to reinforce Commodore George Dewey* in the Philippines.* *Monterey* left San Francisco* on 11 June 1898 in company with a necessary collier and did not arrive at Manila* until 4 August 1898. She nonetheless served as an important reinforcement to Dewey.

Despite the fact that *Monterey* had more modifications made to her than any of the other monitors of the period, she was designed and launched earlier than the others, commissioned on the water of San Francisco Bay on 13 February 1893. She lasted until 1922, when she was sold.

REFERENCE: John D. Alden, *The American Steel Navy* (Annapolis, MD: Naval Institute Press, 1972).

MONTERO RÍOS, EUGENIO
(1832–1914)

Eugenio Montero Ríos was born near Madrid and studied in a Catholic seminary but did not follow an ecclesiastical career. Instead, he became an advocate of progressivism and embarked on a political career in which he became very influential. It was Montero Ríos who in early May 1898 urged Práxides Mateo Sagasta,* head of the Spanish government, to seek peace negotiations with the Americans. Sagasta, however, rejected the idea.

After the peace protocol was signed on 12 August 1898, Sagasta chose Montero Ríos to head the Spanish contingent of the Peace Commission.* The protocol itself ceded Puerto Rico, and Spain also had to relinquish Cuba. Thus, the real issue of the peace negotiations was the fate of the Philippines. Montero Ríos maintained that the United States was not sovereign in the Philippines. Another volley was his attempt to get the United States to shoulder the Cuban debt. He also later introduced a need to compensate Spain for the eventual loss of the Philippines. The Duque de Almodóvar* instructed Montero Ríos to delay while the Americans argued over whether to annex all the Philippines. Discussions between Almodóvar and Montero Ríos included walking out of the sessions, in which case Spain feared a resumption of hostilities against the homeland, the Canary Islands,* or both. Montero Ríos came up with three more propositions. Meanwhile the Sagasta government accepted the McKinley ultimatum, which left Montero Ríos in an unfavorable light in Spain. He wrote *El Tratado de Paris* in 1899 to justify his actions.

At the death of Sagasta, Montero Ríos led the Liberal party.

REFERENCES: Whitelaw Reid, *Making Peace with Spain* (Austin: University of Texas Press, 1965); Eugenio Montero Ríos, *El Tratado de París* (Madrid: Valesco, 1904).

MONTGOMERY (ship)

The U.S.S. *Montgomery,* along with her two sister-ships *Detroit** and *Marblehead,** was authorized on 7 September 1888. *Montgomery,* commissioned on 21 June 1894, displaced 2,094 tons. Armed with nine 5-inch plus smaller-caliber weapons and three above-surface torpedo tubes, *Montgomery* was termed an "unprotected" cruiser, in reality only a little larger than many gunboats of the era.

Montgomery was early included in Admiral William T. Sampson's* blockade of Cuba and in the search for Admiral Pascual Cervera's* Spanish squadron. At 19 knots, *Montgomery* was often planned to be tactically employed against torpedo boats,* but such employment never materialized during the war. The cruiser participated in the bombardment of San Juan,* Puerto Rico, on 12 May 1898, when *Detroit* and *Montgomery* steamed back and forth sending rounds into several military targets without suffering any damage. *Montgomery* returned to the blockade and was later included in the expedition against Puerto Rico.*

REFERENCE: H. W. Wilson, *The Downfall of Spain* (New York: Burt Franklin, 1971).

MONTOJO Y PASARÓN, PATRICIO
(1839–1917)

Admiral Patricio Montojo y Pasarón was a man of diverse abilities and experience. He had previously served in the Spanish navy at the Battle of Callao and had been stationed in Puerto Rico* and Havana.* A lover of literature, he wrote novels as well as professional tracts. At the opening of hostilities in 1898, Rear Admiral Montojo commanded the Spanish naval force in the Philippines.* Of the thirty-seven Spanish ships in the Philippines, most were small launches of 40 tons or so or lightly armed vessels of less than 600 tons. In sum, Montojo possessed only seven vessels with which he could defend against Commodore George Dewey's* Asiatic Squadron.* Like General Fermín Jáudenes,* Montojo, faced political as well as military challenges. Tactically the best solution to Montojo's dilemma might have been to disperse his fleet among the islands in hope of a protracted search, thereby affording the possibility of relief from Spain; in practical terms Montojo found it impossible to leave Manila* unprotected. He was not optimistic of a Spanish victory: Some of his ships could not steam under their own power, he had few mines, and the political situation required him to face battle at a great disadvantage. It was Montojo's plan to make a stand at Subic Bay,* but when he inspected the defenses on 26 April, he found that almost nothing had been done to prepare a land battery, mount artillery, or stock ammunition. After a council of war with his captains, Montojo decided to defend at Cavite* inside Manila Bay. Although Montojo and his force fought gallantly—even heroically—they were outfought tactically and numerically. Montojo, along with Jáudenes, surrendered Manila on 13 August 1898 after a brief land battle.

Upon his return to Spain, Montojo was seized and court-martialed. He was convicted of dereliction of duty, but because he had fought bravely was merely cashiered from the navy.

REFERENCE: French Ensor Chadwick, *The Relations of the United States and Spain* (New York: Russell & Russell, 1911).

MORET Y PRENDERGAST, SEGISMUNDO
(1838–1913)

Segismundo Moret y Prendergast came from an old Andalucian family. He studied law and quickly distinguished himself politically as well. When Práxides Mateo Sagasta* was recalled to power, Moret was made ministro de ultramar, or colonial minister. Moret was in favor of autonomy* for Cuba, and as author of the plan for Cuba, announced in fall 1897, he took keen interest in subsequent events. Moret also proposed a commercial treaty with the United States. He adamantly maintained that his pacification plan would work. Even as events deteriorated later in March, Moret clung steadfastly to his plan and worked through diplomatic channels to attempt to maintain peace. Optimistic until commencement of hostilities, Moret cabled Spanish authorities in the Philippines that the reported impending attack by Commodore George Dewey* might just be a visit by a friendly naval power.

After the commencement of hostilities and particularly the ignominious defeat at Manila,* Moret found himself under attack. In this crisis Sagasta appealed to Spanish nationalism and reorganized the government. Vicente Romero Girón replaced Moret as minister for the colonies. Moret later served as prime minister of Spain.

REFERENCES: Jerónimo Bécker, *Historia de las relaciones exteriores de España durante el siglo XIX,* vol. 3 (Madrid: J. Rates, 1926); Ernest R. May, *Imperial Democracy* (New York: Harcourt, Brace & World, 1961).

MORGAN-CAMERON RESOLUTION

United States Senators John T. Morgan and Donald Cameron jointly proposed a resolution—overwhelmingly passed on 6 April 1896—that attempted two things: (1) achieve recognition of Cuban belligerency* and (2) through President Grover Cleveland's* executive power work with Spain to effect a peace in Cuba on the basis of Cuban independence. Although this resolution expressed only congressional opinion, it sent a clear signal to Cleveland and his Secretary of State Richard Olney* that the Cuban crisis needed attention.

REFERENCE: Philip S. Foner, *The Spanish-Cuban-American War and the Birth of American Imperialism* (New York: Monthly Review Press, 1972).

MORRO CASTLE AND HEIGHTS

Morro Castle sits atop a bluff some 200 feet above the narrow *boca* (mouth) leading into the harbor of Santiago de Cuba.* The castle and the Morro battery command the eastern bluff and the Socapa battery commands the west. The narrow and thus easily defended channel between them meanders northward and at its narrowest is only about 350 feet wide. Mines,* the Estrella battery, and the Puerto Gorda battery complete the fortified naval defenses of Santiago.

The defense of Morro Heights rested upon the Spanish garrison. A land assault could carry the castle and battery and with it control of the channel. In June 1898 Admiral William T. Sampson* in fact proposed to General William R. Shafter* just that: His Fifth Corps* would seize Socapa Heights and Morro. Sampson's navy could then clear the mines and engage Admiral Pascual Cervera's* ships in the harbor, and the Spanish garrisons would be without any support from Spain. Shafter, however, opposed the plan and instead conceived of an attack on the city itself, which was considerably north of the channel. After the landing at Las Guásimas,* Shafter was even more convinced of his plan's wisdom. Shafter also planned a feint at Morro with General Calixto García's* insurgent troops to lead the Spanish into believing that the main attack would occur at Morro Castle, where the Spanish had a garrison of 411 men. Neither Shafter nor General Joseph Wheeler* called for naval gunfire on the batteries of Socapa or Morro—a curious oversight.

After Cervera's sortie on 3 July and his squadron's destruction, Captain

French Ensor Chadwick* asked Shafter again about devising a plan to force the entrance to Santiago. Marines* would land at Cabañas* and march on Socapa; Shafter's troops would take the Morro. This plan of 6 July never occurred because the Spanish capitulated a few days later.

REFERENCE: French Ensor Chadwick, *The Relations of the United States and Spain* (New York: Russell & Russell, 1968).

MOSQUITO SQUADRON, U.S. NAVY

The Mosquito Squadron, or fleet, referred to a group of armed tugs and old monitors.* It was used for coastal protection, quarantine duty, and minefield protection. Commonly called ''mosquito'' in official publications and reports, this force was also referred to as an auxiliary naval force.

N

NANSHAN (ship)

Nanshan was a ship of 5,059 tons launched in 1896 at Grangemouth, Scotland, for use as a collier in the Far East. Purchased on 6 April 1898 at Hong Kong* for use with Commodore George Dewey's* Asiatic Squadron,* *Nanshan* sailed with the squadron on 24 April and coaled Dewey's ships until Manila* was occupied on 13 August. She carried one 6-pounder and served in the Pacific most of her naval career until sold in 1922.

REFERENCE: *Dictionary of American Naval Fighting Ships* (Washington, DC: Navy Department, 1979).

NASHVILLE (ship)

The U.S.S. *Nashville* was a 1,371-ton gunboat commissioned on 19 August 1897. *Nashville*'s armament consisted of eight 4-inch guns, four 6-pounders, and some smaller-caliber weapons. *Nashville* also carried good rate of speed: 16 knots. She was initially attached to Admiral William T. Sampson's* blockade* of Cuba and distinguished herself by capturing the Spanish steamers *Buena Ventura* and *Pedro* on 21 April 1898 and, on the twenty-ninth, the *Argonauta* off Cienfuegos.*

On 11 May *Nashville*, cruiser *Marblehead*,* and cutter *Windom* tried to cut telegraph cables from Cienfuegos to Santiago.* *Nashville* provided supporting and suppressing fires while sailors in launches attempted to sever the cables. Spanish fire from the beach was accurate and plentiful, and only two of the five cables were cut. *Nashville* maintained a blockade of Cienfuegos, awaiting the possible arrival of Admiral Pascual Cervera's* fleet from Curaçao. *Nashville* and *Marblehead* were reinforced by the *Castine*ined* when it was thought Cervera was going to Cienfuegos.

On 26 July *Nashville* occupied Gibara on the northern coast of Cuba.

After the war *Nashville* was sent to the Asiatic station, and in 1921 she was sold and converted to a barge. She was scrapped in 1957.

REFERENCE: H. W. Wilson, *The Downfall of Spain* (New York: Burt Franklin, 1971).

NATIONAL GUARD

The impending conflict with Spain spurred numerous forms of strategic planning within the U.S. Navy, but parallel efforts in the U.S. Army were difficult to discern in the years immediately prior to the conflict. Part of this lack of activity derived from a traditional defensive viewpoint; the army existed to defend the patria from external attack. The resultant thinking emphasized a highly professional but small regular force that could be augmented quickly in time of war with troops from the state militias. Because of this mindset, very little preparation was done by the army or the War Department until April 1898. The administration of William McKinley* issued no directives to either army or navy, which seemed to give weight to the army's inertia. The navy, on the other hand, proceeded to plan and to develop battle-ready forces without directives. Part of This disparity partly boils down to the fact that the navy had a clearly defined mission in the upcoming war: to find the Spanish fleets and destroy them. The army was without such clearly defined spheres of action; its roles could be multiple: This can perhaps explain the Army's seeming unreadiness at the inception of hostilities.

When the army finally began to plan, estimates from its planners, working under the direction of Russell A. Alger,* considered a force of less than 100,000 necessary. They anticipated that the army would play a modest part in the conflict. Nevertheless, to augment the regular army of about only 28,000 officers and men, legislation was necessary. Military reforms considered by General Emory Upton* included an expansible army,* that is, a larger standing army; reforms of the existing organization; and a federal reserve force. Legislation to effect such reforms was sponsored by John Hull.*

Simultaneous to the development and introduction of the Hull Bill, General Nelson A. Miles,* commander-in-chief, proposed an army of 50,000 volunteers, 62,000 regulars, plus additional troops, bringing the total to 162,000. With this plan, dated 9 April, the War Department went to Congress* for negotiations.

Before these negotiations proceeded further, on 15 April the War Department decided to gather regular army units into camps* for possible offensives in Cuba. These troops began to marshall in Tampa,* New Orleans, and Mobile.*

Many Americans were eager to go to war, but in state units with their own elected leaders rather than as anonymous units commanded by strangers. The Hull Bill and War Department plans threatened these regional units and also failed to take into sufficient consideration the political power wielded by the states and the increasingly militant National Guard. The regular army and the National Guard also clashed over organizational issues, deployment, number and type of units, and the like. The conflict resulted from differing points of view about the war's aims: The regulars thought in terms of national needs and strategic needs, whereas the guard units thought in terms of home defense and local political expediencies. These differing points of view could not be reconciled politically. The divergence of thought converged on the Hull Bill, which the National Guard felt (rightly) would divest it of its place in the developing volunteer army. Some guard units passed resolutions to go to war only in their own units with their own officers. The regular army's dream of a federal reserve force faded into obscurity in the face of impassioned congressional debate. The Hull Bill failed. Dilatoriness in Congress and political maneuvering by the National Guard then frustrated War Department plans for compromise legislation. As a result of the confusion, the assembly and encampment of troops became unnecessarily complicated. Unable to recruit until the declaration of war, the regular army was still 10,000 men short when the fighting stopped in August. Shortages of equipment,* untrained soldiers, and bureaucratic bungling kept most of the National Guard out the fighting war anyway.

REFERENCE: Graham A. Cosmas, "From Order to Chaos: The War Department, the National Guard, and Military Policy, 1898," *Military Affairs* 29 (Summer 1965): 105–121.

NATIONAL VOLUNTEERS

Emory Upton* and others struggled with the political and practical problems associated with transforming the American army and armed forces reform. One problem facing military reformers and planners was that the National Guard* was rife with politics—and state politics at that. Upton's argument detailed that providing an efficient and effective fighting force necessitated that all such forces be under federal control. To feed into regular units and to provide for a rapidly expansible army,* Upton called for a national militia or national volunteers under federal jurisdiction. These volunteers would be closely linked to regular army units and would be trained, equipped, and paid by the national government. The idea, publicized in Upton's own writings, became one of the articles of faith of U.S. Army* reformers.

Such ideas ran counter to the politically powerful National Guard, which had a stake in maintaining the status quo. Although little was done during the Spanish American War to develop a federally run program of national volunteers, the war did heighten awareness of reform issues among the military establishment. With the exception of the Rough Riders*—exceptional in several ways— volunteer units generally and the National Guard in particular did not play a significant battlefield role in the few battles of the war.

REFERENCES: Stephen E. Ambrose, *Upton and the Army* (Baton Rouge: Louisiana State University Press, 1964); Graham A. Cosmas, *An Army for Empire* (Columbia: University of Missouri Press, 1971); Emory Upton, *The Armies of Asia and Europe* (New York: Greenwood Press, 1968); Emory Upton, *Military Policy of the United States,* (War Dept. Doc. 290 (Washington, DC: Government Printing Office, 1912).

NAVAL MILITIA

The U.S. Navy did not have the manpower challenges that faced the U.S. Army for two reasons: poor prior planning by the navy and the difficulty of rapidly expanding the number of American surface vessels. Nevertheless, approximately 2,600 men were called up from the militia for regular service and an additional 1,800 were called up for coast defense, auxiliary, or coastal signal service. These men were naval personnel of prior experience listed on the rolls of individual states. Many were sent to merchant steamers like *Yankee,** *Yosemite,** and *Dixie.**

REFERENCE: *Annual Report of the Navy Department, 1898* (Washington, DC: Government Printing Office, 1898).

NAVAL WAR BOARD

The Naval War Board was essentially a board or committee organized by Navy Secretary John D. Long* to provide a body of expertise on naval and technological issues. The navy had no general staff, and the Naval War Board bridged that gap. Members were Captain Arent S. Crowninshield,* Admiral Montgomery Sicard,* Captain Albert S. Barker, and Captain A. T. Mahan.* The Naval War Board involved itself in strategy, intelligence operations,* and even tactics. The board formulated opinions and studies that resulted in numerous operational activities and was one of the ardent discussants on maintaining the fleet intact by lessening undue risk to capital ships.

REFERENCE: John D. Long, *The New American Navy* (New York: Outlook, 1903).

NAVAL WAR COLLEGE

Established at Newport, Rhode Island, in 1884, the Naval War College sought to enhance naval studies and naval doctrine through lectures, discussion, and learned interpretation. One of the means of developing and presenting new ideas was the development of hypothetical situations and war games. In 1894 the academic problem of a hypothetical war with Spain was presented by Lieutenant Commander Charles J. Train. Another plan was proposed by Lieutenant William Warren Kimball* in 1896. These early attempts at planning led to more serious efforts by the Navy Department in 1897. Another Naval War College plan developed in 1897. Although details of these plans differ, all assumed a predominant role for the navy, a blockade* of Cuba and Puerto Rico, an effort against Manila,* a land assault against Havana,* coastal attacks against Spain, confrontation with commerce raiders, and further colonial assaults. As late as February 1898 Theodore Roosevelt* was rehearsing war plans with Kimball.

REFERENCES: John A. S. Greenville, "American Naval Preparations for War with Spain, 1896–1898," *Journal of American Studies* 2 (April 1968): 33–47; David F. Trask, *The War with Spain in 1898* (New York: Macmillan Publishing Co., 1981).

NAVY

Any comparison, no matter how abbreviated, between the U.S. Navy and the Spanish navy of 1898 reveals that the U.S. fleet overmatched that of the Spanish.

The naval battles of 1 May 1898 at Manila Bay* and 3 July at Santiago* were so one-sided in favor of the Americans that many lost sight of the fact that American prewar assessments by both the populace and the U.S. naval hierarchy itself were not so sanguine. In actual numbers, the Spanish fleet had the advantage. Early East Coast panic kept the Northern Patrol Squadron* and the Flying Squadron* close to home to protect American cities from the depredations of Spanish naval cruisers; these depredations never materialized. Unknown to U.S. naval planners at the time was that on paper the Spanish fleet appeared formidable, but operationally, this apparent strength masked serious deficiencies. Both Admiral Patricio Montojo* and Admiral Pascual Cervera* complained of low levels of training, poorly maintained equipment, shoddy, unreliable ammunition, and an almost unreliable logistics system.

Montojo was forced to give battle mostly at anchor because some of his vessels were inoperative. Cervera, who knew full well the deficiencies of his squadron, repeatedly asked for resupply and for a change in the strategic venue—both in vain. Like a descant to this Spanish dirge, Cervera knew he had significant strategic disadvantages operating without an effective naval base while the Americans had Key West* just 90 miles from Havana.* Even the Spanish Eastern Squadron* under Admiral Manuel de la Cámara* fell victim to poor planning and supply and had to scurry back to Spain to defend against a putative American raiding squadron. Administrative ineptitude and vacillation negated the potential advantage of Spanish bravery: A consistent thread of American commentary on Spanish heroism and bravery punctuated eyewitness accounts from the major battles.

Some of the minor naval engagements produced different results. In Cuba, particularly, small actions at Caibarien, Nuevitas,* Cienfuegos,* Nipe Bay,* Cárdenas,* and Manzanillo,* tell a mixed tale by no means one-sided in favor of the Americans.

The U.S. Navy in 1898 was ascendant. New ships and new ideas were being tried. Some, like *Vesuvius,** were not tried again, but the salutary ferment of experimentation and training were impressive, especially considering the changes that had been made in just a little over a decade. The Spanish American War brought great advantage to the American navy: Morale soared, the country uniformly praised its performance, better recruits signed on, and the war essentially ushered in a new respect for the navy.

REFERENCES: John D. Alden, *The American Steel Navy* (Annapolis, MD: Naval Institute Press, 1989); Pascual Cervera y Topete, *The Spanish American War* (Washington, DC: Government Printing Office, 1899); United States Office of Naval Intelligence, *Notes on the Spanish American War* (Washington, DC: Government Printing Office, 1899).

NAVY DEPARTMENT, U.S.

The U.S. Navy Department is the administrative arm of the navy. The secretary of the navy, a civilian, is its chief. John D. Long* fulfilled that responsibility during the Spanish American War. Long had Theodore Roosevelt* as assistant until May 1898, when Charles H. Allen* succeeded him. The department's duties revolved around the political nexus of Congress,* the president, and the navy. The department also manages and administers naval appropriations, supplies, and so on, through its various bureaus such as the Bureau of Navigation, Bureau of Equipment, Bureau of Yards and Docks, Bureau of Construction and Repair, and the Marine Corps.*

Long was instrumental in developing the Naval War Board* as a staff function for advisory purposes in preparing war plans, coordinating the work of the bureaus, and studying strategic problems. The Office of Naval Intelligence* operated under the auspices of the department. As such, the department played a signal role in every aspect of the naval war with Spain, from buying ships domestically and abroad to the creation of an auxiliary naval force of colliers, yachts,* tugs, and armed merchant auxiliaries,* and the provision of ordnance for them. Controversial promotions such as that of Admiral William T. Sampson* to the North Atlantic Squadron* over the more senior William S. Schley* and that of George Dewey* to the Asiatic Squadron* were also within the domain of the department.

Much of the success of the department was due to the steady influence of Long and the prior planning for the conflict done by the Naval War College.* The relative success of the Navy Department (compared to the army) stems from this prior planning, capable leadership, and the strategic advantage enjoyed by the U.S. Navy.

REFERENCES: John D. Long, *The New American Navy* (New York: Outlook, 1903); Charles Oscar Paullin, *Paullin's History of Naval Administration, 1775–1911* (Annapolis, MD: U.S. Naval Institute Press, 1968).

NEW ORLEANS (ship)

Purchased as *Amazonas** from Brazil in 1898, *New Orleans* was built at the Elswick Yard, Newcastle-on-Tyne, England, by Sir W. G. Armstrong, Whitworth & Co. She was purchased on 16 March 1898 from Brazil, commissioned on 18 March as U.S.S. *Amazonas,* and on 15 April 1898 renamed U.S.S. *New Orleans. New Orleans* was attached to Commodore Winfield S. Schley's* Flying Squadron.* When orders were received on 13 May to sail, *New Orleans* remained in Hampton Roads,* Virginia, for a few days before continuing on to Key West.* There she joined Admiral William T. Sampson's* fleet in an attempt to engage the Spanish fleet under command of Admiral Pascual Cervera.* Sampson placed *New Orleans* into the second order of battle, and she joined in the blockade.* *New Orleans* participated in bombardments of Spanish positions at Santiago de Cuba* on 6 June. On 14 June and 16 June *New Orleans* also engaged the Socapa battery* and the Morro battery* in company with the *Vesuvius.** After the surrender of Santiago, *New Orleans* was to be dispatched to bombard the Spanish coast, but General Nelson Miles* asked for a strong naval escort for his expedition to Puerto Rico.* Sampson ordered *New Orleans* to Puerto Rico, where she assisted in blockade and gunnery support.

New Orleans was stricken from the navy on 13 November 1929.
REFERENCE H. W. Wilson, *The Downfall of Spain* (New York: Burt Franklin, 1971).

NEW YORK (ship)

After the U.S. Navy and the U.S. Congress finally agreed to modernize the navy, the armored cruiser *New York* was built for the new navy. Preceded by the battleships *Texas** and *Maine,** *New York* was the premier cruiser of a new breed of warship that represented the best thinking and materials available. Fast—she set a world record at her trials—and offensively and defensively formidable, the *New York* set a new standard for her class of warship when commissioned on 1 August 1893. She mounted six 8-inch and twelve 4-inch rapid-fire guns in the main battery and, in addition to higher standards of weaponry and armor, also employed significantly more sophisticated propulsion machinery. First used in Italian battleships, the system consisted of four engines, two of which could be manually uncoupled for more efficient low-speed operation, greater range, and fuel economy. At double the tonnage of previous American cruisers, *New York* was faster yet economical.

For these reasons, among others, *New York* was a very desirable command, and her roster of captains included many of the navy luminaries of the day, including French Ensor Chadwick,* Robley Evans,* and Winfield S. Schley.* On 26 March 1898, William T. Sampson* hoisted his flag aboard *New York.* Congress declared war on Spain on 25 April 1898, and *New York* became flagship of the North Atlantic Squadron.* This squadron had previously been divided by the creation of the Flying Squadron* under Schley in *Brooklyn.* The Flying Squadron's initial mission was to prevent Spanish forces under Admiral Pascual Cervera* from attacking the eastern seaboard of the United States. On 27 April Sampson received word that the Spanish were fortifying Matanzas*; *New York* immediately sailed from Key West* with *Puritan** and *Cincinnati** and bombarded the fortifications. Sampson again sallied from Key West* on 4 May in search of the Spanish fleet, arriving at San Juan, Puerto Rico,* on 12 May. The North Atlantic Squadron bombarded the forts of San Juan.

The same day, word reached Key West that Cervera's fleet had been spotted at Martinique.* The Americans failed to intercept the Spanish forces, and Cervera safely arrived at Santiago de Cuba* on 19 May. Upon finally ascertaining the whereabouts of Cervera's fleet, a formidable force took up the blockade* of Santiago on 1 June. The blockade consisted of maintaining station coupled with daily bombardments of fortifications in and around Santiago. Meanwhile the U.S. Army* had landed on 22 June. Suffering the ravages of disease and concerned about Spanish reinforcements from the north, the U.S. Army was in some peril. A conference between General William R. Shafter,* army commander, and Admiral Sampson was scheduled for 3 July, the same day Cervera chose to break out of Santiago. *New York* steamed the 9 miles east to the conference site at Siboney* early in the morning of the third, thus almost missing the sea battle at Santiago. At about 9:35 A.M., Sampson spotted gunfire and smoke coming from the entrance to Santiago Harbor. Without consulting Captain Chadwick, Sampson turned *New York* back to Santiago and demanded more speed from the engines in an attempt to catch the battling fleets moving west. *New York* steamed past *Gloucester,** a converted yacht,* in a hot engagement with the Spanish destroyers *Plutón** and *Furor.** *New York* opened fire on *Furor,* the only shots she fired in the battle. *Gloucester's* shots struck *Plutón's* boilers and she exploded. *Gloucester* also ran *Furor* onto the beach. Bending on 16 knots, *New York* tried to catch the fleeing *Vizcaya** and *Colón,** but *Brooklyn* and *Oregon** dispatched both Spanish vessels. Lamentably, *New York* never quite got into the fray.

New York continued supportive missions after the defeat of the Spanish fleet and, of course, assisted in the continuing blockade. After the war *New York* assisted in navy support efforts in the Philippine Insurrection.*

Renamed twice during her long career (*Saratoga,* 1901; *Rochester,* 1917), she survived until December 1941, when she was scuttled at Subic Bay,* Philippine Islands, to prevent her falling into the hands of invading Japanese.
REFERENCE: Ivan Musicant, *U.S. Armored Cruisers: A Design and Operational History* (Annapolis, MD: Naval Institute Press, 1985).

NEWARK (ship)

The U.S.S. *Newark* was a protected cruiser of 4,083 tons capable of 19-knot speeds and armed with twelve 6-inch guns in her main battery. Commissioned on 2 February 1891, she was the last U.S. protected cruiser with a complete sailing rig in addition to her steam propulsion unit. She was also one of the first modern cruisers in the navy.

After an extensive overhaul *Newark* sailed for Key West* and then Cuba, joining the blockade* on 30 June 1898. *Newark* shelled Manzanillo* on 12 August but missed the battle of Santiago,* being away at Guantánamo* coaling. She did shell the beached hulks after the battle, however.

After the war *Newark* was posted to the Asiatic Station serving in the Philippines* and China, conspicuously during the Boxer Rebellion. During World War I she served as a quarantine hulk at Newport, Rhode Island. She was sold in 1926.
REFERENCE: *Dictionary of American Fighting Ships* (Washington, DC: Navy Department, 1979).

NEWPORT (ship)

The yachtlike U.S.S. *Newport* was an iron-framed, wood-hulled, barkentine-rigged gunboat of the *Annapolis** class commissioned in 1897. She could steam at 13 or 14 knots and displaced about 1,000 tons. *Newport* participated in the blockade of Cuba and captured or assisted in capturing nine Spanish vessels.

After the war she served as a Naval Academy training ship and in other training roles until transferred to the city of Aberdeen, Washington, State by act of Congress in 1934.

REFERENCE: *Dictionary of American Fighting Ships* (Washington, DC: Navy Department, 1979).

NEWSPAPERS.
See THE PRESS AND THE WAR.

NINTH CAVALRY

The Ninth U.S. Cavalry Regiment was organized on 28 July 1866 and served as one of six all-black regular army units commanded by white officers. All were known as the "Buffalo Soldiers." They performed a variety of duties in the West, but mostly as Indian fighters. In April 1898 the unit was stationed at Fort Robinson, Nebraska, where it received orders from the War Department* to make preparation to proceed to Chickamauga Park, Georgia. Late in April the regiment was ordered to the Port of Tampa,* where it remained for several weeks before departing with the other units of the Fifth Army Corps* to Cuba. Upon leaving Nebraska for service in Cuba, the Ninth received rousing support from the citizens. However, when the regiment arrived in Tampa, racial hostilities provided a grim lesson on prejudice.

During the Santiago* campaign, the Ninth Cavalry was brigaded with the Third and Sixth Cavalry to form the First Cavalry Brigade under the command of General Joseph Wheeler's* Cavalry Division. During the first part of the campaign, most of the unit was assigned to unload transports and build roads for the artillery. Other troops of the Ninth were sent on patrol and guard duty. At the end of June the unit saw its first real action in the assault on San Juan Hill.* During the fighting the Ninth performed skillfully in supporting Teddy Roosevelt's* Rough Riders* while suffering relatively few casualties.

After the cessation of hostilities and the surrender by Spain, the Ninth Cavalry along with the entire cavalry brigade moved from San Juan Hill to nearby El Caney* and established Camp Hamilton. The regiment remained at the camp until mid-August, when the brigade left for Santiago to prepare for return to the United States. Home was a welcome sight for the unit, whose members suffered badly from heat exposure and tropical fever.

REFERENCES: Herschel V. Cashin, *Under Fire with the Tenth U.S. Cavalry* (New York: F. T. Neely, 1899); Bernard C. Nalty, *Strength for the Fight: A History of Black Americans in the Military* (New York: Free Press, 1986).

MITCHELL YOCKELSON

NIPE BAY, CUBA

Nipe Bay is a sheltered inlet about 14 miles long and 8 miles wide located in northeastern Cuba, 50 miles north of Santiago.

Nipe Bay was part of Lieutenant Commander Charles J. Train's prewar plan for the reduction of Spanish forces on Cuba. Train assumed a war between the United States and Spain; he excluded other European powers. He also assumed that control of the sea would be the deciding factor in the conflict. Nipe Bay figured in Train's plan as a naval rendezvous, coaling facility, and anchorage. Nipe Bay was never to play that role, however.

During hostilities Nipe Bay was the anchorage of an old Spanish cruiser, *Jorge Juan* (935 tons), which had been anchored so long she could no longer get under way. In addition, the small gunboat *Baracoa* lay at anchor. The latter had sown thirteen mines in the narrow entrance to Nipe Bay (American reports exaggerated these mines to around thirty), and apparently, the Spanish trusted that the mines would keep the Americans out of the bay.

On 21 June 1898 the gunboats *Annapolis** and *Topeka,** the auxiliary gunboat *Wasp,* and the armed tug *Leyden* entered the bay without striking any mines. At 12:45 P.M. *Jorge Juan* opened fire on *Wasp,* which returned fire. *Annapolis* then aggressively engaged the Spanish ship. The poor condition of the Spanish ship's guns made the exchange very one sided. *Jorge Juan* got off only a few rounds before her crew scuttled her. The *Baracoa* steamed up the Mayari River, where her crew also scuttled the ship. Both Spanish crews escaped in their respective ship's boats. Meanwhile, *Topeka* shelled Spanish installations near the bay. The action was over in less than an hour, and no casualties were reported on either side. This action was the result of orders Secretary of War Russell A. Alger* gave to Admiral William T. Sampson* to seize Nipe Bay as a staging area for the invasion of Puerto Rico.* However, General Nelson Miles* had already decided to use the bay at Guantánamo* for this purpose, so the action at Nipe Bay had little strategic purpose.

REFERENCE: Augustín Rodríguez González, "Operaciones menores en Cuba, 1898," *Revista de Historia Naval* 3, no. 9 (1985): 125–146.

NORTH ATLANTIC SQUADRON

The North Atlantic Squadron (renamed North Atlantic Fleet on 21 June 1898) was the source of most of the ships used in the Cuban blockade,* the Puerto Rican expedition, and the Cuban expedition. The North Atlantic Squadron also possessed the bulk of the large armored vessels (save only *Oregon,** which steamed from the West Coast) that were to engage Admiral Pascual Cervera* at the Battle of Santiago.* The squadron was commanded by Admiral William T. Sampson.*

NORTHERN PATROL SQUADRON

Initially the coastal defense of the eastern seaboard consisted of eight districts, the most significant of which was the Northern Patrol Squadron under the command of Commodore John A. Howell.* Consisting of the cruiser *San Francisco* and *Yankee,** *Yosemite,** *Prairie,** and *Dixie,** the squadron was to provide protection to the coast from Maine to Delaware. As the likelihood of armed Spanish naval raids evaporated, these ships were sent South.

REFERENCE: John D. Long, *The New American Navy* (New York: Outlook, 1903).

NUEVITAS, CUBA

Nuevitas lies on the north shore of the eastern side of the island of Cuba about 45 miles east-northeast of Camagüey. A small bay at Nuevitas makes it an attractive focus; indeed, it was discovered by Columbus on his first voyage in 1492, and Sir Henry Morgan raided the area in 1668.

On 16 August 1896 Nuevitas was the site of a filibustering expedition* by the redoubtable Captain "Dynamite Johnny" O'Brien.* Commanding *Dauntless,* O'Brien landed a force near Nuevitas.

Nuevitas also figured in strategic terms as one of the eastern limits of the northern naval blockade* of Cuba by American forces. The blockade in its eastern extremities was effective, but due to an insufficient number of ships, not as effective as desired.

General Nelson A. Miles* proposed several plans (or several variations of one plan) in which Nuevitas would serve as a staging area for U.S. infantry and cavalry preliminary to a major overland assault on Havana.* Although Miles was insistent, his plan was never accepted by William McKinley's* administration.

For the Spanish part, Nuevitas was defended by the gunboat *Pizarro* and the armed launches *Golondrina* and *Yumuri.* After the fall of Santiago,* the Spanish army concentrated its forces and Nuevitas was quickly abandoned. The three vessels were scuttled with their armaments and stores and the port evacuated on 31 July 1898, leaving behind only a string of mines at the mouth of Nuevitas Bay.

REFERENCE: David F. Trask, *The War with Spain in 1898* (New York: Macmillan Publishing Co., 1981).

O

O'BRIEN, "DYNAMITE JOHNNY"
(1837–1917)

Born in New York City on 20 April 1837 of Irish immigrant parents, Johnny O'Brien ran away from home at age thirteen to begin a life working on ships. During the U.S. Civil War he got his first experience as a filibuster* helping to deliver arms to the Confederacy, although he worked for both sides during the war. Working after the war as a pilot for boats traveling through Hell Gate, the perilous body of water connecting Long Island Sound and the East River, he became known as "Daredevil Johnny."

By the mid-1880s he had once again become active in filibustering activities, running arms and ammunition to various Latin American and Caribbean nations. The nickname "Dynamite Johnny" was given him during an expedition an 1888 in which his cargo was a dangerous load of dynamite.

O'Brien had become involved by the mid-1890s in helping the insurgents in Cuba, directing several filibustering expeditions during the insurrection.* Ships he commanded included *Hawkins, Commodore, Bermuda, Laurada, Dauntless,* and *Three Friends.* O'Brien claimed to work for the Cuban rebels out of sympathy for their cause, not for any financial reward involved; he had been unsympathetic to U.S. administrations under Cleveland and McKinley before the United States entered into hostilities with Spain.

In August 1896 O'Brien was involved in smuggling American artillery expert Frederick Funston* to Cuba aboard *Dauntless,* along with the Hotchkiss gun Funston had been trained to use. As with other filibustering expeditions, this one required elaborate evasive tactics even before leaving the United States. On this voyage of *Dauntless,* for example, the empty *Commodore* was used to lure federal revenue cutters away from the loaded *Dauntless.* The Cuban junta* obtained the help of sympathetic wealthy Americans, including some railway executives, to help them elude American authorities. Railroad cars of the Plant

Lines* and the Florida East Coast railways were at the disposal of O'Brien and the junta to transport them on the U.S. mainland.

Another celebrated incident took place in December 1896 aboard *Three Friends*. Its cargo included arms, troops, and an elaborate, jeweled ceremonial sword to be presented to General Máximo Gómez* by reporter Ralph D. Paine of the *New York Journal* on behalf of William Randolph Hearst.* When a Spanish gunboat attacked off the southern coast of Cuba near the mouth of the San Juan River, O'Brien ordered return fire using a Hotchkiss gun being smuggled aboard *Three Friends*. The single shot frightened the Spanish enough for them to give up the chase, but the landing of the filibusters in Cuba had to be aborted. The story of the skirmish, reported by the correspondents on board (Paine and Ernest W. McCready of the *New York Herald*), became greatly exaggerated in the U.S. press, being proclaimed as a major naval battle.

Long after the war O'Brien was given the position of chief of Havana harbor pilots by the Republic of Cuba in recognition of his aid during the insurrection. In 1912, when the wreck of the *Maine** was raised from the bottom of Havana Harbor, towed out to sea, and sunk in deep water, Johnny O'Brien was chosen as the pilot to guide it out of the harbor on 16 March. From a post on the hulk of the *Maine,* he gave signals to the two tugs steering it. When the *Maine* was flooded and began to sink, O'Brien was the last person to leave it.

He died in New York on 21 June 1917.

REFERENCES: " 'Dynamite Johnny' O'Brien Dies at 80," *New York Times,* June 22, 1917; Horace Smith, *A Captain Unafraid: The Strange Adventures of Dynamite Johnny O'Brien* (New York: Harper & Brothers, 1912).

MARK A. THOMAS

O'DONNELL Y ABRÉU, CARLOS
(1834–1903)

Carlos O'Donnell y Abréu, duke of Tetuán and count of Lucent, was the Spanish foreign minister under Antonio Cánovas del Castillo.* Descendant of Irish who had long lived in Spain, O'Donnell played a pivotal role in the maneuverings before the war. He served as foreign minister from 28 March 1895 to 29 September 1897. O'Donnell endeavored to address two initiatives: autonomy* in Cuba and support for the Spanish army's attempt to crush the developing Cuban rebellion. At Cánovas's request, O'Donnell initiated talks with the heads of the European powers in a protest against possible American belligerancy and intervention in the Cuban Insurrection* of 1895. The so-called O'Donnell Memorandum articulated what one author has called a "domino theory": If America intervened and Cuba were lost to Spain, then the Spanish monarchy would fall. If the Spanish monarchy fell, how safe would be the monarchies of Russia, Germany, and England?

Sir Henry Drummond Wolff, British ambassador to Spain, slyly informed Hannis Taylor,* U.S. minister to Spain, of O'Donnell's memorandum, and Taylor was able to stop O'Donnell's initiative, but only after a minor diplomatic fracas. After Cánovas's assassination, the duke of Tetuán left office.

REFERENCE: G.J.A. O'Toole, *The Spanish War* (New York: W. W. Norton & Co., 1984).

BRIAN B. CARPENTER

OFFICE OF NAVAL INTELLIGENCE

The U.S. Navy organized the first agency devoted to gathering systematically information on foreign governments and their capabilities. Begun in 1882, the Office of Naval Intelligence, as it was called, was the government's most consistent source of information for three decades. Originally collecting information overtly, by the Spanish American War the intelligence needs of the navy and the government spawned covert intelligence operations* under William S. Sims,* John C. Colwell,* William H. Buck,* Henry H. Ward,* and others.

Earlier the office performed vital strategic planning functions that led to the naval strategy during the war under the leadership of Lieutenant Commander Richard Wainwright* and America's irrepressible navalist Theodore Roosevelt.* Wainwright and Roosevelt shared strategic views, and the latter besieged the office with requests for intelligence on legions of topics. Roosevelt also encouraged the office to emphasize war planning, a relatively new notion. Wainwright willingly accepted the charge and focused earnestly on two potentialities, each of which saw implementation in the Spanish American War. The first of these to achieve focus was Japan.* The office had concerns about Japan in regards to Hawaii,* Korea, and several Pacific regions. The office sent Lieutenant John M. Ellicott to Hawaii* in an attempt to develop counterplans to the perceived ambitions of Japan in the Pacific.

The main thrust of prewar planning concerned the potential of war with Spain. Wainwright ordered his senior analyst, William W. Kimball,* to work with the Naval War College* in preparing a study of the possible conflict with Spain. Kimball's study, completed in 1896, argued for the reduction of Spanish power in the Philippines* and a simultaneous Cuban naval blockade* to control the Caribbean.

Wainwright also utilized a loosely organized system or network of naval attachés strategically located as listening posts in major European capitals. One of these sent reports back to the office warning of Germany's* designs in the Caribbean and the western Pacific—also presaging future frictions.

A huge explosion on the U.S.S. *Maine** on 15 February 1898 destroyed the ship, and the resultant yellow journalism* convicted Spain in the minds of many Americans. Again spurred by Roosevelt, the office armed for the conflict by taking covert as well as overt measures to strengthen the navy and the intelligence community. Roosevelt and the office sent reams of requests for information from naval attachés in London and elsewhere on the possibility of acquiring foreign warships, colliers, munitions, and arms. When Britain declared neutrality on 23 April 1898, two days before the declaration of war, attachés contrived to ship munitions under foreign flags by disguising crates of guns with fraudulent labels. Thus in the early days of the war, the Office of Naval Intelligence was instrumental in acquiring the wherewithal to augment the waging of war. The office had become sufficiently useful to become part of high-level deliberations with the newly created Naval War Board.*

The quality of intelligence and its analysis varied dramatically, and there was an overestimation of Spain's capabilities that led to some interesting and dramatic reports. The office continued to use attachés as gatherers of intelligence, and networks of agents sprouted in Europe (paid for by a large fund set up by the office for that purpose). These efforts extended after the war into the Pacific; specifically, into the Philippines, Japan, Hong Kong,* and China.* The office and its efforts were valued to the extent that in October 1898 the Chief of the Bureau of Navigation, Arent S. Crowninshield,* argued successfully for the incorporation of the Office of Naval Intelligence by law under the bureau in the Navy Department because, as Crowninshield observed, the intelligence need was "permanent."

REFERENCE: Jeffery M. Dorwart, *The Office of Naval Intelligence* (Annapolis, MD: Naval Institute Press, 1979).

OFFICERS, U.S. ARMY

The regular officer corps in the U.S. Army* was divided into bureaus or departments. Promotion within was generally by seniority, although the Spanish American War, like all wars, provided unusual opportunities for advancement. The training of junior officers had little in the way of formal regimen; although there were examinations through captain, the chief planners and those experienced in troop movement were Civil War veterans who had not seen large-unit action for over thirty years. The army itself saw its own role as primarily defensive, a continuation of most of the nineteenth century.

The officer corps led reform efforts for better training, strategic manpower planning, expansion, staff creation, and the like. The regular officers, like Emory Upton,* began to think strategically; they monitored the Cuban Insurrection,* believing it might provide the necessary fulcrum for a Central American canal. Shortages of trained officers during the Spanish American War underlined the arguments of reformers.

In addition to regular officers were the numerous officers of volunteer units who often competed with the regulars for rank and distinction. Frequently well-connected politically, some of these volunteers fared very well. Although the volunteers as soldiers were generally praised, their officers elicited not praise but general disgust. Poorly trained or worse, the volunteer officers and their relatives besieged Secretary of War Russell A. Alger's* office with petitions for commissions, their petitions frequently reinforced by recommendation by politicians and congressmen. Because many volunteer officers were in fact politicians who feared to alienate voters, discipline in many units was poor.

Nevertheless, the war not only expanded the officer corps but gave it experience and a new organizational structure that served as the basis for ongoing reform into the next century.

REFERENCE: Graham A. Cosmas, *An Army for Empire* (Columbia: University of Missouri Press, 1971).

OJEDA, EMILIO DE
(?–1911)

Emilio de Ojeda was a Spanish diplomat of wide experience when he was appointed secretary to the Spanish commission at the peace negotiations* in Paris. Ojeda arrived in October 1898. As secretary, Ojeda served as a go-between serving the American and Spanish commissions, in this capacity producing minutes, proposals, preparation of articles, and the like.

REFERENCE: *Spanish Diplomatic Correspondence and Documents, 1896–1900* (Washington, DC: Government Printing Office, 1905).

OLIVETTE (ship)

Olivette was a commercial passenger steamer owned by the Plant System.* Before the war it ran on a regular route between Tampa,* Key West,* and Havana,* making three round trips each week.

This ship was the setting for an incident made famous by a story and accompanying illustration appearing in the *New York Journal* in 1897. The article was based on a dispatch from correspondent Richard Harding Davis.* While traveling on the *Olivette* back to the United States after his first trip to Cuba, Davis dined with Clemencia Arango,* one of three Cuban women exiled from Cuba by the Spaniards for suspected aid to the rebels. He learned that before she and her companions left the island, authorities had stripped and searched the women at home, then again at the customs house, and finally aboard the *Olivette* before it left Havana Harbor.

Davis's dispatch to New York from Tampa on 10 February did specify that the women had been searched on the ship by a police matron while male officers waited outside the cabin. *Journal* editors were quick to assume that men had performed the search and excitedly published a page-one story on 12 February declaring that ''refined young women [were] stripped and searched by brutal Spaniards while under our flag on the *Olivette.*'' A large illustration by Frederic Remington,* who had not been on the ship during the incident, appeared on page two, showing several Spanish officers searching the clothing of the young woman standing disrobed among them.

The *Journal*'s circulation skyrocketed, and the American public was outraged. Reporters from Joseph Pulitzer's* *New York World* were sent to interview señorita Arango so the *World* could salvage something of the sensational story. They happily discovered, however, that in fact the search had been performed by a woman. Davis had by this time learned about the *Journal*'s misleading account of the story; furious with Hearst, he wrote a letter to the *World* to set straight the facts. The *World* gladly published his letter as a competitive response to the *Journal*'s circulation-building story, accusing the *Journal* of being "guilty of deliberate falsehood." Davis refused to work for Hearst ever again. Even twenty years later, during World War I, he would not allow his syndicate to sell any of his dispatches to Hearst publications.

Later it was *Olivette* that brought back to Key West from Havana the uninjured survivors of the explosion on the *Maine*.* Because of its regular run, *Olivette* also shuttled divers and technicians back and forth to the wreck and carried prewar dispatches and reports on intelligence operations* in Cuba. Then, during hostilities with Spain, *Olivette* served as a hospital ship. It accompanied General William Shafter's* invasion forces from Tampa to Santiago* in June 1898, carrying medical personnel as well as many of the correspondents following Shafter's forces. During the hostilities at Santiago the ship anchored off the coast at Siboney,* where it received the sick and injured.

REFERENCE: Charles H. Brown, *The Correspondents' War* (New York: Scribner's, 1967).

MARK A. THOMAS

OLNEY, RICHARD
(1835–1917)

Perceived as a loyal Democrat from New England, Harvard-trained lawyer Richard Olney found his way into President Grover Cleveland's* cabinet as attorney general. Upon the death of Walter Gresham, Cleveland chose Olney as his new secretary of state.

Olney's tenure faced complex challenges: antiforeign rioting in China, the Venezuelan dispute with Great Britain, and the perpetually gnawing Cuban situation. None was more persistent and less soluble than the problems Olney faced in Cuba. Cuban Americans routinely violated neutrality laws by arming rebels in Cuba. Spain demanded gun-running police to protect Spanish interests. Jingoists and American expansionists inflamed public sentiment through the American press.* The result consisted of a series of small emergencies that collectively became quite a burden to Secretary of State Olney. He assiduously protected the Americans' rights and property without undue investigation into the veracity of alleged citizens. By holding Spain liable, this reactive policy worked in the interests of the United States. Not that Olney defined U.S. interests well in the successive Cuban crises, but by keeping the records open and clear, Olney fostered communication and exerted pressure upon Spain to do something about the Cuban insurrection.*

Olney did not just pursue a reactive policy; he also vigorously attempted to address reform measures that Spain might employ to pacify the seething Cuban situation. In a series of conversations and memorandums with Dupuy de Lôme,* the Spanish minister in Washington, Olney urged Spanish reforms in Cuba because the "United States cannot contemplate with complacency another ten years of Cuban insurrection." Olney's goal was not intervention but amelioration and pacification of the Cuban situation. Of particular importance was a note of 4 April 1896 that Olney sent to Dupuy de Lôme holding out hope for reforms but steadfastly reiterating that the United States viewed the Cuban situation with gravity. Continued fighting and brigandage jeopardized not only the political but the economic future of Cuba; and next to Spain itself, the United States was the chief investor in Cuba. The thrust of the message was an earnest attempt to resolve the Cuban crisis without U.S. intervention. The Spanish reply, dated 22 May 1896 but not delivered to Olney until early June, was a message of refusal, and as such it took the relationship between Spain and the United States one step closer to armed conflict.

REFERENCES: Gerald G. Eggert, *Richard Olney: Evolution of a Statesman* (University Park: Pennsylvania State University Press, 1974); Henry James, *Richard Olney and His Public Service* (New York: Houghton Mifflin, 1923).

OLYMPIA (ship)

Admiral Patricio Montojo y Pasarón* guarded the Spanish-held Philippines* with a miscellaneous squadron of cruisers and gunboats in 1898. Some of Montojo's ships could not get underway.

Opposing Montojo was Commodore George Dewey,* who had been anchored at Hong Kong* then removed to Mirs Bay* in China to assemble the mixed force of protected cruisers *Olympia, Raleigh,* *Boston,* and *Baltimore*** in company with the gunboats *Concord*** and *Petrel*** and the revenue cutter *McCulloch.* On 1 May 1898 Dewey steamed his squadron into Manila Bay.* At 5:41 A.M. *Olympia* opened fire with her forward 8-inch guns, and the rest of Dewey's line followed suit. The results were catastrophic to the Spanish vessels, which lost all their vessels and suffered 371 casualties. The American force lost no ships and suffered only eleven wounded.

After the battle *Olympia* remained in a blockade of the port until Dewey's force was reinforced by *Charleston,* *Monadnock,* and *Monterey*** and then joined by U.S. Army units that forced the capitulation of Manila. *Olympia* supported these efforts with bombardments of batteries and forts.

Olympia was a fast (21 knots) protected cruiser built by Union Iron Works at San Francisco and commissioned on 5 February 1895. She displaced 5,870 tons and carried four 8-inch guns and ten 5-inch guns, smaller calibers, and six torpedo tubes. Unique among Spanish American War vessels, she survives as a shrine and museum at Philadelphia.

REFERENCE: John D. Alden, *The American Steel Navy* (Annapolis, MD: Naval Institute Press, 1972).

OQUENDO (ship).
See ALMIRANTE OQUENDO.

ORDNANCE DEPARTMENT, U.S. ARMY

Generally the Ordnance Department was responsible for the development and testing of weapons, their manufacture or procurement, and their issue to troops.

Additionally, the department administered weapons-related equipment such as ammunition, packs, and artillery-horse equipment. Brigadier General Daniel W. Flagler* headed the department from 1891.

The Ordnance Department struggled mightily in 1898, but numbers of rifles and artillery cannot be increased at short notice. Foreign purchases with money from the Fifty Million Bill* and warnings to army suppliers in March 1898 were necessary but insufficient. The early invasion of Cuba was delayed because the 70,000 volunteers assembled were without such necessaries as ammunition. Like the Quartermaster's Department,* Ordnance found itself with stacks for a 25,000-man regular army, but with demand five times the available equipment. Ordnance began to contract with private firms for ammunition, packs, artillery shells, mess kits, and horse equipment. Although Flagler negotiated reasonable prices, inevitably higher costs from private contractors made such arrangements expensive. The greatest challenge came to Ordnance in obtaining smokeless powder, and in many cases it was not available. The difference between smokeless powder and the old charcoal powder had profound implications on the battlefield. The regulars had Krag-Jorgensens,* which could use only smokeless, but almost none of the volunteers could obtain any Krags under the priority system worked out to deal with the shortage. Meanwhile volunteers made do with Springfield rifles.* Much of this difficulty was caused by congressional parsimony over the years; Ordnance just could not overcome initial deficiencies. It was not until mid-August that the department had enough material to equip every soldier, but by mid-August the war was over. Nevertheless, Ordnance-issued equipment received general praise from soldiers in the field, and since the regiments of volunteers were not used, Ordnance avoided most of the scandalous charges in the postmortem.

REFERENCE: *Annual Report of the Secretary of War, 1898* (Washington, DC: Government Printing Office, 1898); *Report of the Commission Appointed by the President to Investigate the Conduct of the War Department in the War with Spain,* 8 vols. (Washington, DC: Government Printing Office, 1900).

OREGON (ship)

The U.S.S. *Oregon* was an *Indiana**-class battleship of 10,288 tons armed with four 13-inch guns, eight 8-inch guns, four 6-inch guns, and numerous weapons of smaller caliber. In addition, she carried six torpedo tubes and enjoyed armor up to 18 inches thick. Her maximum speed was around 15 knots. She was built at Union Iron Works, San Francisco, and commissioned on 15 July 1896.

Oregon is perhaps best remembered for her epic voyage from San Francisco* to Key West,* 14,000 miles in sixty-six days. When the *Maine** exploded, *Oregon* was ordered to reinforce the North Atlantic Squadron.* Departing San Francisco on 19 March 1898, the battleship sailed south, through the Strait of Magellan, north to Florida,* arriving on 24 May. Two days later *Oregon* joined Admiral William T. Sampson's* blockade* of Cuba. An impressive performance for any ship, the voyage also strangled opposition to the Panama Canal: Manifestly, the navy could not expect events to wait for two months until ships from the Pacific could reinforce those of the Atlantic, and vice versa.

In concert with other battleships, *Oregon* participated in Sampson's blockade and shelled the Morro* and Socapa* batteries on 16 June. She also supported the landings at Daiquirí* on 21 June.

During the Battle of Santiago* on 3 July, *Oregon* again distinguished herself by outrunning faster battleships. She was able to speed in pursuit of Admiral Pascual Cervera's* squadron because both her chief engineer and her captain kept fires under all boilers, a practice contrary to the norm. *Oregon* fired on the emerging Spanish ships, received three hits in return, but suffered no damage.

Oregon was detailed to Commodore J. C. Watson's* squadron to assist Commodore George Dewey* in the Philippines.* These orders were changed, and she went to the New York Navy Yard for refit; she did not arrive in the Philippines until March 1899.

Oregon served a variety of roles until the mid-1920s, when she was preserved as a monument to the war and berthed in Portland, Oregon. During World War II the navy reclaimed the ship for scrap inasmuch as President Franklin D. Roosevelt had decided to preserve *Olympia** as a remembrance of the Spanish American War. After a few years as a dynamite barge in Guam,* *Oregon* was scrapped in 1956.

REFERENCE: John C. Reilly, Jr., and Robert L. Scheina, *American Battleship, 1886–1923* (Annapolis, MD: Naval Institute Press, 1980).

OSCEOLA (ship)

A tug, *Osceola* was built at Philadelphia and launched in 1897. Commissioned into the U.S. Navy on 4 April 1898, *Osceola* immediately joined the Cuban blockade.* Of 571 tons and armed with a machine gun and a few 3-pounders, *Osceola* participated in actions at Cabañas* and Manzanillo,* including the capture of the port, and in general blockade duties.

Osceola was sold in 1923.

REFERENCE: *Dictionary of American Fighting Ships* (Washington, DC: Navy Department, 1979).

OTIS, ELWELL STEPHEN
(1838–1909)

Major General Elwell Stephen Otis was born in Maryland and studied at the University of Rochester and Harvard Law School. In September 1862 he obtained a captain's commission with the New York infantry of the Army of the Potomac. He served with distinction and was brevetted a brigadier general. Commissioned a lieutenant colonel in the regular army in 1866, Otis served in campaigns on the plains in Montana, the Northwest, and Colorado. In November 1893 he was promoted to brigadier.

On 12 May 1898 General Otis was ordered to San Francisco to support General Wesley Merritt* and Eighth Corps* in the expedition to the Philippines. He sailed in July with reinforcements for Merritt and succeeded him the next month as commander and also as military governor. On 8 September Otis ordered the Philippine insurgent forces of Emilio Aguinaldo* out of Manila.* Otis then presided over an awkward time when the United States, as yet unsure of its position on the Philippines in the peace negotiations,* maintained sovereignty in the islands as successor to Spain. Otis, therefore, had the unenviable role of upholding the provisions of the peace protocol until the peace conference at Paris concluded with a treaty.*

REFERENCES: Garel A. Grunder and William E. Livezey, *The Philippines and the United States* (Norman: University of Oklahoma Press, 1951); Teodoro M. Kalaw, *The Philippine Revolution* (Kawilihan, P.I.: Jorge B. Vargas Filipiniana Foundation, 1969).

P

PAREDES, JOSÉ DE

Spanish captain of the *Cristóbal Colón,** José de Paredes came under some criticism by Americans because of a significant technicality. At about 11:00 A.M. on 3 July 1898, the remnants of Admiral Pascual Cervera's* fleet, *Colón* and *Vizcaya,** were fleeing westward to Cienfuegos.* *Vizcaya* received the concentrated fire of four American battleships and the cruiser *Brooklyn.** At 11:15, afire, *Vizcaya* turned toward the beach and drifted onto a reef.

Colón did not have its long-range 10-inch gun mounted and so could not effectively reply. Although newer and somewhat faster than the American ships, *Colón* had shipped low-grade coal at Santiago* and her speed diminished. As *Oregon** found her range, Paredes fired a gun and then surrendered at about 1:15 P.M. However, instead of coming to, Paredes turned into shore and beached his vessel at a high rate of speed. Then, as if prearranged, he opened the valves to sink *Colón.* Admiral William T. Sampson* wanted Paredes brought before a board of investigation for this evident breach of the laws of war. Paredes claimed that the battle lost, he steamed onto the beach and then surrendered. *Texas,** *Brooklyn,* and other U.S. ships saw it differently.

REFERENCE: French Ensor Chadwick, *The Relations of the United States and Spain* (New York: Russell & Russell, 1968).

PARTIDO REVOLUCIONARIO CUBANO.
See CUBAN REVOLUTIONARY PARTY.

PASIG RIVER, PHILIPPINES

The Pasig River flows generally northwest from Laguna de Bay through Manila into Manila Bay.* Because the river divides this isthmus north and south, it became an important tactical consideration in the Battle of Manila.* The Old City of Manila was on the south bank, and suburbs stretched from both sides.

On 13 August 1898 General Francis V. Greene* raced Philippine insurgents* along a line paralleling the Pasig. While the Spanish held their lines until the Americans arrived, the insurgents occupied some territory south of the Pasig, Greene occupied territory north of the Pasig and U.S. forces occupied the citadel. REFERENCE: *Annual Report of the War Department, 1898* (Washington, DC: General Printing Office, 1898).

PATERNO, PEDRO ALEJANDRO
(1858–1911)

Among Philippine insurrectionist leaders, Pedro Alejandro Paterno stands out for a variety of reasons. His father was Máximo Paterno, a wealthy Progressive who was deported from Manila in 1872. The son benefited from his father's wealth and position and enjoyed the respect of other Philippine leaders as well as Spaniards. Paterno was the guiding hand in the development of the Pact of Biak-na-Bato* signed on 14 December 1897. According to the provisions of the pact, Paterno went into exile to Hong Kong* with Emilio Aguinaldo.*

After the Spanish defeat in Manila Bay* on 1 May 1898, Philippine politics became volatile. Educated in Spain, Paterno attempted to float an autonomous plan for the Philippines in alliance with Spain. Bent on independence, Filipinos ignored it. The Spanish had weightier matters on their minds and also ignored it. Paterno was elected president of the First Revolutionary Congress and also later helped in the development of the constitution of the Philippine Republic, often called the Malolos Constitution. Paterno also remained active in the revolutionary movement and government. After the new constitution was announced (21 January 1899), Paterno continued publishing and activist work during the developing Philippine Insurrection.* Chosen as president of the revolutionary government in 1899, Paterno proclaimed war against the United States on 2 June 1899.

Paterno was captured and worked to negotiate an armistice; in this he ran afoul of Aguinaldo, who considered some of his activities treasonous to the revolution. Indeed, Paterno seemed more interested in peace than in revolution. He was, in fact, released from prison so he could lead a peace movement with a promise of amnesty. The effort largely failed, however. REFERENCE: Gregorio F. Zaide, *The Philippine Revolution,* Rev. (Manila: Modern Book Company, 1968).

PEACE COMMISSION

After the initial peace negotiations* produced an armistice, a Peace Commission worked out the details of a treaty. Eugenio Montero Ríos* led the Spanish contingent with Buenaventura Abarzuza, José Garnica y Díaz, Rafael Cerero y Sáenz, Wenceslao Ramírez de Villaurrutia, and Emilio de Ojeda* as secretary. The U.S. contingent to the commission was led by William R. Day* with Whitelaw Reid,* Cushman Davis, William P. Frye,* George Gray,* and John Bassett

Moore as secretary. The Peace Commission labored for three months to produce the Treaty of Paris,* which was signed in December 1898.
REFERENCE: French Ensor Chadwick, *The Relations of the United States and Spain* (New York: Russell & Russell, 1911); David F. Trask, *The War with Spain in 1898* (New York: Macmillan Publishing Co., 1981).

PEACE NEGOTIATIONS

It was President William McKinley's* intent from the beginning to force peace upon Spain at the earliest opportunity. The Spanish intention was to drag out the war to achieve success through outlasting the United States. McKinley wanted to distress the Spanish Empire without directly confronting Spain's strength. Attacks on the margin of the empire—Manila Bay* and Santiago* and ongoing attacks in Puerto Rico*—achieved McKinley's aims in a cost-effective manner and convinced Spain that prolonging the war would not be in the empire's interest.

McKinley also had the support of Great Britain.* London served as an unofficial conduit for American proposals to Spain, and commencing in the first week of June 1898, London forwarded American war aims to Spain. This process altered with the ever-changing political and military climate, and the constantly shifting ground became a leitmotif of the negotiations. General Nelson A. Miles's* landing at Guánica* augmented the pressure on Spain for an early settlement—exactly what McKinley wanted.

Spain initiated what became the protocol for ending the war, but it was Washington that deliberated and debated. By 27 June Spain had asked what terms the United States would accept. Meanwhile, obvious U.S. military actions in Puerto Rico and impending land operations in the Philippines threatened to erode the Spanish bargaining position. The possibility of naval action in Spanish waters was also alarming. Intermediaries such as Jules Cambon,* French ambassador in Washington, served Spanish interests by relaying bargaining points. Spain knew that Cuba was lost, but Spain hoped to negotiate on Puerto Rico and the Philippines. Madrid also wanted to introduce indemnification as a negotiating chip.

McKinley for his part knew exactly what he wanted—save only some uncertainty about the Philippines. He was disturbed, understandably, by the publication of the "Round Robin"* which he felt might weaken his own position. The Duque de Almodóvar* had already relinquished Cuba and so had little negotiating capital left. The Americans insisted on Spain's relinquishing Cuba, the cession of other islands in the West Indies, and a base in the Marianas.* As mentioned, U.S. aims in the Philippines were still ambiguous by late July and early August. For this reason, the protocol, a preliminary document to a formal peace treaty, was developed. After much wrangling, the protocol was signed and an armistice commenced on 12 August 1898 late in the afternoon. Commodore George Dewey* and General Wesley Merritt,* unaware of the protocol, attacked Manila on 13 August and secured the Spanish surrender of the Philippines.

The armistice halted hostilities, but it also gave breathing room for a national debate on the Philippines, expansionism,* and moral responsibility. Business interests, military interests, and some religious interests urged expansion to bring American ideals to diverse lands. Anti-imperialists doubted American virtue, pointing to the American treatment of its native race and the former slaves, but they also darkly hinted that the annexation of these diverse cultures would make the United States a mongrel nation.

Compelling to the president were additional arguments and perceptions: China was to be partitioned by Europe, and the United States had a stake in Far Eastern trade. Spanish misrule was a given in McKinley's mind, but German,* British, or Japanese partition of the Philippines could be even more nettlesome. McKinley somewhat reluctantly came to the conclusion that the Philippines could not be divided. The archipelago could not be turned back to Spain, in the American view. Emilio Aguinaldo's* revolution did not have the confidence of U.S. observers—in short, all roads seemed to be mined except that of U.S. annexation. Having arrived at this conclusion, the president then chose a Peace Commission* that would ratify his ideas of a treaty.

On 1 October 1898 the Peace Commission, composed of Spanish and American appointees, held their first meeting in Paris. Since only the disposition of the Philippines seemed in question, the U.S. contingent thought it would be a short exercise. The Spaniards, however, reopened every point in the protocol and particularly seemed intent on linking the Cuban debt to parts of the protocol. Thus it was that the American populace had ample time to debate the Philippine question and to inform themselves on the Philippines. McKinley remained firm in his resolve to acquire the Philippines. Entreated by his commissioners that the result of his resolve might not be effective, McKinley agreed to some concessions, including a $20 million payment, which the Spanish eventually accepted. The Treaty of Paris* was signed on 10 December 1898.

REFERENCES: Margaret Leech, *In the Days of McKinley* (New York: Harper & Row, 1959); Whitelaw Reid, *Making Peace with Spain* (Austin: University of Texas Press, 1965).

PEANUT CLUB

The Peanut Club was the name given to an informal gathering of New York journalists at 66 Broadway, in the offices of Horatio Rubens, a Cuban expatriate lawyer and a leading member of the Cuban junta* in the United States. The group got its name from the large box of peanuts that Rubens kept on hand for snacks. In the 1890s the junta used this forum to disseminate anti-Spanish propaganda to the media.

Members of New York's press* attended each afternoon. Here, they feasted on tales of Spanish brutality and rebel victory recounted in the news releases given them by members of the junta, such as Rubens or Tomás Estrada Palma,* the junta's leader. The reporters seemed little concerned about the understandable biases in these accounts, coming as they were from Spain's antagonists in the struggle, and the fact that many were completely unsubstantiated. Along with these outright fabrications, the stories published in pro-Cuba publications such as the *Journal,* the *World,* and the *Sun* served their purpose to help cultivate anti-Spain sentiment in the United States.

REFERENCE: G.J.A. O'Toole, *The Spanish War* (New York: W. W. Norton & Co., 1944); W. A. Swanberg, *Citizen Hearst: A Biography of William Randolph Hearst* (New York: Scribner's, 1961).

MARK A. THOMAS

PELAYO (ship)

The Spanish battleship *Pelayo* spent part of the Spanish American War in Cádiz harbor as a potential threat. She figured in plans for Cuba* and the Philippines,* but as a threat more than as a combatant. *Pelayo* was a leading element of Admiral Manuel de la Cámara's* squadron on its abortive mission to Manila,* and as a stimulus to the discussions of A. T. Mahan* over the employment of the Eastern Squadron.*

Of 9,900 tons, *Pelayo* was armed with two 12.5-inch heavy guns in barbettes and two others of 11 inches in sponsons on either beam. Numerous smaller guns and torpedo tubes complemented the heavy guns. She had a speed of 15 or 16 knots and a complement of 630 men. *Pelayo* was scrapped in 1925.

REFERENCE: Alfredo Aguilera, *Buques de guerra españoles, 1885–1971* (Madrid: Librería Editorial San Martín, 1972).

PERSHING, JOHN JOSEPH
(1860–1948)

John Joseph Pershing of later Mexican Punitive Expedition and World War I fame, was born in Missouri and studied in his state until securing an appointment to West Point in 1882. He served in the West in several Indian campaigns but had never been under fire until the Spanish American War. He joined the Tenth Cavalry* at Chickamauga Park, Georgia, on 5 May 1898. His unit went to Tampa* and on 14 June departed for Cuba with General S.B.M. Young's* Second Brigade.

On 1 July orders came to General Joseph Wheeler's* division (Second Brigade was in Wheeler's division) to move down the El Pozo*–Santiago Road. The Tenth Cavalry was caught under the observation balloon* and took fire from entrenched Spanish troops. Observers noted that Pershing was very cool under fire. The Tenth advanced on the San Juan* blockhouse and took a large number of casualties.

REFERENCE: Donald Snythe, "Pershing in the Spanish American War," *Military Affairs* 31 (Spring 1967): 25–33.

PETREL (ship)

The U.S.S. *Petrel,* an 892-ton gunboat, was commissioned on 10 December 1889 and armed with four 6-inch guns and an array of smaller rapid-fire weapons. *Petrel* was assigned to the Asiatic Squadron* of Commodore George Dewey.* She was in Dewey's line at the Battle of Manila Bay,* where she helped destroy six Spanish ships. *Petrel* also sailed into Cavite* to force its surrender. On 2 May 1898 *Petrel* caused the seizure of the arsenal at Cavite and captured the Spanish tugs *Rápido* and *Hércules* plus three launches.

Petrel continued service in the Philippines* and Asia through 1899. She also served in Europe and the Caribbean (1912–1919). She was sold in 1920.

REFERENCE: *Dictionary of American Fighting Ships* (Washington, DC: Navy Department, 1979).

PHILIPPINE INSURRECTION

Relations between the two U.S. commanders, George Dewey* and Wesley Merritt,* and the leaders of the Philippine revolution in the summer and fall of 1898 were uncertain. They were uncertain because the peace protocol and on-going peace negotiations* were ambiguous as to whether the United States controlled Manila* and its environs only, or the entire archipelago. The Spanish, even though surrendered, were not cooperative because they assumed, or at least wanted to believe, that the transfer of power was temporary. Compounding the problem was the distrust between Americans. Revolutionary leader Emilio Aguinaldo* wanted independence. American policy makers, for a host of complex reasons, feared that an independent, weak, new Philippine government would be a destabilizing element in the region. The outbreak of hostilities between the insurgents and U.S. forces commenced on 4 February 1899. In its simplest form; the Philippine Insurrection was a continuation of the revolution, but with a different master.

REFERENCES: Brian McAllister Linn, *The U.S. Army and Counterinsurgency in the Philippine War, 1899–1902* (Chapel Hill: University of North Carolina Press, 1989); William Thaddeus Sexton, *Soldiers in the Sun* (Harrisburg, PA: Military Service Publishing Co., 1939).

PHILIPPINES

Initially the Philippines were seen by U.S. planners as strategic target of opportunity to bring pressure upon Spain militarily. The Philippines were weak and distant from Spain or any other source of relief and supply. They presented a relatively safe, but solid, kidney punch to the Spanish Empire. Existing plans developed by the U.S. Navy called for a strike at Manila.* It became obvious to Spanish authorities months before the commencement of hostilities that Commodore George Dewey* was making naval preparations near Hong Kong.* The Spanish naval commander at Manila, Admiral Patricio Montojo y Pasarón,* realized his force could not defend itself against the developing U.S. Navy force, much less launch punitive raids against the United States. Americans knew this also; the panic that gripped the eastern seaboard in April 1898 was virtually unknown on the West Coast.

Dewey's success on 1 May at Manila Bay* had the desired effect. Spain cherished the Philippines and dispatched Admiral Manuel de la Cámara* with a squadron of ships to relieve Manila. Collusion with the British, a potential threat to Iberia itself, and some intriguing intelligence operations* soon enabled the United States to command the situation sufficiently that Madrid, fearing its own vulnerability, recalled Cámara.

Meanwhile, General Wesley Merritt* was building Eighth Corps* in preparation for a land assault on Manila. The assault took place on 13 August, and Spanish authorities surrendered the Philippines.

The third phase of the role of the Philippines in the Spanish American War occurred during peace negotiations.* President William McKinley* led the development of a national debate on expansionism* and arguments for and against acquisition of the Philippines. In addition, the Spanish contingent at the Peace Commission* worked diligently to maintain the status quo ante. While the war was fought to liberate Cuba, conflicting European aspirations in the Far East by Great Britain* and Germany* as well as covetous looks by Japan* gave the Philippines a heightened significance. Spurred by expansionist argument and also by the perceived instability of Emilio Aguinaldo's* revolution, McKinley evolved in his thinking into something of a cautious expansionist through a pragmatic realization that U.S. sovereignty in the Philippines was the best of a lot of bad potential scenarios. The Treaty of Paris* transferred the Philippines from Spain to the United States for a payment of $20 million. The Philippine Insurrection,* a continuation of the Philippine revolution—but against a different master—grew out of the events in the Philippines during the Spanish American War.

REFERENCES: William Thaddeus Sexton, *Soldiers in the Sun* (Harrisburg, PA: Military Service Publishing Co., 1939); Ephraim K. Smith, "William McKinley's Enduring Legacy: The Historiographical Debate on the Taking of the Philippine Islands," in James C. Bradford, ed., *Crucible of Empire* (Annapolis, MD: Naval Institute Press, 1993).

PILAR, MARCELO H. DEL
(1850–1896)

Marcelo H. del Pilar, along with Graciano López Jaena and José Rizal,* was a leader of the Philippine reformist movement. While he was not as influential a propagandist as Rizal, Pilar's essays were much prized. He also edited *La Solidaridad,* which was edited and printed in Barcelona but smuggled into the Philippines. Pilar became one of the voices calling for revolution in 1895. Until his death in Spain in 1896, Pilar was among the intellectual leaders of what became the Philippine revolution.

REFERENCE: Gregorio F. Zaide, *The Philippine Revolution* (Manila: Modern Book Company, 1968).

PLANT, HENRY B.
See PLANT SYSTEM.

PLANT SYSTEM

The Plant System, or Plant Lines, refers to the system of railroads and steamships that were controlled by Henry Bradley Plant. Born in Branford, Connecticut, Plant (1819–1899) built his career in the express business, first on ships and later on railroads. At the beginning of the Civil War, along with other investors he purchased the southern holdings of the Adams Express Company to form the Southern Express Company, a Georgia corporation. After the Civil War the railroads in the South were physically and financially destroyed; Plant seized this opportunity to purchase many of these properties at bargain prices. With an aim to build a unified transportation system, he continued acquiring railroads, steamship lines, and hotels, organizing the Plant Investment Company in 1882 to place his growing number of holdings under single management. The group of transportation companies under his control were known collectively as the Plant System or the Plant Lines.

As the southern terminus of his railroad system, Tampa* was developed by Plant from a commercially unimportant town into a major commercial center. Port Tampa became the home port for Plant's steamship lines and a major transfer point between his railroads and ships. In particular, it was the U.S. port for his ships sailing to Havana,* and as the closest major port to Cuba, it was chosen as the U.S. military's port of embarkation for the invasion of Cuba during the Spanish American War. In fact, one of Plant's chief deputies, Franklin Q. Brown, had visited Cuba shortly before the hostilities to assess business opportunities and to evaluate the threat of war. After his return to the United States, believing conflict was inevitable, he visited President William McKinley* on 14 April 1898 and extolled the advantages of Port Tampa as a possible port for military use. His enthusiasm may have influenced the decision to use Port Tampa as the army's port of embarkation.

In 1898, however, the Plant facilities in the Tampa Bay area were not yet adequate to stage a major military expedition quickly. The elaborate Tampa Bay Hotel,* built by Plant as part of his plan to develop Florida's west coast, was the only major structure; this ensured its becoming local headquarters for the military and press corps. The city was far south of the contemporary railroad network and population centers of the United States. Only two railroads served the city of Tampa, the Plant System and the competing Florida Central and Peninsular. Contrary to the teamwork exercised by most businesses in order to aid the war effort, each of these two companies seemed intent on competing to keep business from the other, to the detriment of traffic flow.

Especially troublesome was the 9-mile stretch of track from the city of Tampa to Port Tampa, a single-track line of the Plant System that became a major bottleneck. Only a single pier existed at Port Tampa for transferring men and supplies from the railroad to ships. Warehouse space in the Tampa area was insufficient, and material remained in boxcars backed up on sidings hundreds of miles north. The congestion reached its peak in May and June 1898 just before the departure of General William R. Shafter's* army for Santiago,* as more and more supplies and volunteer units funneled into Port Tampa. Initial orders to load the ships came on 30 May, but loading was not completed until 8 June, and it was 14 June before the ships actually sailed toward Cuba.

Besides the problems caused by infrastructure limitations, neither the army nor the railroads had experience with a logistical operation of this scale. One journalist, Burr McIntosh, wrote that "an officer . . . told me that night, during a search for clothing for a certain regiment the previous day, twenty-six cars were either unlocked or broken into before the desired articles were found. The cars were opened because there were no distinguishing labels upon them." One newspaper even claimed that every boxcar was labeled merely "Army Supplies Rush."

In addition to Plant's railroads, several of the Plant System's ships were important to the war effort. *La Grande Duchesse, Macotte,* and *Olivette** were chartered by the military during the war and used as transports or hospital ships.

Henry Plant died in New York City on 23 June 1899. In 1902 the railroads comprising the Plant System were absorbed into the Atlantic Coast Line Railroad.

REFERENCES: Richard R. Prince, *Atlantic Coast Line Railroad: Steam Locomotives, Ships and History* (Green River, WY: Richard E. Prince, 1966); *Railroad Gazette* 31, no. 26 (30 June 1899): 481; G. Hutchinson Smyth, *The Life of Henry Bradley Plant* (New York: Knickerbocker, 1898).

MARK A. THOMAS

PLATT, ORVILLE HITCHCOCK
(1827–1905)

Senator Orville Hitchcock Platt of Connecticut studied law and entered the U.S. Senate in 1879. Platt was an energetic congressman associating himself with the system of patents, copyright, bimetallism, and protectionism and taking part in the growing debate over Cuba. In the 1890s Platt was an early and persistent advocate of peace. He was also supporter of President William McKinley* and an ardent annexationist. Platt voted for annexation of Hawaii* and strongly urged for the acquisition of the Philippines.* As chairman of the Committee on Cuban Relations, Senator Platt reviewed the military government of Cuba. Reacting to wartime revolution and postwar experience, and also to the distasteful experience in the Philippine Insurrection,* Platt proposed an amendment to the Army Appropriations Bill in February 1901. His proposal came from discussions with Secretary of War Elihu Root,* the president and others. Known as the Platt Amendment,* his proposal was quickly passed, providing a framework for U.S.-Cuban relationships for decades.

REFERENCE: Louis A. Coolidge, *An Old-Fashioned Senator: Orville H. Platt* (Port Washington, NY: Kennikat Press, 1971).

PLATT AMENDMENT

In 1898, when the United States declared war on Spain, the complexion of the Cuban rebellion changed dramatically. When he delivered his war message to Congress, President William McKinley* ignored the issue of Cuban independence and spoke only of the need for a stable Cuban government capable of maintaining order and fulfilling its international responsibilities. American corporate interests in Cuba did not want independence for the island. They preferred a custodial arrangement in which the United States maintained political control and guaranteed economic stability. In Congress, anti-imperialists claimed that American intervention in the war had less to do with concern for the Cuban masses than with the need of corporate adventurers to use the U.S. government in extending their economic interests. To appease the anti-imperialists, McKinley agreed to the Teller Amendment, in which the United States disclaimed ''any disposition of intention to exercise sovereignty, jurisdiction, or control over said island except for pacification thereof, and asserts its determination, when it is accomplished, to leave the government and control of the island to its people.''

But few Americans actually in Cuba wanted to leave the country to the control of the Cuban people. The United States established a military government over the island in 1899 under the command of General John Brooke* (January–December 1899) and General Leonard Wood* (December 1899–May 1902). Both men believed that Cuba was not ready for independence. To General Brooke, ''These people cannot now, or I believe in the immediate future, be entrusted with their own government.'' Leonard Wood told President McKinley that ''we are dealing with a race that has steadily been going down for a hundred years and into which we have to infuse new life, new principles and new methods of doing things.'' President McKinley concurred. In a message to Congress at the beginning of the military government, he explained that as far as Cuba was concerned, ''our mission . . . is not to be fulfilled by turning adrift any loosely framed commonwealth to face the vicissitudes which too often attend weaker states.''

Two years later, in 1901, when the U.S. military began withdrawing troops as part of the imminent end of the military occupation, few Americans felt any differently. With the U.S. troops withdrawing from the island, Congress granted Cuba independence, but it was an independence without sovereignty because of what became known as the Platt Amendment. Anticipating the American withdrawal from Cuba, Senator Orville Platt, a Republican from Connecticut, had introduced the amendment in Congress in February 1901. It soon passed. The amendment limited the ability of the new Cuban government to contract a public debt and guaranteed the right of the United States to maintain military bases on Cuba. The Platt Amendment also prohibited Cuba from entering into any treaties with foreign governments without the express permission of the United States. Finally, it gave the United States the ''right to intervene for the preservation of Cuban independence, the maintenance of a government adequate for the protection of life, property, and individual liberty, and for discharging the obligations with respect to Cuba imposed by the Treaty of Paris* on the United States, now to be assumed and undertaken by the government of Cuba.''

Cuba was independent but hardly free. Most Cuban nationalists worried that all they had managed to do in the revolution and the war was to trade Spanish colonialism for American colonialism. Juan Gualberto Gómez, the prominent black Cuban general, remarked despondently that the "Platt Amendment has reduced the independence and sovereignty of the Cuban republic to a myth." The Platt Amendment remained in force for more than thirty years, and on a number of occasions during those three decades, the United States intervened militarily in Cuba under its auspices. The Platt Amendment was not dissolved until 29 May 1934, when both countries signed a new treaty formally eliminating it.

REFERENCES: Jules R. Benjamin, *The United States and Cuba: Hegemony and Dependent Development, 1880–1934* (Pittsburgh, PA: University of Pittsburgh Press, 1977); David F. Healy, *The United States in Cuba, 1898–1903* (Madison: University of Wisconsin Press, 1963); Louis H. Pérez, Jr., *Cuba: Between Reform and Revolution* (New York: Oxford University Press, 1988).

JAMES S. OLSON

PLAYA DEL ESTE, CUBA

Near Guantánamo,* Playa del Este was the Cuban end of the cable to Haiti.* On 7 June 1898 a small landing party of U.S. Marines* destroyed the Spanish cable station at Playa del Este. Later, after 27 June, H. C. Corbin,* acting for Secretary of War Russell A. Alger* ordered the cable reestablished. This connection provided valuable and rapid communication to Washington.

REFERENCE: *Correspondence Relating to the War with Spain* (Washington, DC: General Printing Office, 1902).

PLUTÓN (ship)

The Spanish torpedo boat *Plutón,* sometimes classed as a destroyer, was of the *Audaz* class, with about 400 tons of displacement and armed with a few 14-pounders, two 6-pounders, and two torpedo tubes. *Plutón* was a new ship, having been commissioned in 1897, and was capable of 28 knots.

Plutón sailed with Admiral Pascual Cervera's* fleet to the Caribbean on 29 April 1898, after coaling for several days. Following a tumultuous voyage, *Plutón* arrived at Santiago* de Cuba on 19 May in company with *Infanta María Teresa,* *Vizcaya,* *Almirante Oquendo,* and *Cristóbal Colón.*

In the Battle of Santiago on 3 July, Cervera planned that *Plutón* and *Furor* would be the last ships out of the harbor and would engage the U.S. battleships with torpedoes to enable the larger Spanish cruiser to escape. This plan, whatever its merit, was not carried out. Emerging last, *Furor* and *Plutón* encountered the armed yacht *Gloucester.* Although *Plutón* or *Furor* were individually more heavily armed than *Gloucester,* the latter attacked so ferociously that both destroyers turned to run. In addition, a hail of shells from other ships, particularly *Indiana,* struck decisive blows. One of *Indiana's* shots struck *Plutón's* engine room, killing all but two. Out of control, *Plutón* crashed on the rocks shortly beyond the bay of Cabañas.* More than half her crew died either from gunfire or by drowning.

REFERENCE: H. W. Wilson, *The Downfall of Spain* (New York: Burt Franklin, 1971).

POLAVIEJA, CAMILO DE.
See GARCÍA DE POLAVIEJA Y CASTILLO, CAMILO.

POLO DE BERNABÉ, LUIS
(1854–1929)

Luis Polo de Bernabé superseded Enrique Dupuy de Lôme* as Spanish minister to Washington. He arrived in February 1898 and was plunged into the *Maine** enbroglio. On 21 April Polo was recalled. He returned to Spain by way of Canada but left Ramón Carranza* behind to take care of legation business. In reality, Polo was running a spy ring for Spain, which was broken up in a counterintelligence operation.

PONCE, PUERTO RICO

Forty-five miles southwest of San Juan* lies Ponce on the southern coast of Puerto Rico. General Nelson A. Miles,* with part of the Puerto Rican expeditionary force, landed at Ponce on 27 April 1898. The landing was supported by *Massachusetts,** *Dixie,** *Annapolis,** and *Wasp.**

PORTER (ship)

The U.S.S. *Porter* was a torpedo boat* of 165 tons' displacement commissioned in 1897. She was armed with three torpedo tubes and four 1-pounder guns and had a top speed of 28 knots, although in-service, speed was closer to 22 knots. *Porter* served in Admiral William T. Sampson's* blockade* of Cuba, in which activity she captured two schooners. *Porter* also participated in the bombardment of Puerto Rico* and even distinguished herself in that endeavor by working close to enemy batteries without damage.

Porter bombarded the Socapa battery* in support of the landings at Daiquirí* on 21–22 June.

Porter was sold in 1912.

REFERENCE: *Dictionary of American Fighting Ships* (Washington, DC: Navy Department, 1979).

PORT SAID, EGYPT

At the entrance to the Suez Canal, Port Said was the stopping place of Admiral Manuel de la Cámara and his Eastern Squadron.* The foreign office of Great Britain* refused Cámara coal; nor was he allowed to refuel from lighters. Thus the Eastern Squadron, on its way to relieve Manila* after Commodore George Dewey's* naval victory on 1 May 1898, found itself stymied in its progress not only through American efforts (disinformation planted by U.S. agents) and by diplomatic means but also through the efforts of Great Britain.

By 29 June Cámara had been asked to leave Port Said. The naval battle at Santiago de Cuba* on 3 July rendered Cámara's mission secondary to the urgency of protecting Spain. Accordingly, he steamed back across the Mediterranean.

REFERENCE: David F. Trask, *The War with Spain in 1898* (New York: Macmillan Publishing Co., 1981).

POWELSON, WILFRED VAN NEST
(1872–1960)

During the investigations subsequent to the explosion and sinking of the U.S.S. *Maine,** the U.S. Naval Court of Inquiry was initially handicapped because of a dearth of qualified technical experts. Ensign Wilfred Van Nest Powelson had been a student of naval architecture and spent hours with the divers in an effort to piece together what had happened. It was Powelson's testimony that first indicated the explosion may have come from outside the hull. This testimony pointed to an enemy, not to an accident, and American politicians and the people thought the enemy was Spain. The problem is that Powelson was probably wrong.

REFERENCE: H. G. Rickover, *How the Battleship* Maine *Was Destroyed* (Washington, DC: Naval History Division, 1976).

PRATT, E. SPENCER

Exiled from the Philippines,* Emilio Aguinaldo* left for Europe in April 1898. Coincidentally, his ship stopped at Singapore the very day war commenced between Spain and the United States. E. Spencer Pratt, U.S. consul at Singapore, spoke with Aguinaldo and his party on several occasions and even enlisted Aguinaldo's aid against the Spanish. Aguinaldo's version of the interchange is the only surviving account, but Aguinaldo claimed that Commodore George Dewey,* future victor at Manila Bay,* promised independence for the Philippines. Pratt had other discussions with Aguinaldo, with the result that Aguinaldo agreed to cooperate.

REFERENCE: Teodoro M. Kalaw, *The Philippine Revolution* (Kawilihan, P.I.: Jorge B. Vargas Filipiniana Foundation, 1969).

PRESIDIO, SAN FRANCISCO, CALIFORNIA.
See SAN FRANCISCO.

THE PRESS AND THE WAR

It is a commonly held assertion that a sensational press, motivated by a desire for higher circulation, was responsible for the U.S. war with Spain. Variations on this theme range from blaming primarily the New York press to faulting the press in general, based on the assumption that the public and politicians were easily influenced by the media.

Sensationalist journalism, which reached new heights during the Cuban Insurrection* and, indeed, throughout the Spanish American War, was known as yellow journalism. This style of reporting marked a period of cutthroat competition between William Randolph Hearst's* *New York Journal* and Joseph Pulitzer's* *New York World.*

The *World* ran a popular comic strip entitled "Hogan's Alley," created by R. F. Outcault, that featured an urchin dressed in a bright yellow smock. When Outcault was hired by Hearst of the rival *Journal,* Pulitzer got artist George B. Luks to create another version of the comic in the *World;* the two opposing waifs were popularly known as the Yellow Kids. The competition prompted Ervin Wardman of the *New York Press* to identify the class of journalism employed by Pulitzer and Hearst as yellow journalism.

Before radio and TV and the proliferation of low-priced magazines, newspapers were the media of the masses. Seeing potential profits from the dollars of the rising working class, some editors geared their papers to take advantage of this market. Besides commonly engaging in price wars—the *Journal* and the *World* lowered their prices from two cents to one during their fight for readership—the papers specialized in sensational stories meant to grab the attention of the buying public. Their entertainment content was important, perhaps more important than any edifying news they might have carried.

Lavish illustrations and splashy headlines, at the expense of soberly written news stories, were common characteristics of the yellow sheets. When Arthur Brisbane, editor of Hearst's *New York Evening Journal,* found that the brass type available was too small to make the large headlines he desired, he had artists draw huge letters that were then engraved onto metal plates. The largest of these allowed a word of only five letters across the page.

The yellow papers did not hesitate to spend extravagant sums in their bids to outdo rivals. The ego of the owners, and in some cases their political aspirations, may actually have been more important than profits, at least in the short term. Hearst had hired away most of the *World*'s top staff when trying to get his foothold in New York, and during the Spanish American War the major papers paid top dollar to receive the services of famous correspondents, writers, and illustrators. To draw attention to this elite crew, both the *World* and the *Journal* used signed bylines in their articles, an uncommon characteristic at the time. This period represented the rising importance of the reporter and writer and the decline of the importance of the editor in American journalism.

More free spending during the War was evident in the fleets of dispatch boats hired by major papers and news organizations and in the willingness to pay the high telegrapher's fees from Jamaica, Haiti, or Hong Kong in a bid to be the first paper with a new scoop on the war. Publishing multiple editions throughout the day was also costly; the *Journal* and the *World* printed up to forty editions a day at the height of action during the Santiago* campaign.

The yellow sheets were characterized by self-promotion to make their papers seem part of the news rather than just reporters of it. Upon breaking a sensational case, the *Journal,* for example, often emphasized that it acted while other newspapers sat idly by waiting for the news to come to them. In his desire to be part of the action, Hearst went so far as to concoct a secret plot, never carried out, to sink a ship in the Suez Canal, thereby preventing Spanish warships from traveling to the Philippines* to attack Admiral George Dewey.*

Even when they did not make themselves part of the news, the yellow papers often clearly had a cavalier attitude toward the facts, evidenced by their readiness to report biased stories given them by the Cuban junta,* a willingness to publish stories based on rumors, and the outright fabrication of sensational stories. Rather than being concerned with reporting the facts, these papers saw themselves as able to mold public opinion and, it has been said, attempted to do so.

Some biographers of William Randolph Hearst maintain that he was almost single-handedly responsible for U.S. involvement in the war, motivated by increasing circulation for his paper and building his ego. Hearst himself helped to propagate this legend. He supposedly told the bored Frederic Remington,* who wanted to return to the United States shortly after the explosion of the U.S.S. *Maine** when it appeared there would be no military developments, "Please remain. You furnish the pictures and I'll furnish the war." Hearst's bragging became so crass that on 9 and 10 May 1898, in the upper corners of its first page the *Journal* printed the question, "How do you like the *Journal*'s war?"

An alternative to the one-person thesis is that the war developed from the circulation struggle between the sensationalistic yellow papers in New York, with Hearst's *Journal* and Pulitzer's *World* simply leading the way. This assumes that New York newspapers greatly influenced the media in the entire country. Whereas the largest New York papers did have their own wire services, only some of the larger papers around the nation subscribed to them. Many more obtained their stories from the generally less strident Associated Press,* although the *World* and eventually the *Journal* held Associated Press franchises, stories originating with their own reporters were also distributed by the wire service.

George Auxier suggested that although newspapers in the Midwest did contribute to American involvement in Cuba, they did not customarily use sensationalism. In fact, the midwestern press generally held in disdain the yellow press of the East. Rather, editors focused on what was perceived by the U.S. economic and military interests in the Caribbean, on the issue of democracy in the Western Hemisphere, and on propaganda produced by the Cuban junta*; support for intervention was not based merely on a desire for increased circulation.

Following the mood of the country, the press genuinely sympathized with the Cuban cause and supported the precepts of manifest destiny. The United States had a history of supporting the underdog and of opposing the presence of European powers in the Western Hemisphere, especially if that power were a monarchy. Also, besides this predilection to oppose Spain's colonial presence, there seemed no doubt that the public relations machine of the Cuban junta was more effective than that of the Spanish. Editors thus commonly urged some sort of American intervention; however, it became necessarily a military one.

Theories placing upon the press the burden of U.S. involvement in the war hold that the public demanded war, against the wishes of the government and business interests, and that they were urged on by a press that regularly used inflammatory stories as a competitive tactic. Some historians have focused on President William McKinley's* inability to stand up to public sentiment and to congressional leaders' failure to avoid war with Spain. Although the press influenced public opinion, they say, stronger leadership from the White House could have offset negative sentiment to prevent war.

It nonetheless remains debatable whether the press can really mold public sentiment to the degree so often claimed for it in the Spanish American War. There is no doubt that the press was influential in preparing the American public for the war and was involved in spreading misinformation, such as the propaganda distributed by the Cuban junta. As a part of the culture of the time, however, the papers were giving the public what it wanted, and the editorial views of newspapers largely reflected the views of their readers.

REFERENCES: George W. Auxier, "Middle Western Newspapers and the Spanish American War, 1895–1898," *The Mississippi Valley Historical Review* 26, no. 4 (March 1940): 523–534; Charles H. Brown, *The Correspondents' War* (New York: Scribner's, 1967); W. A. Swanberg, *Citizen Hearst: A Biography of William Randolph Hearst* (New York: Scribner's, 1961); W. A. Swanberg, *Pulitzer* (New York: Scribner's, 1967); M. A. Wilkerson, *Public Opinion and the Spanish American War* (Baton Rouge: Louisiana State University Press, 1932); Joseph E. Wisan, *The Cuban Crisis as Reflected in the New York Press* (New York: Octagon, 1935).

MARK A. THOMAS

PRIMO DE RIVERA, FERNANDO
(1831–1921)

General Fernando Primo de Rivera became captain general of the Philippines,* replacing General Camilo García de Polavieja* on 25 April 1897 in that responsibility. On 3 March 1898 Primo de Rivera cabled Segismundo Moret y Prendergast,* Spanish minister for the colonies, that Commodore George Dewey* had orders to move on Manila.* In conjunction with Admiral Patricio Montojo y Pasarón,* the general planned the defense of Manila Bay* with the understanding that Madrid could neither resupply nor reinforce the Philippines. In a surprise move Primo de Rivero was replaced early in April by Governor-General Basilio Augustín Dávila.*

Primo de Rivera was instrumental in securing the Pact of Biak-na-Bato.* The result of negotiations between Emilio Aguinaldo* and General Primo de Rivera, the Pact exiled Aguinaldo to Hong Kong* and established a fund for his support. The general then provided a general amnesty to the revolutionaries. Upon Primo de Rivera's departure in mid-April, the Philippine insurgents* began revolutionary activities again.

REFERENCES: Teodoro M. Kalaw, *The Philippine Revolution* (Kawilihan, P.I.: Jorge B. Jargas Filipiniana Foundation, 1969); Fernando Primo de Rivero, *Discurso pronunciado en el senado el día II de junio de 1898, con motivo de ataques que le han sido dirigidos en el congreso de los diputados . . .* (Madrid: J. S. García, 1898).

PROCTOR, REDFIELD
(1831–1908)

Born in Proctorville, Vermont (a town founded by his grandfather), Redfield Proctor graduated from Dartmouth and the Albany law school. He rose to the rank of colonel during the Civil War and returned to law and business after the war. Proctor served as lieutenant governor and then governor of Vermont and served as secretary of war under President Harrison. Elected to the Senate in 1892 after filling a year-long vacancy, Proctor served until his death.

Proctor accomplished two important acts relative to the Spanish American War. A widely respected businessman who had a reputation for sobriety and efficiency, Proctor sponsored Commodore George Dewey* as commander of the Asiatic Squadron* and was able to convince President William McKinley* of Dewey's worth—a fact of which he reminded the president after the Battle of Manila Bay.* Proctor also traveled to Cuba at his own expense to assess matters. He arrived 26 February 1898 aboard *Olivette* to investigate the *reconcentrado* situation. His report and address to the Senate on 17 March is credited with swaying Congress to act in Cuba's behalf against Spain. The business community, previously ambivalent toward war with Spain, became prowar because of Proctor's speech.

REFERENCES: *Congressional Record,* 55th Cong., 2d sess., 2916–2919; G.J.A. O'Toole, *The Spanish War* (New York: W. W. Norton & Co., 1984); Julius W. Pratt, *Expansionists of 1898* (Baltimore: Johns Hopkins University Press, 1898); Henry B. Russell, Redfield Proctor, and John M. Thurston, *An Illustrated History of Our War with Spain* (Hartford, CT: A. D. Worthington & Co., 1898).

PROSERPINA (ship)

Admiral Manuel de la Cámara* sailed with a fleet from Spain intending to relieve the Spanish forces at Manila.* The fleet included several ships: *Carlos V,* *Pelayo,* *Alfonso XII,* *Buenos Aires,* and the *Audaz*-class torpedo boat *Proserpina.* Built in Great Britain* for Spain, the class also included *Plutón,* which was sunk at Santiago,* and was basically an improved version of the *Furor.* *Proserpina* displaced around 100 tons and carried two 14-pounders and two 6-pounders. She sailed to Egypt and then returned.

REFERENCE: Rafael González Echegaray, ''Suez amargo,'' *Revista General de la Marina* (February 1974): 133–156.

PUERTO RICO

The island Puerto Rico was insular not just geographically but also politically. Desirous of conserving past glories, Spain actively sought to insulate Puerto

Rico from the reform and independence viruses running rampant in Cuba. Puerto Rico possessed three options in the late nineteenth century: assume status as a province of Spain, assume some form of autonomy* within a Spanish colonial framework, or achieve outright independence. For her part, Spain could either crush the growth of independence or foster education, reform, and Puerto Rico's consequent growth and development. Spain had tried both paths but did neither well, and its obvious vacillation represented a de facto policy of "half a loaf." Political leaders and opinion makers on the island found Spain's efforts unsatisfactory. Spain's policies were reactive. The developing Puerto Rican political parties of the 1880s and 1890s were active, if diverse. Like all such fermenting political processes, the local political leadership was united in little (only in that change was necessary) and disunited in almost everything else. Some desired only reforms in Spanish governance, others a charter of autonomy, and yet others independence. There were those who wanted to ally with the United States. Indeed, Puerto Rican factions of the Cuban Revolutionary party and the Cuban junta* were headquartered in New York.

The 1897 accession to power of Práxides Mateo Sagasta,* Spanish prime minister, brought a new autonomous charter to Puerto Rico. Secured by Sagasta on 25 November 1897, it was not proclaimed on the island until January 1898 and the government not inaugurated until 12 February 1898. This new government had barely sat for two weeks before the war commenced.

The new government faced not only political and military challenges but economic malaise as well. Crises multiplied, and none were met effectively. It has been said that the island was in a state of shock—and so it seemed to those Americans under General Nelson Miles,* who landed in the last week of July. In a campaign that lasted less than three weeks, there was little fighting, much cheering—even aid to the U.S. expeditionary force—and even more passive staring. A fringe wanted to stay with Spain. Another group hoped that being brought under the wing of the democratic behemoth to the north would be like a cleansing shower. Both were disappointed. Puerto Rico shared in neither the Spanish autonomy nor the U.S. Constitution. In the Treaty of Paris Spain ceded Puerto Rico to the United States.

REFERENCES: Edward J. Berbusse, *The United States in Puerto Rico, 1898–1900* (Chapel Hill: University of North Carolina Press, 1966); Ángel Rivero, Méndez, *Crónica de la Guerra Hispano Americana en Puerto Rico* (New York: Plus Ultra, 1973).

PULITZER, JOSEPH
(1847–1911)

Born in Hungary, Joseph Pulitzer arrived in the United States before the Civil War, in which he served in the Union army. After successfully building the *St. Louis Post-Dispatch* using a sensationalist style of journalism, Pulitzer moved to New York in 1883, where he saw a niche for a paper geared toward the rising number of the working class. He took over the *World,* turning it into New York's leading paper within a few years with sensational stories, aggressive populism, and reformist sympathies, opposing corporate and Republican interests.

The style Pulitzer developed, which came to be known as yellow journalism,* was well suited to news of the hostilities in Cuba during the insurrection of 1895.* Papers would focus on stories of atrocities, often exaggerating them or engaging in outright fabrication. Also, at this time Pulitzer entered into fierce competition with William Randolph Hearst,* who had recently entered the New York market with his purchase of the *Journal,* further accelerating each paper's production of outlandish stories in a bid for dominance.

Pulitzer never had a personal interest in Cuban independence, as did Charles Dana* of the *Sun* or even Hearst; nor did he have personal political motives behind the publicity, as perhaps did Hearst. The sensational war stories were, to him, merely a way of fighting a circulation battle by being the most entertaining paper that appealed to the most people. After several embarrassing incidents, however, Pulitzer lost interest in the war.

One of these was when Sylvester Scovil,* a *World* correspondent, swung his fist at General William R. Shafter* during an argument at the Spanish surrender at Santiago.* Another was when the *World* was caught copying a story from the *Journal,* a practice in which all the yellow sheets engaged. The *Journal* revealed the story as a fake, merely planted to catch the *World* stealing news from them, and took great pleasure at poking fun at the *World.*

Another disheartening incident involved a Stephen Crane* article published by the *World* suggesting that the men of the Seventy-first New York Volunteers* had been less than enthusiastic in their duties at San Juan Hill.* The *Journal* charged slander against the brave boys of the Seventy-first, but when the *World* tried to atone by raising money for a memorial to the Seventy-first and to the Rough Riders,* the First Volunteer Cavalry, the men of the Seventy-first rejected any favors from the slanderous *World,* while the Rough Riders did not want to be associated with the cowardly members of the Seventy-first.

Besides being demoralized by affairs such as these, Pulitzer was sickly, being nearly blind and extremely sensitive to noise. After the war, he steered the *World* toward more accurate reporting and a less flamboyant style, allowing Hearst to reign as king of the yellow press* in New York.

REFERENCE: W. A. Swanberg, *Pulitzer* (New York: Scribner's, 1967).

MARK A. THOMAS

PUNTA GORDA, CUBA

Punta Gorda lay north of the channel at Santiago de Cuba.* The battery at Punta Gorda was on a small peninsula (the Punta Gorda) above the Socapa* and Morro Castle.* Punta Gorda commanded the channel, and should any enemy succeed in getting past the batteries at the mouth, Punta Gorda was the failsafe point. It possessed four modern breech-loading guns and two venerable howitzers. While potent, the battery was never engaged. Admiral William T. Sampson* fired on Punta Gorda briefly from American ships, but the army's original plan was to take the battery from the land. General William Shafter's* forces halted, however, and when General Nelson Miles* arrived, he revived Sampson's original plan of a combined sea-land attack. Negotiations achieved the capitulation of Santiago on 17 July 1898.

REFERENCE: *Correspondence Relating to the War with Spain* (Washington, DC: Government Printing Office, 1902).

PURITAN (ship)

The largest of the ''modern'' monitors* built ostensibly as makeovers of Civil War vessels, the U.S.S. *Puritan* displaced 6,060 tons, could steam at 12 knots (if the sea was glass) and carried four 12-inch guns, six 4-inch guns, and six 6-pounders as armament. Although laid down in 1874, *Puritan* was not commissioned until 1896. During the war *Puritan* participated in blockade* and bombardment duties in the Caribbean, lobbing shells at Matanzas* on 27 April 1898 in company with *New York** and *Cincinnati.** After the war *Puritan* served a variety of tasks until she became a gunnery target in 1913. She was sold in 1922.

REFERENCE: *Dictionary of American Fighting Ships* (Washington, DC: Navy Department, 1979).

Q

QUARTERMASTER'S DEPARTMENT, U.S. ARMY

The Quartermaster's Department of the U.S. Army equipped the troops with clothing, moved the troops by rail, ship, or mule, and constructed camps.* Rapid buildup of troops necessitated an equally rapid production program and the acquisition of everything from boots to tents to wagons. These pressures forced authority downward, and the War Department* allowed commanders and bureau chiefs greater latitude in determining requisitions because of the wartime emergency. Nevertheless, the capabilities of the quartermaster always lagged behind the needs of the forces. Private contracts proved a necessity, and approximately two-thirds of the army's clothing and tentage came from private contractors. By the time of the signing of the peace protocol on 12 August 1898, all volunteers and regulars were equipped.

The quartermaster general was Marshall I. Ludington.* Ludington's plans were often ambushed by changing War Department demands. The overnight decision to invade Cuba with 70,000 troops instead of General William R. Shafter's* 6,000-man reconnaissance played havoc with transport acquisition and inventories. Ludington also organized a construction force to go to Cuba for camp construction and for repair of docks, harbors, and the like.

REFERENCE: Graham A. Cosmas, *An Army for Empire* (Columbia: University of Missouri Press, 1971).

R

RABÍ, JESÚS
(1846–1915)

General Jesús Rabí was a descendant of Siboney Indians and early became associated with the Cuban Insurrection.* During the Spanish American War General Rabí toured with Admiral William T. Sampson's* envoy, Lieutenant Victor Blue,* around Santiago's defenses. Rabí pointed out the batteries of Punta Gorda,* Socapa,* and Morro Castle.* Rabí's men proved excellent scouts.

General Rabí also led a diversionary attack at Cabañas while U.S. General William R. Shafter's Fifth Corps* disembarked.

REFERENCES: French Ensor Chadwick, *The Relations of the United States and Spain* (New York: Russell & Russell, 1968); Philip S. Foner, *The Spanish-Cuban-American War and the Birth of American Imperialism,* 2 vols. (New York: Monthly Review Press, 1972).

RAILROADS

The U.S. railroads enjoyed an overshadowed but highly significant role in the mobilization effort during the Spanish American War. The existence and efficiency of a large and diverse rail system enabled the timely and effective transport of material and troops. In fact, most problems associated with transport derived from inefficiencies in the War Department* rather than from problems with the railroads per se. Sensing bottlenecks at the various camps,* railroads built extra sidings, depots, and warehouses, usually at their own expense, to accommodate the flood of shipments. Troops traveled in day coaches or sleeping cars when warranted.

The efficiency of the railroads reflected their stature as one of the nineteenth century's most developed industries. Railroads were competitive and aggressive—the only difficulties occurred between railroads that wanted to serve the same depot. The Plant Line controlled the tracks to Tampa* and allowed rival company rolling stock on its rails only after the military threatened seizure of the Plant System's* local assets.

The Long Island Railroad leased land to the U.S. Army near Montauk, New York, which the army turned into Camp Wikoff.* The railroad built extra track depots and other facilities while allowing free use of extant railroad property. The railroad operated twice its normal traffic to help supply the camp, which was a quarantine station for yellow fever* and other maladies. Despite the co-operation of the railroad, Russell A. Alger's* War Department could not relieve the bottleneck from the railroad yard to the camp itself.

Generally, the railroads received praise from military commanders and the administration.

REFERENCE: *Report of the Commission Appointed by the President to Investigate the Conduct of the War Department in the War with Spain* (Washington, DC: Government Printing Office, 1900).

RALEIGH (ship)

The U.S.S. *Raleigh* was a sister-ship to the *Cincinnati** and mirrored her specifications and armament.

On 22 April 1898 *Raleigh* arrived in Hong Kong* to join with Commodore George Dewey's* squadron assembling to attack Manila Bay.* *Raleigh* entered the bay on 1 May fourth in line behind *Olympia,** *Baltimore,** and *Petrel.** *Raleigh* sustained only one hit in the battle—on the whale boat.

On 3 May *Raleigh* and *Baltimore* were sent to capture Corregidor,* which surrendered without resistance. *Raleigh,* which received the surrendering Spanish commander, had unknowingly drifted over a Spanish mined area, which caused the Spanish commander considerable anxiety. However, the mines had been planted so deep that no danger existed.

REFERENCE: H. W. Wilson, *The Downfall of Spain* (New York: Burt Franklin, 1971).

RATIONS, U.S.

See DODGE COMMISSION.

REA, GEORGE BRONSON
(1869–1936)

As journalist for the *New York Herald,* George Bronson Rea visited Cuba in 1895 and 1896 to report on fighting between the Spanish and the insurgent forces. Unlike the majority of reporters who stayed in Havana,* Key West,* or Tampa,* receiving their news from biased press releases from the rebels, Rea actually traveled in the interior of Cuba with rebel troops. During his first visit, from January through September 1896, he spent time with several insurgent leaders, professing the most admiration for Antonio Maceo,* then in charge of rebel armies in the west. As the insurgency was getting more attention in the U.S. press,* Rea returned to Cuba in January 1897 in a race with the *New York World*'s Sylvester Scovel* to be the first to reach rebel general Máximo Gómez,* a pursuit won by Scovel. Rea joined Gómez shortly after and stayed in Cuba through March.

During his visits to Cuba Rea became disgusted at what he came to realize were the gross exaggerations of rebel strength and Spanish atrocities that were distributed as part of the insurgents'* public relations campaign, readily accepted without verification by most U.S. journalists, and the lack of knowledge or dismissal of rebel misdeeds. After returning to the United States, Rea wrote an exposé entitled *Facts and Fakes about Cuba* in which he was strongly critical of most U.S. news reporters, the U.S. press, the scorched-earth military tactics of the rebels, and U.S. politicians. Rea was especially critical of General Gomez, whom he portrayed as a temperamental fool. He had respect for only the few other reporters, such as Scovel, who had actually made the effort to witness the conflict in Cuba firsthand. Besides detailed descriptions of confrontations between the Spanish and insurgents, Rea's book cites many specific examples of false stories in the American press.

REFERENCE: George Bronson Rea, *Facts and Fakes about Cuba* (New York: George Monro's Sons, 1897).

MARK A. THOMAS

RECONCENTRADO(S).
See RECONCENTRATION POLICY.

RECONCENTRATION POLICY
Less than a week after arriving in Cuba, Spanish general Valeriano Weyler y Nicolau* initiated a policy of reconcentration to control Cuban insurgents.* Begun in 1896, the policy required the populace to move to central locations under Spanish military jurisdiction, and the entire island, it seemed, was put under martial law with restricted travel. The point of the policy was to deny succor to the insurgents and to attempt control of the countryside with a system of trenches that divided the countryside.

Because the reconcentration policy struck directly at civilians and only indirectly at the insurgents, the outcry in the United States was particularly virulent and poured into a reservoir of ill-will between the United States and Spain.

REFERENCES: Philip S. Foner, *The Spanish-Cuban-American War and the Birth of American Imperialism, 1895–1902* (New York: Monthly Review Press, 1972); Ernest R. May, *Imperial Democracy* (New York: Harcourt, Brace & World, 1961).

RED CROSS, U.S.
See AMERICAN NATIONAL RED CROSS.

REED, WALTER
(1851–1902)
More than one war was fought during the Spanish American conflict. The press* trumpeted the battles at San Juan Hill* and Manila,* but in hindsight the

battles against disease had a powerful historical impact. One of the chief militarists in the war against disease was Major Walter Reed.

Reed grew up in Virginia, although both his parents were from North Carolina. Completing his medical course at the University of Virginia in a record nine months, he became its youngest graduate. Doctor Reed worked in public health for a few years in Brooklyn before joining the U.S. Army Medical Corps at age twenty-four. Stationed in Indian country at Yuma, then later at Fort Omaha, he participated in a variety of medical experiences. After a stint of study and research at Johns Hopkins, he again went into the field, where his natively curious mind labored on bacteriology and diphtheria.

In May 1893 George Miller Sternberg* was chosen surgeon general of the army. Sternberg had great effect on Reed. Sternberg was an acknowledged specialist on yellow fever* and a meticulous scientist. He saw in Reed more than a frontier medical officer and fostered Reed's scientific enquiry. Reed began a series of researches that honed his methods and brought him the notice of other professionals.

The declaration of war with Spain caught many by surprise—the Medical Corps, also. Sanitation had always been a challenge with troops in the field, and the rapidity of the war coupled with the tropical climates spread typhus, typhoid, and yellow fever. The first year revealed 20,738 cases of typhoid fever with a 7.6 percent mortality rate. Sternberg assigned Reed to chair a board (later a commission) to investigate this public health scandal. Reed and fellow surgeons traveled from camp to camp making inspections and recommendations. His report, along with those of his fellow commissioners, did much to overcome ignorance of typhoid and its causes.

Sternberg next called upon Reed to chair a yellow fever commission in which his fame became secure, but not at cost. Jesse Lazear, a member of the commission, contracted yellow fever and died. The commission was able to identify the mosquito-borne source of the disease, however, and Reed became renowned as a medical hero. He died of acute appendicitis on 23 November 1902.

REFERENCES: William B. Bean, *Walter Reed: A Biography* (Charlottesville: University Press of Virginia, 1982); Howard A. Kelly, *Walter Reed and Yellow Fever* (New York: McClure, Phillips & Co., 1906).

REID, WHITELAW
(1837–1912)

Born in Ohio, Whitelaw Reid studied at Miami University, graduating with honors in 1856. He became a noted journalist and found himself inexorably drawn into politics. During the Civil War he worked as a reporter who came to know and befriend influential men. Among these was Horace Greeley, who took him on at the *Washington Tribune*. By 1869 he was its managing editor. Enhancing his prestige by marrying the daughter of California millionaire Darius Ogden Mills, Reid exploited his cultural connections. In 1892 he ran as Benjamin Harrison's running mate and soon thereafter became a William McKinley* supporter. McKinley, a fellow Ohioan, earned Reid's trust and the *Tribune*'s endorsement. Reid thought he should be in McKinley's cabinet or at least be rewarded with an ambassadorship, but McKinley was shrewder than that.

When the Spanish American War commenced, Reid believed in expansionism,* and McKinley appointed him to the Peace Commission* knowing Reid was an expansionist.

REFERENCE: Whitelaw Reid, *Making Peace with Spain: the Diary of Whitelaw Reid* (Austin: University of Texas Press, 1965).

REINA CRISTINA (ship)

Launched on 21 August 1887, the Spanish cruiser *Reina Cristina* possessed no armor and six 6-inch guns sponsored on both sides of her hull, and along with *Reina Mercedes*,* she had much wooden construction and upperworks. On the morning of the Battle of Manila Bay,* she was quite outclassed by her American antagonists. At 3,520 tons, *Cristina* was Admiral Patricio Montojo y Pasarón's* flagship at Manila and during the ensuing battle steamed bravely toward the American squadron. Consequently, she took tremendous punishment before burning and sinking. In fact, so numerous and damaging were the hits on *Cristina* that neither side could effectively count them. *Cristina* lost 130 killed, including her gallant commander, Luis Cardoso, who died while evacuating wounded from the stricken ship. Indeed, the majority of the ship's officers were killed. In addition, ninety were wounded, including Admiral Montojo, who was struck by a splinter. The captured battle flag of the *Cristina* was returned to Spain three decades later as gesture of respect for the Spanish sailors who died at Manila.

REFERENCE: Alfredo Aguilera, *Buques de guerra españoles, 1885–1971* (Madrid: Librería Editorial San Martín, 1972).

REINA MERCEDES (ship)

Reina Mercedes was a 3,090-ton Spanish cruiser similar to the *Reina Cristina** and launched the same year, 1887. *Mercedes* was sent to Cuba* in 1896 to augment the Spanish squadrons in the Caribbean. Armed with six 6-inch guns and numerous smaller weapons, *Mercedes* was built of iron without armor. Originally stationed at Havana,* she transferred to Santiago de Cuba.* Deteriorating at Santiago, *Mercedes*'s engines became inoperable; and consequently, some of her guns were mounted on shore batteries.

While at Santiago *Mercedes* participated in the *Merrimac** incident, firing four torpedoes at Lieutenant Richmond Hobson's* ship, but missing. *Mercedes* also provided supporting fires for the batteries during bombardments. On 4 July 1898 General José Toral* sank *Mercedes* in the mouth of Santiago Harbor in an attempt to block the channel. He was only partially successful.

In March 1899 the Americans refloated *Mercedes* and towed her to Norfolk, Virginia, to be refurbished for use as a receiving ship. She was later transferred to Annapolis to serve as storeship and brig for errant midshipmen.

REFERENCE: Alfredo Aguilera, *Buques de guerra españoles, 1885–1971* (Madrid: Librería Editorial San Martín, 1972).

REMEY, GEORGE COLLIER
(1841–1928)

George Collier Remey, born in Iowa, graduated from the Naval Academy in 1859. He saw significant service in the Civil War. After the war he rose in responsibility and rank to commodore. In this capacity he commanded the strategically significant U.S. naval base at Key West.* Key West and Remey's command provided all-important logistical communications and maintenance support for the blockade* of Cuba and the subsequent campaign in Puerto Rico.*

Promoted to rear admiral in November 1898, Remey commanded the Asiatic Squadron* during the last phase of the Philippine Insurrection.* He was an officer esteemed by his peers who performed efficiently and effectively in support of the American naval initiative in the Caribbean.

REFERENCES: *Annual Report of the Navy Department for the Year 1898; Appendix to the Report of the Chief of the Bureau of Navigation* (Washington, DC: Government Printing Office, 1898); French Ensor Chadwick, *The Relations of the United States and Spain* (New York: Russell & Russell, 1968).

REMINGTON, FREDERIC SACKRIDER
(1861–1909)

One of the most prolific and influential artists America has ever produced, Frederick Sackrider Remington defined the American West for several generations. Enamored with cowboys, Indians, and military life in general, Remington found little left of his romantic ideals by the mid-1890s. The Indians were on reservations and the military languished in garrisons. Remington longed for the energized life of war, glory, and manliness.

In September 1895 William Randolph Hearst* bought the *New York Journal.* The *Journal* was an "also-ran" among metropolitan dailies, but Hearst had big plans: He would challenge the larger papers head on with a boldness and flash seldom seen. Among stories Hearst thought had marketing value was the developing disaster in Cuba. Accordingly, in December 1896 Hearst sent Remington and Richard Harding Davis* to Cuba to cover stories of atrocity, the reconcentration policy,* and General Valeriano "Butcher" Weyler y Nicolau.* Remington sent back drawings, but after two weeks he had enough.

Meanwhile, Remington drew an imaginatively portrayed and provocative Clemencia Arango* being strip-searched by lecherous-looking Spaniards that was published with an equally provocative Davis report. The public outcry was deafening.

Davis and Remington continued to report on the developing crisis. Remington sailed on the U.S.S. *Iowa* * for a week and sketched. When the hostilities commenced, Remington went to Tampa,* where he sketched officers and soldiers, including Guy V. Henry,* Joseph Wheeler,* William R. Shafter,* and James F.

Wade.* Remington then followed Fifth Corps* to Santiago.* By so doing, he also completed a body of work that is unique in its depiction of the Spanish American War. Both *Collier's Weekly* and Harper & Brothers published histories of the war laced with Remington illustrations. In the absence of action photography, Remington's sketches captured the struggle and its impressions and interpreted the war not just for contemporaries but for subsequent generations as well.

REFERENCE: Douglas Allen, *Frederic Remington and the Spanish American War* (New York: Crown Publishers, 1971).

RESOLUTE (ship)

The U.S.S. *Resolute* was an Old Dominion Line passenger ship bought by the U.S. Navy as a transport for the war. Launched in 1894 as the *Yorktown,* *Resolute* became part of the navy in April 1898 as a troop transport in the Caribbean. Sold to Merchants and Miners Transportation Company and renamed *Powhatan,* she had a collision with the Fall River steamer *Priscilla* in 1902; collided with and sank the schooner *Shenandoah* in 1909; was, in turn, sunk by the British tanker *Telena* in a collision in 1916.

Raised in 1917, *Powhatan* was rebuilt and reengined with turboelectric drive (the first electrically driven passenger ship) and renamed *Cuba,* the sole vessel of the New Electric Line. After a brief stint on the West Coast as *Seneca,* she burned at Hoboken, New Jersey, in 1927.

As transport and store ship, *Resolute* played a role in slowing the U.S. invasion force when she reported seeing Spanish warships in Nicholas Channel, north of Cuba. Secretary of War Russell A. Alger* kept the fleet at Tampa* until these ships could be identified.

REFERENCE: Frederick E. Emmons, *American Passenger Ships* (Newark: University of Delaware Press, 1985).

RESTORMEL (ship)

Restormel, Roath, and *Twickenham* were English colliers chartered by the Spanish government to supply Admiral Pascual Cervera's* fleet with coal.* *Twickenham* was captured by *St. Louis* on 10 June 1898 off Jamaica. *Restormel* was captured by *St. Paul* on 25 May off Santiago de Cuba,* in plain sight of Cervera's ships. The Americans took the cargo but released the ship after the war.

The seizure of *Restormel, Roath,* and *Twickenham* left Cervera with little fuel, and that of poor quality. She was seized right at the mouth of the harbor, and her British captain said his orders were to steam for San Juan.* If the Spanish ships were not at San Juan, he was to go to Martinique,* then Santiago, and finally Cienfuegos.* The American Flying Squadron,* lying 26 miles offshore, could not see into the harbor. While Captain Charles D. Sigsbee* interrogated the British captain, he communicated with Commodore Winfield S. Schley* aboard the *Brooklyn.* Sigsbee should have concluded that there was strong evidence of Cervera's presence at Santiago. However, the opposite was communicated to Schley.

Cervera, meanwhile, believed he was blockaded on the twenty-fifth, with the capture of *Restormel.*

REFERENCE: H. W. Wilson, *The Downfall of Spain* (New York: Burt Franklin, 1971).

REVENUE CUTTER SERVICE

The origin of the U.S. Revenue Cutter Service, today's Coast Guard, dates back to 1790, when a small fleet of cutters was formed to enforce customs and tariffs on maritime commerce. During the Spanish American War the Revenue Cutter Service came under the direction of the Department of the Navy and fought in the Caribbean and the Far East. Eight revenue cutters, carrying forty-three guns, served in Admiral William T. Sampson's* squadron and helped blockade* Cuban harbors. Cutters were also assigned the mission of patrolling the U.S. coast to look for evidence of Spanish ships.

REFERENCE: United States Coast Guard, *Coast Guard History* (Washington, DC: U.S. Department of Transportation, U.S. Coast Guard, 1982).

KEN KEMPCKE

RICKOVER, HYMAN GEORGE
(1900–1986)

Polish-born American naval officer Hyman George Rickover graduated from the U.S. Naval Academy in 1922 and served over sixty-three years on active duty in the navy. Most significantly, beginning in the mid-1940s he founded and served as director of the navy's nuclear propulsion program. In 1976 Rickover authored *How the Battleship* Maine *Was Destroyed.*

Admiral Rickover was motivated to investigate the loss of the U.S.S. *Maine** based upon his own readings on the Spanish American War. Rickover believed that the war was historically important to the United States and also that the navy had failed to conduct a proper investigation into the accident. One specific fault cited by Rickover was the failure of the 1898 Court of Inquiry to call technical experts, relying instead upon the expertise of the court. Rickover drew upon his many years of work in naval engineering in putting together his study, which concluded that "in all probability, the *Maine* was destroyed by an accident which occurred inside the ship." Rickover wrote, "The finding of the court of 1898 appears to have been guided less by technical consideration and more by the awareness that war was now inevitable."

Rickover was strongly critical not only of the 1898 inquiry but also of the conduct of the *Maine*'s commanding officer, Captain Charles D. Sigsbee.* The admiral noted that Sigsbee had failed to sufficiently protect the *Maine* from an accident resulting from the spontaneous combustion of coal, and that two previous vessels Sigsbee had commanded had fared poorly in cleanliness inspections.

Rickover also condemned a second major investigation held in 1911, which while contradicting certain elements of the 1898 inquiry, endorsed the earlier conclusion that the *Maine* had been destroyed by an external explosion. Again, Rickover condemned the investigators' failure to rely upon technical experts in evaluating the accident.

Rickover's strong opinions on this latter point were brought to light in his response (published in the winter 1978 issue of the *Naval War College Review*) to a largely positive review of his study written by Graham A. Cosmas. Cosmas's assertion that although valuable, Rickover's study would "not radically alter the historiography of the coming of the Spanish American War," in that most historians have assumed the *Maine* was not destroyed by a mine, greatly angered Rickover. In his reply he noted that "between a close approach to truth and an assumption of probability there is a great distinction." Rickover went on to criticize professional historians for failing to focus on the important issues he raised in his technical study of the sinking of the *Maine*.

REFERENCES: Norman Polmar and Thomas B. Allen, *Rickover* (New York: Simon & Schuster, 1982); H. G. Rickover, *How the Battleship* Maine *Was Destroyed* (Washington, DC: Government Printing Office, 1976).

ALAN CORNISH

RIZAL, JOSÉ
(1861–1896)

José Rizal was born in the Philippines on 19 June 1861 to a Filipino father and a Chinese mother. The family was very well-to-do. Rizal's father managed a sugar plantation in Calamba, Lagunas Province. He leased the land from a local Dominican order. Rizal's mother had enjoyed the best in Roman Catholic convent education. They had great ambitions for their son and the money to fulfill many of them. José Rizal was educated at the Ateneo, a private secondary school, and at the University of St. Thomas in Manila. He then went on for postgraduate studies at the University of Madrid in Spain.

Prosperity did not, however, insulate the Rizal family from prejudice and discrimination. As mestizo people, they found themselves trapped in a social structure dominated by pure-blooded Spaniards. Top jobs in the imperial government, church, and military were reserved for men born in Spain. When Rizal was growing up, he frequently heard his parents express their frustration and outrage at the arrogance and power of the Spanish elite. They also harbored deep resentments toward Spanish priests, who often abused the Filipino peasants working church land. By the time he was a young man, José Rizal was already imbued with intense anti-Spanish attitudes and a budding sense of Filipino nationalism.

Rizal arrived at the University of Madrid in 1882 to continue his education. He quickly emerged as the political leader of Filipino students in Spain. Rizal traveled widely throughout Europe and the British Isles for the next five years, discussing politics with students and intellectuals in Germany, France, and England. He studied medicine at the University of Heidelberg in 1886 and completed his first novel, *Noli me Tangere,* a work considered seditious by Roman Catholic officials in the Philippines. He condemned the role of the Catholic Church in promoting Spanish imperialism. With the publication of the novel, Rizal found himself under surveillance by Spanish government agents, who even followed him home to the Philippines in 1887. He did not remain long in Manila, where imperial officials took a dim view of his political activities.

Back in Madrid, where Spanish liberals embraced him politically, Rizal continued to write. He edited a new edition of Antonio Marga's *Sucesos de las Islas Filipinas* (1890) and argued that long before Spain ever arrived in the Philippines, the islands had enjoyed a long, distinguished national history. In his second novel, *El Filibusterismo* (1891), and in dozens of articles in political journals, Rizal continued to promote Filipino nationalism, insisting on equality for Filipinos and demanding Filipino representation in the Spanish parliament. In 1892, upon his return to Manila, Rizal established the Liga Filipina,* a political action group that emphasized peaceful change. In spite of the conservative nature of Rizal's nationalism, Spanish officials reacted immediately, arresting Rizal and exiling him to Mindanao.

Rizal made good use of the four years he spent there. He practiced medicine, taught school, recorded his ethnographic observations, continued to write, and collected local specimens of flora and fauna. During his exile on Mindanao, Rizal was out of touch with the Filipino independence movement, which became increasingly violent and revolutionary. He outspokenly rejected the shift in tactics and goals, but when the rebellion against Spain erupted formally in 1896, Spanish authorities arrested him nonetheless. Convicted of sedition, he was executed by firing squad in Manila on 30 December 1896.

Rizal's fame continued to grow after his death. During the first several decades after the revolution, a number of millennial religious cults appeared in the Philippines. In the theology of many of them, Rizal assumed a larger-than-life stature, becoming a saint, a messiah, or even a god. After the Spanish American War and the U.S. purchase of the Philippines, Filipino nationalists reignited violent resistance. Americans saw to it that José Rizal's brand of nationalism—gradual, peaceful change—was emphasized in the schools as opposed to the more revolutionary approach of people like Emilio Aguinaldo* and Andrés Bonifacio.*

REFERENCES: Emilio Reyna, *Rizal: espíritu de libertad* (Havana: NP, 1958); Charles E. Russel, *The Hero of the Filipinos: The Story José Rizal* (New York: Century, 1923).

JAMES S. OLSON

ROOSEVELT, THEODORE
(1858–1919)

Theodore Roosevelt battled physical weakness by developing an affinity for rugged, athletic endeavors. Early in life he became politically active and also scholarly. Publishing the *Naval War of 1812* in 1882, he also became known as a reformer. Roosevelt's characteristic drive, flair for the dramatic, and profound abilities at self-promotion and high visibility served him well throughout his career. As president of New York City's Board of Police Commissioners, Roosevelt gained a reputation as a stalwart reformer and also came to the notice of William McKinley.* After McKinley was elected president, he appointed Roosevelt assistant secretary of the navy in 1897. In this post Roosevelt developed contacts with the foremost naval strategists of his day. He reviewed naval plans for a possible war with Spain, discussed scenarios with A. T. Mahan* and others, maneuvered to get George Dewey* appointed to the command of the Asiatic Squadron,* and in all things showed himself energetic, gregarious, and effective. To the occasional exasperation of his superior, John D. Long,* he also assumed his supervisor's authority from time to time or worked to fulfill his own personal agenda rather than Long's.

In May 1898 Roosevelt resigned from the Department of the Navy and joined Colonel Leonard Wood's* First U.S. Volunteer Cavalry. The Rough Riders,* as the unit was popularly known, was one of the few volunteer units that saw combat in Cuba. Shortly after arriving in Cuba, Roosevelt took over command of the Rough Riders, Wood having been promoted, and led the right wing of the attack on 1 July at San Juan Hill.* Roosevelt's ability to be seen as dashing gave him spectacular press, which he not only courted but enhanced through his own writings in periodicals and books.

Roosevelt was also a participant in the "Round Robin"* affair, which gave him further notoriety. His spectacular flair for publicity and his administrative acumen led him back into political life, and he became governor of New York, McKinley's vice-president, and upon the latter's death, president.

More than any other individual, including even, President McKinley, Roosevelt has been associated with the Spanish American War—largely because of the publicity and tales he himself generated.

REFERENCE: Theodore Roosevelt, *The Rough Riders* (New York: Charles Scribner's Sons, 1899).

ROOT, ELIHU
(1845–1937)

Born in Clinton, New York, Elihu Root achieved an education and eventually was admitted to the bar. Root's role in the Spanish American War was minimal, but he was a man of accomplishment, and after successfully defending Theodore Roosevelt* in an 1898 tax case, he was also a man with significant political connections. President William McKinley* appointed him secretary of war. After the scandals and criticisms of his predecessor Russell A. Alger,* Root had the opportunity to work reforms and develop planning to upgrade the National Guard* to federal standards.

REFERENCE: Philip C. Jessup, *Elihu Root,* 2 vols. (New York: Dodd, Mead, 1938).

ROUGH RIDERS

The First U.S. Volunteer Cavalry, popularly called the Rough Riders, clearly became the most romantic and visible unit of the Spanish American War. Much of this fame was attributed to Theodore Roosevelt,* who served under Colonel Leonard Wood,* the commander of the unit. Roosevelt wrote voluminously and enthusiastically of the exploits of the unit, which originally was to be raised from the Indian Territory, New Mexico, Arizona, and Oklahoma. However, such was the enthusiasm for the war and Roosevelt's magnetism that the unit became an interesting mix of eastern establishment bluebloods, cowboys, Ivy League Club athletes, Indian fighters, New York City police men, glee-club singers, Texas Rangers, and Indians. Wood and Roosevelt quickly organized and outfitted this group. In fact, they were so successful that the Rough Riders became one of the few volunteer units to see action. Marshalling and training at Camp San Antonio, Texas, the unit was ordered on 30 May 1898 to Tampa.* On 13 June 1898 the Rough Riders sailed for Santiago de Cuba.* They joined Fifth Corps,* which was composed of the elite of the regular army and volunteers. Each of the units was highly trained, motivated, and well equipped compared to the other corps.

The Rough Riders distinguished themselves at Las Guásimas* and also the Battle of San Juan Hill.* These exploits were written in epic style by Roosevelt and others and also immortalized graphically by illustrators like Howard Chandler Christy.* The Rough Riders thus became—rather than a footnote in history—the stuff of folklore and legend.

REFERENCE: Theodore Roosevelt, *The Rough Riders* (New York: Charles Scribner's Sons, 1899).

"ROUND ROBIN"

The successes at Santiago* and Manila* had kept the American public buoyed in the glamour of war. But after these events passed, the very real issues of the health of America's sons captured headlines and held them. Yellow fever,* malaria,* and other diseases represented a threat more potent and insidious than any Spanish force. The journalists initiated a crescendo of stories of camp conditions and disease that struck at the emotional vitals of a country proud of the soldiers' efforts. The truly sad part is that much of what the journalists wrote had a basis in truth. There were messages of dire warning sent by General William R. Shafter* to the War Department on 2 and 3 August. To underline the divisional commanders' concern, a letter was drafted expressing that unless the Fifth Corps* were removed at once, it would be annihilated by disease. The letter was signed, round robin style, by nine generals and Theodore Roosevelt.* This "Round Robin," as it came to be called, was somehow leaked to the press* and caused Secretary of War Russell A. Alger* great concern and difficulty. The leak has been attributed to Roosevelt, but no one knows for sure. The effect of the Round Robin was to inflame public sentiment against the War Department.*

REFERENCE: Charles H. Brown, *The Correspondents' War* (New York: Scribner's, 1967).

ROWAN, ANDREW SUMMERS
(1857–1943)

Andrew Summers Rowan was born in what is now Gap Mills, West Virginia, and graduated from West Point in 1881. He was assigned in 1893 to the Military Information Division* of the U.S. Army and became map section chief before the commencement of hostilities with Spain. Like H. H. Whitney,* in Puerto Rico,* Rowan was inserted into Spanish-held areas to gather intelligence. He was a likely choice for the mission, having studied Cuba and even written a book about the island. He joined a group of Cuban insurgents* in Jamaica and secretly made his way to Cuba to meet with insurgent general Calixto García,* who furnished Rowan with maps and intelligence. Rowan departed Cuba accompanied by insurgent officers who would help coordinate insurgent efforts with the expeditionary force then forming in the United States. Thus Rowan's intelligence operation* provided the basic information for the Military Information Division's planning and briefings for the landings of June 1898. Rowan received the Distinguished Service Cross for his efforts in Cuba. Upon his return he served on General Nelson A. Miles's* staff when the latter landed in Puerto Rico* in July.

Rowan's exploits in Cuba became the subject of Elbert Hubbard's* stirring but factually incorrect "Message to García."*

REFERENCES: Bruce W. Bidwell, *History of the Military Intelligence Division, Department of the Army General Staff: 1775–1941* (Frederick, MD: University Publications of America, 1986); G.J.A. O'Toole, *The Spanish War* (New York: W. W. Norton & Co., 1984).

RUBÍN, ANTERO
(1853–?)

Spanish general Antero Rubín commanded about 1,500 troops along the road that ran from Siboney* to Santiago de Cuba.* After a skirmish with Cuban insurgents,* Rubín's forces dug in along a ridge. This was the force that awaited the Americans at the so-called Battle of Las Guásimas.* Rubín executed a withdrawal the Americans believed was a retreat, leading to erroneous claims of a great victory at Las Guásimas.

REFERENCE: French Ensor Chadwick, *The Relations of the United States and Spain* (New York: Russell & Russell, 1968).

S

SAGASTA, PRÁXEDES MATEO
(1827–1903)

Práxedes Mateo Sagasta came from a family of modest means, but he associated himself early with reform and progressive politics in Spain. He worked to develop a coalition after the Restoration of 1875 and, with António Cánovas del Castillo,* traded leadership of the government in amicable fashion. Upon the death of Cánovas on 8 August 1897, María Cristina, queen regent of Spain, recalled Sagasta to power. He was the head of the Spanish government during the hostilities of 1898.

Sagasta attempted numerous reforms to defuse the Cuban Insurrection.* One of them was a policy of autonomy* for Cuba and for Puerto Rico.* He also promulgated an armistice in Cuba and recalled General Valeriano Weyler,* replacing him with the less flammatory Ramón Blanco y Erenas.*

During the war, Sagasta adopted delaying tactics in an attempt to gain time as well as support for European initiatives to end the conflict. Early defeat at Manila* precipitated a crisis in Sagasta's government that necessitated its reorganization. Sagasta also agreed to sending Admiral Pascual Cervera* to Cuba with a Spanish squadron to battle the U.S. blockade.* The failure of Cervera at Santiago de Cuba* and American army successes at San Juan* convinced Sagasta that peace negotiations* had to commence. He chose his representatives for the Peace Commission and instructed them during the proceedings. The ignominy of the loss of Spain's empire weighed heavily upon Sagasta; the criticism intensely affected him. The last few years of his life were spent completely outside the Spanish political arena.

REFERENCE: René Torres Delgado, *La influencia sagastina en la política* (San Juan: Sociedad Histórica de Puerto Rico, 1987).

ST. LOUIS (ship)

Several merchant auxiliaries* were either hired or purchased outright for the use of the navies during the Spanish American War. *St. Louis* and *St. Paul** were sister-ships, liners, leased by the U.S. Navy as fast scout cruisers in Cuban waters. *St. Louis,* of 1,629 tons, had been launched in 1895 and was taken over by the navy from April through October 1898. Because of her speed (20 knots plus), Admiral William T. Sampson* used her for extensive scout work, particularly while searching for Admiral Pascual Cervera's* squadron. During the month of June *St. Louis* performed cable-cutting duties at Caimanera* and Guantánamo.* The liner also carried troops and supplies, and performed other auxiliary work for the expeditionary forces on Cuba.

In addition, *St. Louis* cut cables at San Juan* and Ponce* in Puerto Rico.* She was accompanied in these efforts by *Marblehead** and *Yankee.**

St. Louis was broken up in 1924.

REFERENCE: Frederick E. Emmons, *American Passenger Ships* (Newark: University of Delaware Press, 1985).

ST. PAUL (ship)

St. Paul and *St. Louis** were sister-ships leased to the U.S. Navy during the Spanish American War. *St. Paul* served from May through September 1898, and like her sister was armed with eight 5-inch guns and eight 6-pounders.

St. Paul served in the Caribbean as a fast scout ship to locate Admiral Pascual Cervera's* fleet. On 25 May 1898 it captured the British collier *Restormel** laden with coal for Cervera's fleet. Information from the *Restormel*'s British officers could have provided valuable intelligence for Commodore Winfield S. Schley* and the Flying Squadron.* However, the information was miscommunicated or misunderstood.

On 22 June the Spanish torpedo boat* destroyer *Terror** and *Isabel II,* a small unprotected sloop, attacked *St. Paul* off San Juan,* Puerto Rico.* *St. Paul* struck *Terror*'s steering gear, jamming the rudder. As the Spanish ship turned, giving her starboard side to *St. Paul,* the latter fired a 5-inch shell that struck *Terror* about 12 inches above the water line, wrecking the starboard engine and killing five men and wounding several others. The shell exited below the water line on the port side, and *Terror* began to sink. Running for the port as fast as her other undamaged engine could take her, the ship was in serious danger of capsizing; so her commander beached her on Puntilla shoals. *Isabel II* declined to engage *St. Paul* and returned to port.

After the war *St. Paul* resumed passenger service. In 1908 she collided with and sank the H.M.S. *Gladiator* in the Solent. She was scrapped at Wilhelmshaven, Germany,* in October 1923.

REFERENCES: Frederick E. Emmons, *American Passenger Ships* (Newark: University of Delaware Press, 1985); H. W. Wilson, *The Downfall of Spain* (New York: Burt Franklin, 1971).

SALISBURY, ROBERT CECIL, MARQUESS OF
(1830–1903)

As prime minister and also foreign minister of Great Britain,* Robert Cecil, the Marquess of Salisbury, counseled strict neutrality in the face of a brewing Spanish American War. Great Britain's reluctance to form a joint European overture to halt the war ensured that Spain would receive no material aid from adjoining monarchies. In June 1898 Salisbury offered to carry peace initiatives; John Hay* politely declined Salisbury's offer, indicating that such should come from Spain. María Cristina,* queen regent of Spain, hinted to Salisbury that some land concessions might be forthcoming if Great Britain could negotiate a peace initiative from among Germany,* France, Austria, and others. Salisbury, however, saw no profit in such a move and declined.

REFERENCE: Robert G. Taylor, *Lord Salisbury* (New York: St. Martin's Press, 1975).

SAMOA

An island group in the South Pacific, the Samoas (there are about ten inhabited islands) do not strictly or technically belong within the purview of the Spanish American War. Nevertheless, the diplomatic jousting whereby the islands were divided between Germany* and the United States (Great Britain* relinquished claims in exchange for several Tongan Islands) grew directly out of the negotiations that embroiled these nations upon the breakup of Spain's empire. The American involvement grew out of the need for coaling* and cable stations, which *did* develop in the Spanish American War.

REFERENCE: Alfred L. P. Dennis, *Adventures in American Diplomacy, 1896–1906* (New York: E. P. Dutton, 1928).

SAMPSON, WILLIAM THOMAS
(1840–1902)

A naval officer whose distinguished career began at the U.S. Naval Academy in 1857, William Thomas Sampson served in numerous posts and positions within the U.S. naval establishment for forty years. He was born on 9 February 1840 in Palmyra, New York. Bright, dedicated, and studious, he graduated first in his class from the Naval Academy in 1861. He served for a time as an instructor at the Naval Academy, transferring to Newport, Rhode Island, where he was promoted to lieutenant in 1862.

Sampson's only combat action during the Civil War was as a junior officer serving aboard U.S.S. *Patapsco,* which was part of the Union navy's South Atlantic blockading squadron. He narrowly escaped death when the ship blew up after hitting a Confederate mine in Charleston Harbor, South Carolina, in January 1865. After the war he served in the European Squadron, attaining the rank of lieutenant commander in 1866.

Over the next twenty years of service in U.S. Navy, Sampson established himself as an educator, reformer, administrator, and technological innovator. He served two more terms as instructor at the Naval Academy, 1868–1871 and

1874–1878, the latter as head of the Physics Department. He was promoted to the rank of commander in August 1874. Sampson stressed the hard sciences, mathematics, and engineering in his academic work and as superintendent of the Naval Academy, to which post he was named in September 1886. Previous service included the Asiatic Squadron, where he commanded U.S.S. *Swatara;* two years as superintendent of the Naval Observatory in Washington, D.C. (1882–1884); and commander of the naval torpedo station at Newport, Rhode Island (1884–1886). Sampson was chief of the Bureau of Ordnance from 1893 to 1897; there, his administrative skills and expertise helped bring about innovations in gunnery training and gun design for naval ships. Smokeless gunpowder was also introduced during his tenure.

He received command of the battleship *Iowa** in 1897 on the eve of the war with Spain. After the U.S.S. *Maine** exploded in Havana Harbor on 16 February 1898, President William McKinley* sent a naval board of investigation to Cuba. Sampson served as board president. The board's final report concluded that the Spanish were the culprits. However, modern investigations into the destruction of the *Maine* have generally concluded that the blast was caused by accident, not by an act of sabotage. In late March 1898 Sampson was elevated to the position of acting rear admiral in command of the North Atlantic Squadron* to replace the ailing Montgomery Sicard.* Sampson was promoted over other more senior officers, Winfield S. Schley* among them, which occasioned some tension. When war was declared, Sampson set out to Havana with his squadron to implement a blockade* of the north coast of Cuba. He was also under orders to locate and engage Admiral Pascual Cervera's* cruisers and destroyers.

Leaving several ships to hold the blockade, Sampson cruised east to Puerto Rico.* On 12 May he bombarded the city of San Juan,* after which he returned to the blockade, joined by Commodore Schley and the Flying Squadron.* Sampson sent Schley to reinforce the blockade at Cienfuegos* and Santiago* and to gather intelligence on the movements of Admiral Cervera's fleet. Schley steamed to Cienfuegos on 12 May, and after receiving information from Sampson that Cervera had actually landed at Santiago, he hesitated. Sampson had not trusted his intelligence and passed on a rather vague order for Schley to proceed to blockade Santiago. Compounding this situation, Schley had his own idea of Cervera's whereabouts and acted upon it: He decided his squadron would leave Santiago and steam back to Cienfuegos. For disobeying orders, Schley was almost removed from command by Navy Secretary John D. Long.*

When Cervera was reported at Santiago, Sampson concentrated his forces there to support General William R. Shafter's* landing at Daiquirí* and subsequent land operations at Siboney* and San Juan on 1 July. Early in the morning of 3 July, Sampson steamed eastward in *New York** for a conference with Shafter. Shortly after *New York*'s departure to the east, Cervera sailed from Santiago heading west. As the nominal commander in the absence of Sampson, Schley spurred the U.S. squadron in pursuit of Cervera's squadron. In just a few hours all of Cervera's ships were sunk. Sampson was unable to join the action, yet the Navy Department, a later U.S. Naval Court of Inquiry, and even President Theodore Roosevelt* credited Sampson's discipline, planning, and professionalism with the victory. Schley, however, was lionized by the popular press and a running Sampson-Schley Controversy* raged for several years.

Sampson was one of the three commissioners who governed Cuba until December 1898, when he resumed his command of the squadron. Promoted to rear admiral the following March, Sampson suffered from failing health and died in 1902.

It is unfortunate that Sampson is remembered, if at all, for the fracas with Schley. Sampson was a progressive reformer who reveled in professionalism and technological innovation. His contributions as a reformer, leader, and naval educator were substantial, yet they were overshadowed by the controversy that flamed at the end of his career.

REFERENCES: Joseph G. Dawson III, "William T. Sampson and Santiago: Blockade, Victory, and Controversy," in James C. Bradford, ed., *Crucible of Empire* (Annapolis, MD: Naval Institute Press, 1993); William Athelstane Meredith Goode, *With Sampson through the War* (New York: Doubleday & McClure, 1899).

RICHARD W. PEUSER

SAMPSON-SCHLEY CONTROVERSY

Rear Admiral William T. Sampson* and Commodore Winfield S. Schley* became the celebrated objects of a media debate, a professional debate within the U.S. Navy, and the principals in a personal feud that carried on well into the twentieth century.

Sampson was appointed commander of the North Atlantic Squadron* over several senior captains, Schley included. Schley commanded the Flying Squadron,* which was placed under Sampson's command for the blockade* of Cuba. Wartime communication problems and perhaps intransigence caused Schley to delay leaving Cienfuegos* for Santiago,* thereby missing the arrival of Admiral Pascual Cervera* and his Spanish squadron.

Irritation between the two commanders erupted into anger, professional jealousy, and eventually bitterness. When Sampson sailed on 3 July to confer with General William R. Shafter,* in the *opposite* direction from Cervera's escape attempt later the same morning, the seeds of discord became manifest. It was Schley—not Sampson—who was the commander during the famous running battle that annihilated the Spanish force.

Schley was eager to accept credit for the victory, and much of the media accorded the victory to Schley. However, the navy hierarchy and Sampson himself argued that since the plans and standing orders emanated from Sampson, he should be accorded the honor. The chief impact of this debate, which escalated from bickering to a full-blown inquiry, was to tarnish the honorable careers of two officers.

REFERENCES: Joseph G. Dawson III, "William T. Sampson and Santiago: Blockade, Victory, and Controversy," in James C. Bradford, ed., *Crucible of Empire* (Annapolis,

MD: Naval Institute Press, 1993); Harold D. Langley, ''Winfield S. Schley and Santiago: A New Look at an Old Controversy,'' in *Crucible of Empire; Record of Proceedings of a Court of Inquiry in the Case of Rear Admiral Winfield S. Schley,* 2 vols. (Washington, DC: Government Printing Office, 1902).

SANDOVAL (ship)

The 100-ton Spanish gunboat *Sandoval* defended the bay of Guantánamo* against U.S.S. *Texas,* *Marblehead,* *Yankee,* *St. Louis,* and *Suwanee.* Some thirty-five mines had been sown across the entrance of Guantánamo Harbor. Nevertheless, when *Texas* and *Marblehead* snared their propellers in the cables, they were able to extricate themselves. None of the mines exploded.

Sandoval was scuttled by the Spanish but seized by U.S. forces on 17 July 1898 and subsequently salvaged and used for training for several years thereafter. *Sandoval* and her sister-ship, *Alvarado,** had been built in Great Britain for the Spanish navy and launched in 1895. In 1919, the U.S. Navy sold *Sandoval* and she became a private yacht.

REFERENCE: Augustín Rodríguez González, ''Operaciones menores en Cuba, 1898,'' *Revista de Historia Naval* 3 (September 1985): 125–146.

SAN FRANCISCO, CALIFORNIA

San Francisco was the port of assembly and embarkation for Eighth Corps,* General Wesley Merritt's* command, which was built of regular units ordered to the Presidio on 6 May 1898. Eventually it became the corps that Merritt was appointed to command on 29 May.

San Francisco also served as entrepôt for supplies going to the Philippines. Besides the Presidio, the Bay boasted the Mare Island Naval Station.* *Oregon** began its illustrious passage from San Francisco on 19 March, and coastal defense monitors* *Monterey** and *Monadnock** steamed from the Bay to strengthen George Dewey's* victorious Asiatic Squadron* at Manila.*

REFERENCE: *Correspondence Relating to the War with Spain,* 2 vols. (Washington, DC: Government Printing Office, 1902).

SANITATION IN ARMY CAMPS

Besieged Spanish cities such as Santiago de Cuba* or Manila* had their own sanitation problems as old as the history of warfare itself. Equally old were the problems of U.S. Army camps.* Since sanitation challenges were of ancient origin, why the inordinate criticism of the War Department* relating to matters of sanitation and military health? The answer is deceptively simple: By 1898 there existed not only the means but the public expectation of better sanitation. Second, significant public debate raged over the failings of Russell A. Alger* and the department he headed; sanitation became another arrow in the quiver of his enemies. Third, the positive experience of Major General Fitzhugh Lee* with Seventh Corps* near Jacksonville,* showed what could be done with experienced and enlightened leadership.

REFERENCES: Walter Reed et al., *Abstract of Report on the Origin and Spread of Typhoid Fever in U.S. Military Camps during the Spanish War of 1898* (Washington, DC: Government Printing Office, 1900); *Report of the Commission Appointed by the President to Investigate the Conduct of the War Department in the War with Spain,* 8 vols. (Washington, DC: Government Printing Office, 1900).

SAN JUAN, CUBA

San Juan lies on the outskirts of Santiago.* At this location occurred the principal land battle of the Spanish American War. General William R. Shafter's* Fifth Corps* began to land at Daiquirí* on 22 June 1898 for an overland assault on Santiago. After a brief skirmish on 24 June at Las Guásimas,* Shafter's force continued to advance toward Santiago in a westerly direction.

Brigadier General Jacob Ford Kent* led his First Division on the southern flank toward San Juan Hill. To the north was Brigadier General Samuel S. Sumner's* dismounted cavalry and John Coulter Bates's* Independent Brigade in support of Brigadier General Henry W. Lawton*'s Second Division. These would attack El Caney,* which was on the road to Guantánamo.* The attack would further safeguard against a flank attack by the Spanish at Santiago. Defended by General Joaquín Vara del Rey* and 500 troops, El Caney proved a stubborn opponent, and in the battle of 1 July Shafter was unable to get past San Juan. He incurred some 1,600 casualties. San Juan and Kettle hills were reinforced by Spanish general Arsenio Linares.* Theodore Roosevelt's* Rough Riders* distinguished themselves in the battle (largely through Roosevelt's own writing) and moved on to San Juan Hill. At the conclusion of the battle, the Americans rested, much of the fight in them dissipated. Shafter felt that Lawton's failure to take El Caney was the reason the army could not press on to Santiago proper. Linares was also criticized for failing to meet the U.S. force with sufficient counterforce. After the battles near San Juan there developed an American siege of Santiago intending to starve out the Spanish. The battle at San Juan had convinced Shafter that to take Santiago required 15,000 more troops. Colonel Federico Escario* had arrived with a relief force, but rather than provide relief, his presence accentuated the shortages. Cervera was gone, and insurgents* controlled the countryside. There would be no resupply. Finding resistance pointless, General José Toral* agreed to a surrender of Santiago on 17 July.

REFERENCES: John B. Atkins, *The War in Cuba* (London: Smith, Elder & Co., 1899) (an Englishman's view of the war); *Report of the Commission Appointed by the President to Investigate the Conduct of the War Department in the War with Spain,* 8 vols. (Washington, DC: Government Printing Office, 1900); Herbert H. Sargent, *The Campaign of Santiago,* 3 vols. (Chicago: A. C. McClurg, 1907).

SAN JUAN, PUERTO RICO

A minor element in the Spanish American War, San Juan was bombarded by Rear Admiral William T. Sampson* on 12 May 1898. Sampson had steamed to waters near Puerto Rico looking for Spanish admiral Pascual Cervera.* There was no discernible damage to San Juan's fortifications.

San Juan also served as one of the early objectives of General Nelson A. Miles's* expeditionary force to Puerto Rico. Originally intending to land near the city, Miles felt the Spanish expected him there and so he opted for a landing at Ponce.* The armistice halted hostilities before Miles's troops reached San Juan.

REFERENCE: French Ensor Chadwick, *The Relations of the United States and Spain* (New York: Russell & Russell, 1968).

SAN JUAN HILL.
See SAN JUAN, CUBA.

SANTIAGO.
See SANTIAGO DE CUBA.

SANTIAGO BAY.
See SANTIAGO DE CUBA.

SANTIAGO DE CUBA

Santiago was the second largest city of the island of Cuba. A major seaport closer to Haiti* than Havana,* it lies on the southeast underside of the island just north of Jamaica. Nearby are Cabañas,* Siboney,* Daiquirí,* Las Guási-mas,* and Guantánamo,* which lies less than 50 miles to the east.

In initial planning, even before the war, Santiago was not a primary target of offensive action. It became a strategic target only as a result of naval actions, primarily Spain's. Santiago was never part of the U.S. blockade* of Cuba, for example; the original target was Havana,* the seat of Spanish power in Cuba. American attention shifted from Havana to Santiago when Spanish admiral Pascual Cervera* arrived at Santiago early in the morning of 19 May 1898. His squadron consisted of *Infanta María Teresa,* *Vizcaya,* *Almirante Oquendo,* *Cristóbal Colón,* and the torpedo boats *Furor* and *Plutón.* Although insurgents* and agents in an intelligence operation* in Havana cabled the news to the White House on the same day, confusion and delays kept U.S. forces from taking advantage of this information until Commodore Winfield S. Schley's* Flying Squadron* was able to effect a blockade of Santiago on 28 May. Eventually *Indiana,* *Oregon,* *Iowa,* *Texas,* *Brooklyn,* *Gloucester,* and *Vixen* participated in the sea battle of Santiago. *New York* was absent with Acting Rear Admiral William T. Sampson.* Other American ships such as *Vesuvius* and *Ericsson* came and went for bombardment duty, picket duty, and so on. R. P. Hobson,* with a skeleton crew of volunteers, steamed *Merrimac* into Santiago and sank his ship in a failed attempt to block the channel. Santiago presented a formidable aspect to assault by sea: Morro Castle and Heights* had a battery that commanded the eastern entrance while the Socapa batteries menaced from the west. Inside the channel were Punta Gorda* and the Estrella batteries. The presence of Cervera, the decision in Washington to pursue a potentially less bloody land war (Santiago instead of even stronger Havana), and the defenses of Santiago tilted toward the decision to attack Santiago by land.

The U.S. Army Fifth Corps*, commanded by General William R. Shafter,* assembled at Tampa* and on 22 June began to disembark its transports near Daiquirí for the overland advance on Santiago. The skirmish at Las Guásimas on 24 June was the first action in which Theodore Roosevelt's* Rough Riders* participated. The Spanish force at Las Guásimas made an orderly withdrawal, but the Americans considered the apparent retreat a victory and it was so reported in the newspapers. On 1 July the Fifth Corps advanced on a broad front toward Kettle Hill,* San Juan Heights,* and on the right flank, El Caney.* Spanish general Arsenio Linares* and his troops put up a stubborn defense that cost the Fifth Corps some 1,600 casualties. Nonetheless, Linares knew his situation was desperate: Insurgents kept succor from reaching him overland, and the blockade stopped ocean-borne resupply.

Meanwhile, on 26 June Governor-General Ramón Blanco y Erenas* committed Cervera's squadron to a sortie. The loss of San Juan Heights on 1 July exacerbated Spanish tensions, and at 7 P.M. on 2 July Cervera gave orders for his ships to attempt a breakout the next morning. Personally opposed to the sortie and fearing the worst, Cervera decided to make his run to the west. Several U.S. ships were missing from the blockade: *New Orleans,* *Newark,* *Suwanee,** and *Massachusetts** were coaling at Guantánamo to the east. *New York* (with Sampson aboard), the armed yacht *Hist,** and torpedo boat *Ericsson** also steamed east to Siboney for Sampson's conference with Shafter. Even with these absences, Cervera's squadron of four armored cruisers and two torpedo boats faced four battleships, two armored cruisers, a torpedo boat and three yachts converted to gunboats. All the Spanish ships were sunk or beached by 1:30 P.M.

Except for minor skirmishes, the battle for Santiago was over. The Spanish surrendered on 17 July 1898.

REFERENCES: Jack Cameron Dierks, *A Leap to Arms* (Philadelphia: J. B. Lippincott, 1970); David F. Trask, *The War with Spain in 1898* (New York: Macmillan Publishing Co., 1981).

SANTO DOMINGO (ship)

Santo Domingo was a Spanish merchant ship acting in Cuban waters. She was involved in two incidents that bring her to historical attention. While Admiral Pascual Cervera's* Spanish squadron lay at Santiago* facing certain defeat in the face of overwhelming U.S. naval forces and the 22 June 1898 American landing at Daiquirí* presaged further complications, Cervera received a message from the Spanish ministry of the marine ordering him to sally from Santiago. Governor-General Ramón Blanco y Erenas,* himself a supporter of Cervera's early departure, through a wire to General Arsenio Linares y Pomba* encouraged Cervera to make the sortie. Blanco believed the sortie feasible inasmuch as *Santo Domingo* and *Montevideo* had had no difficulty running the blockade* on 24 June at 2 A.M.

The second incident with *Santo Domingo* occurred off Mangle Point, southwest Cuba, on 12 July. The U.S.S. *Eagle** chased *Santo Domingo,* and the latter, in her haste to escape, ran aground about 2 miles from Piedras Point. While *Eagle* was picking her way through the shoals, a white side-wheel river steamer approached from a nearby town and took off *Santo Domingo*'s crew. *Eagle* fired a warning shot, and the steamer retired rapidly. *Eagle* then fired 104 6-pounder rounds into *Santo Domingo* without receiving a reply. Boarding the vessel, *Eagle*'s men discovered 4.72-inch rifled guns and ammunition (never fired), steam at 170 pounds' pressure, the ship packed with foodstuffs and blankets (even the staterooms), and the midday meal served but partially eaten. Clearly, the crew abandoned *Santo Domingo* in great haste. What has never been explained is that *Eagle,* a converted yacht,* was armed only with 6-pounders while *Santo Domingo* was more formidably armed with the above-mentioned rifled guns, yet the Spanish crew made no use of them.

REFERENCE: *Appendix to the Report of the Chief of the Bureau of Navigation, 1898* (Washington, DC: Government Printing Office, 1898).

SCHLEY, WINFIELD SCOTT
(1839–1909)

A native of Maryland, Winfield Scott Schley graduated from the Naval Academy at Annapolis in 1860. Schley saw action at Mobile during the Civil War and survived the war a lieutenant. After the war he had a variety of duties: at the Naval Academy; at sea, including command of the *Baltimore* during a crisis in Valparaiso when two sailors were killed by a Chilean mob; and on shore, as lighthouse inspector. In February 1898 Schley was promoted to commodore and placed in command of the Flying Squadron.*

The Flying Squadron's mission was to attack the Spanish squadron of Admiral Pascual Cervera.* In May 1898 it was ascertained that Cervera was moving to the Caribbean, possibly to Cuba. Schley was ordered to place his squadron under the command of William T. Sampson,* nominally Schley's junior, for blockade duty of Cuba. On 18 May Sampson ordered Schley to blockade Cienfuegos* and Santiago.* For a variety of logistic problems and owing to communications failures, Schley was unable to move quickly, and Cervera anchored in Santiago Harbor on 19 May. Schley did not arrive at Santiago until 26 May and did not discover Cervera's presence until 29 May. Schley assumed blockade duty under Sampson off Santiago.

On 3 July Sampson sailed eastward from Santiago to rendezvous with General William R. Shafter.* Cervera coincidentally left harbor in single file steaming west; by default, Schley became the commander of the U.S. forces in a running sea battle. Sampson had issued standing orders in the event of action, and the running battle off Santiago was a melee in which all Spanish ships were destroyed. Furthermore, Schley neither issued any special commands nor exerted special authority during the battle. In fact, he turned *Brooklyn** in a tight circle away from Cervera's ships and opposite the direction of the rest of the squadron. As a result of this action, *Texas** had to maneuver sharply to avoid collision. This event was the source of much comment and criticism later.

Because of the engagement's success and Sampson's untimely absence, the press* accorded Schley the victory. Professional and personal pride in both men created an acrimonious rift, the Sampson-Schley Controversy,* which was still raging years later. Eventually the debate unfortunately overshadowed every aspect of Schley's career as well as Sampson's.

REFERENCES: George Edward Graham, *Schley and Santiago* (Chicago: W. B. Conkey, 1902); Harold D. Langley, "Winfield S. Schley and Santiago: A New Look at an Old Controversy," in James C. Bradford, ed., *Crucible of Empire* (Annapolis, MD: Naval Institute Press, 1993); *Record of Proceeding of a Court of Inquiry in the Case of Rear Admiral Winfield S. Schley,* 2 vols. (Washington, DC: Government Printing Office, 1902); Winfield Scott Schley, *Forty-five Years under the Flag* (New York: D. Appleton, 1904).

SCHOFIELD, JOHN MCALLISTER
(1831–1906)

Graduated from West Point in 1853, John McAllister Schofield was commissioned in the artillery. He saw much action in the Civil War, serving with William T. Sherman in Atlanta and with George Thomas in Tennessee. He was a brigadier general of regulars and brevet major general by 1865. Schofield served as secretary of war under President Andrew Johnson. He enjoyed a variety of commands, ultimately becoming commanding general of the army in 1888, a post he held until 1895, when he retired as a lieutenant general.

Schofield understood well the political ramifications of high command and was one of the principal reformers of the 1870s and 1880s who argued for a chief of staff. During his seven-year tenure as commanding general, he worked diligently to put his ideas into practice.

After retirement General Schofield continued to be active. In 1897 he called for war with Spain or at least intervention in Cuba to halt the suffering there and restore economic order. President William McKinley,* who did not trust Schofield's successor, General Nelson Miles,* relied on Schofield for advice in the preliminary crises with Spain. Schofield thus became an unofficial presidential advisor. It was Schofield, in April 1898 who urged the president to dramatically increase the size of the army by over 125,000 men. This was done to appease the National Guard* and to gain passage of the Hull Bill,* which would allow needed army reorganization and growth.

At this point Schofield's presence began to be disruptive. Already ignored by Secretary of War Russell A. Alger* and by Miles, Schofield lost favor with McKinley, who also began to turn to others for advice. Schofield left Washington in June but maintained contact with McKinley. Approached after the war about serving on a war investigation commission, he declined, since he did not see opportunity for reform. General Grenville M. Dodge* headed the commission.

REFERENCES: *Army Reorganization* (Washington, DC: Government Printing Office, 1898); Graham A. Cosmas, *An Army for Empire* (Columbia: University of Missouri Press, 1971); John M. Schofield, *Forty-six Years in the Army* (New York: Century, 1897).

SCHWAN, THEODORE
(1841–1926)

Theodore Schwan came to the United States from Germany in 1857. He enlisted in the army and served throughout the Civil War, being brevetted captain in 1864. He was awarded the Medal of Honor in 1898 for Civil War service in Virginia.

He was appointed brigadier general of volunteers on 4 May 1898. Serving under General Nelson A. Miles,* Schwan commanded the western column in the campaign in Puerto Rico* during the Spanish American War. Schwan arrived at Ponce* from Tampa* on 30 July aboard the transport *Cherokee*. On 6 August Schwan marched with 1,447 troops to Guánica.* From there he was to pass through San Germán and Hormigueros to Mayagüez.* Schwan fought his first skirmish at Hormigueros on 10 August. He pushed on toward Arecibo,* but the peace protocol intervened on 12 August.

Schwan later served in the Philippines and was promoted to major general in 1916.

REFERENCE: Ángel Rivero Méndez, *Crónica de la Guerra Hispano Americana en Puerto Rico* (New York: Plus Ultra, 1973).

SCORPION (ship)

The 775-ton *Scorpion,* formerly the yacht *Sovereign,* was built in 1896 for M. C. Borden and purchased by the U.S. Navy on 7 April 1898. Armed with six 6-pounders and four 5-inch rifles, *Scorpion* joined the Flying Squadron* and participated in the blockade* of Cuba. *Scorpion* was also used as a dispatch and scout vessel and as escort for supply vessels. On 22 June *Scorpion* assisted the landing of American expeditionary forces at Daiquirí* by clearing the beach. On 1 July *Scorpion* and *Osceola** accompanied by *Wilmington** arrived off Manzanillo* and attacked Spanish gunboats. Direct fire was brought to bear against the four Spanish gunboats, and *Scorpion* was so close inshore that sharpshooters attempted to pick off individual Spanish officers on horseback. *Scorpion* suffered no casualties nor was she hit in this engagement.

After Manzanillo *Scorpion* returned to Guantánamo* to refuel and serve as dispatch vessel. She was decommissioned in 1927.

REFERENCE: *Appendix to the Report of the Chief of the Bureau of Navigation, 1898* (Washington, DC: Government Printing Office, 1898).

SCOVEL, HENRY SYLVESTER
(1869–1905)

Henry Sylvester Scovel was a leading war correspondent in Cuba who several times was the center of highly publicized escapades resulting from his aggressive style of journalism. Born in Allegheny County, Pennsylvania, he was trained as an engineer and spent several years after college working in that profession. In 1895, apparently due to his reputation as an aggressive promoter, he obtained a position as a correspondent in Cuba for the *Pittsburgh Dispatch* and the *New York Herald.* After spending about six months with rebel leader Máximo Gómez* in the eastern part of the island, he returned to Havana,* where Spanish authorities ordered him to leave the island. United States officials were also displeased at his contact with the Cuban insurgents* at a time when the United States was officially neutral. Scovel, however, seemed to have ignored instructions to leave; as a result of his notoriety from this episode, he was hired by Joseph Pulitzer's* *New York World.*

He was again behind insurgent lines by early the next year and spent a total of about ten months with the guerrillas during 1896. After only a short time back in New York, in early 1897 he slipped back onto the island to Máximo Gómez, vying with the *Herald* correspondent George Bronson Rea* to locate Gómez first. Although Rea located the general before Scovel and sent back the story first, Scovel met with the insurgent forces shortly thereafter. On 19 January the *World* published Scovel's interview with Gómez in which the general rejected the recent Cuban autonomy* proposal brought forward by the Spanish prime minister, Antonio Cánovas del Castillo.* By this time the Spanish governor of Cuba, Valeriano Weyler y Nicolau,* had posted a reward for Scovel's capture. While attempting to send dispatches out of Cuba by boat from the southern port of Las Tunas in early February, Scovel was arrested for communicating with the enemy and other related offenses.

The *World* exploited his imprisonment to the fullest, helping to create public pressure for the U.S. action against the Spanish. Governor Weyler released Scovel from prison on orders from Madrid, where there was worry over possible U.S. government involvement in Cuba. When Scovel returned to the United States, he was America's most celebrated correspondent.

After several other overseas assignments in 1897, Scovel was sent back to Cuba late in the year as tensions between the United States and Spain again began to increase. This time, the Spanish followed a strategy of ignoring him rather than risking any more public relations debacles. When the battleship *Maine** exploded in February 1898, Scovel was in Havana and was one of the first reporters, along with George Bronson Rea, to arrive on the rescue ship *City of Washington,** hoping to interview the *Maine*'s captain, Charles S. Sigsbee.* Although he did not get the interview, a report of his appeared in the *World* two days after the explosion. He persisted in his attempts to get close to the investigations until the time American reporters were forced to leave Havana on 10 April.

Staying close to the action during the war, Scovel provided much assistance for U.S. Admiral William T. Sampson.* He ran errands for Sampson using *World* dispatch boats, provided valuable information for the navy on Spanish defenses, communicated with the insurgents in the interior of Cuba, and helped smuggle correspondents onto the island. The navy benefited from the useful espionage, and the *World* benefited by the many exclusive stories Scovel was able to provide.

These escapades came into climax in May. Scovel had arranged for correspondent Charles Thrall and artist Hayden Jones to land in Cuba for the purpose of locating the insurgents who were to receive cargo from the ship *Gussie,* but the reporters were captured by the Spanish. When the U.S. Navy tug *Uncas* traveled to Havana under a white flag to negotiate a prisoner exchange, Scovel, always wanting to be in the center of action, was caught as a stowaway. Secretary of the Navy John D. Long* issued an order barring Scovel from all naval vessels and stations, but Admiral Sampson backed his friend Scovel, pointing out the useful services provided by the correspondent. The *World* editorially complained, and Scovel even sought the intervention of President William McKinley.* In any case, he seemed to have successfully ignored the order.

From late May through early June, he took part in a joint operation by the *World* and the *Herald* to sail around the island of Cuba in search of the Spanish fleet under Admiral Pascual Cervera.* The fleet was not located, but upon returning to Key West,* he received word that Cervera was blockaded at Santiago de Cuba.* Scovel made it to Cuero, just east of Santiago, along with reporter Stephen Crane.* They remained in the area during the battle for San Juan Hill* and for Santiago.

It was during the Spanish surrender at Santiago that the most notorious incident involving Scovel occurred. To ensure his inclusion in official photographs of the American flag–raising ceremony, he climbed onto the rooftop of the governor's palace where the U.S. flag was to be raised at noon on 17 July. After reluctantly coming down from the roof at the insistence of U.S. soldiers, he got into an argument with General William R. Shafter* and was arrested after throwing a punch at the general (although missing him). It was feared that harsh punishment for Scovel would produce negative publicity; correspondents especially tended to dislike Shafter and sympathize with their fellow reporters. The army decided it was best just to ship him back home, taking away his correspondent's license, making him now officially barred from covering army as well as navy operations. This affair embarrassed Joseph Pulitzer,* the *World*'s publisher, helping him lose interest in using the war as a device for building the circulation of his paper.

After the war Scovel remained in Cuba. He worked as an engineer and in various commercial endeavors, but he never again played the role of correspondent. He died in Havana on 11 February 1905 at the age of thirty-five.

REFERENCE: Charles H. Brown, *The Correspondents' War* (New York: Scribner's, 1961).

MARK A. THOMAS

SECOND MASSACHUSETTS VOLUNTEERS

Only five regiments of volunteers were able to participate in the hostilities in Cuba. Because of the rapid buildup and the War Department's* preference to equip regulars first, the volunteer regiments were equipped too late to participate

in most of the fighting in Cuba. An exception, the Second Massachusetts formed part of General Henry W. Lawton's* Second Division of the Fifth Corps* and fought at El Caney* and San Juan,* suffering forty-nine casualties. The Second Massachusetts was under the command of Brigadier General William Ludlow.*
REFERENCE: Walter W. Ward, *Springfield in the Spanish American War* (Easthampton, MA: Enterprise Printing, 1899).

SECRET SERVICE, U.S.
The U.S. Secret Service, headed by John E. Wilkie, former editor of the *Chicago Tribune,* engaged principally in counterintelligence work. A Spanish-sponsored spy ring operating out of Montreal was exposed and expelled from Canada. The arrests of George Downing, who hanged himself in his cell a few days after his arrest, and Frank Mellor, another agent, provided grist for a Secret Service success.
REFERENCE: Don Wilkie, *American Secret Service Agent* (New York: Stokes, 1934).

SECRETARY OF WAR
The civilian secretary of war obtained his appointment from the president and was the officer through whom the president exercised his role as commander-in-chief. In addition, the commanding general controlled all uniformed troops and, in theory at least, both the president and the secretary of war issued orders to the troops through the commanding general. Thus the secretary and the commanding general together administered the army units, engineering projects, records, and all other aspects of the War Department.*

In practice, the office of the secretary of war operated independently of the commanding general, and the various agencies or bureaus enjoyed substantial independence also. However, the secretary—usually a political crony of the president—enjoyed a favored role over the general. This favored position often hurt the general's effectiveness. The secretary could and did issue orders independent of the commanding general, and since the latter had no staff, the secretary could and often did ignore the general completely. Line army officers could, therefore, receive conflicting orders via two chains of command. Thus there existed a constant tension between the secretary, adjutant general,* and bureau chiefs on one side, and the combat line officers and inspector general on the other. Such tensions help explain some of the bitter feuding between General Nelson Miles* and other line officers during the beef controversy,* and the pilloried Russell A. Alger,* secretary of war.
REFERENCE: Graham A. Cosmas, *An Army for Empire* (Columbia: University of Missouri Press, 1971).

SEGURANCA (ship)
Launched in 1893 of 4,033 tons by Delaware River Iron Shipbuilding, *Seguranca* first sailed for the United States and Brazil Mail Line and then was purchased by the Ward Line. The U.S. Army chartered *Seguranca* in April 1898,

and the liner served as General William R. Shafter's* headquarters ship during the Cuban campaign. *Seguranca* was broken up in 1921.
REFERENCE: Frederick E. Emmons, *American Passenger Ships* (Newark: University of Delaware Press, 1985).

SEVENTH ARMY CORPS

Under command of Major General Fitzhugh Lee,* Seventh Army Corps was ordered to Tampa* to help with the assembling and organization of the American expeditionary force to Cuba. Before the force could complete assembly however, Lee had moved to Camp Cuba Libre at Jacksonville,* which he considered healthier and less crowded than Tampa. Lee's command was slated for a fall attack on Havana,* but the armistice came before Seventh Corps—some 30,000 troops—could take the field.
REFERENCE: *Report of the Commission Appointed by the President to Investigate the Conduct of the War Department in the War with Spain,* 8 vols. (Washington, DC: Government Printing Office, 1900).

SEVENTH U.S. VOLUNTEERS

The Seventh U.S. Volunteers was a black "immune"* regiment under the command of Brigadier General A. R. Chaffee* in General Henry W. Lawton*'s Second Division. The Seventh suffered 132 casualties in action at El Caney* and San Juan.*
REFERENCE: French Ensor Chadwick, *The Relations of the United States and Spain* (New York: Russell & Russell, 1968).

SHAFTER, WILLIAM RUFUS
(1835–1906)

Born in Michigan, William Rufus Shafter was a schoolteacher at the beginning of the Civil War when he took a commission with a Michigan volunteer unit. He saw much action and by March 1865 was brevetted brigadier general of volunteers. As a lieutenant colonel of regulars, Shafter served on the frontier after the war, and in May 1897 he commanded the Department of California as brigadier general.

In May 1898 Shafter was promoted to major general of volunteers and placed in command of Fifth Corps,* which consisted of most of the regulars in the U.S. Army supplemented by volunteers like the Rough Riders.* Initially Commanding General Nelson A. Miles* ordered Shafter to Tampa* to prepare an expeditionary force. This force would constitute a reconnaissance in force that would, under Navy escort, link itself with and support Cuban insurgents* but avoid pitched battles. These orders were voided within days of issuance when Admiral Pascual Cervera* sailed with his Spanish squadron. Admiral William T. Sampson* could not spare vessels from the blockade* to transport Shafter's force.

Another false start occurred on 9 May when Miles and Secretary of War

Russell A. Alger* ordered Shafter to assemble for an attack on Mariel* as a prelude to an assault on Havana.* Administrative delays and the inability to locate Cervera's squadron postponed the Havana assault. Miles and Alger squabbled over Cuban strategy until Cervera was located at Santiago.* Shafter's command was incrementally reinforced until it numbered 25,000 men by the end of May. But Shafter failed to plan adequately for the embarkation, and 25,000 sweating and angry troops descended upon Tampa to load onto too few transports. Only 17,000 could embark—the regulars, the Rough Riders, and two more volunteer regiments. Left behind on the wharf were much of the hospital stores, horses for the cavalry, wagons, and mountains of baggage. The disembarkation at Daiquirí* and later at Siboney* were just as chaotic. Nevertheless, the army was ashore. Shafter's orders were to capture Santiago, and he pursued that end. Overweight and suffering intensely in the tropical heat, Shafter had marginal physical ability to maintain pace with his forces.

Shafter's battle plan relied minimally on U.S. naval support or upon the insurgent forces of General Máximo Gómez.* He followed a plan suggested by Miles to seize the high ground, San Juan Heights, east of Santiago. The Spaniards were weakened by poor food, short ammunition supplies, and poor internal lines of communication, but Shafter also faced supply problems of significant magnitude. There was only one narrow road from Daiquirí to Santiago. Wagons and draft animals were in short supply; Shafter ordered only ammunition, a few medical supplies, hardtack, coffee, and tinned beef to go forward to the troops. Herein were the seeds of unrest and future scandal. Menacing the entire force were the twin specters of yellow fever* and malaria.*

On 1 July 1898 Shafter threw his force against the Spanish at El Caney* and San Juan. He had hoped to pass quickly through these outer defenses to invest the city proper; however, the battles of 1 July became not only sanguinary but lengthy. Shafter's force fell short of its goal, but it inflicted a serious defeat nonetheless. Actually, fewer than 300 Spanish troops held the perimeter in front of Shafter at the close of day on 1 July. Had Shafter attacked again, he would have carried the city.

On 3 July Cervera's squadron was destroyed and Shafter's position improved. The destruction of the Spanish squadron altered the strategic picture; Shafter no longer felt a desire to risk his command in battle. A series of parleys with General José Toral*—Arsenio Linares* had been wounded—to negotiate surrender strung out until Santiago was given up on 17 July.

Shafter's next challenge was to stop the spread of disease* and to deal with the political implications of the "Round Robin."* On 7 August Shafter began transferring sick soldiers to Camp Wikoff,* at Montauk Point on Long Island. The move weakened the Fifth Corps, which was rapidly replaced with volunteer regiments, the "immunes,"* and a garrison force. By 25 August all of Fifth Corps had left Cuba. Shafter announced its disbanding on 3 October.

Several of Shafter's subordinates believed him unfit for command and used the press* as a vehicle for their complaints. Shafter, whose plans did go awry and who was ill with gout, was unable to direct the battle at Santiago: The battles "fought themselves," as David F. Trask put it.

After the war Shafter served briefly and then retired in October 1899; he was a major general. He moved back to California to a small ranch near Bakersfield, where he lived until his death in 1906.

REFERENCE: Paul Howard Carlson, *Pecos Bill: A Military Biography of William R. Shafter* (College Station: Texas A&M University Press, 1989); David F. Trask, *The War with Spain in 1898* (New York: Macmillan Publishing Co., 1981).

SHERMAN, JOHN
(1823–1900)

A politician and statesman, John Sherman was born on 10 May 1823 in Lancaster, Ohio, the younger brother of William Tecumseh Sherman of Civil War fame. A wild and reckless youth, he settled down to study law under his uncle, Judge Jacob Parker. He was admitted to the bar on 10 May 1844 and at this time became interested in politics. In 1854 he ran successfully for Congress, and for the next forty-four years he served in a variety of public positions, including representative (1855–1861), senator (1861–1877), secretary of the treasury (1877–1881), again senator (1881–1897), and secretary of state (1897–1898). He was conservative in the majority of his political views but was highly criticized by his opponents for inconsistencies on issues ranging from taxation to Negro suffrage. In the presidential elections of 1880, 1884, and 1888, Sherman made futile attempts to capture the Republican party's nomination. His lack of personality, poor public appeal, and inability to utilize political or party patronage helped make him a failure as a candidate.

In 1896, as a member of the U.S. Senate serving from Ohio, Sherman strongly defended his position that the Spanish government should recognize the independence of Cuba. Conditions in Cuba were deplorable, he felt, and sooner or later the United States must ultimately intervene on behalf of the Cuban people. Sherman had some knowledge of the history of tensions between the United States and Spain. In 1870 he introduced a resolution that the United States recognize the existence of a state of war between Spain and Cuba, and that the United States "observe strict neutrality between the belligerent parties." His case was supported by President Grant, who favored intervention. It took Secretary of State Hamilton Fish* to sway the president from this position, so that the United States remained neutral.

When Sherman served as secretary of state to President William McKinley,* he labored diligently for the release of Cuba from Spanish control. But when war became inevitable for the United States, Sherman tried to persuade McKinley that negotiations must prevail over war. At this point McKinley tried to ease Sherman out of the position of secretary of state. McKinley relied more on Assistant Secretary of State William R. Day* to manage the country's foreign affairs. Declining health and overwhelming pressures at this critical point made

Sherman realize his days were numbered. Subsequently, on 25 April 1898, he resigned the position of secretary of state.

Sherman lived out the next two years trying to defend his positions, especially in the newspapers. Bitter and resentful, he openly attacked the administration's policies. He died on 22 October 1900. Sherman was the author of *John Sherman's Recollections of Forty Years in the House, Senate and Cabinet* (1895) and *Selected Speeches and Reports on Finance and Taxation, from 1859 to 1878* (1879).

REFERENCE: Theodore E. Burton, *John Sherman* (Boston: Houghton Mifflin, 1906).

RICHARD W. PEUSER

SIBONEY, CUBA

Siboney lies about 9 miles east of Santiago* between that city and Daiquirí.*

On 22 June 1898 General William R. Shafter* and the U.S. Army Fifth Corps* disembarked at Daiquirí. Later that same day U.S. troops drove the small Spanish garrison out of Siboney and Shafter used Siboney as another landing site. By 26 June Shafter's corps and General Máximo Gómez* had landed. Siboney continued as a landing site until the surrender of Santiago* on 17 July. Engineers rebuilt a short railroad to supplement the road or trail from Siboney Inland. Shafter kept his lines close to Siboney to facilitate supply, but he suffered from an acute transportation shortage and blockage that centered at Siboney and Daiquirí.

In addition, because of poor sanitation and congestion at Siboney, yellow fever* erupted there first among American troops. When General Nelson A. Miles* arrived, he ordered the entire village of Siboney burned in an attempt to halt the contagion.

REFERENCE: *Report of the Commission Appointed by the President to Investigate the Conduct of the War Department in the War with Spain,* 8 vols. (Washington, DC: Government Printing Office, 1900).

SICARD, MONTGOMERY
(1836–1900)

Rear Admiral Montgomery Sicard studied at the Naval Academy and enjoyed command during the Civil War. As chief of the Bureau of Ordnance (1881–1890), he was instrumental in dramatically upgrading naval firepower with new improved weapons. In 1897–1898 he commanded the North Atlantic Squadron* and then went on sick leave.

As the Spanish American war developed, Sicard was appointed to the Naval War Board* along with Theodore Roosevelt,* Arent S. Crowninshield,* and Albert Barker. The board formulated strategy and plans for the navy.

Sicard was also called to the White House on 20 April to form a council of war, which met periodically to advise president William McKinley.*

Sicard retired in September 1898 and died in 1900.

REFERENCES: French Ensor Chadwick, *The Relations of the United States and Spain,*

2 vols. (New York: Russell & Russell, 1968); David F. Trask has also extracted archival material on Sicard in *The War with Spain* (New York: Macmillan Publishing Co., 1981).

SIGNAL CORPS

Authorized as a separate branch of the U.S. Army by an act of Congress on 3 March 1863, the Signal Corps owes its origins to the army's introduction and application of the telegraph during the Civil War. The Signal Corps operated and maintained the army's communication network. Its basic function was to transmit military information, thereby ensuring coordination of command and unified action. In 1870 Congress directed the chief signal officer, through the secretary of war, to take meteorological observations at military stations throughout the country. This function was assigned to the Signal Corps because it had the means and equipment to process and communicate the information to any part of the country. The Signal Corps maintained and expanded this function until the Weather Bureau was established in 1890 under the jurisdiction of the Department of Agriculture. Signal Corps activities were then confined to strictly military matters.

During and after the war with Spain, the Signal Corps rendered an important service in the construction, rehabilitation, and operation of telephone and telegraph lines, including the laying of several cables in Cuban and Philippine waters. The telephone was first used in combat during the war with Spain. It was also during this period that the Signal Corps turned increasingly to the radio as a means of communication, but advances were also made in telephony and telegraphy. The small nucleus of regular Signal Corps personnel, which had carried on telegraphic and meteorological advances during the years of peace, underwent a swift expansion from 60 men to a force of 1,300, mostly volunteers during the conflict. The chief signal officer, Brigadier General Adolphus W. Greeley of Massachusetts, served with distinction as a volunteer during the Civil War and rose through the ranks of the regular army, attaining the rank of brigadier general and chief of the signal service in 1886.

Although the Office of Naval Intelligence* is credited with furnishing invaluable intelligence to the American effort by its intelligence-gathering activities during the Spanish American War, the Signal Corps also had an important role in gathering intelligence successfully, especially on Spanish ship movements. It also coordinated communications via the telegraph between General William R. Shafter's* headquarters in Santiago* and the War Department.*

Telegraph* was the fastest means of communication, and so the corps installed wire to within 400 feet of combat: Troops were organized, deployed, equipped, and maneuvered by telegraph. Eventually ground commanders in Cuba were within twenty minutes of Washington—an impressive feat. In similar fashion, because of an informer network established by Martin L. Hellings,* Washington was aware of the arrival of Admiral Pascual Cervera* at Santiago within one hour; that Admiral William T. Sampson* only partially believed the information and Commodore Winfield S. Schley* did not believe it at all does not diminish the accomplishment. Nevertheless, telegraph reports detailed the number of Spanish ships and their names.

The Signal Corps also ran a balloon* intelligence operation with mixed results. Those in the gondola beneath the balloon were able to telegraph important information to ground commanders, but because of the manner in which the balloon followed the advancing American troops at San Juan Hill,* the Spanish were able to use the balloon as a range finder for their artillery. George Derby* and Joseph E. Maxfield* manned the basket hanging under the balloon and essentially served as dangling targets for Spanish rifles. It was General Shafter's staff officer who ordered the balloon to follow the troops in such an obvious manner.

The Signal Corps was also responsible for censorship of traffic over cables. This was accomplished principally in Key West,* Tampa,* New York, and Washington.

These communications efforts dictated that the Signal Corps was the first army unit in Cuba, and the last to depart.

REFERENCES: *Annual Reports of the War Department for the Fiscal Year Ended June 30, 1898: Report of the Secretary of War, Miscellaneous Reports* (Washington, DC: Government Printing Office, 1903); Graham A. Cosmas, *An Army for Empire* (Columbia: University of Missouri Press, 1971); Howard A. Giddings, *Exploits of the Signal Corps in the War with Spain* (Kansas City, MO: Hudson Kimberly Publishing, 1980); G.J.A. O'Toole, *Honorable Treachery* (New York: Atlantic Monthly Press, 1991).

                                                                RICHARD W. PEUSER

SIGSBEE, CHARLES DWIGHT
(1845–1923)

Born in New York, Charles Dwight Sigsbee graduated from the Naval Academy in 1863 and served with Admiral Farragut in the Civil War. As he was assigned various commands, he rose in rank and became known for surveying and exploration in the Gulf of Mexico (Sigsbee Deep is the deepest point of the gulf). He served in the European Squadron and the Asiatic Squadron* and also taught at the Naval Academy. In March 1897 he was promoted to captain and the next month was appointed to command the U.S.S. *Maine.** In January 1898 Sigsbee steamed into Havana Harbor. On 15 February 1898 the *Maine* exploded. Sigsbee's postexplosion dispatches from Havana were important not only for their information but also for their calm, dispassionate tone.

During the war Sigsbee commanded *St. Paul** and captured *Restormel** (25 May). On 22 June off San Juan, Puerto Rico,* Sigsbee engaged the Spanish destroyers *Terror** and *Isabel* and sank *Terror; Isabel* retired without firing.

Sigsbee later became the navy's top intelligence officer and in 1905 brought John Paul Jones back from France. He retired in 1907 a rear admiral.

REFERENCE: Charles D. Sigsbee, *The* Maine: *An Account of Her Destruction in Havana Harbor* (New York: Century Co., 1899).

SIMS, WILLIAM SOWDEN
(1858–1936)

Born of an American father in Ontario, Canada, William Sowden Sims graduated from Annapolis in 1880. Assigned as the naval attaché in Paris in 1897, Sims operated a network of agents in strategic locales on the Atlantic seaboard and in Europe the Mediterranean. Using a generous $50,000 established by the Naval War Board,* attachés such as Sims were the Office of Naval Intelligence's* key sources of information. Sim's network was not as extensive as Lieutenant John C. Colwell's,* but it was just as lively. Sims's agent in Spain, for example, tried to pry more money from him, while his agent in the Canaries attempted blackmail. Failing at blackmail, the latter challenged Sims to a duel. Sims's chief contribution of intelligence was made during intelligence operations* against Admiral Manuel de la Cámara* and his attempt to relieve Manila.*

REFERENCE: Jeffery M. Dorwart, *The Office of Naval Intelligence* (Annapolis, MD: Naval Institute Press, 1979).

SOCAPA POINT, CUBA

Socapa Point, Socapa Heights, and Socapa battery are located at the western side of the entrance to Santiago de Cuba.* Socapa faced Morro Castle* on the opposite headland. There were two artillery batteries at Socapa: an upper battery that faced seaward, more or less, and a lower battery that faced the direction of Estrella or Punta Gorda.* The batteries were on bluffs over 150 feet above the water. With one exception, none had modern weapons. In addition, ammunition was in short supply. Nevertheless, the existence of the batteries caused Admiral William T. Sampson* to conclude that he could not force the entrance with his ships. Land-based assault on Morro and Socapa would have rendered Santiago virtually indefensible, and Sampson proposed that very plan. General William R. Shafter,* commander of Fifth Army Corps,* did not favor the navy's plan.

After the battles at San Juan* on 1 July and the destruction of Admiral Pascual Cervera's* ships on 3 July, another plan on 6 July called for an attack on Socapa and Morro. However, interservice rivalry and Shafter's preference to besiege rather than attack smothered the proposal.

REFERENCE: David F. Trask, *The War with Spain in 1898* (New York: Macmillan Publishing Co., 1981).

SPAIN

Spain in the nineteenth century endured the same political convulsions as the other western European states. A revolutionary fervor that had become incendiary in Austria, Germany, and Italy had its counterpart in Spain. At midcentury the country became divided into traditionalists who favored the monarchy and the Catholic Church, republicans and progressives who desired a liberal constitution and a "progressive" government, and a developing mixture of Bakuninists, Marxists, and anarchists who were opposed to both. Governments rose and fell with breathtaking rapidity. Some authors have suggested that at its heart, the political turmoil in Spain was really a religious tumult: Was there to continue a national and state religion, or would citizens be able to publicly exercise their consciences? It was an anachronistic Renaissance notion that the Inquisition (or Spanish national policy) had kept at bay. Certainly more complex than that, there was, nevertheless, fundamental disagreement over the very nature of Spain's future. Many conservatives posited that Spain's past greatness was due, in fact, to religious intolerance. Political and national debility grew proportionate to the decline in Catholic religious enthusiasm and the increase of tolerance for heretical ideas, argued the conservatives.

Liberals riposted that only religious tolerance could deliver Spain from backwardness and obscurity; every disaster or calamity that Spain had endured since Ferdinand and Isabella was rooted in religious intolerance. Modernization and progress would be possible only through promoting religious tolerance.

Clearly these two factions had more than a communication problem dividing them. Their differences were polar.

Against this backdrop were also challenges within the monarchy itself. After the restoration of 1874 and then the new constitution of 1876, Antonio Cánovas del Castillo* and Práxedes Mateo Sagasta* took turns as head of government while Spain struggled to find consensus. Alfonso XII, the king, married his cousin, who soon died. He then married the Austrian María Cristina* in 1879. But Alfonso died in 1885, leaving his wife pregnant with the future Alfonso XIII. María Cristina acted as queen regent, ruling for her son until 1902. The queen regent was concerned not just about her government or preserving the government, but specifically with preserving the government for her son.

In addition, frustration with the loss of overseas possessions led many Spaniards of the 1890s to take a hard view of José Martí's* renewed Cuban Insurrection* of 1895. Cuba was one of the last outposts of Spain, and Puerto Rico* and Cuba were Spain's last possessions in Spanish America. Prestige, national honor, military reputation, and economic well-being—Cuba represented significant trade for Spain—were linked by many Spaniards to successfully quelling the Cuban uprising. At the same time, there were troubles in Spanish Africa and an insurrection in the Philippines. The growing harshness of the Cuban struggle and the increasingly strict measures of General Valeriano Weyler* divided further the conservatives and liberals of Spain. Also, for reasons of pride and insecurity, the true state of military unpreparedness was kept from the Spanish populace. The latter was filled with an odd mixture of patriotic fervor and fatalism reminiscent of Don Quixote. Also, Spanish pride and Spanish fantasy imagined the coming conflict with the United States in racial overtones: Saxons versus Iberians.

Little wonder, then, that as news of the defeats at Manila* and Santiago* became known, the Spanish nation was seized by a despair previously unknown in its history. Many Spaniards felt ruined and hopeless; they questioned even the ability of Spain to continue as a historical entity. The Spanish American War initiated a Spanish national self-examination of profound dimensions. A panorama of psychosocial self-examination after the disaster of 1898 ultimately created serious changes in the Spanish world view. An interesting side effect of the war was that Spain and Spanish America, at odds during the nineteenth century as the independence movement grew in the Americas, achieved a mutual sympathy and understanding as the United States grew increasingly aggressive and powerful. This reawakening of Hispanic sympathy became possible because having been decisively eliminated as an imperial power, Spain was no longer a threat to the Americas. The United States, a growing imperialistic and industrial giant, was perceived as a threat. South American, Mexican, and Central American hispanophobes came to be hispanophiles.

REFERENCE: Frederick B. Pike, *Hispanismo, 1898–1936* (Notre Dame, IN: University of Notre Dame, 1971).

SPRINGFIELD RIFLE

Named for the rifle manufactured at the Springfield Arsenal in Springfield, Massachusetts, the .45-70-caliber rifle was issued to the volunteer units when the war began. The Ordnance Department* considered the modern Krag-Jörgenson rifle* as the standard issue arm for the expanding regular infantry units, but a shortage of Krags signaled the repercussion of years of limited appropriations to the War Department* by Congress after the Indian wars. Therefore, the volunteer units called upon to supplement the regular army in 1898 were issued the outdated Springfield. The one exception, the First U.S. Volunteer Cavalry, or Rough Riders,* were equipped like regulars. Their commanding officer, Theodore Roosevelt,* used his political influence to secure Krag carbines for his men.

More than 260,000 of the single-shot Springfield breech-loaders were in storage at the Ordnance Department's arsenals. Inspections of the arsenals often revealed these rifles in poor state of repair, rusty, and hardly capable of firing properly. The Springfield used a charcoal powder that was in great supply, as well as smokeless cartridge, if needed. Although the Springfield was considered a temporary solution to the shortage of weapons, many of the regular army officers considered this rifle to be on par with the Krag. Both had an effective range of about 2 miles, with the Springfield's 500-grain bullet providing a harder impact than the 220-grain Krag bullet.

The real difference lay in the Springfield's lack of a magazine, which limited its ability to fifteen rounds per minute. This factor gave the Springfield a handicap during the delivering and repelling of a charge during battle. In the opinion of many regular and National Guard* officers, the Springfield's simple breech mechanism was ideal for the inexperienced volunteers because it was much easier to operate than the Krag during the heat of battle. However, the volunteer troops often complained that the charcoal powder of the Springfield created clouds of smoke that exposed their positions to the enemy.

REFERENCES: Graham A. Cosmas, *An Army for an Empire* (Columbia: University of Missouri Press, 1971); William H. Hallahan, *Misfire* (New York: Scribner's, 1994).

MITCHELL YOCKELSON

STERNBERG, GEORGE MILLER
(1838–1915)

Disease*—typhus, typhoid, and yellow fever* in particular—played a considerable role in strategic planning during campaigns in Cuba. The Spanish American War was a medical watershed for a host of sanitary and epidemiologic reasons. Prominent in the address of these issues was Brigadier General George Miller Sternberg, physician, careful scientist, and in 1893, surgeon general of the army. A yellow fever victim himself in 1875, Sternberg was keenly aware of the ravages, past and potential, of disease. He was thus uniquely qualified to seize the opportunities the war provided to do serious public health research. Sternberg sponsored Walter Reed* and the Yellow Fever Commission, directed and instructed them, and provided encouragement. It is doubtful that Reed's commission would have been formed without Sternberg's research, interest, and persistence.

REFERENCE: John Mendinghall Gibson, *Soldier in White* (Durham, NC: Duke University Press, 1958).

STOREY, MOORFIELD
(1845–1929)

Moorfield Storey was a Boston lawyer, Harvard graduate, and politico in Massachusetts and Washington. Storey was a mugwump anti-imperialist who labored publicly against annexation of gains from the Spanish American War. Along with the Anti-Imperialist League,* Storey's other interests included the formation of a third national political party, advancement of black Americans, tariff reform, and civil service review. He was president of the American Bar Association and the National Association for the Advancement of Colored People and a Harvard overseer. Storey also authored several books on political issues, including the Philippines (1904 and 1926).

REFERENCES: Robert L. Beisner, *Twelve against Empire* (New York: McGraw-Hill, 1968); William B. Hixson, *Moorfield Storey and the Abolitionist Tradition* (New York: Oxford University Press, 1972); Moorefield Storey, *The Conquest of the Philippines by the United States* (New York: G. P. Putnam's Sons, 1926); Moorfield Storey, *The Importance to America of Philippine Independence* (Boston: New England Anti-Imperialist League, 1904).

STRATEGY, SPANISH

Once war had been declared in April 1898, Spain,* well-aware of the U.S. Army's unreadiness, continued to pursue or solicit European intervention on its own behalf. In effect Madrid stalled, hoping for a third-party solution. Material support for Manila,* Havana,* and San Juan* had not been forthcoming before the initiation of the war, nor did it materialize after. Admiral Manuel de la Cámara's* abortive relief of Manila was a reaction to Commodore George Dewey's* 1 May defeat of Spanish naval forces at Manila, not a strategic initiative. The threat of a raid upon the Spanish coast and the defeat at Santiago de Cuba* of Admiral Pascual Cervera* caused Captain Ramón Auñon* y Villalón* to terminate Cámara's mission. Auñon ordered Cámara home to avoid destruction. Even Cámara's squadron sailed to doom, as Cervera had warned, to satisfy Spanish pride. For example, the newest and largest Spanish battleship did not have its main guns fitted.

In the land engagements on Cuba, Puerto Rico,* and the Philippines, Spanish strategy was to maintain the status quo, that is, to retain each garrison in place, rather than massing its troops and repelling the U.S. Army with Spain's numerically superior forces. Although massing its troops would have been difficult, particularly in insurrectionist Cuba and the Philippines, doing so would have won battles. But without the capability of resupply by sea—for the U.S. Navy commanded the seas—holding the islands indefinitely might have become an overwhelming challenge. It is clear that Spain's strategy bowed almost completely to political, not military, ends. As war clouds gathered, the government of Spain neither worked to prepare its outposts for the war nor materially supplied them.

REFERENCES: Graham A. Cosmas, *An Army for Empire* (Columbia: University of Missouri Press, 1971); U.S. Office of Naval Intelligence, *Notes on the Spanish American War* (Washington, DC: Government Printing Office, 1980).

STRATEGY, U.S.

Owing to prior planning by the Naval War Board* and others, the U.S. Navy had a strategic vision of the war with Spain that went through several iterations before the conflict of 1898. Prior navy planning viewed the war as essentially a naval contest in which the United States would strike Spanish possessions at the extremities of Spain's logistical and tactical reach: The targets were Cuba and the Philippines. Based upon the recent and growing strength of the steel U.S. Navy and the weakness of Spain's naval forces, and given the proximity of U.S. naval bases in Florida (but none for Spain except Cuba), a blockade* of Cuba and the destruction of Admiral Pascual Cervera's* Atlantic Squadron would necessarily mean eventual success in the Caribbean. While details of strategy were added, such as territorial annexation, the basic U.S. strategy remained constant.

A secondary but similar strategy sustained land combat operations. Direct attacks at heavily garrisoned Spanish objectives like Havana* or San Juan* were discarded in favor of more subtle strategy. General William R. Shafter's* Fifth Army Corps* attacked Santiago* as part of the strategy to seize or destroy Cervera's naval forces. Led by General Nelson A. Miles,* the campaign in Puerto Rico was to be an oblique, four-pronged encirclement of San Juan.

The navy had planned a sortie in the Philippines since 1896. President William McKinley* authorized Commodore George Dewey's* attack on 20 April 1898. The Battle of Manila Bay* on 1 May was an resounding success that altered the war objectives of the McKinley administration to include eventual seizure of the archipelago. General Wesley Merritt* supervised the development of Eighth Corps,* ordered into existence on 12 May, which took Manila on 13 August, over three months after Dewey's victory. Even so, Merritt's achievements followed upon the original strategy of naval conflict. That strategy had other repercussions in the annexation of Guam* and Hawaii* and the desire for further coaling* and cable stations. McKinley may have altered his objective from a quick war to free Cuba, to a quick war to create an American trade zone and empire, but his strategy remained the same: Destruction of Spanish naval power by U.S. naval power buttressed by rapidly developed land forces.

REFERENCES: Graham A. Cosmas, *An Army for Empire* (Columbia: University of Missouri Press, 1971); David F. Trask, *The War with Spain in 1898* (New York: Macmillan Publishing Co., 1981).

SUBIC BAY, PHILIPPINES

The narrow harbor of Subic Bay lies west of the Bataan Peninsula on the southwest coast of the island of Luzon* in the Philippines.* In straight-line distance, it is about 50 miles west of Manila.* Concluding that Manila Bay was undefendable, Admiral Patricio Montojo y Pasarón* proposed to retire his weak naval force to Subic Bay, where it would be safer from assault, yet able to counterattack George Dewey's* fleet with the aid of artillery, torpedoes, and land batteries. Arriving at Subic on 26 April 1898, Montojo found that little progress had been made in preparing its fortifications, and support from Spain was not forthcoming. On 28 April he received word that Dewey had departed Mirs Bay* for the Philippines. With no shore battery in place and on orders from the Spanish governor, General Basilio Augustín Dávila,* to return to Manila Bay, Montojo felt his only recourse was to give battle at Cavite.* On the morning of Friday, 29 April, the Spanish fleet left Subic Bay and steamed directly for Cavite, where it anchored in Cañacao Bay to await the arrival of Dewey. When the American navy arrived the following day, Commodore Dewey sent *Boston,* *Concord,* and *Baltimore* to reconnoiter Subic Bay. They returned to report the harbor empty of Spanish ships, and Dewey proceeded on to the Boca Grande of Manila.

REFERENCES: Stanley Karnow, *In Our Image* (London: Century, 1990); David F. Trask, *The War with Spain in 1898* (New York: Macmillan Publishing Co., 1981).

KEN KEMPCKE

SUBSISTENCE DEPARTMENT

The job of the Subsistence Department was to feed the army. It was headed by a regular army officer, Commissary General Charles P. Eagan,* with military and civilian staff and subordinates. Rations were divided into three general categories: garrison rations, consisting of fresh meat, vegetables, and so on; field rations, including hard tack, bacon, tinned vegetables, and the like; and travel rations, which were similar to field rations except with the addition of more canned items. If these rations sound suspiciously similar, it is because they were innervatingly similar. Nevertheless, they represented a balanced diet for the time. Eagan was disinclined to experiment with newfangled concentrates and prepared foods: He did not substantially alter the ration makeup because it was a proven list—it worked. Eagan's wartime innovations were the result of the exceedingly rapid buildup of troop strength and the overseas expeditions.

Prior wars saw American troops herding cattle that were slaughtered as needed along the route of march. Herding was clearly impractical in Cuba, and the unknown situation of the Philippines demanded another alternative. Beef that had been boiled and then canned had been used by hunters, ranchers, and miners since the 1870s. The navy used over one-half million pounds of it annually, and European armies regularly imported tons of tinned American beef for their armies. Greater use of canned beef seemed a reasonable and safe alternative to the impracticality of herding livestock or shipping frozen carcasses to the battlefield. The Subsistence Department had little difficulty in providing rations for the geometrically expanding army; agriculture was America's nineteenth-century business. However, administrative incompetence in the army camps* sometimes created temporary food shortages, and General William R. Shafter's* logistical problems at Santiago* created significant troop unrest. The Department was nonetheless effective. Eagan's career shoaled and then wrecked on a beef controversy* involving scandal over canned beef.

REFERENCE: *Report of the Commission Appointed by the President to Investigate the Conduct of the War Department in the War with Spain* (Washington, DC: Government Printing Office, 1900).

SUEZ CANAL

Steaming at 10 knots, Admiral Manuel de la Cámara's* Eastern Squadron would take approximately thirty days to travel from Spain through Suez to the Philippines to relieve the Spanish garrison at Manila.* Such timing, adding coaling time, would place Camara's squadron in the Philippines some time in August. Without the ability to use Suez, relief of the Philippines via either Cape Horn or the Cape of Good Hope was not a feasible operation. Both American and Spanish strategists realized the vital nature of Suez. The Americans sent *Monterey** and *Monadnock** to Manila* as reinforcements against the eventuality of Cámara's arrival. Additionally, U.S. strategists formulated several plans to halt Cámara's progress. An intelligence operation* spread disinformation about an American squadron readying for an attack on Spain. State Department efforts to discourage neutrals from providing coal effectively halted Cámara's progress and aborted the mission.

REFERENCE: David F. Trask, *The War with Spain in 1898* (New York: Macmillan, Publishing Co., 1981).

SUMNER, SAMUEL STORROW
(1842–1937)

Samuel Storrow Sumner led the Second Brigade, Cavalry Division, U.S. Volunteers, which included the First U.S. Volunteer Cavalry, also known as Theodore Roosevelt's* Rough Riders.* Born in Carlisle, Pennsylvania, on 16 February 1842, Sumner received his education at army posts and private schools in New York State. When the Civil War broke out in 1861, Sumner was appointed to the second U.S. Cavalry. During the course of the war, Sumner was promoted through the ranks from brevet second lieutenant to major of volunteers. After the war Sumner served in numerous Indian campaigns in the West.

When the war erupted with Spain in 1898, Sumner was appointed a brevet brigadier general of volunteers. On 1 July 1898 he was ordered to take command of the Cavalry Division so that General Joseph Wheeler* could exercise better control over this division and Brigadier General J. Ford Kent's* division in the upcoming battles at San Juan Hill* and Kettle Hill.* Sumner's actions, which led to the taking of these hills, earned him a Silver Star citation for bravery and praise from Wheeler. On 7 September 1898 he was promoted to major general.

After the war Sumner served as military attaché to the American embassy in London from 1899 to 1900. He then commanded a brigade in the Boxer Rebellion in China. Afterward he commanded two military districts in the Philippines, including South Luzon,* 1901–1902; North Luzon, 1902; Mindanao, 1902–1903; the Department of the Missouri 1903–1904; the Southwestern Division, 1904–1905; and the Division of the Pacific 1905–1906. He died on 26 July 1937 at his home in Brookline, Massachusetts.

REFERENCES: *Correspondence Relating to the War with Spain,* 2 vols. (Washington, DC: Government Printing Office, 1993), Robert Leckie, *Wars of America, Vol. 1, From 1600 to 1900* (New York: HarperCollins Publishers, 1992); Joseph Wheeler, *The Santiago Campaign, 1898* (Port Washington, NY: Kennikat Press, 1971).

BRIAN B. CARPENTER

SUPPLY, U.S. ARMY

Supply concerns for the Spanish garrisons on Cuba and in the Philippines initially were complex but rapidly became achingly simple. With the tightening Cuban blockade* and the insurmountable distance and difficulty of reaching the Philippines from supply bases in Spain, the Spanish had to survive on existing supplies and the odd successful blockade runner.

The United States, on the other hand, suffered not from a want of items—especially not in the later months of the war—but from distribution difficulties. The Quartermaster Department* and the Ordnance Department* were caught short, on a peacetime footing, when war was declared. In addition, neither department foresaw the rapid buildup of troop strength and both spent the early weeks catching up, out-sourcing, and devising distribution systems. The army, in particular, had difficulty correlating strategic initiatives with logistics. These logistical difficulties were among the reasons (or excuses) for not sending most of the volunteer regiments into action; the regulars were better equipped.

REFERENCE: Graham A. Cosmas, *An Army for Empire* (Columbia: University of Missouri Press, 1971).

SUWANEE (ship)

An armed yacht, sometimes referred to as converted tender, *Suwanee* took part in several naval engagements in Cuba. *Suwanee* was first detailed from Florida* to take up station with the blockade* of Santiago.* *Suwanee* participated in the bombardment of 6 June 1898 and in the seizure of Guantánamo Bay.* *Suwanee* also participated in the incidents around Caimanera* on 10 June. The yacht shelled Cay del Tor, destroying a small fort.

On 11 June Lieutenant Victor Blue,* of *Suwanee,* went ashore at Santiago to reconnoiter Admiral Pascual Cervera's* squadron. With the aid of Cuban insurgents, Blue was able to provide Admiral William T. Sampson* with confirmation of the presence of Cervera's ships.

During the actual engagement with Cervera's ships, *Suwanee* was away east near Guantánamo refueling. However, *Suwanee* participated in the 12 August action at Manzanillo.*

REFERENCE: H. W. Wilson, *The Downfall of Spain* (New York: Burt Franklin, 1971).

T

TAMPA BAY HOTEL

The Tampa Bay Hotel, a lavish resort hotel in Tampa, was the only major structure in the city at the time hostilities between Spain and the United States were initiated. In the weeks preceding the Santiago* campaign the hotel was headquarters for the army as well as home to throngs of journalists eager to get news of the war. Built by railroad and steamship magnate Henry Bradley Plant in 1888, it opened in February 1891. Plant was hoping to develop the west coast of Florida for the tourist trade to compete with the resorts and railroads being established by Henry Flagler on the east coast of the state.

Typical of large resorts of the Victorian era, the hotel possessed an exotic, fanciful architectural style with Moorish themes featuring a wealth of domes, minarets, and archways. Usually only open during the winter tourist season, the hotel was reopened shortly after closing in April 1898 when Tampa was chosen as the point of embarkation for the U.S. Army traveling to Cuba during the Spanish American War. By default it became headquarters for the military; there was really no other choice in Tampa. *New York Herald* correspondent Richard Harding Davis* declared that "it was fortunate that the hotel was out of all proportion in every way to the size and wealth of Tampa. . . . One of the cavalry generals said: 'Only God knows why Plant built a hotel here; but thank God he did.' "

At first only military personnel used the hotel. Soon, however, correspondents, visitors, and family members of the military arrived to wait with the army before it traveled to Cuba. Davis referred to the waiting period of May and June 1898 as the "Rocking-Chair Period" of the war. As the orders to sail for Cuba were delayed again and again, the long and wide verandas and the spacious open areas of the hotel became a meeting place for military officers, war correspondents from around the world, and foreign military attachés. They renewed old acquaintances and the journalists kept alert for rumors, each hoping to be the first to learn of new developments in the conflict. "It was an army of occupation, but it occupied the piazza of a big hotel," remarked Davis.

The hotel struggled on after the war, but it was really too large and opulent to support itself into the twentieth century in competition with resorts on the east coast of Florida and with smaller hotels. The city of Tampa acquired it early in the century, continuing to run it as a hotel. In 1933 it was leased to the University of Tampa; today, after renovation, it serves as the university's student center.

REFERENCES: James W. Covington et al., *Plant's Palace: Henry Plant and the Tampa Bay Hotel* (Louisville, KY: Harmony House, 1990); Richard Harding Davis, *The Cuban and Puerto Rican Campaigns* (New York: Charles Scribner's Sons, 1898).

MARK A. THOMAS

TAMPA, FLORIDA

The U.S. Congress authorized armed intervention in Cuba on 23 April 1898. In preparation for this intervention, on 29 April Secretary of War* Russell Alger* approved the order for Brigadier General William R. Shafter* to prepare an expeditionary force at Tampa. Tampa, therefore, became the focus of American preparations for the eventual landings at Cuba, which occurred on 22 June. Fifth Corps* and Seventh Corps had headquarters in Tampa, and the city was literally overrun with men and material prior to the embarkation. Approximately 25,000 troops, including the famed Rough Riders,* comprised the military contingent in May. In contrast, the civilian population of Tampa comprised only 26,000 at the time.

Located on the Gulf of Mexico, Tampa presented several obvious advantages as a staging area. The bay was deep enough for ocean transports, yet free from Spanish depredations. A large wharf and an existing railhead provided embarkation capabilities—although both proved inadequate.

REFERENCE: *Report of the Commission Appointed by the President to Investigate the Conduct of the War Department in the War with Spain* (Washington, DC: Government Printing Office, 1900).

TAYLOR, HANNIS
(1851–1922)

Born in North Carolina but a practicing attorney in Alabama, Hannis Taylor was appointed U.S. minister to Spain during the critical years of Grover Cleveland's* administration, just prior to the Spanish American War. Appointed on 8 April 1893, Taylor was singularly unqualified for the post, having no Spanish language proficiency nor diplomatic experience whatever. He was, however, a well-respected Democrat, and the appointment was made for patronage purposes.

Taylor enthusiastically took up his duties and served with no little success in mediating or ameliorating tensions between the United States and Spain over disputed claims for damages and rising frictions after the outbreak of the Cuban

Insurrection* in 1895 (*see also* Insurrection of 1895*). The stories of Valeriano Weyler's* alleged atrocities excited Taylor, who then became an ardent proponent of the Monroe Doctrine. He also came to view the Cuban revolt as inevitably leading to independence: Spain could not solve the problem and America must. Such interventionist feelings ran contrary to Cleveland's neutrality policy. He went so far as to publish his views in the *North American Review,* thus assuring Cleveland's mistrust and clouding Taylor's effectiveness. Inasmuch as Taylor never quite understood the Spanish polity nor policy, he was not as effective as he might have been. To his credit, however, he was able to gain American objectives in a variety of diplomatic areas, the most notable being the American filibuster expedition of the *Competitor.** He also endured strong anti-American sentiment during 1896 and 1897 while in Spain. There were anti-American demonstrations in the streets, and he and his family were booed at bullfights. Even his servants were suspect when one of them served his soup in a chamber pot. Lastly, Taylor succeeded in thwarting a Spanish plan to enlist European diplomats in signing a protest against possible American intervention in Cuba. Although tried on more than one occasion, the plan failed in the face of Taylor's persuasiveness. He felt he had a role to play in the freeing of Cuba. Later, in March 1902, Hannis Taylor served as a special advisor to the Spanish Treaty Claims Commission. This commission attempted to settle claims by private citizens who lost Cuban investments during the Spanish American War.

REFERENCE: Tennant S. McWilliams, *Hannis Taylor: The New Southerner as an American* (Tuscaloosa: University of Alabama Press, 1978).

                                                                                    KEN KEMPCKE

TELEGRAPH

By 1898 the telegraph was an essential element of command and control for both Spain and the United States. All communiqués, consultations, orders, and situation reports were sent via this medium, the fastest way to communicate at that time. Establishing cable stations was a strategic necessity.

When war broke out, the U.S. armed forces created telegraph terminals close to the areas of conflict in both Cuba and the Philippines by hooking underwater telegraph cables used for international communication and patching into them. Not having wireless telegraphs, the navy relied on couriers and hand signals for communication. Admiral William T. Sampson* missed the battle with Admiral Pascual Cervera's* fleet while heading to a meeting with General William R. Shafter* at his headquarters due to this limitation. Because these cable stations were usually in the large cities and close to shore, any army operation away from these areas was seriously hampered by a lack of effective communication.

To deny Spain access to this important means of communication, the U.S. Navy was ordered by Washington to dredge up and cut telegraph cables leading from Cuba to Spain. The navy set out to cut these lines of communication and enforce its blockade* of Cuba by using naval tugs and auxiliary cruisers to pull the cables off the bottom and cut them in half. This operation began on 26 April

1898. As a result of the directive to cut cables, crews from *Marblehead** and *Nashville** came under fierce Spanish fire on 11 May while cutting two cables just off Cienfuegos.* A third line could not be cut, which enabled the Spanish government to stay in contact with General Blanco y Erenas* via Jamaica. From 24 to 28 May *St. Louis** managed to cut feeder cables near Santiago de Cuba,* Guantánamo,* and Môle St. Nicolas.* This ship was driven off by Spanish gunners in its first attempt to cut the cable near *Guantánamo,** but later under the protection of the *Dolphin,* it succeeded in cutting this cable.

Telegraph lines were utilized also for intelligence operations.* The Signal Corps* assumed responsibility for much of the cable laying and for cable capability carried with General Shafter and Fifth Corps.*

REFERENCES: James C. Bradford, ed., *Crucible of Empire* (Annapolis, MD: Naval Institute Press, 1993); *New York Times,* various articles related to the subject, April 26–June 25, 1898.

BRIAN B. CARPENTER

TELLER, HENRY MOORE
(1830–1914)

Henry Moore Teller served as U.S. senator from the state of Colorado in 1876–1882 and 1885–1909. He supported the Cuban revolutionary movement before the war and was concerned that other countries around the world would view American intervention into Cuba as an attempt to seize the island and take control of it. In April 1898 Teller offered an amendment to the joint resolution for war with Spain that disclaimed any intention to exercise jurisdiction or control over Cuba except in a pacification role and promised to leave the island as soon as the war was over. The Teller Amendment was adopted in the Senate on 19 April without debate. Although American troops remained in Cuba long after the conclusion of the war and U.S. expansionists called for its annexation, Teller remained a supporter of Cuban independence.

REFERENCES: Elmer Ellis, *Henry Moore Teller, Defender of the West* (Caldwell, ID: The Caxton Printers, 1941); John E. Findling, *Dictionary of American Diplomatic History* (Westport, CT: Greenwood Press, 1980).

KEN KEMPCKE

TENTH CAVALRY

The Tenth Cavalry was organized in April 1866 along with five other all-black regular units, commonly known as the "Buffalo Soldiers." The Tenth served in the West with the primary function of fighting Indians. Upon mobilization for the war with Spain, the regiment was posted to Montana and sent to Chickamauga Park, Georgia, for training in April 1898. A month later the Tenth was sent to Tampa,* where they boarded transport ships for Cuba. Because of space considerations on board the transports, the cavalry divisions had to leave their horses in Tampa and fight dismounted. Brigaded with the First U.S. Cavalry Regiment and the First U.S. Volunteer Cavalry Regiment to form the Second Cavalry Brigade, the regiments were under the direct command of General Joseph Wheeler's* cavalry division. Wheeler's division was attached to the Fifth Army Corps* during the Santiago* expedition in June 1898.

The cavalry units were the first American regiments to come ashore in Cuba. Unfortunately, one of the boats carrying members of the Tenth Cavalry capsized in rough waters and two soldiers in the regiment drowned. Two days after landing the regiment took part in its first battle at Las Guásimas* with satisfying results. Lieutenant John J. "Black Jack" Pershing,* who served as the Tenth Cavalry's regimental quartermaster, credited his men "with relieving the Rough Riders* from the volleys that were being poured into them from the Spanish." A further test of the regiment's battle prowess would arrive during the fight at Kettle Hill and San Juan Hill.* Mass confusion reigned during the assault as cohesion among the volunteer and regulars units broke down due to Spanish guns firing with deadly accuracy. The Tenth held their composure, despite intense enemy fusillade, and helped the American forces drive the Spanish from their positions. For their efforts, five members of Tenth Cavalry Regiment received the Medal of Honor.

After the war, praise was heaped upon the regiment. One newspaper, *New York Mail and Express,* stated that "the war has not shown greater heroism. The men whose own freedom was baptized in blood have proved themselves capable of giving up their lives that others may be free."

REFERENCES: Herschel V. Cashin, *Under Fire with the Tenth U.S. Cavalry* (New York: F. T. Neely, 1899); Bernard C. Nalty, *Strength for the Fight: A History of Black Americans in the Military* (New York: Free Press, 1986).

MITCHELL YOCKELSON

TEN YEARS' WAR

By the mid-nineteenth century, the Spanish Empire was in a state of advanced decline. Santo Domingo achieved its independence in 1865, leaving Spain with Puerto Rico* in the Caribbean, the Philippine and Mariana islands in the Pacific, a few possessions in Africa, and Cuba, "the Pearl of the Empire." Revenues from Cuban sugar plantations were the last real source of wealth in the empire, and Spanish authorities looked down upon any expression of Cuban nationalism. Cuban-born nationalists, known as *criollos,* were increasingly restless, demanding political and economic reform. To appease them Spain established the Junta de Información, which met in Madrid in 1866 and 1867 to discuss the possibilities of political reform. The junta, composed primarily of Cuban *criollos,* recommended Cuban representation in the Cortes, basic civil liberties, gradual emancipation of the slaves, and enactment of civil and criminal codes in Cuba that were the same, procedurally and substantively, as those in Spain. A brief period of euphoria followed among the Cuban representatives, but their hopes were soon dashed. The Spanish government repudiated its recommendations, increased taxes, and prohibited reformist public meetings and publications.

To more and more *criollos,* the need for reform gave way to the need for revolution. Revolution began in 1868, led by Carlos Manuel de Céspedes. A successful sugar planter, Céspedes had spent much of his adult life agitating for Cuban independence. He was a leader of local *criollo* nationalists, especially those active in the Masonic movement. Carlos Céspedes became famous throughout Cuba on 10 October 1868 when he proclaimed independence and the establishment of the Republic of Cuba in the town of Yara in Oriente Province. The proclamation launched Cuba on the Ten Years' War. By the end of October, Céspedes had nearly 15,000 followers, and by early 1860 he was in virtual control of Oriente Province. In 1869 Céspedes convened a constitutional convention that drafted a constitution declaring Cuban independence, abolishing slavery, and annexing the country to the United States. The delegates to the convention also elected Céspedes as the first president of Cuba. The rebellion soon drew a number of individuals who emerged as revolutionary leaders, including Máximo Gómez,* Antonio Maceo y Grajales,* and José Martí.*

Although the rebels enjoyed considerable initial success, the movement soon disintegrated politically. Céspedes did not possess the skills to maintain internal unity. His decision to abolish slavery alienated many conservatives, who were convinced that abolition would destroy them economically. They were even more enraged with Céspedes's October 1969 decision to support Máximo Gómez's proposal to deprive Spain of its economic base in Cuba by destroying sugar plantations. Many conservatives were also disturbed by the power and popularity of Antonio Maceo. An Afro-Cuban, Maceo was a charismatic figure among the black population in Cuba. *Criollos* feared that Maceo's popularity among Cuban blacks would lead to a racial rebellion and a real socioeconomic revolution in Cuba. Bitter political infighting weakened the revolutionary movement. In 1873 Céspedes was ousted from the presidency; he was ambushed and killed by Spanish soldiers in 1874. By that time the Spanish army controlled most of the country and proceeded to crush the rebellion. Rebels retreated to geographically isolated regions and conducted a guerrilla war for the next four years, but by late 1877 they no longer possessed the will or the resources to continue. In February 1878 rebel leaders and Spanish officials signed an armistice, known as the Pact of Zanjón, ending the war. The Pact of Zanjón included a general amnesty for all political prisoners and all political exiles.

REFERENCES: Enrique Collazo, *Desde Yara hasta el Zanjón* (Havana: Instituto del Libro, 1967); Ramiro Guerra y Sánchez, *Guerra de los diez años, 1868–1878* (Havana: Editorial de Ciencias Sociales, 1972).

JAMES S. OLSON

TERESA (ship).
See *INFANTA MARÍA TERESA*.

TERROR (ship)

Two ships by the name *Terror* were engaged in the Spanish American War, one American and one Spanish. The Spanish *Terror* was a torpedo boat destroyer* built in England and a sister-ship to *Furor.** On 22 June 1898, off San Juan,* Puerto Rico,* *Terror* and the small sloop *Isabel II* attacked *St. Paul** shortly after 1 P.M. The attack may have been an attempt to provoke *St. Paul* into steaming within range of the shore batteries. In any event, the attack failed and *Terror* received a 5-inch shell that disabled the starboard engine. *Terror* then steamed to the beach to avoid sinking.

The U.S.S. *Terror* was a monitor* laid down in 1874 (but not commissioned until 15 April 1896) of the *Amphitrite** class and sister to *Miantonomah** and *Monadnock.** Terror differed from her sister-ships in that she had pneumatic systems (instead of steam or hydraulics) for operating guns, turrets, and steering, thus eliminating some of the overheating problems that plagued the class. *Terror* served in blockade* duty at Cuba and participated in the bombardment of San Juan in May 1898.

Stricken from the navy list in 1915, *Terror* was used as a gunnery target until the hulk was sold in 1921.

REFERENCES: John D. Alden, *The American Steel Navy* (Annapolis, MD: Naval Institute Press, 1972); H. W. Wilson, *The Downfall of Spain* (New York: Burt Franklin, 1971).

TEXAS (ship)

The U.S.S. *Texas* was authorized 3 August 1886 as a battleship but was redesignated a second-class battleship before commissioning on 15 August 1895. *Texas* was designed by competitive means, and the award went to Englishman William John. Because the fitting out of *Texas* was more efficiently accomplished than the fitting out of *Maine,** Texas* became the first battleship of the new steel navy. She was armed with two 12-inch guns in two turrets set in sponsons, port and starboard, six 6-inch guns, twelve 6-pounders, and four torpedo tubes, and she displaced 6,315 tons. This odd gun arrangement—projecting sponsons from each side—made it difficult to coal *Texas* at sea.

Texas left Key West* on 19 May 1898 with the Flying Squadron* and patrolled Cienfuegos* and Santiago de Cuba* in the blockade* until 15 June, when she was ordered to Guantánamo.* Upon arriving at Guantánamo and accompanied by *Marblehead,** Texas* bombarded the fort until it no longer replied (about 2:45 P.M.). Both *Marblehead* and *Texas* had contact with mines, but none exploded.

Texas resumed blockade duty, and on 3 July she maintained station off Santiago when Admiral Pascual Cervera* sallied from the harbor. Under forced draft, *Texas* closed the distance against the emerging *Infanta María Teresa,** Vizcaya,** Cristóbal Colón,** and *Almirante Oquendo,** which were followed closely by the destroyers *Furor** and *Plutón.** Texas* engaged the lead Spanish ships with her main battery and, with her secondary battery, fired upon the two trailing destroyers. At *Brooklyn*'s* turn eastward, she almost rammed *Texas,* the latter reversing engines. This maneuver by Commodore Winfield S. Schley,* elicited much professional comment in the ensuing Sampson-Schley Controversy.*

Texas was an antiquated design at the time of her commissioning and so was decommissioned and recommissioned several times until February 1911, when her name was changed to *San Marcos* to enable the new *Texas* (BB-25) to assume the name. *New Hampshire* (BB-25) sank *San Marcos* in the shallows of Chesapeake Bay southeast of Tangier Island in March 1911. *San Marcos* served as a gunnery target through World War II until finally demolished in January 1959 as a navigational hazard.

REFERENCES: *Appendix to the Report of the Chief of the Bureau of Navigation, 1898* (Washington, DC: Government Printing Office, 1898); John C. Reilly, Jr., and Robert L. Scheina, *American Battleships* 1886–1923 (Annapolis, MD: Naval Institute Press, 1980).

TOPEKA (ship)

Built in Kiel, Germany, in 1881 for Portugal, *Diogenes* was not accepted for service by Portugal. Of 1800 tons, *Diogenes* was purchased by the U.S. Navy in England, armed with six 4.7-inch guns, and renamed *Topeka*. *Topeka* served in Cuban waters and with *Annapolis,** *Wasp** and *Leyden,** took the port of Nipe Bay* with almost no opposition.

Topeka served until 1930, when she was stricken from the navy list.

REFERENCE: *Appendix to the Report of the Chief of the Bureau of Navigation, 1898* (Washington, DC: Government Printing Office, 1898).

TORAL VÁZQUEZ, JOSÉ
(1834–1904)

Commander of the Spanish Fourth Army Corps occupying Santiago de Cuba,* José Toral Vázquez and General of Brigade Joaquín Vara del Rey* had originally been in charge of a two-division brigade that made up the garrison at Santiago. Toral replaced General Arsenio Linares y Pomba* on 1 July 1898 after Spanish forces from San Juan* retreated into fortifications on the outskirts of Santiago. Linares had been wounded in a previous engagement and confined to bed. Toral succeeded to command just as the situation turned against the Spanish forces and negotiations for surrender began.

General William R. Shafter* demanded that Toral surrender the city on 3 July, hours before Admiral Pascual Cervera's* attempt to escape Santiago Harbor. Following the defeat of Admiral Cervera's fleet, Toral was told that shelling of the city would begin 5 July, giving adequate time for all foreign nationals to evacuate the area.

The general countered with his own proposal on 8 July, saying he would evacuate the city if allowed to move his army to Holguín.* Shafter responded by informing Toral that bombardment of the city would begin on 10 July if he did not surrender. When Toral again refused, Shafter asked the navy to begin shelling the western part of the city. The navy complied and began firing on the city around 4:00 P.M. on 10 July and continued according to Shafter's instructions until 1:00 P.M., 11 July.

Negotiations with Toral resumed that day. Spanish law did not allow surrender until all stocks of ammunition and food were exhausted; given this stricture and his own sense of honor and loyalty to Spain, Toral did not surrender Santiago but instead continued to offer the counterproposal of moving his troops from there to Holguín. Shafter again rejected this proposal, telling the Spanish commander that the temporary truce begun on 11 July would continue until midday, 14 July, to allow him more time to think about his situation.

The see-saw of proposals and counterproposals continued after 11 July. American forces shut down the water supply to Santiago while Toral also caught pressure from General Ramón Blanco y Erenas.* The government of Práxedes Mateo Sagasta* in Spain entered negotiations, and Blanco refused to admit the possibility of surrender. However, Sagasta's government, reeling from a series of defeats on sea and land, worried that the conflict might expand to Spain itself, and so Blanco was overruled by Madrid.

In negotiating surrender, Toral concerned himself with preserving his reputation—difficult to accomplish while surrendering. Insisting that his troops be allowed to retain their weapons and that the word *capitulation* be utilized in lieu of *surrender,* Toral clearly attempted to save face at home.

Toral was acquitted by a court-martial early in August 1898. Nevertheless, in the press and other public forums his conduct received serious criticism that played a growing role in Toral's mental instability. He died in an asylum for the insane on 10 July 1904.

REFERENCES: Severo Gómez Núñez, *The Spanish American War* (Washington, DC: Government Printing Office, 1899); also obituaries in the London *Times* and the *New York Times,* 11 July 1904.

TORPEDO

Until the 1870s a torpedo was any underwater weapon, including the submarine mine. After the 1870s the military classified torpedoes as all weapons with independent movement. The general public, however, still favored using the word *torpedo* to describe the submarine mine.

What came to be known as the most widely recognized weapon in this class was originally called the "locomotive" torpedo, or "fish." It was developed by an Austrian navy captain named Giovanni de Luppis and Robert Whitehead, a Scottish engineer. The first Luppis-Whitehead torpedoes suffered from poor performance due to short range, slow speed, and small warhead. Although this weapon was not a significant factor during the war, it was nevertheless included on board U.S. and Spanish torpedo boats* and torpedo boat destroyers.* Torpedo design later overcame these faults, and the torpedo became a deadly weapon with a profound impact in future wars.

Torpedoes in the Spanish American War were submarine mines as well as fish. Cruisers and destroyers in Admiral Pascual Cervera's* Spanish fleet carried locomotive torpedos. Cervera also used submarine mines to deny the Americans access to the harbor at Santiago.*

In the Battle of Santiago, locomotive torpedoes did not fare well because they were poorly placed on *Cristóbal Colón,* *Infanta María Teresa,* *Almirante Oquendo,* and *Vizcaya* and the crew lacked operational training with the weapon. Further, on the Spanish cruisers most of these weapons were disarmed and their warheads used as submarine mines or they were destroyed before they could be used. On the destroyers, they were not used because the ships themselves were sunk before the weapons could be brought into action. The submarine mines, however, fared better. It was a submarine mine combined with gunfire from coastal gun batteries that sank the collier *Merrimac* before she could block the mouth of Santiago Harbor. The mines did offer Cervera's fleet psychological protection as long as the ships stayed in the harbor. Other harbors around Cuba had also been mined, but the Spanish mines proved unreliable: when U.S. ships plowed into them, the mines did not explode.

In the Battle of Manila Bay,* Admiral Montojo y Pasarón* used both types of weapons. He converted at least two of his small gunboats into makeshift torpedo boats. The admiral also placed submarine mines at Manila. Both weapons performed poorly in battle. The two torpedo boats tried to attack *Olympia* but were sunk, their locomotive torpedoes causing no damage to the American ship. The submarine mines were insufficient in number and improperly placed in the harbor and therefore inconsequential.

REFERENCES: Adelbert M. Dewey, *The Life and Letters of Admiral Dewey* (New York: F. Hartley Woodfall Co., 1899); George Dewey, *Autobiography of George Dewey— Admiral of the Navy* (Annapolis: Naval Institute Press, 1913 [1897]); Harold Fock, *Fast Fighting Boats, 1870–1945: Their Design, Construction, and Use* (Annapolis, MD: Naval Institute Press, 1978); George Edward Graham, *Schley and Santiago* (Chicago: W. B. Conkley Co., 1902); Edwyn Gray, *The Devil's Device* (Annapolis, MD: Naval Institute Press, 1991); David Lyon, *The Ship: Steam, Steel, and Torpedoes* (London: W. S. Cowell Ltd. for Her Majesty's Stationery Office, 1980).

BRIAN B. CARPENTER

TORPEDO BOAT DESTROYERS

Naval vessels built and designed to hunt down and destroy torpedo boats,* torpedo boat destroyers were later commonly known simply as destroyers. The U.S. Navy began looking at ways to improve upon torpedo boats when it found that they were not stable enough to be used in open oceans and also could not effectively counter the threat of other torpedo boats. A new class of ships would be needed to fulfill this role. The navy asked Herreshoff Manufacturing Company of Bristol, Rhode Island, and other ship designers to come up with a larger and more powerful version of their current Herreshoff torpedo boats. These ships were not built in time to participate in the war.

Spain built also torpedo boats and torpedo boat destroyers. Their designs were based on British ships of this class built by Alfred Yarrow and John Thornycroft. Despite their larger size and better armament, Spanish destroyers faired poorly during the war due to flawed naval tactics and planning.

At Santiago de Cuba* both *Plutón** and *Furor** were sunk by American warships as they tried to escape the harbor during Admiral Pascual Cervera's* sortie. *Terror** was eliminated while trying to leave the blockaded harbor at the San Juan,* Puerto Rico. Admiral Manuel de la Cámara's* squadron also originally had three destroyers—*Audaz, Properia,* and *Osado*—but these ships returned to Spain along with the two steamers *San Francisco* and *Loyola* after they had escorted the fleet as far as Suez. The rest of the fleet returned to Spain to shore up the country's coastal defenses after Cervera's defeat at Santiago.

REFERENCES: William Hovgaard, *Modern History of Warships* (New York: Spon & Chamberlain, 1920); Edwin P. Hoyt, *Deadly Craft: Fireships to PT Boats* (Boston: Atlantic–Little, Brown Books, 1968).

BRIAN B. CARPENTER

TORPEDO BOATS

Thirty-one of these small, maneuverable, but lightly armed and armored ships were built between 1887 and 1905. In the United States, many of these boats were built by the Herreshoff Manufacturing Company of Bristol, Rhode Island, and Columbian Iron Works and Dry Dock Company of Baltimore. Their purpose, as defined by the U.S. Navy, was channel service and harbor defense. Lightly armored compared to other ships of their day, they did possess one weapon system that would assume a powerful role, the torpedo. Because of their narrowly defined role, small size, and limited range, these ships were restricted to coastal operations.

Of the U.S. torpedo boats that participated in the war, only five, *Cushing** (TB-1), *Ericsson** (TB-2), *Foote** (TB-3), *Gwin* (TB-16), and *Winslow** (TB-5) saw action. *Cushing** captured four small Spanish vessels in the Cayman Islands on 7 August 1898. On 11 August she was joined by *Gwin* and together they captured two small ships. Spanish shore batteries fired on *Foote* during the preliminary fighting at Manila Bay.* *Winslow*'s war activities more well known. During an effort to capture three Spanish gunboats at Cárdenas,* *Winslow* was struck three times by artillery shore batteries, wounding three, including the commander of the ship, and killing four men, including Ensign Worth Bagley,* the only U.S. naval officer to be killed in the war. The unfortunate boat's steering gear was also disabled. *Ericsson* rescued survivors from the burning *Vizcaya** at Santiago de Cuba.* Other ships of this designation served as picket boats or messengers.

While U.S. torpedo boats did engage in some combat activities, the same is not true of Spain's. Spain did not send its flotilla of torpedo boats to Cuba, the Philippines, or Puerto Rico because it was afraid this action would leave its shores and harbors unprotected.

Instead, the Spanish government sent to Cuba two of its larger torpedo boat destroyers,* *Furor** and *Plutón,** and three of its cruisers, including the *Cristóbal Colón.** These new cruisers carried their own complement of torpedos. A third destroyer, *Terror,** developed engine trouble and never made it to Cuba. All were destroyed in the battle at Santiago.

In the Philippines, the Spanish navy converted several of its small gunboats into torpedo-carrying boats. Two of these small craft attacked *Olympia** during the Battle at Manila Bay, but their attack was ineffective. One was sunk as it attacked the large American warship, and the other was forced to beach itself after its abortive attack.

The combat record of these vessels, while distinguished, was not a success. Doctrine for the use of these vessels was ill defined, and as a result the vessels were misused and abused in roles unsuited to them. By the end of the war, the U.S. Navy began exploring other ship designs based on the largest of their torpedo boats, *Cushing.* The purpose of these new boats would be to seek out and destroy enemy torpedo boats and to protect ships in the U.S. fleet.

REFERENCES: Víctor M. Concas y Palau, *The Squadron of Admiral Cervera* (Washington, DC: Government Printing Office, 1900); W.A.M. Goode, *With Sampson through the War* (New York: Doubleday & McClure Co., 1899); William Hovgaard, *Modern History of Warships* (New York: Spon & Chamberlain, 1920); J. Moody, ed., *Dictionary of American Fighting Ships: Historical Sketches* (Washington, DC: Government Printing Office, 1981); Severo Gómez Núñez, *The Spanish American War* (Washington, DC: Government Printing Office, 1899).

BRIAN B. CARPENTER

TOWING

Towing was a viable transport method during the steam era. The Spanish American War saw both Spain and the United States employ ships to tow other ships operationally. The monitors *Monadnock** and *Monterey** were towed by colliers at least partially across the Pacific. The monitors *Amphitrite** and *Terror** and the torpedo boat *Porter** were towed by heavier combatants as a fuel-conserving measure. Similarly, the Spanish gunboats *Terror** and *Furor** were towed across the Atlantic to save fuel. The difficulties of bunkering at sea and the paucity of bases necessitated towing for both combatants.

REFERENCE: H. W. Wilson, *The Downfall of Spain* (New York: Burt Franklin, 1971).

TRANSATLÁNTICA LINE

At the conclusion of hostilities in Cuba, after the signing of the peace protocol in August 1898, General William R. Shafter* was anxious to wind things up and began the process of gathering the remnants of the Spanish garrisons in Cuba. Some 24,000 were thus assembled at Guantánamo* and elsewhere. Lieutenant John D. Miley efficiently carried out the assignment of gathering all Spanish prisoners.

The U.S. War Department,* concerned about the cost of guarding and provisioning such a large contingent of prisoners, advertised for bids to repatriate

the Spanish. Without the means itself to repatriate the prisoners, the War Department utilized this unusual expedient. Bids were received from Cunard and from Hamburg-American Line as well as from some others, but the lowest bid, somewhat ironically, came from the Spanish Transatlántica Line at $55 per officer and $20 per enlisted man. Thus the United States expended $513,860 to efficiently repatriate 22,864 Spanish soldiers between 9 August and 17 September 1898. This odd arrangement proved an effective and politically important means of ending all possibility of further conflict over prisoners and justified the decision to offer repatriation as a condition of the surrender of Santiago.*
REFERENCES: R. A. Alger, *The Spanish American War* (New York: Harper & Brothers, 1901); French Ensor Chadwick, *The Relations of the United States and Spain* (New York: Russell & Russell, 1968); John D. Miley, *In Cuba with Shafter* (New York: Charles Scribner's Sons, 1899).

TRANSPORTATION

Mobility has always been an advantage in battle, and in the Spanish American War this advantage was conspicuously absent among Spanish forces. Distance, geography, and insurgents* in Cuba and the Philippines combined to stymie Spanish attempts at supply, reinforcement, and tactical movement. A transportation infrastructure did not exist for Spain in Cuba, in the Philippines, or in Puerto Rico. The blockade* and a shortage of shipping shut down movement by sea in the Antilles, while the Philippines are half a world away from Spain. The difficulties and failure of the Spanish Eastern Squadron* under Admiral Manuel de la Cámara* offer ample testimony to the strategic significance of transportation.

The transportation challenge of the United States was also significant, but for different reasons and with a different effect. Only 90 miles from Havana,* the U.S. forces had easy and ready access to supply wharfage, ship repair, and material depots. A rail infrastructure existed that could carry heavy tonnage; production capacity existed to manufacture wagons, railroad equipment, and rolling stock; and the merchant marine could provide water transport. Missing from the U.S. equation was amphibious experience in this, the first foreign war of the United States. Missing also was the leadership necessary at the War Department* and Quartermaster's Department* to organize and process the unprecedented rapid buildup of troop strength and material and the efficient transport of both to the combat theater. The notable failures occurred in Florida and Cuba, where soldiers in the midst of copious equipment at Tampa* had to sail without it and disembark without sufficient barges, pack trains, and rations. Rapid buildup created unforeseen bottlenecks at Tampa's single track of rail. Inexperience did not foresee the challenges. Improvisation and a rapid learning curve, aided immeasurably by Spain's inability to exploit the situation, quickly resolved the difficulties. The railway bottleneck at Tampa eventually led to Russell A. Alger's* abandoning Tampa as the port of embarkation.

Eighth Corps* at San Francisco was, in contrast, orderly and efficient, highlighting the differences between General William R. Shafter* of Fifth Corps* and General Wesley Merritt* of Eighth Corps.

REFERENCE: Graham A. Cosmas, *An Army for Empire* (Columbia: University of Missouri Press, 1971).

TREATY OF PARIS

Signed on 10 December 1898 by members of the Peace Commission,* the Treaty of Paris obligated Spain* to relinquish sovereignty in Cuba and to cede Puerto Rico,* Guam,* and the Philippines,* the last in consideration of a payment of $20 million. The treaty was the one-sided result of President William McKinley's* unyielding firmness in peace negotiations* with Spain's corresponding impotence to effect any change in the outcome. The treaty was approved by the U.S. Senate on 6 February 1899 and signed by the president the same day. Ratified by Spain on 19 March, the treaty was proclaimed on 11 April 1899.

The treaty and its implications wrought acrid political turmoil in Spain and legislative deadlock; the queen regent, María Cristina,* signed it to break the deadlock.

The U.S. Senate also participated in vigorous debate and passed the treaty by a two-thirds margin, 57 to 27.

REFERENCE: David F. Trask, *The War with Spain in 1898* (New York: Macmillan Publishing Co., 1981).

TROCHA

The *trochas* of Cuba were wide swaths of empty road, perhaps 50 feet wide, periodically fortified with garrisons and blockhouses. They were cut from the Cuban vegetation in an effort to deny the insurgents* access to other parts of the countryside. Initiated by General Arsenio Martínez Campos* and expanded by his successor, Valeriano Weyler,* the *trocha,* combined with the reconcentration policy,* was a Spanish strategic failure. Inflamed U.S. opinion and sympathy for the insurrection and eventual Cuban independence largely resulted from the *trochas* and the reconcentration policy. *Trochas* did contain the insurgents, but at a terrible cost to Spain. Antonio Maceo Grajales* was killed trying to cross a *trocha,* whose tactical utility remained questionable. When General William R. Shafter* and his Fifth Corps* landed, the Spanish—wedded to garrisons on the *trochas*—could not or would not redeploy to overwhelm the Americans.

REFERENCE: Philip S. Foner, *The Spanish-Cuban-American War and the Birth of American Imperialism* (New York: Monthly Review Press, 1972).

TURPIE, DAVID M.
(1828–1909)

David M. Turpie was the Democratic senator from Indiana who, with cosponsor Senator Foraker* from Ohio, offered an amendment to the resolution for war with Spain. The amendment sought formal recognition of the Republic of Cuba. It passed the Senate but was narrowly defeated in the House. A compromise proviso was adopted, however, that required Spain to withdraw from Cuba immediately.

KEN KEMPCKE

U

ULLOA (ship).
See DON ANTONIO DE ULLOA.

UNIFORMS, U.S. ARMY

When preparing for war against Spain, the War Department* suffered the most when it came to properly clothing the army for the tropical temperatures they were sure to face in Cuba. Prior to 1898 no provisions were made for a hot-weather uniform. Soldiers on duty in the American South and Southwest wore the standard blue wool uniform with only minor modifications. However, in 1883 the Quartermaster's Department* issued a brown canvas uniform, which was the closest the army got to a summer uniform.

In April 1898 the commanding general of the army, Nelson A. Miles,* recommended to Quartermaster General Marshall I. Ludington* that he contract for the manufacture of 10,000 experimental canvas suits to be worn by troops sent to Cuba. Typical of army contracts during this period, Ludington failed to secure the uniforms in time for the troops to use them in Cuba. The problem arose when the quartermaster general insisted that the cloth should be manufactured from khaki. Used by the British in warm climates with great success, the closely woven, light brown cotton fabric proved too difficult for an American firm to weave or dye. The quartermaster rejected several bids before settling on an acceptable cloth in June.

To tide the army over until the new uniform could be issued, the quartermaster general reduced the weight of the cloth in the blue uniform in hopes of making it adaptable to the hot climates. He also bought and issued large quantities of a light cotton underwear. The volunteer units fared even worse. While training in the camps, many troops wore their civilian clothes until they could be issued uniforms. In some cases what they received were old, regular army castoffs.

Because of delays in production, only 5,000 of the new uniforms reached

General William R. Shafter's* Fifth Corps* before they left for Santiago. However, a shipload of tropical uniforms arrived off the coast of Siboney in July. Because of a lack of transportation facilities to ship the uniforms, the men continued to swelter in the trenches while wearing wool trousers and flannel shirts. Other regiments fared better, particularly those participating in the invasion of Puerto Rico.*

Those who were lucky enough to be issued the new canvas uniforms complained that they fitted poorly, wore out quickly, and were almost as hot as the regulation blue uniforms. Not until the war ended did Ludington successfully procure a true cotton khaki uniform and issue them to all troops serving in Puerto Rico and the Philippines.

REFERENCES: Graham A. Cosmas, *An Army for Empire* (Columbia: University of Missouri Press, 1971); Gregory J. W. Urwin, *The United States Infantry: An Illustrated History, 1775–1918* (New York: Sterling Publishing Co., 1991).

MITCHELL YOCKELSON

UPTON, EMORY
(1839–1881)

Emory Upton's ideas on infantry strategy and tactics influenced many military officers who served during the Spanish American War. One of his central ideas, the formation of an expansible army,* fell on deaf ears prior to the end of the war. The conventional wisdom was that an army could be created out of volunteers supported by a small cadre of career soldiers.

Congress under the leadership of Representative John A. T. Hull,* a Republican from Iowa, provided the groundwork for an expansible army to come into existence, but change was slow. Congress and the military both knew acceptance of the plan would eliminate the need for militias and thus was a politically hazardous undertaking. During the war the mixed results of infantry actions lead to a rethinking of strategy that lead, in turn, to an expansible army.

The founder of these military theories did not live to see his plans come to fruition. While stationed at the Presidio of San Francisco,* Upton suffered from increasingly severe and debilitating headaches that interrupted his work. He was forced to resign from the army on 14 March 1881, and the following day he shot himself with his service revolver.

REFERENCES: Trevor N. Depuy, ed., *The Harper Encyclopedia of Military Biography* (New York: HarperCollins, 1992); Emory Upton, *Military Policy of the United States* (New York: Greenwood Press, 1968); Emory Upton, *A New System of Infantry Tactics* (New York: D. Appleton, 1867).

BRIAN B. CARPENTER

U.S. ARMY MILITARY INFORMATION DIVISION.
See MILITARY INFORMATION DIVISION.

U.S. ARMY SIGNAL CORPS.
See SIGNAL CORPS.

U.S. ASIATIC SQUADRON.
See ASIATIC SQUADRON.

U.S. CONGRESS.
See CONGRESS.

U.S. NORTH ATLANTIC SQUADRON.
See NORTH ATLANTIC SQUADRON.

V

VAMOOSE (ship)

Vamoose was a speedy yet delicate steam-powered yacht* chartered by William Randolph Hearst* and fitted out as a press boat to carry dispatches from Cuba to the United States for his *New York Journal.* On 24 November 1896 the *Journal* prominently announced the acquisition of the boat; its departure for Key West* with correspondent Charles Michaelson was proclaimed on 6 December. Government officials were suspicious about Hearst's using the ship as a filibuster* and searched it several times on its journey. No arms were found, thus supporting Hearst's claims that it was to be used solely as a press boat to bring back news uncensored by the Spanish. Hearst declared that "the first time she steams out of the harbor of Havana she will carry a cargo more fatal to Spain's hopes than all the dynamite ever made."

Writer Richard Harding Davis* and illustrator Frederic Remington* were hired by Hearst to travel from Key West to Cuba aboard *Vamoose* to join the rebels in Santa Clara Province. After joining the insurgents,* the correspondents were to send weekly dispatches to the Cuban coast, to be picked up by Michaelson aboard *Vamoose* and taken back to Key West. The vessel was delayed from leaving Key West first when the crew went on strike due to fear of arrest by Spanish authorities and later when the captain turned back due to heavy weather. Growing impatient with the repeated delays, on 9 January 1897 the pair of reporters sailed to Havana on *Olivette,* a regular passenger vessel. Rather than sneaking behind the insurgents' lines, they had to settle for an official pass from the Spanish.

Hearst was the first publisher to see the need for press boats; the *Journal* eventually had ten such vessels, which it referred to as its "fleet." Other news organizations had smaller numbers of boats, but the total number was substantial and the cost of acquiring and operating them was a major expense for the newspapers. Although it was the first of many dispatch boats used by the press

during the war, the frail *Vamoose* was unsuited to the task and never made a trip to Cuba.
REFERENCE: Charles H. Brown, *The Correspondent's War* (New York: Scribner's, 1961).

MARK A. THOMAS

VARA DEL REY, JOAQUÍN
(1840–1898)

Brigadier General Joaquín Vara del Rey served under General Arsénio Linares y Pomba* in Cuba, and in the battles for Santiago,* Vara del Rey commanded the 500 troops that defended El Caney.* The spanish general's stubborn defense frustrated American plans to take El Caney. Anticipating a Spanish defense as ineffective as that at Las Guásimas,* Brigadier General Henry Lawton's* division, which outnumbered Vara del Rey's command ten to one, was stymied; Vara del Rey's troops held up further American advances for over eight hours. The Spanish defense collapsed when Vara del Rey, wounded in both legs, was killed while being carried in a stretcher. The brigadier general also lost his two sons in the battle.
REFERENCE: Severo Gómez Núñez, *La Guerra Hispano-Americana,* 5 vols. (Madrid: Imprimería del Cuerpo de Artillería, 1900–1902).

VELASCO (ship)

Velasco was a Spanish gunboat constructed by the British between 1879 and 1881. *Velasco* served as the prototype of a whole class of these gunboats but differed from her sister-ships *Don Juan de Austria,* *Conde de Venadito,* and *Don Antonio de Ulloa* by having three 6-inch guns in the main battery augmented with various smaller calibers. *Velasco* burned at Manila,* another victim of *Petrel,* and was not refloated.

VEST, GEORGE
(1830–1904)

Democratic senator from Missouri from 1879 to 1903, George Vest challenged the constitutionality of the Treaty of Paris.* When Spain ceded Puerto Rico* and the Philippines* to the United States, Vest observed that federal statutes contained no provisions for colonies. He introduced a resolution in the Senate arguing that it would be unconstitutional for the United States "to acquire territory to be held and governed permanently as colonies."
REFERENCES: *Dictionary of American Biography,* vol. 5 (New York: Scribner's, 1937); Stanley Karnow, *In Our Image* (London: Century, 1990).

KEN KEMPCKE

VESUVIUS (ship)

Little technological experimentation occurred during the Spanish American War; the conflict was too short. Nevertheless, earlier efforts at experimentation were given wartime trial. One such previous effort was an attempt at increasing the destructive power of the navy's projectiles. More potent explosives, such as nitroglycerin and dynamite, were available, but they were so unstable as to be impractical for delivery in the systems of the time. *Vesuvius* became an attempt to bridge the gap between high but unstable explosives and jarring delivery systems.

Vesuvius was a ship designed around three pneumatic guns. The guns, 15 inches in diameter and 54 feet in length, lay side by side at an 18-degree angle from the lowest deck (where the guns were loaded) to the muzzles, which protruded from the fore deck. Pointing forward, fixed and aligned with the ship, the guns were aimed by aiming the ship. The guns were fired by compressed air. The air propelled projectiles of dynamite weighing as much as 500 pounds with a range in excess of a mile. Basically, the tubes were huge pellet guns mounted in a ship.

The promoter of this system to the navy was army lieutenant Edmund L. G. Zalinsky, who had an arrangement with the Pneumatic Dynamite Gun Company, and he served as the company's spokesman. For this reason, contemporary literature often referred to the "Zalinsky Dynamite Gun," although he was not the inventor.

Vesuvius had a narrow 26-foot 5-inch beam and a 9-foot draft (shallow for close inshore work) on a long 252-foot 4-inch hull. Launched in 1888 completely unarmored for speed, she handled poorly and rolled prodigiously. On 23 February 1897 *Vesuvius* began Florida-based neutrality patrol, which she continued until she joined the blockade* of Cuba near the end of April 1898. Rear Admiral William T. Sampson* ordered *Vesuvius* to Santiago to employ her guns against Spanish shore batteries. Inasmuch as *Vesuvius* was unarmored and full of dynamite, her officers were naturally reluctant to expose the ship tc desultory fire from the Spanish. Therefore, the vulnerable *Vesuvius* moved inshore only at night. On six nights between 15 and 27 June and the nights of 4 and 5 July, she fired on forts and shore batteries but effected little, if any, serious damage, according to Lieutenant José Müller y Tejeiro, second in command of Spanish naval forces at Santiago. Unimpressed with *Vesuvius*'s performance, the navy decommissioned *Vesuvius* in September. When recommissioned in 1905, she was no longer a dynamite ship but a torpedo-training vessel. Sold for scrap in 1922, the ship ended her career as a naval oddity of the Spanish American War. REFERENCE: John W. Kennon, "USS Vesuvius," *U.S. Naval Institute Proceedings* 80 (February 1954): 182–190.

VICKSBURG (ship)

Vicksburg was the second of the *Annapolis**-class gunboats launched. Commissioned on 23 October 1897, she was armed like *Annapolis* and served in the Havana* blockade with *Annapolis.* Like *Annapolis, Vicksburg* had composite construction; that is, she had a steel frame with wood planking.

Vicksburg transferred to the Coast Guard in 1921 and was sold in 1946.

REFERENCE: John D. Alden, *The American Steel Navy* (Annapolis, MD: Naval Institute Press, 1972).

VILLAAMIL, FERNANDO
(1845–1898)

Captain Fernando Villaamil of the Spanish navy sailed from Cádiz on 13 March 1898 with a troop transport, three torpedo boats,* and three destroyers. They arrived in Caribbean waters before the heavier squadron of Admiral Pascual Cervera.* Villaamil's departure caused some consternation among senior U.S. naval officers, who at one point discussed a preeruptive strike against Villaamil but then abandoned the idea.

Villaamil energetically entered into the debates among Cervera's captains on the tactical plan to utilize Cervera's ships, but like Cervera, he was not optimistic of success. Commanding *Furor** and *Plutón** at Santiago,* Villaamil sortied last in the line and left a gap between the ships—an unfortunate gap inasmuch as Villaamil's two ships were destroyed almost immediately: *Furor* and *Plutón* sank while attempting to beach. Loss of life on the two vessels was high, and Villaamil was one of those killed by a shell that hit the *Furor*'s bridge.

REFERENCE: Víctor M. Concas y Palau, *The Squadron of Admiral Cervera* (Washington, DC: Government Printing Office, 1900).

VILLAVERDE, DOMINGO

A Cuban telegrapher, Domingo Villaverde was strategically located in Havana,* where he could report regularly on Cuban events to his longtime associate Martin L. Hellings.* Villaverde's usefulness came not from what he saw as much as from his ability to communicate to the United States by evading the lax Spanish military censor at Havana. The censor retired at 9 P.M., and Villaverde could then telegraph to Hellings's office in Key West* events he deemed significant. It was essentially a one-way communication inasmuch as messages to Villaverde from Key West would have caused suspicion in even the most lethargic of censors. It is odd, to say the least, that the Spanish authorities kept these cables open and allowed Villaverde, a Cuban in the employ of an American telegraph company, to continue to operate them—more so, even, when one realizes that the cable office was located in the governor-general's palace, where all kinds of sensitive conversations could be overheard. The whole episode begins to sound like something out of a Hollywood movie.

Villaverde's most significant cable arrived in Key West on 19 May 1898. It informed Hellings that Admiral Pascual Cervera* and his squadron had anchored in Santiago,* not in Cienfuegos* as had been expected. Confirmed in the United States within twenty-four hours, this intelligence precipitated events that led to neutralizing Cervera's squadron and the landing of troops on Cuban soil.

REFERENCE: G.J.A. O'Toole, *The Spanish War* (New York: W. W. Norton & Co., 1984).

VIRGINIUS AFFAIR

Americans have always been interested in Cuba. As early as 1762 during the French and Indian War, troops from the North American colonies occupied Havana.* The interest of Americans concerning Cuba varied during the nineteenth century between concern that France or Great Britain might seize the island to annex Cuba to the desire for a free Cuba. A Cuban insurrection* shortly after the American Civil War once again focused the interests of the United States on the island. Filibusters,* of which the *Virginius* affair was one example, seized the national attention.

Virginius was an iron sidewheeler constructed in Scotland in 1864 as a Confederate blockade runner. In 1873 she was employed (and had been since 1870) as a supply vessel for Cuban insurgents. She carried arms, ammunition, and volunteers. Technically a registered vessel of the United States with an Annapolis graduate, Joseph Fry,* as captain, *Virginius* might be better described as a ship of the insurrection. The American owner was only a front for the insurrection, and *Virginius*'s flag locker carried ensigns of many nations. On 31 October 1873 *Virginius* surrendered to the Spanish *Tornado,* herself another Scots-built Confederate blockade runner, and *Virginius* was taken to Santiago. General Juan Berriel, Spanish military governor, declared *Virginius* a pirate and promptly ordered firing squads to execute fifty-three of her officers, crew, and passengers, including Captain Fry. The remaining 155 men of the *Virginius* doubtless would also have died had it not been for the timely arrival at Santiago of the H.M.S. *Niobe* and her captain's (Sir Lambton Loraine's) strenuous protests.

A severe diplomatic wrangle ensued between the United States and Spain. American newspapers called for war, and Union and Confederate veterans volunteered to rid the hemisphere of Spanish autocracy. Secretary of State Hamilton Fish,* a very capable diplomat, negotiated a settlement with Spain in which Spain paid an indemnity.

There were two important results of the *Virginius* affair that directly affected the Spanish American War twenty-five years later. The first is that at the height of the crisis, Secretary of the Navy George Robeson ordered all available U.S. Navy* vessels to Key West. The assembled fleet was a rusty, rotting, motley array of ships that had not seen duty in eight years. The obvious military weakness of the navy left American diplomats no alternative but negotiation. The navy's humiliation left a lasting impression on young officers such as Robley Evans.* Twenty-five years later the U.S. Navy would be modern, robust, and aggressive.

The second impact on the Spanish American War was the negative feeling generated by the brutal and summary executions of Americans at the hands of the Spanish. The press of the day dramatically emphasized the emotional side of the executions by publishing, for example, Fry's farewell letter to his wife. Even though the *Virginius* affair was settled pacifically, a residue of antipathy toward Spain lingered in the American mind. In 1898 the *Virginius* affair was resurrected in the press, receiving almost as much attention as it had a generation earlier.

REFERENCE: Richard H. Bradford, *The Virginius Affair* (Boulder; Colorado Associated University Press, 1980).

VIXEN (ship)

Vixen, of 545 tons, was one of the converted yachts* purchased by the U.S. Navy in a defense measure of 9 March 1898. *Vixen* was part of the American forces involved in Admiral William T. Sampson's* blockade and, along with another armed yacht, *Gloucester** vigorously attacked the Spanish destroyers *Plutón** and *Furor.** After the war *Vixen* served in the North Atlantic Squadron.*

VIZCAYA (ship)

Launched in 1891, *Vizcaya* was one of three sister-ships: *Infanta María Teresa,** *Almirante Oquendo,** and *Vizcaya.* Of 6,890 tons, each was armed with two 11-inch guns, ten 5.5-inch guns, eight 12-pounders, and miscellaneous machine guns and weapons of smaller caliber. Deck armor of 3 inches and an armor belt two-thirds the length of the hull completed her armament. Under forced draft, *Vizcaya* was capable of 20 knots, but in service in Cuba, speed was less. The large main battery was shielded with only 3-inch superior and 9-inch lateral armor. The 5.5-inch guns had only shields, no armor. Thus *Vizcaya* was gunned to fight battleships but armored so that such an encounter would find her weak. The high freeboard and wooden cabins suffered severe damage during the Battle of Santiago.*

Vizcaya visited New York four days after *Maine** blew up in Havana on 5 February 1898. *Vizcaya* departed from New York for Havana on 25 February and anchored beside *Almirante Oquendo.* Both ships then joined Admiral Pascual Cervera's* squadron in the Cape Verdes.*

On 3 July *Vizcaya* was the second ship out of Santiago's harbor in Cervera's attempted escape from the blockade.* *Vizcaya,* the last of the three sister-ships to be destroyed, was engaged by *Brooklyn,** *Texas,** *Iowa,** and *Oregon,** while concentrating her fire on *Brooklyn.* The battle was short, only about six minutes, during which time a storm of American shells fired the ship. *Vizcaya* ran ashore and *Ericsson** ran in to rescue Spanish crew members. The heat of the fires on *Vizcaya* began to explode munitions aboard ship. *Iowa* also sent in boats to rescue the *Vizcaya*'s crew and brought back Captain Antonio Eulate, wounded.

REFERENCE: Alfredo Aguilera, *Buques de guerra españoles, 1885–1971* (Madrid: Librería Editorial San Martín, 1972).

VOLUNTEERS

Volunteers existed on all sides of the conflict. By their nature, the insurgent forces in the Philippines and Cuba were often self-selected. There existed also *voluntarios* or Spanish-sympathizing home guards in Cuba and the Philippines. Often unreliable—understandably so—these played marginal strategic roles in the Spanish American War. The third group, larger and more influential than the first two combined, were the thousands of American volunteers.

Warlike civilians organized into militias with officers representing various states. The National Guard,* by definition a volunteer group, swayed politically to and fro. In the United States, volunteers had a cherished constitutional and mythic link to the ideals of American nationhood, the Revolution, and the Civil War. Veterans of the last-named conflict still existed by the thousands. For some the existence of the regulars, a standing army, constituted a moral decay. Citizen soldiers—the volunteers—were to be America's soldiers, they reasoned. The swirling debate surrounding the Hull Bill, introduced by Representative John A. T. Hull,* was often couched in these moral tones.

In addition, officers in volunteer units often had political ambitions beyond the war. Theodore Roosevelt* and William Jennings Bryan* are two notable examples. Recognizing this fact, President William McKinley* treated the two very differently. An inveterate self-promoter, Roosevelt set himself up for future office with the opportunities handed to him, and the opportunities he seized. Bryan, a colonel of volunteers with a Nebraska regiment, was denied any visible role by his erstwhile political opponent.

The military establishment placed its trust in the regulars. These were tested, trained, and proven, whereas the volunteers were not. For this reason very few volunteer units got into the actual combat. The most notable exception, the Rough Riders,* also the most famous unit of the war, owed its fame and place to its flamboyant leader, Roosevelt.

On 19 April the day Congress authorized intervention in Cuba, McKinley's spokesmen in Congress also introduced bills to create a volunteer army. Compromises worked out between the powerful and politically savvy National Guard and the McKinley administration, these bills recognized that when state units were called up, they could retain identity and officers as state units, yet still be under federal jurisdiction. In addition, volunteer units could be created upon the same basis as regular units. All volunteer generals were to be appointed by the president, and the president could assign a regular officer to any volunteer regiment. Corps commanders could also appoint boards to review incompetent officers. Thus the compromise allowed volunteers and the unit or state identity but brought the whole under federal control and regular command. Most volunteers never left the States, although 12,000 volunteers guarded the eastern seaboard, and General Wesley Merritt's* Eighth Corps,* destined for Manila,* was comprised primarily of volunteers.

REFERENCE: Graham A. Cosmas, *An Army for Empire* (Columbia: University of Missouri Press, 1971).

W

WADE, JAMES FRANKLIN
(1843–1921)

James Franklin Wade served as chief organizer of the U.S. Army and U.S. volunteer troops heading to Cuba from Tampa* and Camp Thomas.* Wade was born in Jefferson, Ohio, on 14 April 1843. Appointed as a volunteer first lieutenant to the Sixth U.S. Calvary on 1 May 1861, he saw action at Beverly Ford, Virginia, and in southwestern Virginia, advancing from first lieutenant to brigadier general of volunteers.

After the Civil War Wade mustered out of volunteer service, became a captain in the U.S. Army, and worked his way through the ranks to brigadier general. On 15 April 1898, shortly after war had been declared on Spain, Wade commanded a troop assembly area at Tampa.* On 26 May Wade took command of Third Corps at Camp Thomas, Chickamauga, Georgia.

After Spain signed the peace protocol in August, Wade was asked on 17 August to be part of the Cuban Evacuation Committee, which would oversee the evacuation of Spanish forces from Cuba* and Puerto Rico. Wade continued to serve in the armed forces until being discharged from volunteer service on 12 June 1899.

Following the conflict, Wade served in the Philippine Islands, from 1901 to 1904, being promoted to major general in 1903. By law he was forced to retire on 14 April 1907. He died at his home in Jefferson, Ohio, on 23 August 1921.

REFERENCE: *Correspondence Relating to the War with Spain,* 2 vols. (Washington, DC: Government Printing Office, 1993).

BRIAN B. CARPENTER

WAGNER, ARTHUR LOCKWOOD
(1853–1905)

Besides his career as army officer, Colonel (later Brigadier General) Arthur Lockwood Wagner was most noted as a progressive reformer of the army.

Born in Illinois and an 1875 West Point graduate, Wagner served in the West but acquired distinction at the Infantry and Cavalry School, where he was instrumental in establishing a professional regimen. Heading the Military Information Division* in early 1898, Wagner also served on the staffs of General Henry Lawton* at Santiago* and General Nelson A. Miles* in Puerto Rico.

REFERENCE: *Webster's American Military Biographies* (Springfield, MA: G. & C. Merriam, Co., 1978).

WAINWRIGHT, RICHARD
(1849–1926)

Of a distinguished American military family, Richard Wainwright graduated from the Naval Academy in 1868 and served in a variety of duties, including that of chief of the Office of Naval Intelligence.* In 1897, while executive officer of the U.S.S. *Maine,** Wainwright directed the recovery of bodies from the wreck and participated in the U.S. Naval Court of Inquiry.

Wainwright later commanded *Gloucester,** a converted yacht,* where he proved an aggressive and able commander. He led the furious charge against *Furor** and *Plutón** at the Battle of Santiago.* He rescued some 200 Spanish survivors from the water, including Admiral Pascual Cervera.*

Wainwright led the American expedition to Puerto Rico, where *Gloucester* captured Guánica* on 25 July 1898.

In 1911 Wainwright retired from the navy, a rear admiral.

REFERENCES: Damon E. Cummings, *Admiral Wainwright and the United States Fleet* (Washington, DC: Government Printing Office, 1962); *Log of the U.S. Gunboat* Gloucester (Annapolis, MD: U.S. Naval Institute, 1899).

WAKE ISLAND

Wake Island is actually one island and three smaller islands in the Pacific Ocean between Hawaii* and Guam.* It lies at 19°17' North and 166°35' East and is about 45 miles long and a little over 2 miles wide. It is a coral island.

The scenes of later heroic action in World War II, Wake Island was a source of contention as soon as the United States acquired the Philippines.* The Americans faced an insurgency in the Philippines that also threatened continued U.S. sovereignty. Japan* and Germany* both lusted for the Philippines. As a result of the acquisition of the Philippines, various effects of the Treaty of Paris,* and the American need for closer communication with its new Pacific acquisitions, Commander Edward D. Taussig of the U.S.S. *Bennington** claimed Wake for the United States on 17 January 1899. The acquisition of Wake Island was for a trans-Pacific cable link, a need that developed directly from the Spanish American War.

REFERENCE: William Reynolds Braisted, *The United States Navy in the Pacific, 1897–1909* (Austin: University of Texas Press, 1958).

WAR DEPARTMENT

Exercising administrative and fiscal jurisdiction over the U.S. Army, 1789–1947, the War Department was an executive branch agency of the U.S. government.

During the 1890s the War Department consisted of a central office headquartered in Washington, D.C., under the supervision of the civilian secretary of war,* and of field components under the direction of a professional military commander whose title was "commanding general of the army." The central office was comprised of ten administrative and supply bureaus under the direct supervision of the secretary of war. These bureaus provided administrative and technical support for the field components. The field components, or the "army in the field," were stationed throughout eight geographical military districts across the country. Their size and boundaries were established by presidential order. Within each military district the army was organized into tactical units, or "troops of the line," namely, infantry, cavalry, and artillery under the direct command of officers in the rank of colonel or higher. These officers were responsible for the overall health and general welfare of the men and the post or station under their command.

The position of secretary of war in 1898 was held by Russell A. Alger* of Michigan, a veteran of the Civil War, who achieved moderate success as a businessman and politician. The commanding general of the army during this period was Major General Nelson A. Miles* who also served during the Civil War but was better known for his exploits during the Indian Wars.

By 1898 the administration of the War Department was carried out by ten bureaus: the Judge Advocate General's Department, the Inspector General's Department, the Adjutant General's Department (considered the most powerful because it handled personnel-related matters and issued all the orders emanating from both the secretary of war and the commanding general of the army), the Quartermaster's Department,* the Subsistence Department,* the Pay Department, the Medical Department, the Corps of Engineers, the Ordnance Department,* and the Signal Corps.* Each bureau chief, however, had considerable independence and autonomy due to vague army regulations operating at that time. The system became decentralized, with each bureau operating independently, without any knowledge of what the other bureaus were doing. The lack of coordination and communication between the bureaus created unnecessary rivalries and slow policy implementation. Accordingly, when war broke out, the mobilization of men, machines, and supplies was chaotic for the first few weeks of the conflict.

Many historians generally agree that the War Department failed to handle adequately the massive mobilization of men to fight an overseas war in 1898. This problem and the organizational flaws of the War Department have been aptly defined and discussed by historians Graham A. Cosmas (*An Army for Empire*), David F. Trask (*The War with Spain in 1898*), and Russell F. Weigley (*History of the United States Army*). Cosmas argues that the War Department sensibly and efficiently handled the problems, including organizational flaws and pressures from the states' National Guards* and Congress. Thus, the department thereby corrected the problems and paved the way for reform provided by the Dodge Commission* and the next secretary of war, Elihu Root.*

The problems of the War Department were many, stemming from organizational flaws and archaic, bureaucratic practices and red tape. Congress contributed to the problem by creating vague rules and regulations that bogged down the War Department in unnecessary paperwork and administrative overkill. Bowing to the pressure exerted by newspapers across the country and by influential congressmen, President William McKinley* appointed the Dodge Commission on 26 September 1898 to look into the matter. Two significant changes that resulted from the recommendations put forth by the committee were the abolishment of the commanding general of the army and the creation of the general staff.

REFERENCES: *Annual Reports of the War Department for the Fiscal Year Ended June 30, 1898: Report of the Secretary of War, Miscellaneous Reports* (Washington, DC: Government Printing Office, 1903); Graham A. Cosmas, *An Army for Empire* (Columbia: University of Missouri Press, 1971); James E. Hewes, *From Root to McNamara: Army Organization and Administration, 1900–1963* (Washington, DC: U.S. Army Center of Military History, 1975); David F. Trask, *The War with Spain in 1898* (New York: Macmillan Publishing Co., 1981); Russell F. Weigley, *History of the United States Army* (New York: Macmillan Publishing Co., 1967).

RICHARD W. PEUSER

WAR, SECRETARY OF.
See SECRETARY OF WAR.

WARD, HENRY HEBER
(1871–1916)

An Annapolis graduate (1889), Ensign Henry Heber Ward served as a decoder in the cipher room of the U.S.S. *Maine.** The destruction of the *Maine* left Ward with a bitterness against Spain that found outlet in a highly dangerous intelligence operation.* Along with William H. Buck,* Ward volunteered to be a covert agent. Traveling to Spain, Ward spied on Admiral Pascual Cervera's* fleet fitting out in Cádiz. He also traveled to St. Thomas and the Madeiras. In June 1898 he journeyed to Puerto Rico* in disguise as a gentleman of British extraction. He was arrested by Spanish authorities, but with the help of local authorities from Great Britain,* he succeeded in convincing them he was not an American spy and continued his adventure.

REFERENCE: Jeffery M. Dorwart, *The Office of Naval Intelligence* (Annapolis, MD: Naval Institute Press, 1979).

WATSON, JOHN CRITTENDEN
(1842–1923)

From Kentucky, John Crittenden Watson entered the U.S. Naval Academy at fourteen and graduated in 1861. Watson had a distinguished record during the Civil War, serving at the side of Admiral David Farragut.

After the Civil War Watson enjoyed command and promotion; he was posted as commodore in 1897. During the Spanish American War, from 6 May 1898 to 21 June 1898 he commanded the northern blockade* of Cuba under Admiral William T. Sampson.* On 27 June Watson was placed in command of the Eastern Squadron.* The creation of this squadron was a successful attempt at threatening the coast of Spain in order to worry the Spanish into recalling the squadron of Admiral Manuel de la Cámara* from relieving Manila.* Promoted to rear admiral on 3 March 1899, Watson served primarily in the Pacific, succeeding Admiral George Dewey* in 1900. He retired in 1904.

REFERENCE: French Ensor Chadwick, *The Relations of the United States and Spain* (New York: Russell & Russell, 1968).

WEAPONS

At the outbreak of the Spanish American War, the United States was provided with an opportunity to experiment with its recently modernized weapons. Since the Civil War the Industrial Age brought about innovative developments in fortifications, automatic weapons, and a new concept in ammunition,* the smokeless cartridge. The newer weapons were the result of American and European studies of recent battles that determined that the more firepower brought onto the battlefield, the better the chance of victory. After years of tests and squabbling by ordnance boards, the United States would have the chance to test this theory against a foreign power.

One of the first efforts made by the War Department* was to renovate the outdated fortifications designed to render an adequate coast defense. In the 1880s Congress authorized a large-scale reconstruction of the forts protecting the nation's primary harbors. The result was the Army Gun Factory, which was capable of producing rifled steel breech-loading cannons of several calibers. Encouraged by new government contracts, private manufacturers increased their capacity to produce gun forgings, carriages, and finished weapons for the revamped forts.

Also in the 1880s, the Ordnance Department* did away with the Civil War–era muzzle loaders and introduced an arsenal of breech-loading steel guns in a variety of calibers. Machine guns were given a high priority as a potential wartime weapon, and Gatling guns* were stockpiled among the arsenals. However, the most significant advancement for the army was a new rifle. The regular army was now equipped with the .30-caliber Krag-Jörgenson,* but there were not a sufficient supply in the arsenals for the volunteer units. The bolt-action, magazine-fed, five-shot weapon was adopted in 1892 to replace the trapdoor Springfield rifle,* which was in heavy use during the Indian Wars. The navy, on the other hand, was using the Lee navy rifle. Ordnance men in the navy believed their .45-70-caliber Lee bolt-action rifle to be superior to the Krag, but they also planned to issue the German Mauser,* a gun rejected by the army.

Because the Krag was in short supply, most volunteer units were issued the obsolete black-powder Springfield .45-caliber rifle. One exception was the First U.S. Volunteer Cavalry Regiment commanded by Theodore Roosevelt,* who used his political influence to secure Krag carbines for his men, the "Rough Riders."* To resolve the ammunition shortage, the Ordnance Department distributed all available smokeless cartridges to units carrying the Krag. Cartridges using black powder* were issued for the Springfields until an ample supply of the smokeless variety could be procured.

The new small arms and artillery would bring about a different style of warfare. No longer would the massive shoulder-to-shoulder fighting of the Civil war era suffice. Instead, soldiers now had to move, shoot, and communicate. To prepare for combat, enlisted men went through intensive training. In order to give the enlisted man the proper instruction, officers were sent to a variety of schools. Depending upon the specialty, officers attended a school for artillery, engineering, cavalry, or infantry. All were designed to provide education in the latest tactics and weapons operations. The navy relied upon the Naval War College* for developing its men and tactics.

The U.S. Navy's fighting capacity during the war included four new armor-plated first-class battleships. Armed with long-range guns firing smokeless powder, the Americans overpowered the Spanish fleet. However, in many cases the navy guns missed their targets and did not take advantage of their superiority over Spain's weaker military.

Although Spain was ill prepared to battle with the United States, it furnished its troops with the most modern small arms. The primary arm used by the Spanish army in Cuba, for example, was the 7-mm Spanish 1893 Mauser rifle. Rejected by the U.S. Army for a variety of reasons, the Mauser used a smokeless powder and was loaded by clip. In addition to the 1893 Mauser, the Spanish also used 11-mm Remington Rolling Blocks and 7.65-mm Argentine Mausers.

The Spanish navy, on the other hand, was badly outmatched by the American naval forces. Their effective fighting force embraced only four armored cruisers and a few torpedo boats* and destroyers, all of which were in some need of repair and underequipped. Although on paper the torpedo boats could race through the water at a fast pace and wreak havoc on larger vessels, the Spanish boats were of little threat during the war. A lack of fuel made them virtually inoperable.

When the war with Spain ended after a very brief period of fighting, valuable lessons were learned by the United States about its lagging technology. Foremost was that black powder had to be eliminated in its entirety. Infantry and artillery weapons firing the charcoal powder were more a hindrance than a help, revealing the firing positions and inviting destructive counterfire by the Spanish. The War Department* also learned that the Mauser proved far superior to the beloved Krag because of its rapid-fire magazine and higher degree of accuracy. The navy realized essentially the same problems as the army. Naval guns were inadequate for fighting a full-scale naval war, which luckily was not the case in the war with Spain. If Spain's navy had been up to par, the outcome of the conflict might have been different. The highly respected Alfred Thayer Mahan* put it best when he warned, "We cannot expect ever again to have an enemy so entirely inapt as Spain showed herself to be."

REFERENCES: Michael Blow, *A Ship to Remember* (New York: Morrow, 1992); Graham A. Cosmas, *An Army for an Empire* (Columbia: University of Missouri Press, 1971).

MITCHELL YOCKELSON

WEYLER Y NICOLAU, VALERIANO
(1838–1930)

Valeriano Weyler y Nicolau was born in the Canary Islands* in 1838 to German-speaking parents who had moved there for business opportunities. Dedicated to a military career, Weyler joined the Spanish army and rose steadily through the officer corps. During the American Civil War, he served as the Spanish military attaché to Washington, D.C. Three years later, when the Ten Years' War* erupted, Weyler was posted to Cuba in command of a division of Spanish troops. In 1888, after the Pact of Zanjón, Weyler was promoted to the rank of general. In 1896, with rebellion spreading throughout the island, Spain named Weyler governor of Cuba.

The days of Spanish vacillation were over. Weyler's political and military mission was to crush the rebellion, restore political order, and revive flagging revenues from the sugar industry. The Spanish government gave him *carte blanche* as far as military tactics were concerned, and because of his status as governor and commander-in-chief, Weyler did not have to deal with any potential civilian-military conflicts. He undertook the assignment with relish. An arrogant European with little respect for Cubans, whom he considered racially and culturally inferior, Weyler was anxious to demonstrate the military power of Spain and suppress the rebellion.

But Weyler soon found himself in the midst of a frustrating guerrilla conflict. He had hoped to employ conventional tactics with the insurgents,* to defeat them in standard, set-piece battles where Spanish firepower would prevail. But the rebel armies lived off the land, mixing in with the civilian population. They required only a tenth of the logistical support Spanish troops needed, and Spanish troops were unable to distinguish the rebel soldiers from the civilian population. The guerrillas ambushed Spanish patrols, using hit-and-run tactics, and then melted into civilian villages. Weyler could not attack them without causing civilian casualties and further alienating the Cuban population.

Like many other military commanders fighting guerrilla wars far from home, Weyler tried to implement a reconcentration policy,* to herd the rural Cuban population into garrisoned towns and concentration camps. There he could control them, and they could provide no assistance to the rebels. No longer worried about civilian casualties in the war zones, Weyler was free to concentrate his firepower on the rebels. In 1896 and 1897 Weyler relocated more than 300,000 people into what he called reconcentration camps. Hunger, disease, and starvation were rampant, and thousands of innocent people died.

Weyler's policies made life more difficult for the insurgents in the short term, but they were political disasters in the long term. In Madrid, Spanish liberals described Weyler's policies as brutal and inhumane. In the United States, the emigré newspapers made the most of Weyler's program, advertising the mass suffering in the relocation camps and supplying a steady stream of similar stories to the large metropolitan dailies in Boston, Philadelphia, New York, and Chicago. Millions of American readers began to sympathize with the rebels in ways that would have been impossible a few years before, and those sympathies found political expression in the attitudes of a number of prominent congressmen. Whatever tactical advantage Weyler enjoyed because of the concentration camps was squandered in the overwhelming political opposition it generated in Cuba, Spain, and the United States.

In the long run even Weyler's heavy-handed tactics were not enough. By 1897 the Filipino rebellion was well underway, and Spain began redeploying some of Weyler's military units to the Philippines. Weyler began to lose ground militarily. He lost more ground politically. In June 1897 Weyler's major political supporter in Madrid—Prime Minister Antonio Cánovas del Castillo*—was assassinated. Cánovas's death eliminated Weyler's political base in Madrid. He resigned as governor of Cuba late in 1897 and returned to Spain. After several military assignments in Spanish Sahara and Spanish Morocco, he retired in 1910. Valeriano Weyler died in 1930.

REFERENCE: Horatio Rubens, *Liberty* (New York: Brewer, Warren, & Putnam, 1932).

JAMES S. OLSON

WHEELER, JOSEPH
(1836–1906)

Joseph Wheeler, who was born on 10 September 1836 near Augusta, Georgia, served as both a soldier and a congressman. He graduated from West Point in 1859 and served as a second lieutenant of dragoons before resigning to join the Confederate army in 1861. During the Civil War Wheeler served diligently as a cavalry commander in the western theater and rose to the rank of lieutenant general.

After the war Wheeler moved to Alabama, where he eventually practiced law, then entered politics. He served from 1883 to 1900 in the House of Representatives, with his major contribution the advocacy of reconciliation of the North and the South. His high degree of popularity helped ease the Confederacy back into the Union.

At the outbreak of the Spanish American War in May 1898, Wheeler offered his services to President William McKinley.* The president appointed him a major general of volunteers, which was applauded as a significant effort to help fuse the North and the South. Wheeler at first reluctantly accepted the position, arguing that his age countered the appointment. At sixty-one years with snow white hair and beard, Wheeler donned his new blue uniform and took the reins as the commander of a dismounted cavalry division.

During the Santiago* campaign Wheeler served as second in command of General William R. Shafter's* Fifth Army Corps.* Troops under Wheeler's command, which included Teddy Roosevelt's* Rough Riders,* won the battle of Las Guásimas* on 24 June and took part in the attack on San Juan* Heights before Santiago. During the fighting, it was reported that an excited Wheeler yelled, "We've got the damn Yankees on the run." Later in the campaign, Wheeler became ill with a tropical fever and was replaced by General Samuel S. Sumner.*

At the conclusion of the Santiago campaign, Wheeler commanded the army convalescent camp at Montauk Point, Long Island, and briefly commanded a brigade in the Philippines (August 1899–January 1900). Although Wheeler's appointment was seen by many as strictly political maneuvering by the president and his victory at Las Guásimas as unimportant, "Fighting Joe" relived his Civil War glory and was chiefly responsible for the final defeat of the Spanish at Santiago.

REFERENCES: Michael Blow, *A Ship to Remember* (New York: Morrow, 1992); David F. Trask, *The War with Spain in 1898* (New York: Macmillan Publishing Co., 1984).

MITCHELL YOCKELSON

"WHITE MAN'S BURDEN"

The term "white man's burden" was coined by Rudyard Kipling,* the English writer and poet who viewed European imperialism in general and Anglo-American imperialism in particular as the salvation of the world. A native of Bombay, India, Kipling was educated in England but returned to the country of his birth in 1882, where he began writing for a local newspaper. During the next decade Kipling became known around the world for his verse and fiction. From 1891 to 1896 he lived in the United States. Astonished at the economic growth and American potential as a world power, Kipling yearned for the spread of Anglo-American institutions throughout the world. The United States, Kipling was convinced, must be a full partner in the quest for empire if the world was ever to be civilized. One of Kipling's most famous poems, "The White Man's Burden," was published in 1899. It celebrated the racial superiority of white people and praised the men and women who carried "white" virtues to the "backward" peoples of the world. Kipling sent the first copy to Theodore Roosevelt,* whom he believed was the one American most likely to appreciate it. Roosevelt did.

Others did too. There was a ready audience in the United States for the message that the Anglo-Saxon world carried a moral obligation to convert the rest of the world to Protestantism, democracy, and capitalism. Some Americans had a particularly acute sense of that responsibility. The idea of American exceptionalism was rooted deep in American popular culture in the late nineteenth century. The "white man's burden" was just the most recent manifestation of early notions of American exceptionalism, such as the Puritan idea of the "city on the hill" in the 1630s and the Manifest Destiny anthem of the 1840s. Josiah

Strong, a prominent Protestant evangelist, wrote *Our Country: Its Possible Future and Present Crisis* in 1885. The book was an instant bestseller, with 170,000 copies in print, and it was translated into dozens of languages. "The Anglo-Saxon race," Strong wrote, "is the representative of two great ideas . . . civil liberty and a pure Christianity. . . . The Anglo-Saxon is divinely commissioned to be his brother's keeper." More than a decade later, as the United States contemplated acquiring an empire in the wake of the Spanish American War, Senator Albert Beveridge of Indiana gave the "white man's burden" even more explicit expression: "God has not been preparing the English-speaking and Teutonic peoples for a thousand years for nothing but vain and idle self-admiration. . . . He has given us the spirit of progress to overwhelm the forces of reaction throughout the earth. He has made us adept in government that we may administer government among savage and senile peoples."

Protestant missionaries carried that message around the world in the late nineteenth and early twentieth centuries. They preached a Protestant version of salvation but also preached a temporal gospel as well, praising such lofty American virtues as democracy and capitalism, as well as the more material comforts of sewing machines, ready-to-wear clothing, cotton underwear, and electrical appliances. The savage, uncivilized regions of the world needed the benefits of true religion, American technology, and democracy. The idea of the "white man's burden" was music to the ears of American businessmen, who were anxiously looking abroad for new markets and new sources of raw materials. Arguing for imperial expansion as the salvation of the industrial economy, they endorsed the missionary gospel as well. The vision of American businessmen and the vision of American clergymen together shaped public opinion in the 1890s and created a powerful momentum for the acquisition of an empire.

REFERENCES: Julius W. Pratt, *Expansionists of 1898* (Baltimore: Johns Hopkins University Press, 1936); Daniel B. Schirmer, *Republic or Empire* (Cambridge, MA: Schenkman, 1970); Leon Wolff, *Little Brown Brother* (New York: Longmans, 1961).

JAMES S. OLSON

WHITNEY, HENRY HOWARD
(1866–1949)

Henry Howard Whitney graduated from West Point in 1892 and in 1896 was assigned to the U.S. Army's Military Information Division.* One month after the· commencement of hostilities, Whitney was sent to Puerto Rico* to gather intelligence. Arriving on a British merchant ship, Whitney discovered that his mission had been leaked to the press. Disguising himself as a stoker, Whitney eluded Spanish authorities, took an alias, and traveled the island. Whitney's reports of Spanish military preparedness, lack of artillery, and surface warships materially aided General Nelson A. Miles,* who landed with an expeditionary force in July 1898.

REFERENCE: G.J.A. O'Toole, *The Spanish War* (New York: W. W. Norton & Co., 1984).

WILDMAN, ROUNSEVELLE
(1864–1901)

The U.S. Consul at Hong Kong,* Rounsevelle Wildman met with Emilio Aguinaldo* and urged him to return to Manila* and aid Commodore George Dewey* in abolishing Spanish control of the Philippines. Meeting with Wildman on 4 May 1898, Aguinaldo vacillated. His colleagues, however, united in support of Wildman's proposal. Wildman also facilitated the Philippine revolutionary's purchase of 2,282 rifles and 176,500 cartridges. When the administration subsequently resolved to remain aloof from entanglements with the insurrectionists, Wildman gratefully stepped back. Philippine sources state that Wildman represented Dewey in his discussions with Aguinaldo, but there is not unanimity on that point.

REFERENCES: David F. Trask, *The War with Spain in 1898* (New York: Macmillan Publishing Co., 1981); Gregorio F. Zaide, *The Philippine Revolution* (Manila: Modern Book Company, 1968).

WILHELM II, KAISER OF GERMANY
(1859–1941)

Wilhelm II was the German kaiser and king of Prussia who succeeded to the throne in 1888 and ruled until his ouster in November 1918, following Germany's defeat in World War I.

According to historian David F. Trask, Wilhelm II strongly opposed U.S. efforts in 1897 to pressure Spain into granting Cuba independence or autonomy.* However, the German foreign minister, Prince Bernhard von Bülow, urged Wilhelm to adopt a course of neutrality, partly because of the inevitability of American victory in a war with Spain. In March 1898 Germany failed to offer support to Spain upon learning of the U.S. intent to attack the Spanish fleet in the Philippines.

REFERENCE: David F. Trask, *The War with Spain in 1898* (New York: Macmillan Publishing Co., 1981).

ALAN CORNISH

WILKIE, JOHN ELBERT
(1860–1934)

Head of the U.S. Secret Service,* John Elbert Wilkie engaged in counterespionage against Lieutenant Ramón Carranza.* Taking office in 1897, Wilkie worked to disarm agents at Tampa* and to neutralize Spanish intelligence operations* emanating from Montreal.

REFERENCE: Don Wilkie, *American Secret Service Agent* (New York: Frederick A. Stokes, 1934).

WILLIAMS, OSCAR FITZALAN
(1843–1909)

Oscar Fitzalan Williams had been U.S. consul at Manila* since January 1898. He provided Commodore George Dewey* with erratic information on Spanish intentions and deployment. It was Williams who reported to Dewey that the Spanish fleet at Manila had removed to Subic Bay.* Williams arrived at Mirs Bay* on 27 April 1898, and that very afternoon Dewey's Asiatic Squadron* sailed for Manila. Williams accompanied Dewey to Manila and telegraphed Dewey's ultimatum to Spanish governor-general Basilio Augustín Dávila.*

REFERENCE: David F. Trask, *The War with Spain in 1898* (New York: Macmillan Publishing Co., 1981).

WILMINGTON (ship)

Wilmington-class gunboats, like *Wilmington* and *Helena*, were almost new vessels in 1898, designed expressly with very shallow draft, just 9 feet, for river operations in China. Twin screws and oversize rudders made them very maneuverable. Commissioned in 1897, they displaced 1,397 tons and rolled like drunks in a seaway. For this reason, postwar duty kept them on the Yangtze or in South China. Both *Helena* and *Wilmington* participated in the blockade* of Cuba and in various convoy and military actions near Manzanillo,* Cárdenas,* and Santa Cruz.

REFERENCE: John D. Alden, *The American Steel Navy* (Annapolis, MD: Naval Institute Press, 1972).

WILSON, JAMES HARRISON
(1837–1925)

A graduate of West Point in 1860, James Harrison Wilson saw significant action in the Civil War, rising to the rank of brevet major general. Mustered out in 1866, Wilson was appointed lieutenant colonel. His strengths in command and engineering served him well during his long career.

At the outbreak of war with Spain, Wilson was again appointed major general of volunteers and given command of the Sixth Corps,* which was never organized.

Wilson then served under General Nelson Miles* in the Puerto Rico* campaign. With 3,500 troops, Wilson embarked from Charleston, South Carolina, on 20 July 1898 and arrived off Guánica* a week later on 27 July. Eschewing Guánica for Ponce,* Wilson disembarked and occupied the port and city with only token resistance. Miles divided his considerable force and directed Wilson to march up the road to Aibonito,* one of the four columns in Miles's plan. Wilson's command experienced the first real engagement of the campaign at Coamo,* commencing on 9 August. Wilson prepared to outflank Aibonito and was in the process of preparing to develop the situation when news arrived of the peace protocol on 12 August. Hostilities ceased, and Wilson's First Division halted.

Subsequently, Wilson was an occupation commander in Cuba (Matanzas and later Santa Clara departments), and later, second in command to General A. R. Chaffee* in the relief of Peking. He retired as a brigadier general of regulars in

1901 and was promoted to major general on the retired list in 1915.

REFERENCES: French Ensor Chadwick, *The Relations of the United States and Spain* (New York: Russell & Russell, 1968); James H. Wilson, *Under the Old Flag* (New York: D. Appleton & Co., 1912).

WILSON, JOHN MOULDER
(1837–1919)

West Point class of 1860, John Moulder Wilson served with gallantry during the Civil War and then worked as an engineer on river and harbor improvements. Appointed chief engineer in 1847, Wilson worked to provide coastal defense,* coast artillery, and the mining of harbors in the event of Spanish attack. Wilson's department was one that escaped censure in the postwar scandals.

The U.S. Army Corps of Engineers* had received significant funding from Secretary of War Russell A. Alger,* and Wilson had his officers working on defense as early as January 1898. Although never utilized, the defenses developed by the engineers were significant: Twenty-eight major Atlantic harbors were mined and hundreds of coast artillery emplacements were manned and mounted.

REFERENCE: Graham A. Cosmas, *An Army for Empire* (Columbia: University of Missouri Press, 1971).

WINSLOW (ship)

On 8 May 1898 the little 142-ton torpedo boat *Winslow* steamed into the bay at Cárdenas* firing her three 1-pounders at Spanish tugs and gunboats (*Alerta, Antonio López, Ligera*) in an effort to either cut them out or draw them outside the shallow bay, where *Wilmington* and *Machias** were cruising. The effort failed.

On 11 May *Winslow* tried again in company with *Hudson.** The Spanish gunboats and concealed shore batteries riddled *Winslow,* killing one officer, Ensign Worth Bagley,* and wounding the other and killing or wounding 25 percent of the crew. *Hudson* had to tow *Winslow* out of range.

Winslow was then sent to Mobile for repairs. She had been commissioned in 1897 and was sold out of the service in 1911.

The Cárdenas action resulted in several unusual events: Ensign Worth Bagley was the first officer killed in the Spanish American War, and Chief Gunner's Mates George P. Brady and Hans Johnsen and Chief Machinist T. C. Cooney received the Medal of Honor.

REFERENCE: *Dictionary of American Naval Fighting Ships* (Washington, DC: Department of the Navy, 1981).

WOOD, LEONARD
(1860–1927)

Leonard Wood came from New Hampshire and received an M.D. from Harvard in 1884. Securing an appointment with the U.S. Army two years later, he served in the Arizona Territory under Henry W. Lawton,* distinguishing himself as a medical and line officer and in March 1898 receiving a Medal of Honor.

Appointed physician to President Grover Cleveland* in 1895, Wood also became a close friend of Theodore Roosevelt.* In May 1898 Wood and Roosevelt organized the First U.S. Volunteer Cavalry Regiment, which Roosevelt's public relations acumen promoted as the Rough Riders.* Wood was the commander and led the unit at the battle of Las Guásimas* on 24 June. When General S.B.M. Young* became ill, Wood was appointed to take command of his cavalry brigade (the Second Brigade) consisting of the First and Tenth U.S. Cavalry and the First U.S. Volunteer Cavalry. Wood commanded the Second Brigade under General Joseph Wheeler* at San Juan.* After the surrender of Santiago* on 17 July, Wood was appointed military governor of the city and engaged in a vigorous sanitation campaign. Working with William C. Gorgas, Wood instituted significant civil and sanitation reform as governor of Cuba and relinquished his office to civilian Tomás Estrada Palma.*

In 1898 Wood was a captain; by 1903 he became a major general. He later served as commander in the Philippines and as chief of staff.

Blunt and outspoken, Wood possessed unquestioned skills, but his later career was shrouded in some political controversy.

REFERENCES: Herman Hagedorn, *Leonard Wood: A Biography* (New York: Harper, 1931); Jack C. Lane, *Armed Progressive* (San Rafael, CA: Presidio Press, 1978).

WOODFORD, STEWART LYNDON
(1835–1913)

Born in New York City on 3 September 1835, Stewart Lyndon Woodford graduated from Columbia and was admitted to the bar in 1857. Active in Republican politics, he served as a lieutenant colonel in a New York volunteer brigade and was the first military governor of Charleston, South Carolina. Immediately after the war Woodford served as lieutenant governor of New York (1867–1869), but he was defeated for governor in 1870. He served a term in Congress but primarily practiced law in private practice until the new McKinley* administration appointed him minister to Spain in 1897.

As minister to Spain Woodford had his diplomatic hands full, managing the deteriorating relationship between the United States and Spain. Some have said that his influence helped bring Práxides Mateo Sagasta* to power and rid Cuba of General Valeriano Weyler y Nicolau.* He negotiated for belligerent rights of those in the Cuban Insurrection.* Although Woodford labored well, events overtook him when war was declared. He practiced law upon his return to America and died on 14 February 1913.

REFERENCE: Alfred L. P. Dennis, *Adventures in Diplomacy* (New York: E. P. Dutton, 1928).

ϒ

YACHTS

The commencement of hostilities found both Spain and the United States unprepared. Nothing unusual there; to a greater or lesser degree the initiation of hostilities is always accompanied by surprises. Battleships, cruisers, and torpedo boats* existed on both sides in various states of readiness. What was universally lacking, however, were the necessary naval auxiliaries. This lack was particularly pronounced among the American forces that had to rush to acquire merchant auxiliaries* for troop transport, dispatch, hospital, and cruiser duties. A specific subgroup of auxiliaries was needed to serve as tenders to the ships on blockade,* shoal-draft reconnaissance craft to go where warships could not, pickets in an offshore role, and boats for harbor patrol duty. The Naval Auxiliary Board examined a very large number of vessels for these duties: from large passenger liners to small tugboats and yachts. For the above-mentioned subgroup, the board acquired twenty-seven steam yachts, mostly by purchase. These yachts were converted to wartime configuration through the installation of small-caliber guns, reduction of rigging, and rearrangement of cabins and stowage to increase bunker capacity, and provide munitions lockers and larger crew spaces. Some of these converted yachts were spectacularly successful: *Gloucester** and *Vixen** at Santiago,* for example. Many others, like *Mayflower,** *Hist,** *Yankton, Eagle,** *Hornet,* and *Scorpion,** were very serviceable.

At first blush, yachts in prolonged sea service seem ill advised. Lightly built, and for comfort, with only nominal speed and short range, yachts might have proved to have been a hindrance rather than a help. The decks had no reinforcement for the weight and recoil of the guns, there was no distilling apparatus, and cruising ranges were short. Nevertheless, these yachts often served with distinction, particularly in the small engagements in inlets, bays, and such that received little press coverage or historical attention. In fact, so successful were some of these vessels that there developed a dialogue in navy circles of the desirability of a class of vessels that were neither gunboats nor torpedo boats but naval auxiliaries of 200 to 800 tons.

Some of these yachts also had distinguished former owners: J. P. Morgan's* *Corsair* was converted to an auxiliary along with F. Augustus Schermerhorn's *Free Lance* and William Randolph Hearst's* *Buccaneer,* among others. At the close of hostilities, most were returned to private pursuits, but *Gloucester, Scorpion, Vixen, Mayflower,* and a few others remained in commission, some for many years. Others were transferred to naval militia duty.

REFERENCE: W. P. Stephens, "The Steam Yacht as a Naval Auxiliary," *Transactions of the Society of Naval Architects and Marine Engineers* 6 (1898): 89–113.

YALE (ship)

Yale was a liner built in Scotland in 1889. At the outbreak of hostilities, the U.S. Navy had a need for merchant auxiliaries* to supplement its forces. *París* (as she was launched) was renamed *Yale* and chartered to the navy. Commissioned on 2 May 1898, she was a 10,699-ton ship lightly armed with four 6-pounders and four 3-pounders.

Yale was initially sent looking for Admiral Pascual Cervera's* squadron near Puerto Rico.* On 8 May *Yale* captured the Spanish cargo ship *Rita* and sent her with a prize crew to Charleston, South Carolina. *Yale* got into a scrap with a more heavily armed transport off San Juan* and had to withdraw. She sailed to Haiti with *St. Paul** and then took up station off Santiago.* After the battle, *Yale* ferried troops, many of whom were diseased with typhoid.

Yale was decommissioned on 2 September and returned to merchant service. She was scrapped at Genoa in 1923.

REFERENCE: *Appendix to the Report of the Chief of the Bureau of Navigation, 1898* (Washington, DC: Government Printing Office, 1898).

YANKEE (ship)

Built in 1892, *El Norte* was a passenger steamer for the old Morgan Line and was acquired 6 April 1898 as a merchant auxiliary* for the U.S. Navy. Renamed *Yankee,* she was armed with ten 5-inch guns, six 6-pounders, and some smaller guns. *Yankee* took up the blockade* in Cuba, patrolling and occasionally bombarding shore batteries. On 7 June *Yankee* joined *Marblehead** and *St. Louis** to attempt to cut cables in the bay at Guantánamo.*

Yankee also inspected merchant vessels as part of patrol duty and while off Cienfuegos* gave chase to the Spanish gunboat *Diego Velázquez.* A running gun battle ensued with *Velázquez, Lince,* and shore batteries, but without effective result. Several other such inconclusive engagements showed Yankee to be an aggressive cruiser.

REFERENCE: *Dictionary of American Naval Fighting Ships* (Washington: Department of the Navy, 1981).

YAUCO, PUERTO RICO

Located in southwestern Puerto Rico,* Yauco lies less than 20 miles west of Ponce* and 6 miles northwest of Guánica,* where General Nelson A. Miles* arrived from Cuba on 25 July 1898. Upon arriving, Miles sent Brigadier General George A. Garretson* and seven companies to seize Yauco (through which ran a railroad line) in anticipation of seizing Ponce. After a brief skirmish—the first action in Puerto Rico—Garretson's troops secured the town on 26 July.

Yauco also served as the assembly point for Brigadier General Theodore Schwan's* advance toward Mayagüez.* Schwan left Yauco on 9 August bivouacking at Sabana Grande that evening.

REFERENCE: *Annual Reports of the War Department for the Fiscal Year Ended June 30, 1898* (Washington, DC: Government Printing Office, 1898).

YELLOW FEVER

Among the enemies that both Spanish and Americans had to contend with were a variety of diseases.* The foremost among these was yellow fever, an ancient disease with a misty and unrecorded past. Frequently in history the tolls taken upon armies by typhus, typhoid, and various fevers far exceeded anything an opposing force could accomplish. Yellow fever was particularly perplexing and threatening because no one understood its mode of transmission, yet mortality rates could be as high as 85 percent.

The disease is transmitted by mosquito—a theory first promulgated by Cuban physician Carlos J. Finlay. Surgeon General and Brigadier George M. Sternberg* followed these events, and upon the commencement of hostilities in 1898, Sternberg appointed Doctor James Carroll and Major Walter Reed* to study yellow fever. The surgeon general was very concerned that an invasion of Cuba might result in disease losses of 50 percent. General Nelson A. Miles* was also concerned about the possible effects of yellow fever in future campaigns; the threat of disease colored much of the strategic and tactical planning in the Cuban and Puerto Rican campaigns. The disease swept through the U.S. Army's Fifth Corps* shortly after the assault on San Juan Hill.* By 9 July there were confirmed cases diagnosed, and within a few weeks thousands were sick.

The Yellow Fever Commission was organized in 1899 and composed of Walter Reed, James Carroll, Jesse W. Lazear, and Aristides Agramonte. The commission experimented with identification and transmission of the fever. The commission also suffered casualties: James Carroll contracted yellow fever in his laboratory in Havana.* Doctor Lazear also contracted the disease and died subsequently. Nevertheless, the commission members felt they had demonstrated that mosquitoes transmitted the disease and they had identified an incubation period. Thus the Spanish American War provided a theater for the investigation of one of the world's oldest plagues.

REFERENCE: Howard A. Kelly, *Walter Reed and Yellow Fever* (New York: McClure, Phillips & Co., 1906).

YELLOW JOURNALISM.
See THE PRESS AND THE WAR.

YOSEMITE (ship)

Like *Yankee*,* U.S.S. *Yosemite* was built in 1892 for the Morgan Line and originally named *El Sud.* Of 6,179 tons, *Yosemite* was armed with four 5-inch guns and six 6-pounders. *Yosemite* sailed on 30 May 1898 for Key West* and then to Havana* convoying *America,* which was carrying ammunition. On 8 June she convoyed *Panther,* loaded with U.S. Marines, to Santiago.* While disembarking marines, *Yosemite*'s whaleboat crew captured a Spanish field gun of small caliber. Sailing to Kingston, Jamaica, *Yosemite,* in a comedy of errors, failed to capture *Puríssima Concepción,* a Spanish troopship also carrying much gold. A lookout reported her to the deck officer three times, yet she was allowed to pass by without so much as a hail. She was in neutral waters, however.

Yosemite replaced *St. Paul** in the blockade* of San Juan,* Puerto Rico. On 28 June at about 5 A.M., lookouts identified the Spanish *Antonio López* and fired a shot across the latter's bow. *López* ran for the harbor and *Yosemite* pursued. A hot engagement followed: The American fired 5-inch guns while receiving fire from three Spanish gunboats, *Isabella II, Concha,* and *Ponce de León* and occasional fire from Morro Castle.* A storm blew in, shielding *Yosemite* from Morro Castle. Meanwhile, fearing the rapid advance of *Yosemite,* López beached herself. *Yosemite* achieved a firing rate five times that of the Spaniards. *Yosemite* continued blockade duty until relieved by *New Orleans** on 15 July.

After the war *Yosemite* served as a station ship at Guam* in the Pacific. Damaged in a storm, she was scuttled in 1900.
REFERENCE: Joseph S. Stringham, *The Story of the U.S.S. "Yosemite"* (Detroit, MI: NP, 1929).

YOUNG, SAMUEL BALDWIN MARKS (1840–1924)

Brigadier General Samuel B. M. Young began life in Pittsburgh, Pennsylvania. He served with distinction in the Civil War, being brevetted to brigadier in April 1865. After the Civil War he joined the regular army as a second lieutenant and received regular promotions, becoming a colonel of the Third Cavalry in June 1897. In May 1898, on the outbreak of the Spanish American War, he was again promoted to brigadier and commanded one of General Joseph Wheeler's* brigades in Cuba. At Las Guásimas,* Young was given the opportunity to initiate the first army action in Cuba. Backed by information and support from Cuban general Demetrio Castillo, Young took two regiments of regular cavalry, the First and the Tenth, and advanced northward along a road to the east of his other regiment, the Rough Riders.* The dense undergrowth made contact between the units impossible; nevertheless, after an arduous night march, Young's troops were in position early on the morning of 24 June 1898. The Spaniards, under General Antero Rubín, had orders to retreat to Santiago* to avoid being cut off. Young's troops carried the day, in their own minds at least, being unaware of Rubín's orders to retreat.

General Young was among those who were soon taken sick, and he retired to the rear. Eventually, he was sent back to the States, and on 5 August he arrived at Montauk, New York, with orders to build a camp for convalescing soldiers. The camp, named Camp Wikoff* after Colonel Charles Wikoff,* became a yellow fever* quarantine station.

After the war Young served in campaigns in the Philippine Insurrection* and as military governor of Luzon District. In 1901 he was named president of the War College Board; and in 1902, president of the Army War College. During 1909–1910 he was also president of the board of inquiry that investigated the Brownsville, Texas, riots of black soldiers. He died in Helena, Montana.

REFERENCE: French Ensor Chadwick, *The Relations of the United States and Spain* (New York: Russell & Russell, 1911).

YUCATAN CHANNEL

The channel between western Cuba and Yucatan (Mexico) figured in the U.S. Navy's efforts to locate Admiral Pascual Cervera's* Spanish fleet. Both the Flying Squadron* and Commodore Winfield S. Schley,* along with other elements of the blockade,* patrolled the Yucatan channel looking for Cervera. The dynamite ship *Vesuvius** and the protected cruiser *Cincinnati** steamed back and forth in the channel in a fruitless search for the Spanish ships. Cervera, who had been expected to steam to either Cienfuegos* or Havana,* went instead directly from Curaçao* to Santiago de Cuba.*

Z

ZAFIRO (ship)

Commodore George Dewey's* anticipated attack on the Spanish squadron at Manila* required some significant logistical planning. Far from any U.S. base, Dewey needed a small fleet of transports and colliers to resupply his squadron. On 9 April 1898 Dewey purchased *Zafiro* at Hong Kong. A 1,062-ton collier built in Scotland in 1884, *Zafiro* had only one navy officer aboard, the commanding officer, and served a variety of resupply and coaling missions during the Spanish American War and the subsequent Philippine Insurrection.* *Zafiro* traveled the length and breadth of the Philippines. She was decommissioned on 15 January 1906.

REFERENCE: *Dictionary of American Naval Fighting Ships* (Washington, DC: Navy Department, 1981).

ZOGBAUM, RUFUS FAIRCHILD
(1849–1925)

Action photography was yet in its infancy in 1898, and the news-hungry public still looked to illustrators to provide images and impressions of significant events. Besides Frederic Remington,* Rufus Fairchild Zogbaum perhaps became more closely associated with the Spanish American War than any other popular illustrator. However, whereas Remington remains a household name among artists and illustrators, Zogbaum remains obscure. Despite the parallels between Zogbaum's and Remington's careers, Zogbaum's predated Remington's, and Zogbaum became known as essentially a military artist, devoting almost his entire twentieth-century output to naval and military subjects. Between the years 1885 and 1890 Zogbaum published over fifty illustrations for *Harper's Weekly,* the leading periodical of the day. Zogbaum specialized in drawings of cowboys, westerners, Indians, and the military on the frontier. His work appeared in fiction, as well.

With the coming of the Spanish American War, Zogbaum's western work virtually disappeared, and like Remington, he devoted his skills and talents to depicting the heroic scenes of Santiago* and naval subjects. Unlike Remington, however, he continued to devote his energies to military subjects; among contemporaries, he achieved considerable renown. Rudyard Kipling* wrote a poem about Zogbaum's work after both visited Captain Robley Evans,* ''Fighting Bob.''

Zogbaum died on 22 October 1925 in New York City.

REFERENCE: Robert Taft, *Artists and Illustrators of the Old West, 1850–1900* (New York: Scribner's, 1953).

Bibliographical Essay

Any bibliographical discussion of the Spanish American War should begin with extant bibliographical efforts. For the war with Spain there are few. The principal works are Thomas E. Kelly III, *U.S. Army and the Spanish-American War Era, 1895–1910* (1974) and Anne Cipriano Venzon, *The Spanish-American War: An Annotated Bibliography* (1990). By skimming through both, a rough overview of the primary and secondary sources on the war comes into focus. The Kelly bibliography, done at Carlisle Barracks, understandably emphasizes the U.S. Army's participation. Although more than two decades old, it is still very useful. The Venzon bibliography is much more recent, broader in treatment (there are sections on biography, army, navy, the press, medicine, ethnic treatments, fiction, music, and more) but less comprehensive. Since it is selective, the Venzon bibliography has some built-in limitations. Nevertheless, Venzon's annotations can provide important signposts for the Spanish American War novice. The chief shortcoming of both the Kelly and Venzon bibliographies is that they are almost wholly oriented to the U.S. sources and points of view.

Much of the grist and grunt of historical research on the war lies in contemporary government publications and contemporary summaries of these government-issued reports. The secretaries of the navy and the army both issued an *Annual Report* for 1898 that contains a wealth of detail. In addition, the *Annual Report* of the War Department (1898), the Navy Department (1898), the two-volume Adjutant General's Office *Correspondence Relating to the War with Spain . . .* (1902), the U.S. Senate's *Report of the Commission Appointed by the President to Investigate the Conduct of the War Department in the War with Spain* (1900), and the *Appendix to the Report of the Chief of the Bureau of Navigation* (1898) could all be read with profit.

Official Spanish government reports are equally valuable, but scarce in this country. Fortunately, many of these were translated and then published by the U.S. government, thus affording significantly greater access. Among these are *Spanish Diplomatic Correspondence and Documents, 1896–1900, Presented to the Cortes by the Minister of State* (1905); Admiral Pascual Cervera y Topete, *The Spanish-American War: A Collection of Documents Relative to the Squadron Operations in the West Indies* (1899); and Víctor M. Concas y Palau, *The Squadron of Admiral Cervera* (1900). The last-named title might better qualify as a secondary source: Concas served in the West Indian theater under Cervera, but he attempted a broader analysis than his own experience provided. The other principal Spanish history of the war is Severo Gómez Núñez, *La Guerra Hispano-Americana* (1899–1902). Lamentably, with Gómez Núñez, Spanish scholarship on the war all but ceased.

The best accounts by American contemporaries utilizing the above-mentioned documents are French Ensor Chadwick, *The Relations of the United States and Spain: The Spanish American War* 2 vols. (1911 and reprint 1968, an immensely useful work); and H. G. Davis, *The Downfall of Spain* (1900 and reprint), an underutilized naval history. Interesting, also, is Russell A. Alger, *The Spanish American War* (1901), which is Alger's self-defense of criticisms leveled at the War Department. These are the most useful general accounts by contemporaries.

In addition to these general and contemporary publications, the numerous memoirs of prominent individuals such as Joseph Wheeler, Theodore Roosevelt, and George Dewey, as well as others not so famous, enrich the bibliographic record dramatically. Some of the small-unit actions, cutting-out expeditions, which were numerous in Cuba, and anecdotes of war can be found only in these memoirs. A missing element in present-day scholarship on the Spanish American War is the kind of social and military history possible only from a review of such personal accounts and individual unit histories. The bulk of published Spanish American War history actually looks at the war from the bottom up. Unit histories, personal memoirs, and ship histories are legion in variety, even if only sparsely held in the nation's libraries.

The secondary sources, while important, nevertheless make a short list. The long-time standard was Walter Millis, *The Martial Spirit* (1931), which is still useful. However, the best overall history of the war is David F. Trask, *The War with Spain in 1898* (1981). Trask provides a balanced view of the evolving political, economic, social, and military crises that created the war and spun it to conclusion. Another general history, G.J.A. O'Toole, *The Spanish War* (1984), is more anecdotal than comprehensive, but it is particularly useful for intelligence operations, among other things. Philip S. Foner, *The Spanish-Cuban-American War and the Birth of American Imperialism, 1895–1902* (1972), is excellent for Cuba. Teodoro M. Kalaw, *The Philippine Revolution* (1925 and reprint), and Gregorio F. Zaide, *The Philippine Revolution* (1968), are useful studies for the Philippines. In addition, there are studies of Puerto Rico in the war (Carmelo Natal, *Puerto Rico y la crisis de la Guerra Hispanoamericana,* 1975; and Ángel Rivero Méndez, *Crónica de la Guerra Hispano Americana en Puerto Rico,* 1973), and even little Guam has its specialized history (Henry Beers, *American Naval Occupation and Government of Guam,* 1944).

Another specialized history, but essential reading, is Graham Cosmas, *An Army for Empire: The United States Army in the Spanish American War* (1971), which is clearly the best exposition of the U.S. Army's role and development through the war. Further necessary reading includes Margaret Leech, *In the Days of McKinley* (1959), and H. Wayne Morgan, *William McKinley and His America* (1963), both of which plow new interpretive ground in their persuasive assessments of McKinley the president and statesman.

Index

Page numbers in **boldface** indicate the location of the main entry.

About the Editor and Contributors

DONALD H. DYAL holds a Ph.D. and is the author of several books and articles, including *A Special Kind of Doctor* (1991) and *Guide to the Courthouses of Texas* (1993). He is the director of the Cushing Library at Texas A&M University (Special Collections, Manuscripts & Archives) which houses, among other collections, a vast military history collection.

BRIAN B. CARPENTER received a B.A. from the University of Tennessee (Chattanooga) and an M.S.L.S. from the University of Tennessee (Knoxville). He is the patents and trademarks librarian at Texas A&M University.

ALAN CORNISH served in the U.S. Navy Nuclear Propulsion Program for six years prior to pursuing a B.A. in history from Texas A&M University and an M.L.I.S. from Louisiana State University. Presently, he is coordinator of Electronic Reference Services at Texas A & M University Library.

KEN KEMPCKE received a B.A. in history from Eastern Illinois University, an M.A. in American Studies from Purdue, and an M.L.S. from Indiana University. Currently, he is the Social Science Reference Librarian at the Sterling C. Evans Library, Texas A&M University.

JAMES S. OLSON received a B.A. from Brigham Young University and an M.A. and Ph.D. from the State University of New York, Stony Brook. He is currently serving as chair of the history department at Sam Houston State University in Huntsville, Texas. Professor Olson is the author of more than twenty books in U.S. history, including *The Cuban Americans* (1995) and *John Wayne, American* (1995).

RICHARD W. PEUSER received both a B.A. and M.A. from the University of Scranton, Scranton, Pennsylvania. He is an archivist with the Military Reference Branch, National Archives and Records Administration, Washington, DC, specializing in nineteenth- and early twentieth-century navy, army, and maritime records.

MARK A. THOMAS received a B.A. in economics from Rice University and an M.A. in Library Science from the University of Texas at Austin. Presently a research librarian for the Texas Transportation Institute, he previously worked as a government documents librarian at Texas A&M University.

MITCHELL YOCKELSON received a B.S. from Frostburg State University and an M.A. from George Mason University. He is a reference archivist in the Military Reference Branch of the National Archives, Washington, DC, where he specializes in army records from the period of the Spanish American War through World War I.

ISBN 0-313-28852-6

9 780313 288524

HARDCOVER BAR CODE